Barons,
Brokers,
and
Buyers

Barons, Brokers, and Buyers

The Institutions and Cultures of Philippine Sugar

Michael S. Billig

University of Hawai'i Press
Honolulu

© 2003 University of Hawai'i Press
All rights reserved
Printed in the United States of America
08 07 06 05 04 03   6 5 4 3 2 1

Library of Congress Cataloging-in-Publication Data
Billig, Michael S.
　Barons, brokers, and buyers : the institutions and cultures of Philippine sugar / Michael S. Billig.
　　　p. cm.
Includes bibliographical references and index.
　　ISBN 0-8248-2561-6 (hardcover : alk. paper)
　　1. Sugar trade—Philippines.　I. Title
　　HD9116.P61 B46 2003
　　338.4'76641'09599—dc21
　　　　　　　　　　　　　　　　2002005536

University of Hawai'i Press books are printed on acid-free paper and meet the guidelines for permanence and durability of the Council on Library Resources.

Designed by Santos Barbasa Jr.

Printed by The Maple-Vail Book Manufacturing Group

*To those who toil in
the fields under the
hot Philippine sun.
May your children
know security,
prosperity, and peace.*

Contents

Acknowledgments ix

Acronyms and Special Terms xi

1 Introduction 1

2 The Legacy of Colonialism and Neo-Colonialism 32

3 Production, Financing, CARP, and the U.S. Quota 60

4 Property Rights, *Quedans,* and the SRA 101

5 The Great Importation War 148

6 Rationalization, Groupism, and the Chinese 201

7 Conclusion: The Institutions and Cultures of Philippine Sugar 251

Notes 275

References 291

Index 305

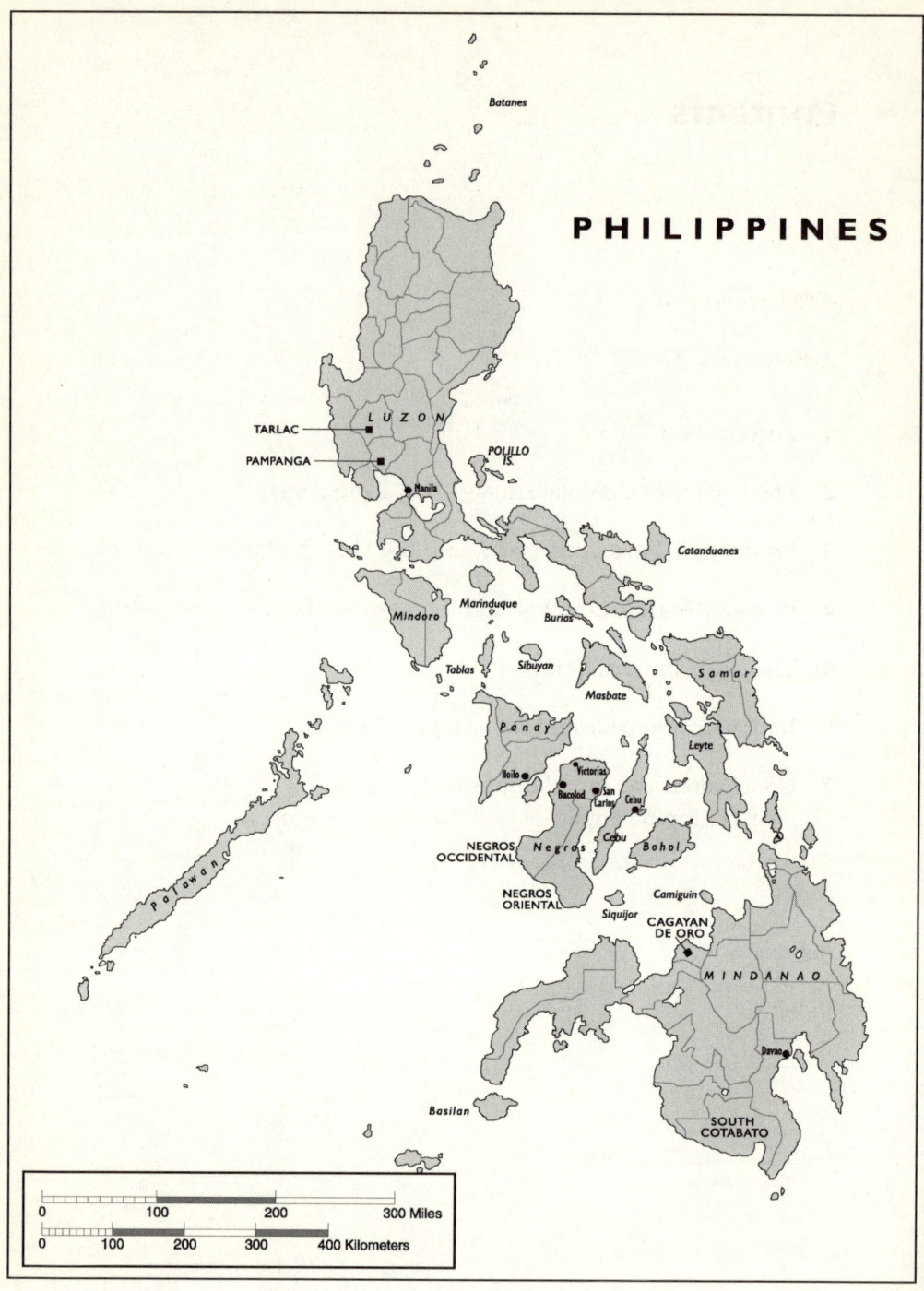

Fig. 1 Map of the Philippines highlighting sugar-producing areas.

Acknowledgments

As with all works based upon long-term field research, the list of those who merit acknowledgment and thanks is very long—consider this the abridged version.

My parents, Adele and Arnie, did not always quite get what it meant to be an anthropologist, but they supported my decision to become one and pushed me to do good work in whatever field of endeavor I chose. My desire to make my late father proud is never far from my mind.

My darling daughters, Shira and Monica, suffered through two periods in the field with relatively good humor. That neither has any interest in becoming an anthropologist is understandable, but I do hope they come to appreciate the ways in which these field experiences enriched their lives.

Teaching at a liberal arts college can sometimes try one's patience, but I have been blessed with wonderful students from whom I have learned a great deal. A few deserve special recognition: Hilton Robinson, Sarah Dugan, Kim Heiser, Brian Pompeo, Ilias Islamov, Fred Fournier, Amy Leicht, and Emily Green. Dan Reichman is the kind of student and person who comes along once in a teaching lifetime. I have also been privileged to work with brilliant, stimulating, and supportive colleagues and friends: Jim Taggart, Misty Bastian, Jan Zeserson, Mary Ann Levine, and Jim Delle. For fourteen years, Arlene Mimm made it easy to organize our work and lives. Franklin and Marshall College helped finance some of my earlier research in the Philippines and granted me a sabbatical in 1993–1994.

While in the midst of writing this book, I was diagnosed with CLL (chronic lymphocytic leukemia). After six rounds of chemotherapy and a stem cell transplant, I returned to teaching and writing with a new dedication and fire (as well as entirely new blood cells). Doctors in Lancaster (Swapna Deshpande and H. Peter DeGreen) and at Johns Hopkins (Ian Flinn) saved my life, and a mere "thank you" seems wholly inadequate. Outstanding nurses made my cancer saga bearable: Robin, Theresa, Jean, Barb, Mary, Jane, Evelyn, Amy, Anna, Carol, Marylu—I could go on at great length, and could wax prolific about their kindness. My family and friends who encouraged, rooted, and prayed for me kept me going through this ordeal. My sisters, Ronda and Melinda, and my cousin and chronicler, Bill Glovin, were constant sources of rock-like support.

Obviously, my work in the Philippines would have been impossible but for the hospitality of friends, the good will of informants (of which there were nearly four hundred), and the financial help of the Fulbright Scholar Program, which granted me a Senior Research Award in 1993–1994. I could not have carried out the research without the help of friends in the Philippines, including Sally and Boybo Villanueva, Dory and Ed Ledesma, Maribel and Boy Lim, Helen Mendoza, the late Dading Ledesma, Boygie Gallardo, Sally and Boy Ledesma, Tony Rustia, Fred Lopez, Echel and Remo Ramos, Clara Lapus, Nanette and Chick Garcia, Fr. Niall O'Brien, Joe Marie Zabaleta, Gov. Lito Coscolluela, Rafael Abello, Chap Ykalina, Ben Lopue, Jr., Franklin Fuentebella, and (most especially) Anne and Phil Abello. Alex Calata, the director of the Philippine-American Educational Foundation (PAEF), which administers the Fulbright Program in the Philippines, was an endless font of information, contacts, and encouragement. Violeta Lopez-Gonzaga of the University of St. LaSalle in Bacolod and Rolando Dy of the University of Asia and the Pacific in Manila were gracious hosts at those institutions. Tom McHale was a terrific teacher on both sides of the Pacific. Fellow Fulbrighters and wonderful scholars Rick Meixsel and Andrea Esser helped make my time in Manila both entertaining and intellectually stimulating.

It has been a pleasure to work with Pamela Kelley at the University of Hawai'i Press and Esther Pacheco at Ateneo de Manila University Press. Thank you both for your wisdom and your faith in me. The five anonymous reviewers of my manuscript impressed me with their erudition, knowledge, and insights, and their comments helped make this a far better book. I could not imagine a wiser or better copy-editor than David Akin. John Svatek, graphic designer *extraordinaire*, gave invaluable assistance in cover design, slide preparation, and the map of the Philippines.

My wife, Jane Rossetti, is my best friend, my staunchest supporter, and my most constructive editor. She is the "caregiver" to whom I owe my survival and recovery. She buoys my spirits when things are not going well, and pushes me gently to do and be better. Although I could never live up to her example, she provides me with my model of a wonderful human being. She makes my life worth living. There is so much of her in this book.

Acronyms and Special Terms

A-sugar	Sugar destined for the U.S. market under the U.S. sugar quota
ADB	Asian Development Bank
AIM	Association of Integrated Millers (a now defunct millers' organization)
ASEAN	Association of Southeast Asian Nations
B-sugar	Sugar immediately sellable in the domestic market
BIPA	Binalbagan-Isabela Planters' Association
BIR	Bureau of Internal Revenue (Philippine government)
BISCOM	Binalbagan-Isabela Sugar Company (a sugar mill)
BUSCO	Bukidnon Sugar Company (a sugar mill)
C-sugar	Reserve sugar portion to be converted by later sugar orders
CAFGU	Citizens' Armed Forces Geographical Unit (a security force on farms)
CARP	Comprehensive Agrarian Reform Program
CB-bills	Bills issued by the Central Bank of the Philippines
CCC	Commodity Credit Corporation (guarantees crop loans to U.S. farmers)
CONFED	Confederation of Sugarcane Planters (one of two confederations)
CPP	Communist Party of the Philippines
CY	Crop Year
D-sugar	Sugar destined for the world market
DA	Department of Agriculture (Philippine government)
DAR	Department of Agrarian Reform (Philippine government)
DENR	Department of Environment and Natural Resources (Philippine government)
DIWA	Democratic and Independent Workers' Association (labor union)

DOF	Department of Finance (Philippine government)
DOLE	Department of Labor and Employment (Philippine government)
E-sugar	Sugar intended only for authorized exporters of processed food
EDSA	Epifanio de los Santos Avenue (site of the EDSA Revolution in Manila)
EU	European Union
FAO	Food and Agriculture Organization (of the United Nations)
GATT	General Agreement on Tariffs and Trade (supplanted by WTO)
GSP	Generalized System of Preferences (U.S. government trade program)
IMF	International Monetary Fund
MSG	Monosodium glutamate
m.t.	metric tons
NACUSIP	National Congress of Unions in the Sugar Industry of the Philippines
NAFTA	North American Free Trade Agreement
NASUTRA	National Sugar Trading Corporation (Marcos-era sugar trading agency)
NEDA	National Economic Development Authority (Philippine government)
NFSP	National Federation of Sugarcane Planters (one of two confederations)
NFSW	National Federation of Sugarcane Workers (labor union)
NGO	Non-government organization
NPA	New People's Army
NSO	National Statistics Office (Philippine government)
P	Philippine peso
PA	Planters' Association

PAEF	Philippine-American Educational Foundation
PASON	Planters' Association of Southern Negros
PASRI	Philippine Association of Sugar Refiners, Inc.
PCFM	Philippine Chamber of Food Manufacturers
PD	Presidential Decree (Marcos-era decree)
PHILEX	Philippine Exchange Corporation (Marcos-era monopsony)
PHILFOODEX	Philippine Food Exporters Association
PHILSUCOM	Philippine Sugar Commission (Marcos-era sugar monopsony)
PHILSUTECH	Philippine Sugar Technologists Organization
PNB	Philippine National Bank
PSA	Philippine Sugar Association (colonial-era organization)
PS/Ha	Piculs of sugar per hectare
PSMA	Philippine Sugar Millers' Association
PSTC	Piculs of sugar per ton of cane
PVO	Private voluntary organization
RP	Republic of the Philippines (or Republika ng Pilipinas)
RPB	Republic Planters Bank
RSB	Roberto S. Benedicto (Marcos-era sugar "czar")
SIFI	Sugar Industry Foundation, Inc.
SO	Sugar Order (action of the SRA)
SRA	Sugar Regulatory Administration (attached agency of the Department of Agriculture)
T-bills	Treasury bills issued by the Philippine government.
TC/TS	Tons of cane needed to produce one ton of raw sugar
TS/H	Tons of sugar per hectare
TRQ	Tariff-rate quota (U.S. government sugar quota; not *really* a quota)
URSUMCO	Universal Robina Sugar Milling Company (a sugar mill)
USAID	United States Agency for International Development

USDA	United States Department of Agriculture
VAT	Value-added tax
VICMICO	Victorias Milling Company (the nation's largest sugar mill)
VOS	Voluntary offer for sale
WTO	World Trade Organization

Introduction

For more than a century the sugar industry was a dominant force in the economic and political life of the Philippines. Perennially among the top three exports of the country, sugar wielded clout far beyond what one would have predicted based upon the number of people the industry employed. The so-called "Sugar Barons"—wealthy *hacendero* planters located mainly in Central Luzon and on the Visayan island of Negros—were reputed to be a well-organized bloc of power brokers who controlled vast networks of clients and who used their economic might to achieve political ends. Their patterns of conspicuous consumption and attention to the social graces dominated society pages of national newspapers and set the pace for the Filipino cultural elite. That sugar was almost entirely produced for overseas markets and financed with foreign capital required planters to associate with foreign traders, financiers, and officials. Consequently, planters considered themselves to be the most cosmopolitan of Filipinos who were, by virtue of their sophistication and Western-style education, the natural leaders of their more benighted countrymen. Although the hacienda system was described by some as being "feudal" or "quasi-feudal," industry leaders proudly proclaimed their modernity by pointing to their up-to-date agricultural methods, the technologically sophisticated "centrals" (i.e., mills), and the entrepreneurial genius of the industry's founders and leaders.

In the 1970s and 1980s, however, things began to unravel. Expiration of the post-War U.S. quota and a precipitous and unanticipated decline in world-market sugar prices left producers holding thousands of tons of sugar that they could not sell. By the mid-1980s Negros was being referred to in the international media as a "social volcano" and "Asia's Ethiopia." As the profitability of sugar planting declined, hundreds of thousands of workers were idled, half the sugar land went unplanted, and sugar-producing areas became hotbeds of malnutrition, displacement, and political violence. In the wake of roller coaster price fluctuations on the world sugar market, the Marcos administration stepped in to "rationalize" the trading and marketing of Philippine sugar. The unsurprising result was that the industry became yet another cash cow for the president and his cronies, and in the process a major independent power base was emasculated (a gendered trope that planters themselves use) at the hands of superior power and cunning. Sugar could not regain its former position after the 1986 EDSA Revolution that overthrew the Marcos kleptocracy, even though former President and People's Power heroine Corazon Aquino is a member of one of the nation's wealthiest sugar-planting families.

In the 1990s, however, the industry did make something of a comeback. Much of the idled land was brought back under production, there were infrastructural improvements, Philippine sugar consumption (mainly in the form of soft drinks) grew rapidly, and sugar's price on the domestic market was consistently above the cost of production. Most important, the hunger and violence in sugar-producing regions largely abated. Bacolod, the main city of Negros Occidental province which produces more than 50 percent of the nation's sugar, experienced a considerable economic boom.

And yet, sugar is widely perceived in the Philippines as a "sunset industry." The great majority of planters today have fairly small land holdings and no longer lead lives of glittering luxury. Annual sugar production is considerably lower than it was in the 1930s, and almost every mill operates well under capacity. Only a small proportion of sugar is exported to foreign markets at high prices by quota or preferential agreement; most goes to satisfy domestic demand at more competitive prices. In some recent years a substantial proportion has been "dumped" on the surplus world market at prices well under production cost, while in others production has failed to cover domestic demand, and the Philippines has had to import sugar. Most of the mills are antiquated and inefficient, and overall farm productivity now lags far behind the first rank of cane sugar-producing countries.

The relative power and influence of the various sectors within the industry has also shifted. The trading sector has proliferated to the extent that the greatest profits are being made in the industry's least materially productive activity. No longer can sugar planters deliver large blocks of votes; many can no longer command even the votes of their own workers. In political squabbles on the national and even local scenes the sugar industry now has difficulty uniting to accomplish common purposes. In recent battles with industrial food processors, bankers, free-market oriented government advisers, and agencies of the Philippine state, the industry has been portrayed as a "pampered" group of elites whose demise as a potent political force would be a boon to Philippine democracy. While most government officials are reluctant to express hostility toward an industry that still employs over half a million people, today's politicians know there is no political advantage in being perceived as doing sugar's bidding, and the industry loses more battles than it wins. In short, today's industry is characterized by extreme disunity, not only among the different sectors but among the planters themselves. They fight more and more acrimoniously over smaller and smaller stakes. But this is hardly unique to the sugar industry.

One of the main arguments advanced in this work is that, despite what has been written and said by some scholars about the continued hegemony of landed oligarchs, the Philippines is currently undergoing a rapid shift from the economic and political dominance of rural agrarian elites to that of urban-based commercial, industrial, and financial interests. Power in the Philippines increasingly resides in Makati—the glittering financial center of Metro Manila—rather than in Negros, Pampanga, or Tarlac. And with that shift in power come cultural changes in the way most Filipinos perceive "the good life," how they think of justice and fairness, how they frame their aspirations for the future, and how they conceive of themselves and their society. And as these new cultural attributes spread throughout the different classes and status groups that comprise Philippine society, younger members of agrarian elite families begin to take on values, norms, and behaviors different than those of their parents. For example, the vaunted Filipino value of personalizing all social relations (e.g., Lynch 1964, 1984; Yengoyan 1984) is giving way to a greater appreciation for abstract, bureaucratic rules and relations. Philippine society is today in the midst of a fascinating period of rapid change, reformulation, and contestation in which the economic, political, and (especially) cultural influence of agrarian elites is diminishing. By adopting the more "bourgeois" values that characterize the ascending elite reference groups, those agrarian elites are unwittingly cooperating in their own disempowerment. In other words, it is not simply the case that one dominant elite class is replacing another. To a considerable extent, the children of the older elites are struggling to *become* members of the new dominant class, thereby expediting the decline of their parents' hegemony. And most are doing so with their parents' encouragement.

This study attempts to explain the decline of the sugar industry within the dynamic context of contemporary Philippine society. Perhaps it is easiest to describe what this book is about by eliminating what it is not. It is not a history. It is necessary to situate the industry within local, national, and global historical context (chapter 2), but doing so is not the main thrust of the book, and most of the historical sources I rely on are secondary. The book is also not, properly speaking, a traditional ethnography—least of all one of life on a sugar hacienda. Although much of the description and explanation will be presented in the form of narrative, and my field method is certainly a form of participant observation, the sugar industry is too macro-level a unit of analysis to rely exclusively on fine-grained ethnographic study (Gregory and Altman 1989). Neither is the book an economic analysis, at least in the way such analyses are typically understood. Although many of the phenomena considered are "economic" in a broad sense, one of my key arguments is that it is futile to abstract such discrete categories out of their social and cultural contexts, then reify them as not only real but as uniquely important.

Although this study is specifically about the Philippine sugar industry, it also speaks to broader features of Philippine culture, society, economy, and politics. The main focus is the interaction among "institutions," "power," and "culture," and the sugar industry is viewed as being illustrative or symptomatic of issues of wider import for the Philippines and perhaps for other developing countries. But these general implications and comparisons will be broached infrequently and with a light hand. What comparative generalities emerge are "rather closer to the ground" (Geertz 1973: 24) and firmly rooted in the specific empirical case being examined. Neither the Philippines nor certainly the Philippine sugar industry can be taken as microcosms of "capitalist transitions," "modernization," "globalization," the effects of "colonialism," or any other overarching processes or world historical forces. As is true of most works in economic anthropology, the narrative is most heavily weighted toward interpretation and explication of things I learned from my informants during my fieldwork. General questions—why institutional inefficiencies persist, why collective action becomes difficult within certain cultural contexts, why power tends to shift toward urban activities, and whether a certain kind of "civil society" is a prerequisite for democratic political life—will be concretely developed mainly in reference to the specific "organizational field" of the Philippine sugar industry. My theoretical points about economic culture, narrative knowledge, and the nature of class conflict have broader relevance than this particular study, but those implications also will not be extensively or directly developed in this work. Rather than attempting to understand the Philippine sugar industry within a comparative perspective, I concentrate on particular, micro-level descriptions and analyses of this single organizational field, alluding to comparative cases only when clearly warranted. For the most part, such comparisons will have to wait for later works and, of course, be supplied by my readers.

Before I first visited Negros in January of 1990, I read all I could find about that troubled island.[1] Although I knew that the causes of the crisis had to be more complex than I had understood from my reading, I arrived half expecting sugar planters to be the very personifications of evil. Or if they were not personally malevolent, I supposed they would at least be selfishly dedicated to preserving a system and a way of life that had oppressive consequences for workers, peasants, and the civic health of their nation. The reality, of course, turned out to be far murkier. While most previous researchers had understandably concentrated on the hacienda workers, my research increasingly embodied the principle of "studying up" (Nader 1972), getting at the sources of power by focusing on elites.[2] As my focus of analysis shifted from Negros to the sugar industry itself I found myself increasingly interviewing, observing, and befriending not only workers but also planters, milling company executives, traders, food processors, exporters, union leaders, Planters' Association officials, priests, politicians, bureaucrats, and journalists. As individuals, these are mostly decent people trying to do what they perceive to be best for themselves, their families, their communities, and (in a few cases) their country. Many of them readily express that they too feel "trapped" within a system that offends their moral sensibilities, but which for a variety of reasons they are obligated to participate in and reproduce. It is one of my goals to portray these conflicting perspectives, pressures, and sensibilities sensitively and realistically. In order to accomplish this it has been necessary to sublimate as much as possible my own culturally constructed sense of good and evil.

Influences and Perspectives—
The Neo-Weberian Approach

This is a work in the emerging tradition that I have identified as "Neo-Weberian Economic Anthropology" (Billig 2000). After almost two decades in which Marxist approaches dominated the field, economic anthropologists are increasingly looking to Weber as the venerable ancestor who asked the most prescient questions about the relationship between economy and culture. Rather than viewing culture as part of the epiphenomenal superstructure determined "in the last instance" by material forces, these neo-Weberians integrate a meaning-centered view of culture into their institutional and social analyses and view all of social life—including economic life—as animated by culture. Whereas an older tradition viewed economic life as being embedded in the social and the cultural only in non-market-oriented societies, neo-Weberians see cultural embeddedness in all societies, even the most urban, complex, capitalist ones. The neo-Weberian approach is, in this sense, an economic anthropology more in tune with the interpretive turn in many contemporary social sciences. Although in true Weberian fashion this perspective is diverse, non-prescriptive, and still being defined in practice, some of the characteristic features of neo-Weberian economic anthropology include causal eclecticism, political neutrality (in the specific sense discussed below), a penchant for inductivism, and self-consciousness about building models. All neo-Weberians stress the importance of culture, but they do not consider culture as either a discrete and isolated "box" apart from social, political, and economic life or a looming set of traditions, values, and precepts immune to the innovative actions of individual agents. It is, in a way, an attempt to forge a middle ground between those structuralist, neo-Marxist approaches, which (idiosyncratically in anthropology) have come to be called "political economy," and interpretive, meaning-centered approaches to economic life.[3]

Of course, this does not imply any sort of dogmatic devotion to Weber's particular answers. I agree with Peter Berger when he asserts that, "But even if some of Weber's answers are doubtful, there can be no doubt that his questions continue to be highly relevant today. Weber's opus remains a very important building block for any theory of modernity and ipso facto any theory of capitalism" (1986: 28). Weber has been rightly and appropriately criticized for his endless typologizing, his view that increasing rationalization of a certain kind is the most salient feature distinguishing the West from other, particularly Asian, societies (Goodell 1995; Goody 1996), and his failure to appreciate the irrational elements of bureaucracy (Herzfeld 1992). And, of course, anthropologists wish that Weber had not expressed such somber doubt about the ability of people in one society to understand those in another. The Weber that remains vibrant and alive, at least in economic anthropology, is the Weber who:

- Stressed the need to study meaningful social action in order to understand what motivates people.
- Insisted that we create the ideal types that enable us to classify, compare, and contrast institutions and societies, and that we must take responsibility for those ideal types and not reify our own abstractions.
- Viewed the social sciences as being more akin to narrative history than to physics.
- Was neither materialist nor idealist, and rejected *a priori* causal determinism in favor of a complex, eclectic approach to causality that included the innovative actions of individuals.
- Enjoined us to remain as ethically and politically neutral as possible when we are doing social science.
- Saw the human condition as resulting from particular, unguided, and undetermined history and rejected grand schemes that overgeneralize how history proceeds, in favor of probabilistic unintended consequences and "elective affinities."
- Saw social life more in terms of conflict over competing "interests" than as prevailing consensus and order.
- Taught that we must not reduce all conflict to relations among classes, and that if people think that status, party, race, and ethnicity are important distinctions, they act as if those distinctions matter.
- Focused on elites and their competing values.
- Focused on the confluence between the institutional environments that we create and the values, morals, and symbols that allow us to live as sentient social beings.

To understand the arguments that follow, it is necessary to explain briefly some of these attributes. One of the major tenets of the neo-Weberian approach is causal eclecticism. There has been a tendency, especially in the United States, to view Weber as an idealist antidote to Marx and Marxism. I believe that such a reading is misguided. Of course, the subject to which Weber himself most famously applied his causal eclecticism (and which has proven most open to alternate interpretation) was the initial transition to capitalism in northern Europe and the absence of such a transition in China, India, and Mediterranean antiquity. Whereas many members of the "culturological" school—those who focus on the cultural traits that predispose some peoples and indispose others to capitalism (whatever that means)—tend to favor the "strong thesis," idealist interpretation of Weber's *Protestant Ethic*, I strongly agree with Collins (1986a) that when viewed within the context of Weber's more mature work, as well as Weber's own later discussion of the *Protestant Ethic*, the "weak thesis," causally eclectic reading is far more plausible. The strong-thesis perspective suggests that Calvinist values, most especially salvation anxiety, were the primary reasons that northern Europe in the sixteenth to eighteenth centuries made the transition to capitalist relations of production and exchange. The weak thesis, on the other hand, stresses Weber's point that these values arose initially for reasons that had nothing to do with economic life, but that once they arose they had unintended, even ironic "elective affinities" with the pursuit of economic gain in distinctly capitalistic ways. These values may have been necessary preconditions at least to the *initial* emergence of a certain kind of capitalism, but they were by no means sufficient. The strong-thesis interpretation views Weber as an idealist; the weak-thesis interpretation sees him as a causal eclectic fighting against all simplistic determinisms and preferring to focus on unintended consequences, historical accidents, individual action, and the particularism of sociological understanding. That latter interpretation is the Weberianism I favor in this work and in general.

The social science and historical literatures are replete with theories and analyses relying upon prime movers (single major causes) of, and generalizable scenarios about transitions to and within capitalism. Micro-level studies such as this one provide particularly valuable lessons about the wisdom of *avoiding* such simplified causal accounts and "in the last instance" determinisms. One prime-mover perspective is the aforementioned culturological school (e.g., Sowell 1994, 1996; Harrison 1985, 1992; Huntington 1996; Pye 1985; Fukuyama 1995; Gilder 1981, 1984; Fallows 1987, 1994; Kaplan 1996; Himmelfarb 1999; and Harrison and Huntington 2000) whose adherents focus mainly on development-promoting versus development-inhibiting cultural attributes of certain countries or sub-units within countries. Other prime-mover theorists stress secure property rights (De Soto 2000—who takes strong exception to the culturological school), formal legal institutions (North and Thomas 1973; North 1990; Rosenberg and Birdzell 1986), the exploitation of poor countries and regions (Frank 1967; Wallerstein 1974), the relative ability of commodity prices to find their market-clearing levels (Schultz 1978; Timmer 1986), and the co-optation of the state by self-aggrandizing elites (Thompson 1966; Wolf 1999). There are also a host of fringe racialist, climatological, individual genius, and divine destiny prime-mover theories. One common feature of such strongly causal analyses is that they tend to be broadly historical and comparative rather than ethnographic. At such high levels of aggregation it is more practicable to assert causal priority by keeping non-favored elements out of clear focus, emphasizing certain factors held to be important *a priori* and ignoring others. Empirical, ethnographic studies, however, most often find it is impossibly difficult to tease apart discrete elements (e.g., colonial exploitation, the world sugar market, the values of elites, the structure of national politics and the state, the economic "system") and unambiguously evaluate some as being more causal than others. This does not constitute a weakness or flaw but is rather a positive natural concomitant of active engagement with the complexity of real lives as people actually live them. Such engagement makes one reluctant to impose simplistic causal explanations of other people's lives no matter how appealing it may be to offer such facile accounts. Particularlism, eclecticism, and ethnographic knowledge are inextricably linked elements of the same package.

Another cornerstone of the neo-Weberian perspective is the idea that society and culture at any one point in time reflect the many compromises among conflicting viewpoints, individuals, and sectors with differential degrees of power. As my fieldwork proceeded I found myself increasingly concentrating on the many conflicts within the sugar industry over such issues as the allocation of property rights, serving consumers versus protecting producers, and the nature of and need for "rationalization." This book is organized mainly according to the conflicts that I believe most clearly illustrate the institutional forms, the cultural precepts, and the political contingencies of the Philippine sugar industry today. Such a "writing the conflicts" approach was the hallmark of Gluckman's Manchester School (Gluckman 1955), and attempts by such scholars as Dahrendorf (1958), Collins (1975), and Mills (1956) to forge a "conflict sociology" through syntheses of Marxian and Weberian modes of analysis, and has become increasingly common in contemporary American anthropology (e.g., Wells 1996; Ginsburg 1998; McCay 1998; Finn 1998; Newman 1999). A focus on conflicts affords one the opportunity to view cultural precepts and the dynamics of power at critical junctures and is a natural concomitant to any interest in the mutual construction of institutions and culture. The positions individuals take on contested issues within the various sectors are not always predictable based upon any outsider's prior assessment of the "objective interests" that people within that sector should pursue in an abstractly rational world, nor do they always reflect an outsider's view of the relative power of the parties involved. At times, debates within sectors are as fierce as those between sectors, and how people perceive their economic and political interests is the most manifest way for outsider analysts to apprehend the values of their ethnographic subjects. These constructed interests are most easily and profitably analyzed in situations of conflict. Fortunately, at least for my research, the sugar industry in the 1990s provided ample opportunity to scrutinize such conflicts.

It will be clear at many points in this work that it is more useful to conceive of even a seemingly self-contained entity such as "the Philippine sugar industry" as a heterogeneous set of interests, cultures, and forms rather than as a monolithic unity. To name only a few of the elements in this raucous mix, the industry consists of one highly diverse sector organized around individual actors with severe collective action problems (the planters), one sector with a corporate form of organization (the mills), one very competitive sector that functions much like a bazaar economy dominated by small family enterprises (the traders), and a thoroughly bureaucratic state agency (the Sugar Regulatory Administration, or SRA) charged with representing consumers as well as producers but dominated by planters and millers. In addition, there are the workers, labor unions, industrial consumers, multinational food companies, non-government organizations (NGOs), banks, politicians, and the thousands of families whose livelihoods depend upon sugar. With the collapse of the fixed milling districts, the truckers have become a powerful and influential independent sector that has recently organized to promote its interests. Within each of these sectors there is great diversity in size, complexity, and influence. For instance, referring to "the planters" as a single sector lumps together the hundreds of small farmers who plant sugar with the far fewer but more powerful *hacenderos*. These different sectors, and even groups within the same sector, not only have different modes of organization and perceived interests, but also different "cultures" in the sense of norms, goals, ideologies, and perceptions. To complicate matters further, there has been increasing spillover between sectors, such as the important and controversial recent trend of wealthy traders purchasing mills.

Too often in contemporary social science the study of conflict is pursued in the service of advocacy for a particular political position. That the Philippine sugar industry is characterized by extremes of wealth and poverty and by social relations that may be considered oppressive presents difficulties in this regard for the non-Filipino researcher. My neo-Weberian predilection and my experience in studying this industry have made me skeptical about "advocacy," "action," or "critical" anthropology. Social scientists who begin their research in a spirit of moral condemnation rather than "objective" detachment tend to understate the causal complexity of the world's ills, and in so doing provide simplistic and facile accounts and solutions. This is not to say that it is possible or even desirable to be amoral or completely neutral in the light of injustice, nor do I perceive myself as occupying a magisterial position outside of my own cultural and personal background. Admittedly, I chose to study the sugar industry in part because my moral sensibilities were offended by the gross inequalities fostered by the system that I beheld. I was morbidly fascinated by a place and a "system" so famous for simultaneously embodying profound misery and grand opulence. But once I began to do the *research* on that system, it was more productive—particularly as a foreign scholar—to get on with understanding how it works than it would have been continually to denounce its "oppressive" and "exploitative" nature. In fact, given the highly polarized atmosphere of the sugar industry, I would have been denied the access that allowed my research to progress if my informants had not been convinced that I was a neutral party who treated their words and ideas with respect (and in Negros in the early 1990s a contrary perception might have exposed me to physical danger). For how could one hope to understand, empathize with, or even take seriously, the motivations, thoughts, and perceptions of human actors when one has already made negative moral judgments about those motivations, thoughts, and perceptions? Not only does the pursuit of objective understanding facilitate our research, but in the long run we gain moral authority, both individually and collectively, by trying our best to be scrupulously non-judgmental about the subjects we study *when we are conducting social scientific research.* In other words, the provisional and pragmatic pursuit of objectivity enables social scientists not only to understand the world better, but by positioning ourselves as "expert witnesses" rather than as advocates it also affords us the credibility and respect required if we hope to change it (Billig 1997, 1999).

Weber himself denied the possibility of any truly objective or value-free social science in the absolute sense, but he maintained the need for practitioners to aspire to greater *relative* objectivity in their research and teaching. In *Science as a Vocation,* Weber states: "I am ready to prove from the works of our historians that whenever the man of science introduces his personal value judgment, a full understanding of the fact *ceases*" (Gerth and Mills 1946: 146). Those whose only exposure to Weberian social science is through the work of interpretive anthropologists might be surprised to learn that Weber —as well as Dilthey, the other founder of interpretavism—ardently believed that the analysis of thought, value, and symbol must be objective and rigorous, though both made a sharp distinction between the characteristic methods of the natural and human sciences. Again, both Weber and Dilthey taught that social scientists need to be "expert witnesses" rather than advocates. Objectivity is a goal for which we strive. To claim that we *achieve* it would be preposterous, and I make no such claim about my own research. But it is equally fallacious to claim that because the goal can never be fully achieved there is no virtue in the striving.[4]

Another model for the non-judgmental study of elites is the work of Eugene Genovese (e.g., 1969, 1974, 1992, 1994). Genovese is an eminent culturally oriented Marxist historian who has written famously about the values, perspectives, and ideas of slaveholders and conservative thinkers in the American south. Needless to say, Genovese has no sympathy for slavery or for slaveholders as such. But by taking elite culture *seriously* he has provided us with a far deeper and richer understanding of the complexities of the intellectual and cultural traditions (as well as the political economic circumstances) within which slavery was embedded. He is able to establish and convey *empathy* with his subjects' views despite his having no *sympathy* whatsoever for those views.

Although excessive reflexivity can become self-indulgent and tedious, one of the salubrious effects of the postmodern movement in the social sciences has been to sensitize us to our own presence within our research and the need for honesty about its effects. My own view of the pursuit of objectivity involves relatively more reflexivity rather than the (now fairly discredited) omniscient authorial persona as exemplified by, say, Evans-Pritchard. It will be clear from what follows that I was no fly on the wall or automated camcorder. Try as I might to remain detached, there were times when my informants expected me to become a "player" in the conflicts within the sugar industry, and times when my research and writing fed back on the topics being discussed and analyzed. As I will discuss at several points, it is sometimes impossible for an anthropologist to *study* conflict without being drawn into the vortex. To conceal these moments from one's readers would be disingenuous and distorting. Rather than glossing over them I have written about them, because they too tell us much about the cultures of Philippine sugar.

This work departs from those panglossian perspectives that view economic, political, and cultural developments as being inevitably progressive over the long term. Economic organizations and institutional forms arise and persist partly for reasons of efficiency and profitability, but also because of differential power, competing interests, and the cultural-historical context within which they exist. The "demand" for new institutional forms (a trope commonly applied in the New Institutional Economics literature; e.g., Feeny 1993) need not ensure the "supply" of those forms if cultural and political impediments stand in the way. Forms that are maladaptive—from the point of view of economic efficiency—commonly endure through sheer inertia and because they serve the interests (themselves defined within a cultural context) of powerful individuals or groups.[5] Often, members of powerful groups do *not* actually benefit from older forms in any absolute sense, but they work to sustain them in order to prevent other groups or individuals from challenging or overtaking them. For example, most Philippine sugar planters realize that the extant method of apportioning property rights to milled sugar leads to inefficiency, high transaction costs, and low capital investment; but they refuse even to discuss alternative methods in part out of fear that they would enhance the power of the millers. Although planters admit that the current method empowers the trading sector relative to both themselves and the millers, the historical animosity between planters and millers continues to be a paramount source of both conflict and stasis within the industry.

Often, people act to sustain institutional forms that undermine their own economic interests because they perceive these forms as possessing deep-rooted moral and emotional legitimacy. Certain ways of conducting business become taken for granted as right, just, and proper, and suggestions that other ways would reduce transaction costs or increase incentives for capital investment can be met with shrugged shoulders or vociferous defensiveness. People evaluate their "interests" only within the context of the possibilities defined by those extant institutional forms.

Although many people inside the sugar industry can describe changes that need to be made to "rationalize" the industry and ensure its future success, most of them are extremely pessimistic about whether these changes can be carried out before the industry collapses. As we will see, aspects of the industry's institutional structure that foster inefficiency also open doors for maverick entrepreneurs, allowing them to pursue innovative strategies that exploit structural flaws to their own advantage. Such strategies may generate coordinated efforts to thwart the innovators by those whose "interests" are compromised or whose moral sensibilities are offended. But these strategies may also generate new institutional forms which will themselves become the new foci of conflict and contestation as groups re-form, loyalties shift, and interests are reconceived in a never-ending, irresolvable dialectic. Ironically, such seemingly hidebound, structurally rigid social entities as the Philippine sugar industry are the ones most open to the innovative action of individual agents. But the new institutions and organizational forms that emerge often produce unintended consequences that ramify throughout social systems and create new and unpredictable incentives for future action.

Property rights are among the most significant class of institutional forms discussed in this study. A central—albeit hardly original (e.g., Hann 1998)—argument here will be that the way rights to land, raw materials, finished products, and capital are apportioned has critical significance for the power relations among the different sectors, the profitability of the entire industry and its various components, and the moral claims made by different groups and constituencies. Property rights manifest themselves not only in the ownership of milled sugar, but also in such issues as the allocation of work on the overcrowded haciendas, the "right" of industrial consumers to purchase cheaper imported sugar, and the Comprehensive Agrarian Reform Program (CARP)—the loophole-ridden, largely unenforced land reform program instituted under the Aquino administration.

The case of CARP is a useful illustration of the ramifying consequences of changing property rights and contested claims to property. In part because of the residual power held by sugar planters, land planted in sugarcane has been among that least avidly pursued by the government department charged with implementing the law. The unintended consequences of creating a law but hedging on its implementation have redounded throughout the agricultural sector. Firstly, agricultural land has become effectively unsellable, thereby ensuring that many younger members of planting families are forced to continue to plant despite their desire to pursue other careers. Secondly, the potential for agricultural diversification has been stymied by the less-than-earnest enforcement of CARP for sugar land as compared to land used for other crops. Planters who want to exploit high prices for other crops or to experiment with alternative crops are reluctant to do so for fear that such diversification would make their land more vulnerable to appropriation. Thus, the next generation continues to plant, and plant sugar. Diversification into industry or commerce has been further slowed because agricultural land no longer serves as viable collateral for individuals or families who need loans to start new non-agricultural enterprises, precluding potential entrepreneurs from transforming land into productive capital (De Soto 2000). In addition to the many implications of different property rights regimes that will be analyzed in this work, the conflicts over these issues and the discourse within which those conflicts occur will be explored in some depth.

Chapter 4 will examine another important example of the cultural underpinnings and ramifications of property rights, explaining how the peculiar way of apportioning ownership of sugar and molasses between planters and millers leads to inadequate investment in infrastructure, technological lag, inefficiencies in both the farm and the mill, failure to develop ancillary products made from sugar cane, and prohibitive transaction costs due mainly to the existence of a large and unproductive secondary trading sector. To understand why such a clearly "inefficient" property-right system persists one must dig deeper to uncover the shared meanings, the contradictory and shifting perceptions of interests, and the conflicting norms and values of the different individuals, groups, classes, and sectors. One must delve into the historical experiences that have formed the attitudes and beliefs that motivate the participants to sustain the current system, despite their awareness that it has a corrosive effect on the industry by preventing (what they most often refer to as) "rationalization." The story of one institutional entrepreneur's attempt to impose a new and different property-rights system will provide a fascinating illustration of the possibilities and limits of individual action to effect change within a deeply embedded institutional and cultural context.

Use of the Culture Concept

It should be obvious from the foregoing discussions that the culture concept is an "essential" (pun intended) component of the analytical arsenal used in this work. "Culture" is an abstraction that we impose upon our informants' words, ideas, behaviors, language, and symbolism in order to simplify and comprehend the complex realities that we confront through our engagement with individual lives and minds. Although those individual lives and minds are real—things of nature—"culture" must be created, specified, and treated as the abstraction that it is. "Culture" is, in other words, an ideal type, and "culture concept" is a second-order abstraction referring to the way we use this ideal type as a discrete element in our analyses.

The past decade or so has witnessed a paradoxical occurrence in the life of this concept. While the word "culture" has become hotter than ever in the academy and in popular sensibilities all over the world, anthropologists have begun to treat it almost as our dirty little secret. As Sahlins phrases it: "So pretty soon everyone will have a culture; only the anthropologists will doubt it" (1999: 402). It is no coincidence that while "cultural studies" sections of mass-market bookstores have been growing, anthropology sections have been steadily shrinking. In the past the culture concept was associated both in and out of the academy with the discipline of anthropology. Today, anthropologists are shying away from it and attacking it while other disciplines, interest groups, and ethnic entities embrace it as their own (Mintz 2000). In this work I use the culture concept forthrightly and frequently. But first I need to specify and defend that usage, after providing some background.

The assault on the culture concept has many strands. It has, with some justification, been linked to nationalism, colonialism, romanticism, and naive positivism. But the more pertinent, and in the long-term more consequential, assault on the culture concept concerns a well-placed but overstated concern with essentialism (e.g., Asad 1983; Clifford 1988; Clifford and Marcus 1986; Crapanzano 1986; Barth 1987, 1989; Abu-Lughod 1991; Vayda 1994). I will admit that I feel deep ambivalence about this critique. On the one hand, I myself have written in opposition to the static, ahistorical, reified use of the culture concept—what I call the "800-pound gorilla" view—that characterizes much of the new concentration on culture in some disciplines (Billig 1994, 2000). On the other hand, I feel strongly that the fact that the culture concept has been used to promulgate essentialist descriptions of other people's values, ideas, and ways of living should impel us to devise a better culture concept rather than discarding it altogether. That "culture" is an analytic abstraction of our own creation—a "meta-narrative," if you will—in no way diminishes its explanatory and descriptive power. Whatever culture is, it does have real and important effects, and we discard the concept at our peril.

The view of culture expressed by the new cultural determinists is well-illustrated by the following quote from Harrison (1992: 43): "In Argentina . . . 'entrepreneurship' has usually taken the typical Hispanic American mercantilist form of a preference for commerce over industry, dependence on governmental protection, avoidance of competition, concentration on the domestic market and low export growth, emphasis on low volume and high prices, reluctance to innovate, and a generalized mistrust that has kept business at family scale. Behind these manifestations lie an authoritarian, individualistic, present-time-focused, antiplanning, and antiwork value and attitude system typical of Hispanic America."

Note how the logic works: These words—authoritarian, individualistic, present-time-focused, etc.—characterize this *thing* called Hispanic American culture and lead inexorably to "maladaptive" types of economic activity. And they exist as a value and attitude *system*, fitting together to form a coherent (Hegelian) whole rather than as, in Lowie's famous phrase, "a thing of shreds and patches." These values and attitudes exist in the shared consciousness of Hispanic Americans and result in a business ethos that obstructs the type of enterprise we see in more successful countries, presumably ones that have prior cultural traits that foster a "better" kind of economic activity.

What we have here is reification of abstracted "traits," post hoc fallacy, extreme methodological holism, reification, and a disregard for history that leads to a view of culture as a fixed constraint oppressively looming above the real actions of real people (i.e., the 800-pound gorilla). In such a perspective, culture is seen as a discrete, identifiable sphere of human activity that gains causal priority over other discrete spheres (e.g., economy, politics), rather than as an analytic category whose current form can only be understood as resulting from a complex and dynamic historical interaction with all manner of human action, thought, and perception. Of course, I have not even touched the issue of whether Harrison's description of Argentina's capitalism is fair, or whether it is reasonable to ignore macroeconomic distortions, oligarchic political structures, colonial exploitation, the dynamics of power, class differences, and all the other untidy historical and institutional facts that have interacted with past and present manifestations of culture, leading to the current economic situation.

When Asian countries, likewise, were economically backward relative to those of Europe and North America, many Western observers—following a simplistic understanding of Weber—attributed this backwardness to the development-inhibiting, anti-entrepreneurial cultures of Asia. But now that many Asian countries have become or are becoming economically prosperous, there is a tendency to reinterpret their cultures as being somehow development-promoting and pro-entrepreneurial. The history of these patently *post hoc* explanations should itself indicate to us that the views of culture and of the relationship between culture and economy they espouse are too one-dimensional and static (Hofstede 1980; Fallows 1987; Fukuyama 1995).

And yet, the culture concept need not be so. The overstatement of uniformity and coherence is not intrinsic to its meaning. To reject such a useful concept because it might lead to essentialism or, worse yet, structuralism is to throw the baby out with the bathwater (Sahlins 1999). While no one would defend stereotyping or the unwarranted assumption that people are merely cultural automatons, a certain amount of abstraction and even essentialism is a necessary concomitant of communicating with symbolic language. Cultures are dynamic, and their boundaries are fluid. Within even relatively homogeneous societies there are cultural differences by gender, age, class, ethnicity, region, and many other axes of distinction. It is trite and nonsensical to ask which group in a country like, say, the Philippines possesses the most "authentic" Philippine culture. Is it wealthy sugar planters in Negros, poor urban squatters in Manila, middle class schoolteachers in Zamboanga, or even Filipino-American nurses in Los Angeles? Surely, Philippine culture is an analyst's conception of the rich and heterogeneous amalgam of meanings, values, and thought patterns of all these groups and many more—and we gain our understanding of this amalgam through interactions with only a small sample of individuals, none of whom possesses Philippine culture in any meaningful sense, but all of whom bear its imprint. That individuals are the repositories of culture and yet no one of them can represent the entirety of culture is only a contradiction for the reified, thing-of-nature conception of the term. It is true that when we speak about culture, we are inevitably essentializing, but this in no way suggests that culture does not matter, or that we must avoid the term. Culture influences us; in important ways, it forms us. Our self-interest, for example, is only self-interest insofar as we perceive it as such, render it meaningful, and think about what ways are appropriate to pursue it. And these processes are always cultural. That self-interest is culturally constructed makes it no less real a motivation for action.

But how can we essentialize culture without reifying it, implying static stereotypes, or ignoring individual agency? One answer is to be entirely open and clear about the process by which we create these conceptions from our informants' quite real words and deeds; in other words, to employ Weber's still-useful notion of "ideal type." The ideal type is an analyst's construct, an intentional simplification, a working model of reality. It is, in other words, a self-consciously essentialized reality. We choose and must specify its boundaries and its properties. We create the ideal type's specific meaning in every instance in which we use it. If culture appears to be coherent and systematic that is because we ourselves make it to be so in our ideal type. Culture is neither intrinsically systematic nor chaotic and conflictual, for ideal types have no intrinsic properties outside of our creation. Is there such a thing as Negros sugar-planter culture? Yes, if we define an ideal type for one. Is there a Philippine culture? Yes, of course, but, though such an ideal type may be useful for some analytic purposes, we must expect it to be an even greater simplification as we expand its boundaries and attempt to incorporate greater complexity. This is one reason the title of this book refers to the "cultures" rather than the "culture" of Philippine sugar. As Geertz asserts in his famous "thick description" essay (1973), theoretical constructs such as culture are most powerful when they remain relatively close to the ground, local, and concrete. Although culture must not be treated as a reified reality—a misplaced concreteness, as the philosophers say—we must not allow the inordinate fear of essentialism to rob us of the most important tool for the creation of ideal types in our theoretical arsenal.

Attempts to reduce culture to elements of "practical reason" frequently amount to understanding an abstraction by invoking other abstractions. To argue, for example, that "in the last instance" differential power underlies tastes, values, and sensibilities fails to appreciate the extent to which power itself requires a cultural, symbolic context in order to have any meaning (as argued so brilliantly by Geertz 1980). Power, however, cannot be entirely reduced to symbolism. Some people really do have the power to influence (or even destroy) lives more than others, and this cannot be ignored. Formal institutions, likewise, may be grounded in informal "values," but not all values become codified or institutionalized. Powerful individuals, classes, and groups cannot always readily impose their wills on others in any way they see fit, owing to institutional and cultural constraints as well as the interplay of power itself. Not only "culture" but also "power," "economy," and "institutions" are themselves useful ideal types for thinking about social life. None is more ontologically real than the others. None offers an objectively better or sharper reflection of the seamless way that social lives are actually lived. That we deal with ideal types and analytic abstractions is another argument in favor of Weberian eclecticism, modesty, and particularism.

A few examples of the use of ideal types by myself as well as by my informants themselves will help to illustrate the use of ideal types, to show how that use fits with the discussion of conflicts within the sugar industry, and to push ahead in outlining my arguments. Debates that occur in the industry today—and in much of the rest of Philippine society—are often framed in terms of familiar symbols and emotionally laden concepts. But such words and ideas of course mean different things to different groups and individuals, and the use of these symbols often itself becomes the central focus of debates among the different sectors. This is not surprising, since it is through these symbols that various groups, factions, and classes differentiate their own values and commitments from those of competing groups. In order to gain legitimacy for their causes, groups will typically appropriate words such as "capitalism," "the free market," "sustainability," and "democracy" that have positive resonance in the larger society (or so the sloganeers imagine). Conversely, they attempt to label competing groups with terms such as "communist," "feudal," "foreign," "irrational," and "corrupt." In the land reform debate, for example, planters will argue that they represent the true force of "capitalism" insofar as they are the sentinels of "private property," and those who support land reform are "communists." Advocates of land reform, on the other hand, argue that poor farmers desire only to be good "capitalists" and would do so if only they could gain access to some private property of their own, property currently in the hands of "feudal" barons. Planters often point to the century-long success of sugar on Negros and the failure of every past effort at agricultural diversification as evidence that sugar is the most "sustainable" crop given the island's environment and social realities. Others decry the environmental and social degradations that result from the unsustainable "monocrop economy." Although these different groups and individuals share much by virtue of their being Filipino and involved with sugar, it is essential that the heterogeneity of the factions, sectors, and groups be stressed throughout, for it is this diversity that provides the raw material for the dynamic compromises and tentative understandings that are constantly being negotiated, reproduced, and renegotiated.

Perhaps the local term that has the most diverse, even contradictory, meaning is "rationalization." This widely used word connotes to some people in the industry more competition and greater exposure to the "free market." Among those who apply that meaning, some favor "rationalization" of one or all sectors of the industry, while others oppose it. But the more I talked with people in the industry, the more I heard the term "rationalization" applied to an entirely different vision. Many millers, planters, and government officials explicitly advocate "rationalizing" the industry by *reducing* competition and exposure to market forces, by having the government take a far stronger hand in controlling supply, demand, and marketing, by re-establishing a government sugar-trading monopsony,[6] by setting producer prices and establishing strict production quotas across the board, and by reverting to fixed milling districts in which planters have no choice about which mill to send their cane. In other words, for these people "rationalization" entails a control economy and artificially guaranteed profits for the entire industry. They equate the "free market" with chaos, excessive and debilitating competition, and shared poverty. In part this conception stems from the Marcos-era "rationalization" of sugar by strong government control, which greatly "rationalized" the pillage and destruction of the industry by the Marcos kleptocracy. But in greater part, this control and rent-seeking conception of "rationalization" represents the legacy of the U.S. colonial era in which fixed milling districts, fixed prices, and strict production quotas were imposed on the Philippine industry. This was done partly to mollify American sugar interests and partly to attract Filipino planters into the industrial-colonial world of international sugar.

One set of arguments in this work will perhaps be controversial. They concern the extent to which various aspects of the organization and current state of the sugar industry reflect cultural precepts widely shared in the Philippines, or among members of particular class and status groups. I argue, for example, that the industry's difficulties with collective action must be viewed within the context of a "groupism" that characterizes Philippine culture. Not only is there hostility and mistrust between the different sectors of the industry, but there is also constant squabbling and jockeying for position among different groups and leaders within each sector. There is a tendency for groups to fission, to coalesce around new leaders, and to form internal factions based upon personal or familial loyalties rather than upon positions on issues.

These shifting sands of group formation and change, driven by the constant rise of new leaders around whom groups coalesce, illustrate the "personalism" and "familism" that are often and with some justification said to characterize Philippine social relations. Such personalism makes it particularly difficult to develop formal institutions and organizations that facilitate collective action in a way that bridges the disparity between self-interest and the common good.

Although Filipinos are justly proud of the gains their nation has made in establishing the "rule of law" in recent years, many still regard themselves as more likely to act out of personal and familial loyalty than out of abstract principle or authoritative codes of moral conduct. I was surprised to find that many Filipinos themselves complain about their own (and their countrymen's) difficulty in sublimating the personal and the familial to overarching or nationalist principles. They typically assert this in a way that suggests that it is a kind of cultural weakness; they wish it were not so, but admit that it is. Anyone who has worked in or studied the Philippines is sure to have heard the "crabs-in-a-barrel" metaphor dozens of times.

The groups that tend to form within the sugar industry are not the kinds praised in social science literature for promoting a healthy "civil society." Putnam (1993) describes *weak* civil society as the situation in which the groups that form tend to be hierarchical, unstable, focused on gaining advantage for their members, and based upon the primacy of individual leaders—a fair description of most groups within the sugar industry, and a major reason why I describe the ideal type "groupism" as emerging out of the more primary "personalism." Wolfe (1989: 114–120) sharply differentiates between those groups that sublimate or restrain their own self-interest from those—such as rent-seeking "special interest groups"—which exist entirely to further their own interests. In other words, a plethora of groups attempting to seek government favors and gain privileged access to markets, contracts, licenses, and resources may well be symptomatic of cultural norms that inhibit altruism, democratic citizenship, and social trust (e.g., Fukuyama 1995).

However much these distinctions may hold in comparative perspective, I will argue that such abstract, highly theorized dichotomies lack cultural context and ignore the dynamic aspects of civil society. The same cultural impetus that underlies the Filipino predilection to form unstable interest groups also, in my experience, underlies the formation of NGOs, Private Voluntary Organizations, Parent-Teacher Associations, religious groups, and sports associations. Filipinos rarely, if ever, go "bowling alone" (Putnam 2000). While such groups may also form around individual leaders, organize according to kinship and fictive kinship, and tend toward frequent fissioning, many of them do impressive work. Despite the country's reputation for personalism and "amoral familism" (à la

Banfield 1958), I would be highly reluctant to conclude that the Philippines has an objectively weaker (note the linear implication of that term) or less healthy (note the moralism of that one) civil society than, say, my own country. Whether, on balance, Filipino groups do or do not provide the nation with the "crucible of democracy" (in Tocqueville's famous phrase about civil society) is an imprecise, debatable, and almost meaninglessly abstract question. If civil society theory is to have any analytic import, it must be applied within the context of particular cultural and institutional orders.

One of the most widely discussed ideal-type cultural themes in the Philippine studies literature is "patron-client relations."[7] Traditional conceptions about the mutual obligations, interdependence, and proper modes of behavior and address among different sectors and classes within the sugar industry remain very much alive, and are reflected in the organization of the industry. However, there is increasing anxiety, self-consciousness, and disgruntlement about them. Some regret the loss of certainty and predictability that comes with the erosion of these norms, while others decry the continued persistence of such inegalitarian and illiberal norms. Still others manage to express both of these sentiments without recognizing the logical contradiction. Perhaps the most surprising thing I witnessed regarding the cycle of obligation, debt, and deference that is often rendered by the shorthand phrase "patron-client relations" is the extent to which the so-called patrons feel as confined by these norms as the clients do. Most of the planters with whom I spoke say that they would like to be able to hire only the number of workers they need, to relocate workers' families in order to turn their haciendas into farms rather than villages, and to have more professional relationships with their workers. In other words, they would prefer to be employers rather than *amos* (roughly, "bosses" or "masters"). However, change of such a radical nature simply cannot be achieved, and it would be irresponsible to try. While the planters clearly possess greater bargaining power than the workers and there are no explicit laws that would preclude such actions, few can imagine "rationalizing" their farms at the expense of workers. Such actions would not only be considered shameful by one's peers, but they would dishonor the memory of fathers and grandfathers who took their responsibilities as *amos* seriously. I will discuss in chapter 6 a notable incident in which one of the country's wealthiest and most controversial tycoons *did* "rationalize" his agricultural land, including his sugar hacienda in Negros. Not only did this cause hostility among the displaced workers (for whom simple houses were built in a nearby town as recompense for the ones they lost on the farm), but he lost considerable respect from his fellow planters.

This is not to imply that the relationship between patrons and clients is not changing. Today most planters no longer live on their haciendas or experience the lives of their workers, and many of the ritualized formalities of the patron-client relation are no longer practiced. There are an increasing number of grievances about irresponsibility, shirking, and duplicity on all sides. On the farms I visited, one needed only to scratch the surface to witness the subtle forms of resistance that the relatively powerless workers employ toward the owners (Scott 1985, 1990). But there are many dyadic relationships—between planters and workers, politicians and constituents, suppliers and customers, producers and traders—in which the metaphor of patron-client relations continues to serve as a useful heuristic device or ideal type for understanding complex mutual ties.

Among unions that have tried to organize workers, there is also great ambivalence about the meaning and future of patron-client relationships. It is not surprising that these unions advocate what is best for sugar workers, come what may, and this often cannot be framed as whether patron-client ties are good or bad in an ideal world. Union leaders criticize planters for creating and sustaining a system in which workers are rendered dependent, are treated like children, and are expected to demonstrate extreme deference. And yet, those planters who do not take sufficient "care" of their workers are criticized for failing to fulfill their obligations, even though union officials acknowledge that fulfilling these obligations serves to reproduce the conditions of dependency that they decry. What unions want are higher wages, better conditions, more work, private garden plots to grow food, livelihood projects, and access to land. Several activists have expressed the belief that it will take at least a generation for sugar workers to overcome the attitude of subservience that makes them incapable of independent decision-making. This perspective ironically mirrors the culturological school's notion that a sense of dignity and self-worth is a precondition of economic success, political consciousness, and full-fledged human equality. I was astonished to hear union leaders and pro-labor social activists say, often rather imperiously, that sugar workers *are* like children, and that therein lies the biggest obstacle to their empowerment.

The Rise of Urban Elites

A major argument developed in this work concerns the changing political economy of the Philippines. Specifically, Philippine economic and political life—long dominated by rural-based elites oriented toward export agriculture—is increasingly controlled by Manila-based industrial, commercial, and financial interests. Within the sugar industry this is most apparent in the growing power, influence, and reputation of the traders and industrial consumers (particularly beverage companies and export-oriented food processors) at the expense of the once-mighty planters. This shift has been accompanied by concomitant shifts toward more "bourgeois" attitudes about the nature of success, legitimate authority, the "national interest," the definition of "fairness," and the proper aspirations for young people. Many planters do still believe that their industry is capable of protecting itself through concerted political action no matter how uncompetitive and inefficient it becomes. But it is obvious even to casual observers that sugar's political clout and ability to organize to wield power effectively are largely features of the past. National political figures, in fact, are reluctant to be associated with an industry that serves as the archetype of the old order, one whose public image among the rapidly growing "middle class" is increasingly that of privilege, protectionism, and anti-consumerism. Many in the sugar industry persist in the belief that they are among the most powerful political forces in the nation. But those with real power consider that claim laughable in today's Philippine political economy. More political capital can be gained from disparaging the "sugar barons" than from advancing their interests.

And yet, in their effort to portray the Philippines as a neo-colonized, exploited, and "feudal" cog on the periphery of the global world capitalist system, many Philippine scholars have missed or understated this important trend. By stressing the "restoration of planter power" (McCoy 1991), the "survival of privilege" (Angeles-Forster 1995), the "anarchy of (elite) families" (McCoy 1993), "ersatz capitalism" (Kunio 1988), "booty capitalism" (Hutchcroft 1998), or "cacique democracy" (Anderson 1987), scholars have conveyed the impression that the old rural oligarchs have preserved their preeminence in unabated form, or at least that all Philippine elites are pretty much alike in how they relate to the state.[8] Journalistic accounts (e.g., Chapman 1987; Collins 1989; Jones 1989; Kessler 1989; Timberman 1991; Goodno 1991) are even more stark in their portrayals. For them the Philippines is a "changeless land" and a "land of broken promises," dominated by fabulously rich rural elites able to direct political life unfettered by competition from other elites with other values and unconcerned with the greater national good. Such images of changelessness and unabated landlord power are the norm in popular accounts of the Philippines.

I am not claiming that those perspectives are entirely mistaken, only that today's Philippine reality is far more complex. Where rural elite families have managed to maintain their status and power, they have done so by adapting to radically different circumstances, by making new alliances, and by using their wealth and influence to pursue different strategies of gain. Those oligarchic families who have clung to the older methods of wielding influence have largely ceded ground to the *nouveau riche*. Most important, urban businessmen and financial wizards have increasingly become the dominant reference groups for ambitious young people.[9] One would be hard-pressed today—even in Negros—to find a young member of a planter family who would admit to aspiring to a life of rural leisure and inherited "success." Whereas in the past successful traders who aspired to social respectability had to purchase land and take on the social trappings of the country gentleman, now the children of planting families major in "commerce" (the most popular subject in Philippine universities), aspire to start their own businesses, and look up to those who have succeeded through trade and finance. Entrepreneurship has become a hot buzzword among young Filipinos, even those outside of the large cities (Billig 1994).

Although patrimonial capitalism endures in the Philippines, I argue that the shift from landlord dominance to the dominance of urban businessmen is critically important as a harbinger of future change in politics, economy, and culture. While it may appear at first glance that all Philippine elites are alike, that elites from different sectors pursue different strategies of domination and advocate different sorts of policies has consequential implications.

Many on the Philippine left see signs that the next "ruling class" will consist of former peasants or proletariat. But it seems far more plausible, given current trends, that what is evolving is the more typical historical progression: replacement of an old elite class by a newer one with different interests and sources of power, even though many of the individuals and families are the same. Despite the many works decrying the static composition of Philippine elites and the bipolarity of Philippine society, I argue that this shift is affording an unprecedented amount of upward mobility and the rapid growth of a Filipino "middle class."[10]

Of course, there is an ethnic component to this shift. One increasingly hears young people say that Filipinos need to be more aggressive, more frugal, and more future-oriented; in other words, more like the "Chinese." While there is still considerable animosity toward Chinese traders, and negative stereotypes about the habits and business practices of Chinese families persist, the overall tone is increasingly one of respect and emulation.[11] Indeed, successful Chinese businesspeople have come to be among the most important reference groups for young Filipinos. One sugar planter told me: "Those Chinese guys we used to hate, and most people still do—they had it right all along."

There is also a decided gender component to the rise and respectability of entrepreneurship and bourgeois values among sugar elites. During the crisis years, the wives of sugar planters took leading roles in organizing Private Voluntary Organizations, in instituting livelihood projects, and in starting enterprises that could employ idled workers. The Association of Negros Producers, for example—often touted as the paragon of quality and diversification in the province—has an overwhelmingly female membership. The younger generation of women from elite sugar families have pursued non-agricultural professions even more avidly than the men and have led the way in manufacturing, commerce, and small business growth. Many of these young women have also migrated to Manila and the United States to pursue lives and careers outside of what they often perceive to be the stultifying atmosphere of elite rural society. Whereas many young men are obligated to stay home and continue their families' agricultural operations, young women have avidly exploited their relatively fewer constraints by pursuing higher education and urban professions, and by starting many of the businesses that have fostered economic growth in sugar-producing areas.

It will be clear throughout this work that events within the sugar industry cannot be adequately understood without considering how global economic forces impinge upon it. To properly convey the many ways global forces affect this one industry in this relative economic backwater would require a much larger work devoted entirely to the subject. Sugar is a major world commodity traded in

New York, London, and Tokyo, is produced on every continent, and is subject to intense political machinations in all of the world's major markets. It is also a key ingredient in many processed foods and beverages which are themselves important world commodities produced by powerful multinational companies. Sugar is produced in the tropics and sub-tropics chiefly from sugarcane, and, since the nineteenth century, it has been made in temperate climates from sugar beets. The sugar market has been severely affected by the growing use of corn syrup for beverages, by the invention and extensive use of aspartame and other sugar substitutes, by various dietary fads, by nutritional research, and by world politics. In most years, the supply of sugar is greater than the worldwide demand, and action by governments and international regulatory organizations is required to keep prices remunerative for producers. Increasingly, poorer tropical countries such as Thailand, Indonesia, and the Philippines regard processed foods as potentially lucrative exportable products capable of jump-starting export-led economic growth. Not surprisingly, high prices for domestically produced sugar are typically perceived as encumbrances to food processing businesses, pitting the interests of sugar producers against those of expanding enterprises with real value-added export potential. Such conflicts between sugar producers and their biggest consumers occur all over the world, and they have been worked out either through creative compromises or the more successful marshalling of power by one of the factions. In different countries these "solutions" include import quotas, price supports, price guarantees, and special sugar import licenses granted to producers of exportable food products.

Both Philippine and American sugar producers argue, with some justification, that it is unreasonable to compare their prices to those of the "world market." This is because the world market functions more as a residual market for surplus (or "dumped") sugar than one that truly reflects worldwide supply and demand. The overwhelming majority of international trade in sugar occurs by quota or special agreement that circumvents the world market. The Philippines has yet to devise a regular and predictable system for balancing the interests of the various factions, and their endless disagreements will be prominent in the present work. But these sugar wars do not occur in a vacuum—sugar policies of the United States, the European Union, Japan, Australia, Cuba, and other countries form the all-important backdrop against which these debates take place. Sugar producers and industrial consumers ignore this larger context at their peril; any analyst of sugar who does so risks profound distortion.

Although many of the conflicts that form the foundation of this book are intimately related, and many of the players and positions overlap the different conflicts, I have chosen for the sake of coherent narrative to tease them apart and treat each conflict as a discrete "issue." After a chapter of historical background, and another describing the current state of the industry and how the international sugar business affects Philippine sugar, I begin the conflict chapters. Choosing the order of presentation proved more difficult than I anticipated, in part because these conflicts are more chronic than chronological. My final choice was most determined by the information I needed to supply readers with to allow them to follow the positions and the players. The first, chapter 4, is about the way ownership rights to sugar are apportioned among planters, millers, and traders. It includes a discussion of a controversial recent attempt to change the allocation system that has been in force since the 1920s. The case illustrates the mutual constructedness of culture and institutions, and argues against the proposition that economic institutions are driven to ever-greater states of efficiency.

Chapter 5 explores the conflict between the sugar producers and the industrial food processors (the major consumers of sugar) over the right to import foreign sugar into the Philippines. Some of the key players in this conflict employ the neo-liberal rhetoric of "free markets," "comparative advantage," and "value added," but they do so in particularly Filipino ways. This conflict is emblematic of the struggle between the agrarian elites, who dominated Philippine economic and political life for much of the nation's history and who are struggling to maintain or reassert that dominance, and urban industrial, financial, and commercial elites. The latter are younger, wealthier, and more "Chinese," and are just beginning to exercise political and economic muscle to advance their interests. Chapter 6 follows with a focus on the conflict or conflicts over whether and how the sugar industry needs to be "rationalized" and what it would mean to do so. As noted earlier, rationalization is a ubiquitous buzz-word in the industry, but conceptions of its meaning vary widely between and even within different sectors. The chapter also presents analyses of "groupism" and collective action, the position of the Chinese, and the case of one sugar planter whose biculturalism made him an especially perceptive, if agonized, interpreter of planter culture. The book culminates in a chapter of conclusions.

In my office there are three entire bookshelves of documents pertaining to my research on the Philippine sugar industry. These consist of newspaper and magazine articles, technical journals, reams of published and unpublished data, statistical compendia, position papers, studies, strategic plans, "doomsday scenarios," "boomsday scenarios," legislation, international agreements and treaties, information about sugar technology, international sugar comparisons, conference proceedings, forecasts, adversarial pieces, and copies of letters to bureaucrats, government officials, and rivals. I have read all of this material, I cite much of it, and there is no question that this paper record informs much of what I have written in this book. But I have tried very hard not to be overwhelmed by the reams of paper and not to inundate my readers with unnecessary numbers and citations to sources mostly unavailable to the public. More important, I have endeavored to privilege the voices of my informants and to communicate views, perspectives, and facts that were given to me orally over the course of more than four hundred interviews. Sometimes an informant would tell me something that contradicted the written data, and I have tried to convey such instances to my readers. These misapprehensions, alternate perceptions, and varying perspectives are themselves among the most important "data" that I possess, and portraying the sugar industry realistically as an agglomeration of the agencies of real human actors with highly disparate views is among my most important goals. Neither the institutional forms nor the cultures of the sugar industry reside in those written documents; they are ultimately to be found in the thoughts and actions of the individuals who constitute it. It is my task to construct and interpret the institutional forms and cultures as ideal types derived from my interactions with the limited sample of those people whom I have come to know. This concentration on living, thinking actors in the here and now, I still believe, is among the most important methodological distinctions between anthropological works and historical ones. Although this work is hardly a "traditional" ethnography, it is anthropological through and through.

The Legacy of Colonialism and Neo-Colonialism

For most of its history under Spanish rule (1521–1898)[1] the Philippines remained an unprofitable "friarocracy," more important as an entrepôt between China and the Spanish empire than as a producer of commodities in its own right.[2] Although some export crops were grown from the earliest period of Spanish colonialism, it was only in the late eighteenth century that commercial products such as sugar, abaca, tobacco, indigo, and coconut became the economic foundations of the colony.

Sugar cane cultivation was already widespread in the Philippines prior to the arrival of Magellan in 1521. Pre-Hispanic Filipinos drank both fresh and fermented cane juice but did not produce crystallized sugar. Only gradually did domestically produced sugar replace crystallized sugar imported from China (Larkin 1993: 21). Sugar was exported from the Philippines as early as the seventeenth century (Larkin 1993:1) when more sophisticated technology introduced by Spanish friars and Chinese entrepreneurs made it economically viable. But it was not until the late eighteenth century, when extraction methods became more efficient and demand more regular, that sugar became anything more than a luxury crop. In 1793, only one annual cargo was exported, totaling around 5,000 piculs.[3] By 1795, a British merchant was able to procure 40,000 piculs, remarkable considering that the port of Manila was first opened to non-Asian vessels in 1785 (Quirino 1974: 6).

The modern, recognizable sugar industry began in the nineteenth century as a cash commodity whose main markets were the metropolitan centers of Europe and North America. Following the shock of the British occupation of Manila (1762–1764) during the Seven Years War, Spain began to liberalize colonial commercial policy by stimulating local production for export. By the time the famed Manila Galleon trade between Acapulco and Manila ceased in 1815 (when Mexico—Spain's most valuable colonial possession—won its independence), export crops had supplanted entrepôt trading in economic importance. The Spanish government granted foreign firms residence rights in 1814, against the militant opposition of the religious orders who denounced foreign merchants as "Protestants," "Masons," and "Jews" (Aguilar 1998: 17), and who equated commerce with evil and heresy. In 1829 foreigners gained permission to enter Manila as the equals of Spanish traders (Hawes 1987: 21), and in 1834 the *Real Compaña de Filipinas* went bankrupt, thus forfeiting any remaining share of its previous trading dominance (Aguilar 1998: 233). Of course, the Spanish had compelling reasons for this new approach; they had lost their Latin American empire and desperately needed to make the distant Philippine colony a profitable concern. Mexican silver—the commodity most demanded by the Chinese—was no longer available to the Spanish, and, with the mechanization of cloth production, the market for Chinese textiles had declined in Europe and the Americas. Wealthy merchants who had prospered from commerce, as well as fortune-seeking Spaniards newly arrived from Latin America, were encouraged to procure tracts of land to produce export crops on a commercial scale. A repeal of the ban on rum production in 1823 succeeded in its goal of spurring more sugar production, as did the practice of foreign merchants advancing credit against the next crop. Nonetheless, Spanish colonial officials in the mid-nineteenth century decried the reluctance of Spaniards in the Philippines to invest their energies and capital in agriculture, and the development of export-oriented production was slow relative to that in British, Dutch, and French colonies. Still, by 1841, sugar—produced mostly by small planters and sold mostly to the United States and Great Britain—was the colony's leading export; by 1850, production was up to 457,927 piculs. This was mostly from Central Luzon (Quirino 1974: 25), but soon the focus of production would shift south to the Visayas.

The Negros Story

Negros entered the world economy rather late, even for the Philippines. Up to the 1840s it remained a peripheral frontier relative to the rest of the Spanish colony, subject to frequent violent raiding by Muslims from the south. It was a sparsely populated, densely forested island of Malay agricultural chieftainships (or *datuships*) in the lowlands and Negrito foragers in the uplands.[4] By mid-century, a small number of mostly poor migrants from Panay, Bohol, and Cebu had established small farms on which they grew rice, corn, and some cash crops (Larkin 1993: 60). Though the Spanish friars had made some headway in bringing the lowlanders "under the bell," a significant proportion of the population remained outside the authority of colonial church, state, and army. Over the next century, however, a powerful migration flow from Panay brought about displacement and assimilation as the natives were forced into the uplands, absorbed into the hacienda labor force, or murdered outright. The peasant farmers who had initially opened up this frontier by claiming and clearing forested land were themselves displaced by wealthy landowners who established the sugar haciendas that remain today.

As the threat of Muslim piracy waned in the 1830s and 1840s, the Spanish became increasingly interested in opening up the Negros "frontier" for commercial agriculture. Don Agustin Montilla, a Philippine-born Spaniard married to a member of the Iloilo-based Chinese mestizo Locsin family, established a successful agricultural settlement at Bago as early as 1844, but he planted no sugar. An Iberian Spaniard political refugee named Eusebio de Luzuriaga began farming profitably in what is now Bacolod in the mid-1840s. French sugar expert Yves Leopold Gaston appears to have been the first to recognize the potential for growing sugar on Negros and to convince other pioneer farmers (including Montilla and Luzuriaga) to follow his lead (Larkin 1993: 40–41).[5] Spanish Recollect friars, who began their mission to Negros in 1848, had also begun small-scale sugar production (Lopez-Gonzaga 1987a: 5). By that year Negros production had already reached 3,000 piculs (Larkin 1993: 40–41).

Because Negros was far from Manila and had no good harbors or ports, it would not have become a major producer of export crops but for a watershed event in 1855: the opening up of provincial ports to foreign trade.[6] In that year, the thriving city of Iloilo, on the island of Panay facing western Negros on the Guimaras Strait, was opened to foreign commerce for the first time. Iloilo had been a prosperous textile-producing town since the mid-eighteenth century. Enterprising Chinese mestizo merchants living around its sheltered harbor exported textiles made from cotton, silk, pineapple fiber, and abaca produced locally mainly by female weavers on a contract basis similar to Europe's "putting out" system (McCoy 1982: 302). For their return trips these merchants would purchase European goods to sell in markets around Iloilo. So successful was Iloilo's textile industry that, at its peak in 1857, the city was second only to Manila in size and commercial importance. In 1856, a young man named Nicholas Loney became the British vice-consul in Iloilo. Loney's mission was strictly commercial, and his actions would change the Visayas irrevocably. He flooded the local market with cheaper, machine-made British cottons, and thereby oversaw the destruction of Iloilo's economic base. Loney encouraged the expansion of sugar cultivation on Negros both as a profitable return cargo for British ships landing in Iloilo and as a way to channel the energy and capital of the region's elites whose textile business was crumbling.[7]

Iloilo's textile exports to Manila dwindled from 141,420 *piezas* in 1863, to 30,673 in 1864, 12,700 in 1869, and 5,100 in 1873 (McCoy 1982: 307). By contrast, sugar exports rose from 12,000 piculs in 1855 to 2,470,400 piculs in 1898. From the 1870s onward—the time when sugar ceased being a luxury in the West and became a necessity for people of all classes (Mintz 1985)—sugar would comprise over 90 percent of Iloilo's exports. By the mid-1880s, Negros had surpassed Pampanga as the Philippines' leading producer of sugar. The price that producers received for sugar was high, credit provided by export firms and foreign banks was plentiful, and the milling machinery needed was relatively simple and inexpensive. Although Loney was not the first to exploit Negros' sugar-growing potential, it was he who facilitated the systematic channeling of capital, labor, and skill from Iloilo textiles into Negros sugar. The fledgling sugar industry, unlike the older textile business, was thoroughly dependent upon foreign capital. Loney and the foreign trading firms that entered the Iloilo-Negros sugar business lent money at the low rate of 8 percent (moneylenders charged 30 to 40 percent) and provided state-of-the-art milling equipment at cost, under the condition that their companies be sole purchasers of the produce. The dependence on credit, particularly the practice of borrowing money in advance of the next year's crop—not a widespread practice in Philippine agriculture—has persisted in Negros to the present, even during the period in which Negros *hacenderos* were the wealthiest farmers in the nation. Another feature that has continued from the nineteenth century is the persistent complaint by planters that "foreign" traders manipulate the market in order to extract a disproportionate share of the profits.

McCoy estimates that the population of Negros rose from 18,805 in 1849 to 308,272 in 1903. Most of the migrants were *indios*—native Filipinos of Malay stock—who came from the poor weaving villages of Panay. The *hacenderos,* or large plantation owners, were mainly Chinese mestizos from the towns of Jaro and Molo (today parts of

Iloilo), a few Chinese entrepreneurs, Spanish political refugees and fortune-seekers (such as Luzuriaga), Philippine-born (or creole) Spaniards and Spanish mestizos (such as Montilla), and other Europeans (such as the Frenchman, Gaston). The colonial state was weak in enforcing tenancy relations, and the Spanish disdained the role of rural patron in an environment where tenants still had some bargaining power owing to the scarcity of labor. Both factors opened the way for Chinese mestizo dominance of commercial agriculture throughout the Philippines (Aguilar 1998: 87). Within a few generations, however, extensive intermarriage would blur most of the ethnic and national distinctions among the Negrense elite, though the perceived distinction between planter and worker would never be so blurred. Still, as is common in frontier areas, nineteenth-century Negros was characterized by a degree of ethnic intermingling uncommon elsewhere in the Philippines (Aguilar 1998: 106).

Aside from the expansion of the sugar industry itself, the migration flow was also facilitated by the defeat of Muslim pirates in the Guimaras Strait by Governor Emilio Saravia in 1857, and the subsequent government decision to station two steam gunboats in the strait to deter future raiding (Larkin 1993: 61).[8] Finally, Negros had become important enough to warrant military protection.

There were obstacles to the acquisition and consolidation of land to form the haciendas. Spanish policy prohibited settlers from appropriating native land and prevented Filipinos from gaining title to land outside of their native provinces. These laws were circumvented by bribing local officials and creating close financial relationships between the holders of capital and political power. One common method of acquiring the land of small farmers used in many parts of the archipelago was the *pacto de retrovendendo* (generally called *pacto de retro*) in which land was sold for less than its true value, usually by a poor farmer, with an option to buy it back up to some specified future date with additional interest payment. In the interim, the seller was allowed to remain on the land paying a fixed rent, but he could rarely earn enough to exercise the repurchase option and ultimately became a sharecropper on land that he had once owned (Lopez-Gonzaga 1991: 16). Another method was to lend money at prohibitive rates to the occupants of land and then claim the land in lieu of payment. Some land was acquired by simple purchase, and some by shamelessly manipulating the law and the courts, and much was taken through outright and often violent appropriation. The English term "land-grabbing" still has great potency in Negros. Over the course of half a century, the island went from having little formal land ownership and few legal land titles to having most of its prime land held in fact if not in law by a small, elite class of planters who had come from elsewhere. In 1869 a Spanish official would complain in a letter to his superior about the small proportion of Negros land holdings that were legally titled, the high number of illegal occupations, and the rapid dispossession of lands formerly held by the "Indians" (Lopez-Gonzaga 1987a: 18). But the colonial state was too weak to prevent or reverse these land machinations. By the 1890s most of Negros' coastal forests had been cleared and most prime land had been acquired—one way or another—by the new class of *hacenderos,* who had already begun to fashion themselves as aristocratic *Dons* and *Doñas* (Aguilar 1998: 117). As holdings became more concentrated, an increasingly high proportion of land was devoted to sugar rather than subsistence crops. The era of the hacienda had arrived on Negros and the peasants, many of whom had come to make their fortunes, were drawn into a system that would render them even more dependent and susceptible to hunger, mistreatment, and indebtedness.

Sugar is a labor-intensive crop, but labor remained in short supply on Negros up to the 1920s. Early on, debt bondage and share tenancy were the main methods of procuring permanent plantation labor. Potential workers on Panay would be given cash advances to relocate to Negros, only to find themselves saddled with an unrepayable debt to the *hacendero.* The internal passport system had been put in place since the 1840s in order to limit geographic mobility, and was an impediment to the enticement of labor to Negros from other islands. Town officials and priests on Panay and Cebu were often reluctant to part with workers and residents, and the Negros *hacendero* was frequently required to pay off any tributes the potential worker owed to the colonial state. Much of the initial recruitment of labor by Negros sugar farms was, in fact, in violation of Spanish law (Aguilar 1998: 128). Since debt bondage created disgruntlement among the workers, overseers commonly resorted to whipping and beating with clubs, sometimes to death, to maintain discipline. Security patrols were formed, often in league with the *Guardia Civil,* to track down and punish the large number of escapees (McCoy 1982: 323). Many of those who eluded capture joined the growing ranks of "undocumented persons" living on Negros; others signed on to work for other *hacenderos* who were more than willing to hire them.⁹ Planters would often confiscate the identity papers *(cedulas)* of workers to prevent flight, a practice declared illegal by the colonial authorities.

Other haciendas began as clusters of sharecropped *(agsa)* holdings with approximately half the produce kept by the sharecropper and half going to the landlord. Such tenancy relationships, either on a fixed-rent or share basis, were the norm in most regions of the Philippines, including the sugar haciendas of Central Luzon.¹⁰ In Negros, however, this would change in the early twentieth century. Once most prime land was cleared, debt bondage and share tenancy proved inadequate to the task of recruiting and keeping a labor force on the haciendas and gave way to the fixed-wage rate that persists today. Since planters needed to supplement their regular labor forces by hiring day and seasonal laborers, the medium of cash payment, often given in advance of the work, became the norm. By 1939, only 14 percent of sugar hectarage on Negros was still farmed by sharecroppers (Aguilar 1998: 218). After World War II, most of the remaining tenants had little choice but to become resident wage laborers, or *dumaans*. The prevalence of cash transactions and wage labor in Negros helped make that island a major center for cockfighting, one of the few activities that transcended class distinctions (Aguilar 1998). Even today, most flights from Bacolod to Manila have cargo holds laden with fighting cocks bred and raised in Negros headed to the big-time arenas in the capital city.

One of the advantages of the older *agsa* system of sharecropping had been that the *hacenderos* themselves did not have to concern themselves unduly about the details of sugarcane agriculture. But the new wage-labor system required more sustained and knowledgable coordination of production. As early as the late nineteenth century, owners of larger haciendas preferred to live in the bigger towns with more modern amenities. Most commonly, they would leave a paid overseer *(encargado)* and foremen *(cabos)* in charge of running the farm, some of whom would aggrandize themselves at the expense of both the *hacenderos* and the workers. In many other cases, all or part of a farm would be managed by a leaseholder who paid the landlord a portion of the total sugar produced (Larkin 1993: 73–75). While much farm leasing goes on today, it is now almost entirely transacted in cash, and the farms are managed by salaried supervisors.

During the first half of the twentieth century the *hacendero* typically maintained a splendid home on the plantation (in addition to one in town) and provided his workers with clothing, medical care, marriage and funeral expenses, and rice during the May through September "dead season," albeit usually deducted from their already low wages. Workers purchased their food and supplies from *cantinas* owned and operated for profit by the *hacenderos*. Despite the supposed "cradle to grave security" afforded by this system, workers have always been readily laid off and forced to fend for themselves during tough years. So while this was ostensibly a wage-labor system, hacienda laborers functioned and appeared much like subsistence workers bound to their haciendas for life (Larkin 1993: 78–79).

Given the persistent shortages of labor, it was also a system in which landowners worked hard to convince their workers that they were partners in a common enterprise (Aguilar 1998: 145). For many *hacenderos*, this "fair treatment" of workers became a point of honor, one that persists to this day. What may from one perspective be viewed as paternalism and the creation of dependency may from another be perceived as humane and fair treatment. The sugar planters of the late nineteenth and early twentieth centuries were adept at living in two cultural worlds simultaneously: they could be strictly devout Catholics, yet converse knowledgeably about the spirit world; they could host "elegant European-style dinner parties served with exquisite napery and imported silverware with guests, and eating in the native fashion, using bare hands, the older ones squatting on the floor chewing red cuds of betel, when by themselves" (Aguilar 1998: 187). Not until the American period would the cultural distinction between *hacendero* and worker become an insurmountable chasm.

None of the methods employed to secure an adequate labor supply at cutting time were entirely successful, and substantial portions of the crop would often be lost due to a shortage of cutters. This created the need for the *sacadas*, or seasonal laborers, who would be imported from nearby provinces (most numerously from Antique, Panay's poorest province) just for the harvest season. One well-known sugar technologist estimated that Negros required 20,000 *sacadas* to harvest the 1931 crop (Larkin 1993: 179). The *hacendero* would arrange with a *contratista* to deliver a specified number of laborers. The *contratista* would give cash advances that would have to be repaid by piece-work *(pakyaw)* labor at extremely low rates.

Although planters often complained about the poor discipline of the *sacadas* and the cheating of the *contratistas,* many *sacadas* ended up worse off after a harvest than before. To this day, the plight of the *dumaans* who reside on the hacienda is difficult, but that of the *sacadas* is worse. In recent times, however, Negros has experienced a large surplus of labor and fewer *sacadas* have been hired (Lopez-Gonzaga 1984). Their role has increasingly been filled by *pangayaws,* or casual workers, many of them women and children who work on a *pakyaw* basis (Lopez-Gonzaga 1988: 7). Nonetheless, *dumaans* continue to complain that at the one time of the year in which adequate work opportunities are available, the hiring of *sacadas* and *pangayaws* undermines the earning potential of those who should have first priority to the work.

The rise of the beet sugar industry in Europe caused the first of many crises in the Philippine sugar industry as prices tumbled and many smaller planters went bankrupt. A production rebound in the 1890s resulted from the diversion to Asian markets (particularly China and Japan) of much of the sugar that had previously been exported to Britain and continental Europe.[11]

Most sugar planters had become anti-Spanish well before the uprising in Luzon in 1896. The Spanish government was ineffective at keeping order and merely an inconsequential annoyance as an economic force. The execution of Jose Rizal on the penultimate day of 1896 further radicalized many *hacenderos* as it had other groups throughout the Philippines. After the fall of Manila to American forces in August 1898, the Spanish colonial government relocated to Iloilo. The *hacenderos,* led by the now-legendary Juan Araneta and Aniceto Lacson, armed and organized their workers to attack Spanish garrisons on Negros (Aguilar 1998: 172). The Spanish were outmanned and tricked by subterfuge into thinking they were outarmed—they surrendered without a fight.

But the sentiment reflected by this attack was far more anti-Spanish than anti-colonial. In order to protect their interests, the planters sent a message to the negotiations in Paris (which concluded the Spanish-American War) expressing their preference for the United States to establish protectorate status in the Visayas. Many planters supported U.S. forces against those of the Malolos Republic during the war that followed the American annexation of the islands (Lopez-Gonzaga 1989; Sa-Onoy 1992). Having enjoyed a considerable *de facto* autonomy under the inept Spanish administration, Negrense elites feared being subsumed "as part of a grand *Republica Filipina*" as much as they hated the prospect of continued Spanish rule (a real possibility for the Visayas and Mindanao during the Paris negotiations) (Aguilar 1998: 178). For a brief time Negrenses established a "Federal Republican Government of the Canton of Negros Island"—granting citizenship only to owners of land and capital—to avoid becoming incorporated into the fledgling republic (Lopez-Gonzaga 1989; Aguilar 2000). Their support of the United States against the Luzon-based Aguinaldo government pitted the Negros elite not only against the "revolutionaries," but in many cases against their own workers and tenants.

Throughout the 1880s and 1890s there arose in the Western Visayas a sequence of what would become an uninterrupted history of "peasant protest movements with messianic, revivalistic and nativistic overtones" (Cullamar 1986: 74), many of which incorporated *babaylanismo,* or pre-Christian spirit worship. These rebellions were typically led by charismatic individuals who claimed to command powerful spiritual forces and frequently took on the title *"Dios"* or *"Papa"* (one female *babaylan* called herself "Virgin Mary"). One well-armed rebellion in Negros led by Papa (or Pope) Isio lasted from 1896 until 1907; it began as a workers' revolt against the Spanish, the friars, and the spread of sugar haciendas, but soon became a holy war against the *hacenderos* and the Americans until it was defeated by U.S. forces.[12] Isio, who saw himself as the rightful successor to Spanish rule, surrendered in August 1907 and died in a Luzon prison in 1911 (Aguilar 1998: 182–183). Legends persist throughout the region that some of these charismatic *babaylans,* including Papa Isio, are still alive and awaiting the proper time to return and exact their revenge.

The Pampanga Story

Due to its proximity to Manila and its fertile volcanic soil, the province of Pampanga was the center of Philippine sugar production for much of its history. But Pampanga would never develop a monocrop economy like that of Negros. For by the time sugar expanded in the nineteenth century, Pampanga was already a densely populated, economically diverse province with many links to the archipelago's largest and most cosmopolitan city. The concept of a land market and individual ownership of land came relatively early to the provinces near Manila (Aguilar 1998: 74). Moreover, the system of land tenure and owner-worker relations that emerged in Pampanga was the classic tenancy, patron-client system that characterized the more established provinces of the Philippines rather than the wage-labor *hacendero*cracy that emerged on "frontier" Negros. As Larkin phrases the difference: "Whereas (Pampanga) began with communities upon which the sugar industry was grafted, in Negros the social units were a creation of that industry" (1993: 145). Although much of the sugar land in Pampanga *was* blazed from forest or wilderness, it was opened "mainly under the aegis of an indigenous elite rather than under that of outsiders" (1993: 85). While the elite continually incorporated new individuals and ethnic elements (especially Chinese mestizos), its shared identity, mode of land acquisition, and methods of controlling the labor force would remain conservative throughout the nineteenth and twentieth centuries.

Early on, Pampanga exhibited the rather archetypal colonial social order of having a Spanish governor *(alcalde mayor)*, Spanish priests who exercised both religious and secular responsibilities, and some Spanish soldiers, but also a substantial native elite *(principalia)* that ". . . possessed ample opportunity to maintain jurisdiction over the population, collecting taxes, assigning corvee duties, administering justice, and, in general, serving as buffer between the ruling Spaniards and the bulk of the Capampangan" (Larkin 1993: 30). During the seventeenth and eighteenth centuries, this *principalia* would increasingly use their economic and political power to "reduce the population to share tenants working on lands controlled by the elites" (Larkin 1993:31). By the late eighteenth century the *samacan* contract—the tenancy arrangement in which landowners provided seeds, tools, some food, and high interest loans to increasingly indebted workers *(kasamac)* in exchange for a share of the harvest—would be widespread throughout Pampanga. Spanish law tried to encourage the maintenance of a communal property system, but an informal and inequitable system of private ownership increasingly emerged, and was widely abused by those with power. For while sharecropping typically affords tenants a degree of autonomy from the discipline of the landowner, it is crucial to remember that sugar production is an industrial process as well as an agricultural one. Since the landowners owned and controlled the on-farm mills, the autonomy of the tenants typical of rice farming in the Philippines was far less secure with sugar.

By 1603 a community of Chinese merchants resided in Pampanga, having arrived following a massacre of Chinese in Manila. By the mid-eighteenth century, a new mestizo elite had emerged and come to occupy a dominant place in the social order. This new elite would gradually come to dominate the early sugar industry of Luzon, first as traders, then as credit suppliers, then as owners of sugar land and sugar producers (Larkin 1993: 33). Up to the late nineteenth century most goods moved out of Pampanga from the Chinese-dominated Manila Bay port of Guagua. But the opening of the Manila-Dagupan railroad in 1892 gave direct access to Manila and opened up many new parts of Pampanga and Tarlac as viable sugar lands.

There are many important contrasts between the sugar business in Negros and that of Pampanga. Whereas the Negros elites used credit from foreign sources to get their sugar enterprises started, Capampanga elites relied more heavily on indigenous credit sources, particularly rural credit associations and the *pacto de retro* contract between relative equals.[13] Pampanga's sugar lands were generally settled as smaller, fragmented holdings rather than large haciendas. Not surprisingly, the largest holdings existed in the less-populated areas of northern Pampanga and Tarlac. A typical owner of sugar land in the north also owned rice land in the more established southern part of the province. Most importantly, the Capampanga landowner generally imported the *samacan* system of recruiting labor to the new sugar lands, but—unlike with rice—payments would commonly be conducted in cash once the year's sugar production was completed. The owner generally provided credit, land, cane points, mill equipment, and mill workers. The tenant provided tools, carabaos (the ubiquitous water buffalo), and labor, including paying and/or feeding any additional hired or mutual-help laborers. The landowner would sell the finished sugar to Chinese merchants and then pay the *kasamac* his share of the cash, most often 50 percent (Larkin 1993: 89). The two systems were similar in one way: both worked to the overwhelming advantage of the landowners, and were characterized by severe inequalities between holders of the different factors of production. Perhaps the most debilitating aspect of the *samacan* system was the crushing debt load that most peasants bore, perpetuated because children inherited their parents' debts. In both provinces, peasant debt was manipulated to allow landowners to increase their holdings at the expense of the poor.

A final contrast between the systems concerns the relative flexibility, openness, and independence of nineteenth-century Negros as compared to the conservatism of socioeconomic relations in Pampanga. As world tastes changed, technology improved, and markets shifted, Negros sugar production proved resilient and continued to expand, while the Pampanga industry often seemed on the verge of failure. Still, the sugar business did bring unprecedented levels of wealth and worldliness, and inequality, to late nineteenth-century Pampanga. As in Negros, Pampanga's elite avoided manual labor and came to view land ownership as the only proper form of economic activity for people of high social status. In both provinces, the elected and bureaucratic offices available to natives under the colonial regimes were dominated by members of the planter class.

The Philippine Revolution and the war against the United States had a more direct impact and caused more suffering on Pampanga than on remote Negros. Although some members of the Pampanga elite were leaders in the Malolos government and loyalties were shifting and complex throughout the revolutionary period, beginning in early 1901 most elites began to back the United States against the Republic. Whether backing the Spanish against the early revolutionaries, the Republic against the Spanish and later the Americans, or the Americans against the Republic, Pampanga's elites appeared to side with whichever force gained the upper hand and afforded the best guarantee for preserving order and the sanctity of property (Larkin 1993: 120–121).

The American Period

In the waning years of the nineteenth century there were signs that the glory days of the sugar industry were coming to an end. The increased production of beet sugar in temperate areas, the growth of sugar cane industries in Australia, Java, Formosa, India, Hawai'i, Cuba, and Puerto Rico, and the leveling off of sugar consumption in Europe and the United States led to worldwide oversupplies of sugar. The Philippine Revolution caused disruptions at the port of Manila in 1898 and 1899 and closed the country's only refinery. To make matters worse, an 1897 rinderpest epidemic devastated the population of carabaos, so essential for both farming and milling (Larkin 1993: 51–53).

U.S. colonial rule transformed the Philippine sugar industry. The American colonial state was favorably disposed toward the sugar planters both because of sugar's moneymaking potential and because of the support planters had given to annexation. In the wake of the rinderpest epidemic, U.S. agricultural officials arranged the importation of large numbers of inoculated carabaos from China and Indochina. An effort to rid sugar provinces of locusts was largely successful. Roads were built in sugar provinces to facilitate transport of cane, farm inputs, and sugar, and the port of Pulupandan was opened in Negros Occidental, thus permitting direct transport of sugar out of the province (i.e., circumventing Iloilo) for the first time (Aguilar 1998: 195). In 1919, American agricultural officials introduced tractors to sugar growing areas, and through the 1920s most large farms retired their carabaos and switched to "power farming" (Aguilar 1998: 194). An Agricultural Bank, capitalized by the colonial government, was created in 1907, largely in order to facilitate channeling credit to cash-starved sugar planters. When the Agricultural Bank ran out of funds in 1913, the governor-general of the colony authorized 1.5 million pesos be deposited in the privately owned Bank of the Philippine Islands "to be used exclusively . . . for the specific purpose of making loans on growing crops to tide the Hacenderos of Negros and Panay over the present crisis" (Aguilar 1998: 196). The expectation of credit advanced on the future crop backed by the authority of government (rather than merchant houses or traders) remains today, and one still frequently hears the accusation—voiced early on by colonial officials—that many planters use these loans for personal consumption rather than improving sugar production.

Powerful American sugar interests at first advocated applying the protectionist Dingley Tariff to Philippine sugar in order to protect Cuban, Puerto Rican, and Hawaiian interests, but they backed down once strong political pressure was brought to bear. At the persistent urging of President William Howard Taft—a former Governor of the Philippines and a major figure in the consolidation of U.S. rule there—the sugar interests finally acquiesced in the passage of the Payne-Aldrich Act of 1909. This Act provided for duty-free importation of many Philippine goods (in exchange for free entry of U.S. manufactures into the Philippines), and led to the easy credit for planters that would help generate another boom for Philippine sugar (Lopez-Gonzaga 1991: 34–54). The lobbying of Negros and Pampanga elites for Payne-Aldrich pitted them against many Philippine nationalists who worried that the Act would make the Philippines more reliant on the United States and delay independence.

And yet, despite the tariff concessions, Philippine sugar could not at first compete with other sources because its quality remained low at a time when the demand in Europe and America was for sugar of higher purity. Indeed, the Philippines was by then the only major producer in the world without centrifugal milling and advanced refining to produce high-purity, refined white sugar. Refiners throughout the world increasingly accepted only high-quality centrifugal sugar.

The most radical change that took place in the 1910s and 1920s concerned the arrival of this new technology and its attendant mode of organization, and the subsequent division of labor in the industry. During this period, private investment flowed into the construction of sugar "centrals," or large centrifugal mills, still among the most prominent features of the Negros and Pampanga landscapes. This moved milling out of the haciendas, where it had been done by small, inefficient moscovado mills, into large industrial factories.[14] Between 1914 and 1927, 820 hacienda mills in Negros alone were replaced by seventeen mostly American-owned centrals and their associated rail networks (McCoy 1982: 326). In the country as a whole, by 1922 there were twenty-six centrals turning out 233,770 tons of centrifugal sugar. By 1934, forty-five centrals were producing 998,123 tons. During that same period, sugar hectarage increased by 27 percent (14 percent in Pampanga; 44 percent in Negros Occidental) and exports grew fourfold (Larkin 1993: 149–150). These were the first mills to use the "share system," in which the mill processes and transports the sugar in exchange for a share of the finished product rather than outright purchase of the raw cane. This system is still in use today, and will be discussed in considerable detail in chapter 4.

In most other countries the mills themselves lease or own the agricultural lands that provide the cane, but the U.S. colonial government tried to prevent non-Filipino ownership of large tracts of land. This was partly out of deference to Filipino elites who felt strongly that the Philippines should not become a plantation-based economy, and partly to create a nation of yeoman farmers. It also reflected the concerns of U.S. beet sugar interests and American investors in Caribbean and Hawaiian sugar.[15] Despite the recommendation of Governor Taft and the Philippine Commission to limit foreign land holdings to 25,000 hectares, the U. S. Congress set the limit at only sixteen hectares for individuals and 1,024 for corporate entities, a type of restriction not found in Cuba, Puerto Rico, and Hawai'i (Aguilar 1998: 198). The limits made it difficult for a central to secure an adequate cane supply throughout its designated milling season. This problem had to be solved so as to encourage investment in the costly new factories (Larkin 1993: 57). The solutions—unique to the Philippines—were the fixed milling district and the share contract. Most sugar land was divided into milling districts so that all planters in a district had to mill with the central of that district. Since sugar was transported almost entirely by rail, a planter could not choose to send his cane to a different central. Contracts between millers and planters typically ran for five to thirty years, and mills received from 25 to 50 percent share of the milled sugar.[16] Each planters' association, therefore, dealt with a single monopsonistic mill (Quirino 1974: 84–86). Once this system was in place, investment money for the construction of centrals flowed in from Hawai'i, California, and Spain, Spanish residents of the Philippines, and native elites backed by the Philippine National Bank (PNB),[17] all with the support of the colonial government. Although the colonial state and foreign capital were essential to the financing of most centrals, that there were Filipinos among the owners and managers led to the widespread perception that the centrals represented "the great awakening of the Filipino capitalists" (Aguilar 1998: 201) and they became potent symbols of nationalist pride.

Despite their disparate backgrounds, the central owners proved to be the most politically organized sector of the industry. In the subsequent years, many of the most important political leaders in the sugar-growing provinces emerged from the ranks of the *centralistas*. The Philippine Sugar Association (PSA), originally established in 1922 as a clearinghouse for technical information, soon became a powerful lobbying organization for Philippine sugar, most especially the milling sector. Despite many *centralistas* having originally come from the ranks of the *hacenderos*, the Confederation of Associations and Planters of Sugar Cane (founded in 1924) often took an adversarial position toward the PSA, though the planters were rarely as united or effective as the millers. Today the milling districts have largely broken down and most cane is now transported by truck to mills that must compete for cane supplies. Nonetheless, relations between planters' associations and centrals remain among the most contested aspects of sugar politics, and the anti-competitive consequences of the old milling districts still plague the industry.

The shift to centrifugal mills had many important effects. By greatly expanding production capacity it created a surging demand for land that resulted in further acquisition of the land of small farmers and expansion into even more marginal acreage.[18] This further exacerbated the already sharp social and economic distinctions between the owners of large haciendas and the majority of farmers with small and mid-sized holdings. The advent of the centrals created a sizable class of industrial laborers and the consequent beginning of a trade union movement. It made the local economy more dependent upon U.S. capital and the American market, and it helped create two new and powerful elite segments of Philippine society: the sugar millers and the sugar traders. From the start, traders and bankers tried to manipulate prices. The PNB even opened an office in New York City to lobby for the best possible prices for sugar produced by the bank-financed centrals (Aguilar 1998: 201). The larger planters and millers formed a bloc to fight for their interests but soon conflict between these two groups broke out over the terms of milling contracts. In 1929–1930, the Federation of Planters of Negros Occidental threatened to reduce their cane production unless their share was increased by five percent, to 60 percent, and they even attempted—unsuccessfully—to force this change by legislative action (Larkin 1993: 186). It was colonial government policy to encourage *hacendero* investment in the centrals in order to prevent conflict between the agricultural and industrial sectors, but despite this the equity owned by the planters in the mills remained small and conflict broke out frequently. American colonial officials had defined the factory mill surrounded by independent farms as a "cooperative" mode of organization in which the mill regulated the timing and pace of production, yet "the mill-*hacienda* relationship, from the outset, was seen in oppositional terms" by the planters who resented having lost so much of their autonomy (Aguilar 1998: 209).

Growth was slower in Pampanga, but that province also experienced a sugar boom the 1910s and 1920s. Although the first central in Pampanga was built with American money—by the same group that had earlier built a mill in Laguna province to the south—the second was built by a cooperative group of native landowning families with financing from the PNB. Members of this group and other elite planters offered their own land as collateral to secure the loan. When these centrals opened, many planters switched from rice to sugar and on-the-farm moscovado production virtually ceased (Larkin 1993: 97–98). As in Negros, the supply of cane was guaranteed mainly through the milling contract and the share system rather than the large integrated sugar estates that characterized other cane-growing countries.

Although the new centrals were efficient, state-of-the-art industrial factories, Philippine productivity in the agricultural sector was the lowest of any major sugarcane producer (Larkin 1993: 55). Some landowners did experience significant productivity gains through improved field techniques, the introduction of new cane varieties (often developed at government-sponsored research facilities), and the adoption of new methods financed by the centrals. However, the majority did not know enough about the agricultural side of the business to improve their yields (Larkin 1993: 104). Most did not even keep cost account records (Aguilar 1998: 109). Sugar "planters" —especially those with significant interests in the new centrals — had easy access to credit, low labor costs, cheap and abundant land, large profits, and sumptuous lifestyles; farm productivity and precise bookkeeping seemed inconsequential.

Although credit remained easy for the planters, it was widely known during this period that the PNB was virtually insolvent. The bank had given loans collateralized with heavily mortgaged properties, and had written off millions of pesos of bad debt—especially to the bank centrals—and it was on the verge of collapse by 1926. An examiner recommended that "'a competent American [manager] who will be in absolute control of operations' be installed in the Bank Centrals, along with 'a competent auditor'" (Aguilar 1998: 203). American officials increasingly worried that this "great awakening of the Filipino capitalists" was fraught with corruption and incompetence. The conservative and unpopular Governor-General Leonard Wood tried to pursue a policy of weaning the PNB from its financial dependence on the colonial government, largely because of his hostility to the bank centrals. Still, the overall trend through the 1920s and 1930s was a decreasing role for American and European capital and management in the sugar mills and an increasing debt burden for the bank centrals. By 1935, American capital amounted to only 10.5 percent of investment in Philippine sugar, and Spanish capital 9 percent, whereas fully 79 percent was Filipino (Aguilar 1998: 207).

During this period, the Philippine "sugar barons" became legendary for their glamour, love of gambling, and conspicuous consumption (Lopez-Gonzaga 1989: 18). Profits from sugar were enormous owing not only to the new centrals but also the 1914 opening of the Panama Canal (which reduced transport costs to east coast refineries), duty-free exports to the United States, a price surge that occurred when European beet sugar—by then the largest contributor to world supplies—declined during World War I, and the construction of new railroad and port facilities by the colonial government. A large portion of these profits went toward the purchase of automobiles and mansions, foreign travel, education in the United States or Europe, cock breeding and cockfighting, and opulent high-society events. The *hacenderos* become known for their reliance on credit during years when the price of sugar was low, and lavish spending when it was high. Saving and frugality were regarded disdainfully as "tradesmen's" values. Planters themselves seemed to relish cultivating the image of the devil-may-care gambler willing to live life to its fullest in the here and now. The sugar business was often portrayed as the ultimate game of chance, though, of course, there was very little real risk involved for the larger planters.

Some of the profits were used to further improve transportation and other infrastructure (thus reducing the almost complete isolation of most hacienda communities), but few of the benefits accrued to the workers, who experienced food scarcity, disease, and the constant threat of displacement. In fact, "the industrialization of milling and mechanization of much farm work during the 1920s reduced the demand for agricultural labor for the first time in the province's history, creating a surplus and depressing wages" (McCoy 1982: 329). The writings of American officials of this period are filled with reports of injustices perpetrated against the poor, even while high profits and glittering luxury were the norm among the elite.

But the charmed life of the early American years would come to an end. In the early 1930s the price of sugar plummeted owing to the worldwide depression and the overproduction encouraged by U.S. tariff policies and the provision of ample credit. The Timberlake Bill to limit importation of sugar was narrowly defeated in the U.S. Congress despite being strongly promoted by increasingly protectionist American sugar producers. As the amount of direct American investment in Philippine sugar declined, American sugar interests increasingly perceived the Philippines as a foreign competitor. The debates over the two Philippine independence bills (Hare-

Hawes-Cutting and Tydings-McDuffie), which would end the duty-free status of Philippine sugar, created a furor among Philippine producers. Many U.S. banks, which held interests in Cuba, were strong advocates of the bills, which stipulated a ten-year Commonwealth period followed by complete political independence. The U.S. Congress passed the bills despite President Hoover's objection that the transition period was too short. The Philippine legislature, led by Manuel Quezon, rejected the initial independence bill, partly because of its proposed tariffs and partly because of provisions guaranteeing a U.S. right to retain Philippine naval bases. The PSA —the powerful millers' organization—instituted a per-picul lien to pay for its extensive lobbying effort to advance its interests. In 1933, the PSA hired the just-retired Senator Hawes—former chairman of the Senate Committee on Insular Affairs—to head its Washington, D.C. office. While the initial independence bill set and enacted a quota of 800,000 tons of centrifugal and 50,000 tons of refined sugar (duty-free for the first five years), fierce lobbying by the PSA and its friends led to a slight increase of the quota (to 982,000 short tons raw value) in the subsequent Jones-Costigan Act of 1934. After a record year in 1933–1934 (1,431,920 m.t.), Philippine sugar production dropped precipitously the next year (to 631,142 m.t.) due to the imposition of the new quota. This created ripples of hardship throughout sugar-producing provinces as standing cane fields were burned and workers idled (Quirino 1974). And yet, within a few years of the quota's imposition production would rebound and the never-ending cycle of boom and bust would continue. The complete dependence on the U.S. market was underscored in 1937 when, as part of the London International Sugar Conference (which sought—without success—to restrain global overproduction), the Commonwealth government agreed not to export any sugar to any country other than the United States so long as the quota remained in force. This agreement hardly disturbed those in the industry, for although Philippine sugar had become considerably more expensive than sugar from other countries, the United States committed itself to buying the Philippine product in the stipulated amounts.

The quota led to favoritism and further consolidation of wealth and power within the industry. The Philippine Sugar Administration (later the Sugar Quota Administration) granted portions of the quota to milling companies that, in turn, apportioned quotas to planters within their districts. Although the insular government administered the quota fairly and with minimal political influence (Larkin 1993: 203–204), larger planters prospered at the expense of others, and the owners and managers of centrals wielded even greater clout than before. Although the quota put an end to the voracious expansion of sugar acreage at the expense of food crops (Aguilar 1984: 19), it was a major factor in the further stagnation of the oligarchy in sugar-producing areas. Once in place, the quota amounts were fixed, and a planter could not get credit or even a milling contract without a share of the quota. One could only gain a larger share by buying or leasing it from someone else, and parents bequeathed their shares to their children. The industry languished since there was no incentive to improve production methods or increase efficiency. Although some of the wealthiest planters began to diversify their interests and investments into other pursuits, most continued to view commerce and marketing as unnecessary, declassé, and "Chinese." Competition was minimal, the centrals and the PNB supplied ample credit, the crop was profitable, and the quotas were in place; the sugar elite —whose fathers and grandfathers had been the risk-taking "cowboys" of the Philippines—lost their entrepreneurial drive to the lure of luxury and the pursuit of political advantage (Billig 1994). While the planters complained to government officials about their financial difficulties, it was hard to take them seriously given their lifestyles and spending habits.

The late 1930s was a period of heightened conflict between planters and millers. The centrals were becoming increasingly consolidated, powerful, and closely allied with the Quezon administration. With the opening of the Manila stock market in 1927, equity shares in sugar centrals were bought up by a few very wealthy investors amidst allegations of insider trading (Aguilar 1998: 213). By 1937, seven families or corporations controlled two-thirds of all Philippine sugar milling. The Aranetas and the Lopezes in particular made vast fortunes from sugar milling and began to diversify into industries in Manila. The planters, despite their own consolidation as large landowners bought up quota shares of smaller ones, were faring less well during this extended period of low prices; and the quota made it difficult for them to find new ways to improve their circumstances (Larkin 1993: 210–214). Planters, most of whom did not bother to learn how the centrals' technology or accounting worked, reasoned that since the centrals were so much more profitable than they were, the share was inequitably apportioned and should be adjusted in their favor. Accusations of cheating became widespread, and planters' associations began once again to demand an increase in the planters' share of the finished sugar. Negros and Pampanga politics became increasingly and often violently polarized between factions representing the interests of these two powerful opposing forces. As planters fared increasingly badly through the late 1930s and early 1940s they cut wages, economized labor costs, and attempted to force tenants to accept a lower share. This led to a series of worker protests, strikes, and acts of vandalism. And yet, the planters frequently cited the need to provide for their workers and tenants when they pressed their claims to the colonial and (after 1935) Commonwealth governments. In 1933, the colonial government enacted a sugar tenancy law that required owners of tenanted land to provide tenants with accurate receipts for farm expenses and an accounting of the amounts of sugar in the planters' shares (Aguilar 1998: 221). The law, which proved difficult to enforce, was obviously intended to curtail the widespread cheating of tenants, especially in Pampanga. In 1938, President Quezon ordered that the Philippine Constabulary force in Pampanga be augmented, but the police could not restore order and the landowners formed a violent vigilante group which intimidated strikers and tenant organizers. The constant threat of violent resistance in Luzon largely prevented the Pampanga sugar industry from making the transformation from tenancy to wage labor, as had been successfully accomplished in Negros.

The sugar industry was decimated by the Japanese occupation and World War II. Many fields reverted to subsistence crops or weeds and many centrals were scuttled for parts.[19] Only three of the forty-two pre-war centrals were left intact in the immediate aftermath of the war (Aguilar 1998: 214). As part of the post-war package granting independence to the Philippines, the U.S. Congress created the Rehabilitation Finance Corporation and passed the Bell Trade Act of 1946, restoring duty-free trade until 1954. Also restored was the generous sugar quota of 982,000 short tons per year (Hawes 1987: 90). But in order to gain the desperately needed reconstruction assistance, the Philippines had to agree to onerous concessions on currency exchange, military bases, and privileged American access to the Philippine economy. Many Philippine nationalists bristled especially at the "parity clause" that gave Americans equal rights to exploit natural resources and operate public utilities (Larkin 1993: 239). The reestablishment of the old dependency relations was solidified when the Philippine Congress passed a resolution in 1952 once again barring export of sugar to any country other than the United States. Also reestablished was the animosity between planter and miller that again became the main focus of politics in sugar-growing areas.

The Bell Act and the ready availability of funds to repair the damaged centrals caused a revival of sugar production, and the social organization of the industry quickly reverted to pre-war patterns. The smaller, less efficient centrals remained closed, and the milling sector consolidated even further than it had in the 1930s. The planters scored a political coup in 1952 when the Philippine Congress legislated an increase in the planters' share to 60–70 percent, depending upon the productivity of the mill (Aguilar 1998: 215). The *kasamac* of Luzon and the *dumaan* of Negros gave up their subsistence crops and, for the most part, went right back to planting sugar at the behest of landowners.

An important post-war move affecting the sugar industry was the Laurel-Langley Trade Agreement of 1954, which extended the Bell Act's provisions, granting Philippine sugar a high quota for entry into the United States on an accelerating tariff schedule up to 1974. This, more than anything else, led to boom years for sugar in the 1950s, 1960s, and early 1970s. The souring of U.S. relations with Cuba following that country's revolution led to an additional increase in the quotas of all other sugar exporting countries. In 1961, the Philippines was given 15 percent of the Cuban share, causing another surge in demand for land. Between 1962 and 1977, nineteen new centrals were built, many outside of Negros and Central Luzon in areas that had not previously produced sugar (e.g., Mindanao, Bicol, the Cagayan Valley). Meanwhile, another important trend was emerging: Philippine domestic sugar consumption increased in every year after the war. Today, the largest portion of Philippine sugar is consumed at home, and the domestic market continues to expand.

The Marcos Years

All through the glory years of sugar, planters, millers, and traders were among the most influential people in the country. Many national political figures sprang from the ranks of the sugar barons, and others were beholden to them in one way or another.[20] Although many sugar people supported Ferdinand Marcos initially and some played key roles in getting him elected, they, like most Filipinos, would come to regret this support. Marcos was intent upon curbing the power of the sugar industry. He largely succeeded in doing this during the martial law period by creating a government monopsony that was used to aggrandize cronies and siphon off much of the sugar profits into bank accounts in Switzerland and the United States. Planters fared poorly, but the workers, as usual, bore the brunt of the disaster.

When the Laurel-Langley Agreement expired in 1974, sugar producers lost their guaranteed access to the U.S. market. Most assumed that the quota would be extended beyond the expiration date as it had been in 1954, but U.S. sugar interests won the day. With the quotas no longer in effect, the placid sugar industry entered into its most turbulent years. Upstart farmers began to plant sugar, some planters' groups banded together to purchase mills,[21] and, as the old milling districts began to break apart due to truck hauling[22] and the decreased power of the post-quota centrals, mills now had to compete for limited supplies of cane. After fifty years of easy credit and duty-free quotas, Philippine sugar was suddenly forced to participate in the world market during one of the most volatile periods in the history of commodity trading.

At first, there were few complaints since the world-market price of sugar in 1974 reached a historic high of U.S. $0.67 per pound.[23] Citing rumors that large traders were forming a cartel to manipulate the price of sugar, the Marcos administration nationalized the sugar trade by placing all trading functions in the hands of the Philippine Exchange Company (PHILEX), a subsidiary of the PNB. Many planters supported this move, thinking that a consolidation of trading under a single unit would eliminate most of the unproductive trading activity and lead to higher profits for the producers. They believed Marcos when he said that his aim was to lend "rationality to the marketing process effecting in less manipulation by traders" (Sa-onoy 1984: 10). The planters preferred a "rational" government trading organization to the machinations of powerful "Chinese" traders, whom many feared had the financial clout to control the industry. PHILEX's managers speculated that prices would go even higher, so they kept as much of the 1974 sugar as possible out of the market and in the centrals' *bodega*s, but they were proved wrong. By 1975, a worldwide glut was caused by the high prices as well as the entry of large quantities of heavily subsidized European beet sugar into the world market. This forced prices to plummet to $0.30 per pound, a price at which there were no world-market buyers of Philippine sugar (Dacanay 1982). People in Negros still talk about 1975–1978 as the years in which surplus sugar had to be stored in swimming pools, schools, and even churches in order to clear the *bodegas* for the new crop.

Prices continued to decline so that by August 1978 they briefly reached as low as $0.07 per pound. Planters protested when prices were set at P75 per picul at the beginning of the 1977–1978 crop year, which was significantly below production cost. In addition to low prices, planters were being squeezed by rapidly escalating fuel and fertilizer prices caused by the Arab oil embargo. The PNB had to take over several of the newer mills that had been built with its funds, and even the bank joined in the clamor to return trading to the private sector. But instead, Marcos activated a different government monopsony: the Philippine Sugar Commission (PHILSUCOM), with its trading arm, the National Sugar Trading Corporation (NASUTRA), under the directorship of his close friend, Roberto S. Benedicto.[24] The mandate of this organization was to control domestic pricing, local distribution and marketing, and all export functions. Benedicto became the czar of the industry, using his personal Republic Planters Bank to dispense patronage to relatives and friends. He was able to stifle dissent in the industry by having his bank give ample crop loans on very little collateral. If a planter could not repay, as was often the case in those years, he would either lose a marginal plot of land or simply have his debt restructured and continue to borrow. Although many planters were deeply in debt to the crony-controlled banks, few actually experienced foreclosure. But crossing Benedicto would have been an unwise strategy for a planter interested in keeping his land. And, of course, the centrals were hardly faring much better. By 1986, twenty-two of the nation's forty-one centrals were controlled by the PNB (Hawes 1987: 96), and none could afford to invest the capital required for even routine maintenance.

In case the wealthy and powerful planters and millers did not get the message, there was always the example of the Lopez family to consider. Fernando Lopez, a member of one of the nation's wealthiest and most influential sugar families, had been Marcos's vice president prior to the declaration of martial law. After 1972, the government seized many of the Lopez family's diverse assets (including their media empire) and arrested or exiled several prominent members (Hawes 1987: 97). Many people in the sugar industry regarded the destruction of the Lopezes as an example for the rest of them of what would ensue if they attempted to resist.

Most of the profits being made in the industry were in the trading sector, now controlled by Benedicto and his loyal minions. As world prices began to rise in the early 1980s, Philippine producers realized that the price at which they were selling to NASUTRA was barely rising at all. Although NASUTRA was very secretive about the terms of its transactions, the agency was buying sugar from the planters at P180 per picul and selling it abroad at P500. It soon became clear that PHILSUCOM's main purpose was to divert profits into the hands of Marcos and his cronies and to emasculate planters and millers who represented a threat to the authority of the administration. The descriptions of the lavish lifestyle Benedicto was able to lead at the expense of the industry are truly extraordinary.[25] All the while, the government continued to print and borrow money with impunity, nearly leading to the government-owned banks being closed down by the IMF.

It is estimated that the industry lost more than fifteen billion pesos between 1975 and 1987. Hectarage planted in sugar declined from a high of 573,150 hectares in 1977 to a mere 215,640 hectares by 1988 (FAO 1998). Total production of centrifugal raw sugar plummeted from 2.84 million tons (m.t.) in 1976 to 1.20 m.t. in 1987 (FAO 1998). Unemployment increased three-fold during this crisis period. By the mid-1980s, Negros had become a noteworthy spot on the "international charity map" (Ofreneo 1987: 162). Attention was properly focused upon the workers; on Negros alone 400,000 of them had lost all sources of income in an economy that proffered no viable alternatives (Meenahan 1985: 17). Between 1975 and 1981 real income for the average sugar worker declined by 33.5 percent, and the worst was still to come (Aguilar 1984: 33). In a 1982 survey, the mean annual income for unskilled sugar workers was $187 (Lopez-Gonzaga 1983: 19). The result was malnutrition on a massive scale. In a 1982 study, nearly 70 percent of 177,373 children weighed on Negros were suffering from malnutrition (Ofreneo 1987: 162). In 1985, 83.7 percent of families were earning less than the poverty threshold (Lacson 1988: 1–2). Meanwhile, the government-sanctioned labor union with the sole right to speak on behalf of sugar workers took out full-page advertisements in national newspapers thanking God for guiding Marcos and Benedicto in their "efficient and effective management of the sugar industry in crisis" (Hawes 1987: 99).

Martial law, with its heightened power of the military, the absence of a free press, and the suppression of independent unions had strong effects on life in sugar-producing areas. These were widely reported in the West. During this time "salvaging," or the brutal execution of those on the opposite sides of disputes or in other factions, was rampant (Berlow 1996). At the height of the crisis, the Philippine military listed Negros as having the second worst insurgency problem in the nation (Lacson 1988: 4).

In this environment, the Catholic Church in Negros, led by Bishop Antonio Fortich, became a leading voice for the poor. The Church established its own NGOs, set up kibbutz-like "Basic Christian Communities," and even founded a small mill in a remote part of southern Negros to foster self-sufficiency among peasants and workers. Priests citing the "preferential option for the poor" became ardent advocates for social justice, and several of them were imprisoned, framed, or even killed (McCoy 1984; O'Brien 1987). Bishop Fortich was able to convince Pope John Paul II to add Negros as a stop on the Pope's pastoral visit to the Philippines in 1984. In front of a massive throng on the main plaza in Bacolod (and in the presence of Imelda Marcos), the Pope asserted: "Injustice reigns when within the same society some groups hold most of the wealth and power while large strata of the population cannot decently provide for the livelihood of their families even through long hours of backbreaking labor in factories and in the fields . . ." (O'Brien 1987: 195).

The leftist rebels in the hills (mostly associated with the New People's Army, or NPA) grew increasingly bold and recruited many new members, a few of them priests but most desperate young people. The planters, many of whom displayed bravado by becoming self-styled "warlords," responded by organizing vigilante forces of their own, and bands of bizarre *fanaticos* pursued "communists" with mystical and gruesome fervor. Negros became a polarized and militarized powder keg, and thousands of refugees were forced from their homes by the violence.[26] This tense situation lasted into the 1990s, and occasional flare-ups of the violence continue to occur. The Ramos administration's amnesty and negotiation program went a long way toward abating the NPA threat, and the banning of private armies helped allay the tension in rural areas. But to this day, many planters resent the negative image that Negros received during this period, feeling that it exaggerated the magnitude of the problem.

NASUTRA ceased functioning in 1984 and PHILSUCOM was dismantled in 1986 because of pressure from the World Bank. Since then, the economic plight of the planters has improved and many of the outward signs of starvation have diminished. Thanks to rising sugar prices as well as many health and nutrition programs run by highly active NGOs and PVOs, the immediate crisis was defused. But malnutrition remains a problem, the majority of the population live in great poverty, and political violence remains an ever-present threat. Planters are still waiting for the implementation of the noble-sounding Restitution Law (Republic Act 7202), which ordered "restitution of losses by sugar producers from crop year 1974–1975 to crop year 1984–1985 due to actions of government controlled agencies." Most believe that the government does not have the resources or will to implement such a law, and everyone has given up hope that the Marcos' personal wealth will ever find its way back into the Philippine treasury. The implementation of the restitution law is complicated by the existence of CARP, the agrarian reform program, which specifies a preference for foreclosed land to be redistributed to tenants and workers. But since the restitution law protects the "owners" of foreclosed land, land-reform advocates point out that it works at cross-purposes with the well-intended, but ineffectual agrarian reform law.

The plight of the industry since the fall of Marcos takes me to the following chapters.

Production, Financing, CARP, and the U.S. Quota

No matter how one measures productivity, the Philippines is no longer one of the world's most prolific or efficient producers of cane sugar, and the situation shows little sign of reversing itself. In 1997, sugar was grown on 367,000 hectares in the Philippines, down from a peak of 573,000. Total mill capacity is less than three million tons. Over the last twenty-five years—a period in which sugar consumption in the Philippines itself has increased rapidly— Philippine production has fallen from 3.3 percent of total world production to 1.3 percent. The United Nations' Food and Agriculture Organization estimates worldwide production in 2000 at 127.20 million m.t.; Philippine production was 1.68 million m.t. in that year, making the country eighteenth in world sugar production, just behind Italy and ahead of Ukraine.[1] In 1975, when the world produced 79.64 million m.t., Philippine production was 2.62 million m.t., while Thailand only produced 1.14 million m.t. and Australia produced 2.86 million m.t. That year the Philippines was the world's eleventh leading producer with 3.3 percent of global production.

Some simple contrasts serve to illustrate not only the stagnation of Philippine production but also the declining position of the country among the sugar producers in its own region. Philippine production in 1971, 1981, 1991, and 2000 was (in million metric tons): 2.06, 2.40, 1.74, and 1.68. Australian production in those same years was: 2.79, 3.44, 3.11, and 5.78. Thai production was: 0.41, 1.64, 4.05, and 5.72, reflecting that Thailand has made a concerted effort to boost its production of sugar over the last four decades. While sugar production varies from year to year in every country, the secular trend for the Philippines has been downward, contrasting with the decidedly upward trends in Thailand and Australia. In the 1990s, the most productive year for Philippine sugar was 1993 (2.13 million tons); the least productive (owing to an El Niño-related drought) was 2000 (1.68 million tons) (FAO).

The relative inefficiency of Philippine sugar production is evident in the low yields. Dividing sugar tonnage by the number of hectares planted in sugar gives a rough approximation of the yields in the three countries. For 1994, 1995, 1996, and 1997 the values (in tons per hectare) are as follows: Philippines—4.66, 6.00, 4.83 and 4.84; Thailand—5.01, 5.97, 6.29, and 5.78; Australia—13.92, 13.18, 14.11, and 13.80.[2] Thailand has a slightly lower farm yield of cane per hectare than the Philippines, but far more efficient mills and more productive cane varietals. This means that despite having a lower cane yield per hectare, the Thai yield of actual *sugar* per hectare is higher than in the Philippines. Australia has the highest farm yields and most efficient mills of any sugarcane-producing country (data from FAO). Whereas the Philippines needs, on average, eleven tons of sugarcane to produce one ton of raw sugar, the Australians need only seven tons of cane (SRA Administrator Arsenio Yulo, interview).

While the trend in other countries is toward more efficient mills, Philippine centrals are large, superannuated, highly polluting dinosaurs that continue to use older technology, to depreciate rapidly, and to function at low-capacity utilization. The average age of centrals in the Philippines is over fifty years; in Thailand less than twenty years. While other countries' extraction efficiencies are high and increasing, Philippine extraction rates are low and declining. In sugar-producing areas, the most often discussed statistic is PSTC, piculs of sugar per ton of cane. Overall Philippine PSTC was 1.31 in 1989, 1.46 in 1990, and 1.33 in 1991.[3] In mid-1998, Victorias Milling proudly announced that it had reached 1.49 PSTC—the highest of any of the twenty-three still-operating mills in the nation (*Balita-L listserve*, 10 July 1998). In contrast, Thailand, whose farms are not more efficient than those of the Philippines, has an average PSTC above 1.7. But even more striking than the contrast with other countries is the temporal contrast within the Philippines itself. In the five-year crop period 1946/7–1950/1, Philippine PSTC was 1.81. Ten years later (1956/7–1960/1) it was 1.79, then (1966/7–1970/1) 1.51. Twenty years later, it was down to 1.33 (figures from Covar 1990: 27; and SRA: final production CY 1990 to 1991). Today, PSTC in the very best mill is .32 lower than the average fifty years ago.

One sugar technology consultant told me that he believes one important factor in the decline of mill efficiency has been the erosion of technical knowledge and management practices in Philippine centrals. The recent trend of traders purchasing mills (discussed in the next chapter) has meant that people with no expertise in sugar production are increasingly running the mills, and they are highly reluctant to hire Filipino engineers who know more than they do. I met this particular consultant when he was in Negros helping a new trader-owner organize and retool a mill that had been "run into the ground." Education in sugar technology—once a respectable course of study for the scions of the sugar industry—is no longer popular as more and more young people from planting and milling families major in business and commerce. The consultant was "quite certain that the levels of technical competence, research, and management in the milling sector have declined precipitously since the 1960s."

There is one positive consequence of mill inefficiency: the production of highly prized molasses. Molasses is a by-product of sugar milling, but an efficient mill will produce molasses with a low sucrose content because a greater proportion of the sucrose will be recovered in the sugar. Since Philippine mills have low sucrose recovery, the molasses they produce tends to be particularly sweet, averaging 58 percent sucrose as compared to 40 percent for Thai molasses (procurement manager, Ajinomoto Philippines, pers. com., 1994). Although molasses is not as lucrative a product as sugar, alcohol distilleries and Japanese producers of monosodium glutamate regard Philippine molasses as being of particularly high-quality (though not high-purity)—much to the embarrassment of the sugar mills.

Perhaps even more troubling than the declining efficiency of the mills is diminishing farm productivity. One cause of this is the deterioration of the cane itself. It is not clear why this is occurring, though it is probably a combination of factors. One agricultural scientist blames the lack of trace elements in fertilizers; others cite the decay of irrigation networks and canals, El Niño, the overlong milling period that forces farmers to mill during the lower-sucrose wet season, depleted soil fertility due to monocropping and poor soil management, and increasing salinity of the soil and groundwater due to deforestation, excess runoff, and prawn cultivation. While many planters continue to blame the mills for the increasingly poor extraction, mill efficiency could not possibly have degenerated so rapidly. Cane today simply has less sucrose in it; from only 1986–1987 to 1988–1989, the sucrose percentage in cane declined from 11.96 to 10.45, and the ratio of tons of cane to tons of sugar rose from 10.22 to 12.07 (Covar 1990: 49). The Philippines is one of the only sugar-producing countries in which most farmers plant sugarcane in the same fields every year with no fallow periods or crop rotation.

Further, while in most producing countries fields are fully plowed and new cane points are planted every year or every other year, Philippine farmers rely more on "ratooning," in which previously planted points are left in the ground to regrow for several years. Some small farmers might even attempt five or six ratoons before planting new cane points, with the productivity, sucrose percentage, and pest resistance of the cane declining each year.[4] Since there is great variation in the cost of cane points by cane varietal, many farmers choose to plant less productive varietals and save money. Others complain that they would plant better varietals, but none are available.

One legendary farmer on Negros described to me what he felt was wrong with sugarcane farming practices. First, the varietals that were available and that people plant are too old and unproductive, and the propagation of new varietals is appallingly slow. Although his farm averages 150 piculs per hectare, he claimed he could probably get 200 if only he had access to a cane varietal recently produced by Victorias but not made commercially available. Second, harvesting methods have deteriorated, particularly in the way that cane is typically cut too quickly and unskillfully (resulting in high trash content) but loaded too slowly (resulting in sucrose loss from desiccation and inversion). Third, people tend to mill too early, trying to "make the quick buck," even though the cane is not yet fully ready for harvesting. Fourth, he contended that the five or six *laksa* (10,000 cane points) per hectare that most people plant is too high a density. Three *laksa* per hectare actually yields more and healthier cane. Fifth, planters fail to use many of the natural, "sustainable" sources of fertilizer available to them and rely instead on more expensive commercial fertilizers. Sixth, planters rarely assess the appropriateness of the land to grow sugar. He himself plants sugar only on land that has potential to grow cane well, and on other land he plants rice and fruit trees. He is convinced that rice can be at least as profitable a crop as sugar, but only if one erects—as he did—a rice mill to process one's own *palay*. (Clearly, most rice farmers could not afford such an expensive capital outlay). Finally, he criticized his fellow planters for their failure to mechanize land preparation, inter-row cultivation, fertilization, and other functions (besides harvesting, for which he still uses manual labor). He claimed that his workers "have no problem" with his greater degree of mechanization because he has provided his resident workers with five hectares on which they can plant anything they please, and sell the produce themselves. He also gives his workers a 5 percent profit share and productivity bonuses. This planter told me that he wished, "there could be a kind of land reform that took the land away from planters who inherited it but know nothing about farming and gave it to knowledgable farmers who will be good stewards of the land. If people perceive good farming as a sacrifice, then they aren't cut out to be farmers. The land should belong only to those who love it, not to the traders and politicians who are afraid to get their shoes dirty. Farming requires one to study and pursue excellence just like any other noble profession. It seems to me that the higher the prices we get for sugar, the more ignorant our planters become. Complacency will be our downfall."

The 1997 Report of LMC International divides world sugar producers into four cost categories. Australia is included among the low-cost producers, Thailand the low-to-medium-cost producers, and the Philippines the medium-to-high-cost producers (LMC International 1997). Although prices and costs fluctuate, the average cost of sugar production in the Philippines today is between $0.13 and 0.15 per pound, not including the "cost of money" in an industry that relies heavily on bank financing. In contrast, costs in Thailand average $0.10 and in Australia 0.06. In other words, when the Thais and Australians sell on the world market, where the price generally ranges from $0.10 to 0.14 per pound, they make money. The Filipinos, on the other hand, lose money when they sell on the same market. No wonder the Filipinos so value their share of the U.S. quota, which guarantees a price of $0.18 per pound but typically yields 0.22 or higher. A further computation shows that if average Philippine PSTC were 1.7, as in Thailand, costs would be approximately $0.11 per pound. So while the higher input costs might explain half the difference in overall cost of production between Thailand and the Philippines, the other half is due to mill efficiency, cane quality, and the other components of PSTC. Lizares (1993) claims that Philippine labor costs on the farm are higher than Thai labor costs. According to him, Philippine sugar farm laborers made on average P80.50 per day, while Thai laborers made only P51.00 per day. These numbers are impossible to confirm given the difficulty in assessing the degree to which employers actually pay the legally mandated minimum wages, the seasonality of sugar work, and the widespread use of piecework and migrant labor for certain tasks at certain times of the year.

Although sugar has traditionally been one of the Philippines' major exports, this has not been the case for more than a decade. Through the 1960s, sugar typically accounted for 20 percent or more of all Philippine exports by monetary value (Dacanay 1982). But between 1973 and 1982 it accounted for just 12 percent, and by 1985 only 4 percent (World Bank 1987). While it was still the third largest Philippine export in dollar value in 1979, by 1991 it was only ranked seventeenth, up from eighteenth in 1987 (Paxton 1982; National Statistics Office 1992). Whereas the Philippines was the world's second largest exporter of sugar in 1970 (far behind Cuba and just ahead of France), by 1991 it had dropped to nineteenth (*Asiaweek*, 1 Dec. 1995: 24) despite having the third largest U.S. import quota. In contrast, during the same period Thailand advanced from forty-fifth to fifth place among the world's sugar exporters.

In 1999, the Philippines exported 142,852 m.t. of raw centrifugal sugar—almost all to satisfy its U.S. quota—making it the world's thirty-seventh leading exporter.[5] But in the same year the Philippines *imported* 396,864 m.t. of sugar owing to a serious shortfall in the domestic market. To illustrate how rapidly things have changed, in 1993 the Philippines exported 324,808 m.t. and imported nothing, at least officially. In 1975, the Philippines exported 972,217 m.t. (making it the world's fourth leading exporter) and imported nothing (figures from FAO). The Philippines continues to try to satisfy its American quota to the fullest extent possible because of the high prices offered by the United States and fear of the prospect of having that quota reduced if the country proves incapable of fulfilling its "obligations." But whenever Philippine production is under about 2.2 million m.t. annually, it must import sugar in order to satisfy domestic demand. The issue of importation (discussed in chapter 6) has been the focus of one of the most contentious political debates surrounding sugar in the last decade. But clearly, the days in which the Philippines was one of the world's major sugar exporters have ended.

The leading Philippine exports recently, by a wide margin, are garments, electronic components, and coconut oil. In 1991 the values of exports in millions of U.S. dollars were: garments = 1,860.59; electronics = 1,751.21; and, coconut oil = 298.53. In that same year, the value for sugar was 114.62 million. Philippine sugar producers rightly claim that today's much smaller sugar exports are more than offset by the rapid growth of domestic sugar consumption. The USDA estimates that Philippine sugar consumption grew 40 percent between 1990 and 1997 alone (Lord and Suarez 1997). The 1994 estimate of Philippine consumption was 22 to 23 kilograms per capita per year. Many industry insiders claim that since consumption in some developed countries is over 40 kilograms (even in Malaysia it is 35 kilograms), and the Philippines population continues to grow around two percent per year, there is significant growth potential in the domestic sugar market.

Given the disintegrating state of affairs in the sugar industry, it is particularly unfortunate that the research and extension functions of the government's Sugar Regulatory Administration are in such disarray. A visit I made to the SRA's La Granja Agricultural Research and Extension Center in July 1992 illustrates the problem. The director described the almost total lack of financial support. Although the SRA is theoretically self-sustaining because of the 50-centavo-per-picul lien paid by every sugar producer, that money still goes into the government general fund and must be budgeted to the agency. In 1991–1992, the SRA was allocated P120 million, but only half of that was actually released by Congress, and almost all of that was earmarked specifically for salaries. In other words, salaries could be paid, but there was nothing left over for operating expenses; clearly, a serious hardship for a research and extension facility! At La Granja, there was a nematode lab with no nematodes, a rodent lab with no rodents, and the research farm had not been fertilized at all. The micropropagation lab is critically important since micropropagation can decrease the time it takes to turn newly bred varietals into commercially available cane points.[6] I was shown a beaker that needed to be stirred constantly. Since the test-tube shaker was broken, someone occasionally passed by and gave the beaker a shake. Many of the chemicals in the lab (mostly supplied by USDA) were beyond their expiration dates. In other words, virtually no agricultural science was being brought to bear on the problem of deteriorating varietals. While a new varietal might have high sucrose content, yield high tonnage, and be resistant to common cane diseases, these traits —especially resistance to disease and fungus—tend to erode over time. New varietals must constantly be produced to prevent production levels from falling. I was told that the third most commonly planted varietal in the Philippines was bred in 1956, and that it has seriously deteriorated. The administrator of the SRA told me himself that the La Granja facility was "pathetic." He said that it was impossible even to communicate with La Granja because the facility had no working telephone.

In addition to the lack of varietal production, little was being done to improve soil management, to maintain and upgrade water supply and irrigation, or to disseminate new techniques of fertilization and pest-control. I asked the director of La Granja whether it would have been possible to lay off some employees in order to concentrate on a few critical areas of research. He replied that any earmarked money not spent on salaries would revert to the general fund and could not be used for operating expenses. Other SRA officials stated openly that budget decisions were purely political, often reflecting internecine squabbling among members of Congress. An SRA official told how one senator in particular had scuttled the SRA's research budget after a dispute over the use of the agency's helicopter. In the meantime, while the industry languished, the La Granja facility retained its full complement of staff; many held Ph.D.s in agricultural science, but few had anything of substance to occupy their time. Even more amazing was that the other SRA research facility (in Floridabanca, Pampanga) continued to have its full complement of salaried staff two years after it had been destroyed by the eruption of Mt. Pinatubo!

There was talk among planters and millers of starting a private foundation, funded by an additional P5 lien, to support the La Granja facility and get research and extension back on track. Indeed, Executive Order 18—the act that created the SRA—explicitly stated the goal of eventually privatizing the research and development functions. Nothing came of this initiative due to continued squabbling over which planters' group would manage and control this foundation. Mills that do produce their own cane varietals in their own laboratories (e.g., Victorias in Negros and Luisita in Tarlac) are often quite reluctant to share those "trade secrets" with planters in other regions and districts. One enterprising planter became so fed up with the lack of new varietal production that he set up a nursery on his property and earned P750,000 selling cane points.

The problem of institutional bloat affects more than research and development. It is widely claimed that agencies of the Philippine government, for example, are filled with political appointees who fulfill no necessary functions. When I asked the administrator of the SRA why so many of the employees at that agency's headquarters in Manila were reading newspapers, he confided that most of them really had nothing to do. There were over one thousand employees of the SRA even though the agency would function better if had less than three hundred. "Every day I get one or two calls from some congressman or political big shot asking me to hire his nephew or the son of some supporter. I cannot refuse." He feared that making an enemy of an important politician would redound negatively on the agency's budget and his own career. He complained that it was impossible to fire anyone, but he must go on hiring.

Another highly controversial issue and difficult dilemma concerned mechanization on the farm. From the mid-1970s to the mid-1980s there was a lot of discussion about mechanizing planting, weeding, loading, and even harvesting, and some planters made serious efforts to do so. Many planters took trips to northern Australia,[7] entrepreneurs began to market machines, and Roberto Benedicto became an ardent advocate of mechanized farming. Not surprisingly, this led many scholars, clerics, and union leaders to decry the trend as causing unemployment and hardship among workers (Lopez-Gonzaga 1983, 1986; Aguilar 1984). But since then the trend has largely been halted, and even reversed. The equipment sellers are gone, the workers are again planting, weeding, and cutting by hand, and the machines purchased by PHILSUCOM for its model farm rust in the back lot of SRA headquarters. Philippine topography is considerably rougher than that of Queensland, Philippine land holdings are smaller, and the availability of hard currency and credit is more limited. But most important, Philippine labor is more abundant and wages are much lower. In fact, if the Philippines retains one competitive advantage in producing sugar it is just that: low wages. But therein lies a dilemma. If the Philippine sugar industry continues to deteriorate, its workers could find themselves massively more disadvantaged than they are even today. But some of the things the industry needs to do to recover would require decreasing its reliance on abundant low-paid, poorly treated workers. Is it better to advocate continued inefficiency to protect the short-term interests of workers, or is it better to advocate improvement for the long-term gain of fewer workers, as well as all other sectors of the industry? Discussions of long-term interests and the need for "rationalization" ring hollow to workers living at the edge of subsistence. This issue will be developed in chapter 6.

In addition to technical inefficiency and institutional stasis, Philippine sugar is always at the mercy of natural disasters. Typhoon Ruping caused the 1991 harvest in the Visayas to be 20 percent lower than projected. Typhoons Iliang and Loleng had major effects on the crop throughout the country in 1998, and Mount Pinatubo had a serious impact on production in Pampanga and Tarlac perhaps for all times. In 1996, 1997, and 1998 droughts caused by the El Niño phenomenon lowered production, and subsequent La Niña rains were almost as debilitating. Yet despite the country becoming a net importer of sugar, some Filipino sugar producers consider the last several years to have been successful ones owing to the high prices for the commodity. Given the continued growth of domestic demand, the generous portion of the U.S. sugar import quota, and the protected nature of the market, production shortfalls translate directly into higher prices. In 1991, when prices on the world market were P380 per picul, the price of domestic sugar exceeded P700. One might imagine that the natural disasters, on top of the declining productivity of the land, the increasingly inefficient mills, deteriorating sucrose content of the cane, skyrocketing costs of inputs such as fuel, fertilizer and spare parts, and a sharp increase in the mandated minimum wage for agricultural workers, would have had a negative impact on sugar producers. That they did not illustrates the unreality of the industry. Despite these vicissitudes, and the inability of the industry to satisfy growing domestic demand, many producers seem unfazed. Still, there is a pervasive feeling that the good times cannot last, and unless the systemic problems of the industry are addressed soon the provinces that depend upon it could enter another period of crisis, perhaps even worse than the last one. The SRA seems well aware of the long-term problems. In the Forward to the 1988–1989 *Annual Synopsis of Philippine Sugar Factories Performance Data*, Administrator Arsenio Yulo wrote: "In the near term, the prospect of the sugar industry looks bright. But, when we turn our sights at the long term, the picture appears to be a little bit hazy. The sugar industry has not caught up with technological acceleration going on in various sugar producing countries all over the world. As a result, mill extraction fell below standard, sucrose losses and overall recoveries continue to leave much to be desired. Even our product quality in terms of color, grain size and sometimes polarization does not meet the standard requirements for raw-sugar quality. Lately, our sugar shipments to the U.S. had been slapped penalties due to high dextran content."

None of this is to imply that there have been no recent improvements in the sugar industry. One positive development has been the construction of several new refineries. In the days when all Philippine sugar was exported to the United States there was no need for refineries, since many developed countries, including the United States, will only buy raw sugar from foreign sources as a way to protect their large refining companies. Although Singapore grows no sugar, Singaporean refiners and traders are among the world's major sellers of refined sugar, made from raw sugar that they purchase at world market prices. But since most Philippine-made sugar today is sold domestically, and many major consumers demand high-quality refined sugar, the construction of refineries has been a key priority for milling companies and traders. Moreover, the value-added on refined sugar as compared to raw sugar makes the refined product more profitable, especially since all the additional profits go to the milling companies rather than the planters. So far, only a few of those refineries have managed to meet the stringent quality standards of large industrial consumers such as Coca-Cola, Pepsi-Cola, and San Miguel, and the market for packaged sugar is dominated by only two companies, Victorias and Luisita. But newer refineries are increasingly requesting that their products be tested for quality, and industrial consumers would like nothing more than to certify as many refineries as possible to increase the reliability of supply.

In 1990 the Board of Investment (BOI), an arm of the Department of Trade and Industry, instituted tax incentives for the improvement of the sugar industry. Up to 1992 only mills were covered, but in 1993 the program was extended to new refineries and planters who owned more than twenty hectares of land. An individual or company had to register with BOI to qualify for these incentives. To upgrade mills and farms, these incentives included duty-free importation of capital equipment as well as a tax credit for domestically produced equipment. New refineries were given a tax holiday for four years. By 1993, eighteen mills, five new refineries, and seven planters had registered with BOI for the incentive program. The governor of the BOI admitted to me that while P875 million in potential tax revenue had been foregone as a result of the program, the executive branch was extremely displeased about the poor registration from the agricultural sector. Most sugar planters, he opined, just could not afford to purchase new capital equipment, incentive or no. Most planters with whom I spoke had never heard of the BOI incentive program. The few that had stated that it was not relevant to them since they did not plan to buy capital equipment. The seven farmers who did register used the incentive mostly to purchase trucks, and a few also purchased tractors. Registration for the program closed at the end of 1993, and it expired as originally scheduled at the end of 1994.

Refineries are expensive, costing millions of dollars to erect. The refining process extracts far more molasses and impurities than does mere milling, and it requires conditions that are far more sanitary. Of course, one major difficulty has been that the quality of refined sugar is directly related to the quality of the raw sugar that gets refined, and this has been deteriorating in the Philippines. The quality parameters for refined sugar are more elaborate than those for raw sugar, and there is a lot more that can potentially fail. Unless the quality of raw sugar improves, it is not likely that the new refineries will be able to produce a product that consistently meets international quality standards even though many of the refineries are state-of-the-art facilities.

There has also been something of a shakeout in the milling sector, with a significant number of the less efficient, less productive mills closing in the last decade or so. In 1993, there were still thirty-nine centrals operating in the Philippines: ten in Luzon (two in Pampanga; two in Tarlac, two in Batangas, and one each in Cagayan, Camarines Sur, Pangasinan, and Laguna); eighteen in Negros (fifteen in Negros Occidental; three in Negros Oriental); two in Cebu; five in Panay; two in Leyte; and two in Mindanao. There were nine sugar refineries: four in Luzon; two in Negros; one in Panay; and two in Mindanao (PSMA 1993). By 2000, sixteen of the centrals were either temporarily idled or permanently closed. The twenty-three remaining centrals are: five in Luzon (five closed); nine in Negros (nine closed); one in Cebu (one closed); three in Panay (two closed); two in Leyte; and three in Mindanao (one additional mill opened) (PSMA website). Needless to say, the average capacity utilization of the still-operating mills has increased significantly since the closure of those sixteen.

There has also been a geographical shift in the distribution of the sugar industry. Production by region varies in any given year, but the distribution up to around 1990 was 22–26 percent of Philippine sugar coming from Central Luzon, 50 percent from Negros, with the remainder coming from Panay, Cebu, the Eastern Visayas, Bicol, the Cagayan Valley, and Mindanao. While Negros still accounts for 50 percent of the production, the fastest growing mills and hectarage are now in Mindanao, much of which has excellent soil conditions for growing sugarcane. Plus, some of the nation's largest producers of sugar-using processed food (e.g., Dole and Del Monte) have their plantations and processing plants in Mindanao. Increasing population density and the eruption of Mount Pinatubo have had disastrous effects on sugar production in parts of Pampanga and Tarlac, and the focus of Luzon sugar production seems to have shifted to the district around the well-managed Don Pedro central in Batangas, despite the relatively small average land holding in that district. I interviewed one planter with a 263-hectare farm in Pampanga, only a few miles from the erstwhile Clark Airbase. He related how his farm was spared the immediate effect of the Pinatubo eruption but had been virtually obliterated by the slow-moving lahar, or volcanic mud that takes years to clear away. He was looking to sell all or part of his land to any takers. I myself was staggered by the enormity of lahar damage on several of the farms I saw in Pampanga. Although there are still functioning mills in Panay, Cebu, and Leyte, these are increasingly peripheral. The manager of a Negros mill who managed a mill in Cebu for many years confided that Cebu was too rocky to grow sugarcane, and that it would better if the mills on that island closed down.

The manager of Peñafrancia mill in Camarines Sur, Bicol, told me that his small production mill stayed in operation mostly because sugar was a more profitable crop than rice or corn for the small, poor farmers in his typhoon-prone region. The mill had a four-month milling season, and in 1993 produced only 381,000 50-kilogram bags. (or 19,050 m.t.) of raw sugar. He admitted that the mill had been a chronic money-loser, but he was optimistic that the new owners, the Bicol Agro Producers Cooperative, would manage it better and begin to turn a profit. But by 2000 the Peñafrancia mill was closed, and no central was operating in Bicol.

The manager of the Canlubang mill in Laguna, not far from Manila, told me that his mill would be closing down within three years. A mere decade before Canlubang had milled one million tons of cane, but in 1994 its volume declined to less than half that amount. The provinces of Laguna and Cavite—never the most productive sugar land—were becoming too densely populated and industrialized for planters to hang on. Planters were only netting P5,000–7,000 per hectare, and even the very best could do no better than P12,000–15,000 per hectare. Farmers were increasingly selling out to real estate developers and industrialists looking to relocate near, but not in, Metro Manila. The Canlubang mill itself had deteriorated, but the company could no longer afford to make the investment needed to bring it back up to speed, especially considering its insufficient cane supply. He voiced an opinion heard often among millers that the Department of Environment and Natural Resources had been too aggressive in insisting that sugar mills conform to new air and water pollution regulations, and it would be prohibitively expensive to make the improvements necessary for the mill to become less polluting. This had been the last straw for Canlubang's management, and now the problem was to decide "how to close shop gracefully" and protect the mill's workers. The consolidation of the overcrowded milling sector is probably good for the long-term health of the industry, but the closing of sixteen mills in less than seven years generated thousands of unemployed workers and made planting sugar impossible for hundreds of small planters that had come to rely on the crop. There is little gracefulness in that.

This shakeout does not mean that the milling sector is becoming appreciably healthier. Perhaps the biggest shock to the sector in recent years was the 1995 bankruptcy of the Victorias Milling Company, by far the nation's largest central. The bankruptcy was accompanied by a spate of indictments of company officials for financial malfeasance. Although the Victorias management blamed competition from cheap imported sugar—a refrain heard frequently among sugar producers—that was not a major factor in the mill's downfall. Rather, Victorias had been operating significantly under capacity for many years, had borrowed heavily to invest in mill and boiler rehabilitation and in diversification schemes (e.g., into prawns, poultry, animal feeds, cut flowers), and had over-extended in the trading sector through its poorly run trading arm, North Negros Marketing Corporation. Moreover, the company had been badly managed, perhaps criminally so. In 1997, the Philippine Securities and Exchange Commission approved Victorias' petition to suspend payment on its P5.07 billion ($192 million) debt to thirty-two bank creditors, as well as North Negros' separate petition to suspend P2.20 billion in debt payments. The alternative seemed to be foreclosure on many of the company's assets and a probable closure of the mill (*Financial Express* 10 July 1997). In 1999 the Philippine Stock Exchange threatened to de-list Victorias shares, the trading in which had been suspended in 1997 because the company had failed to pay its maintenance and listing dues, and had failed to file annual and quarterly financial reports. After the company paid its P100,000 fees plus P25,000 in penalties, the exchange backed down. In the report filed by Victorias in wake of the de-listing threat, the company made public that its losses had been P2.05 billion in the fiscal year ending August 1997, P903 million in the next fiscal year, and P570 in the most recent year (*Philippine Daily Inquirer* 16 Sept. 1999).

I recall an interview I had in 1994—a year before the bankruptcy—with the manager of a Luzon mill. He told me that he thought Victorias was spending too much to rehabilitate its A mill. Victorias was relying on expensive Australian components and technical help, while this manager's mill was upgrading with far less expensive Czech equipment. He also expressed puzzlement at the way Victorias seemed to be so rapidly diversifying rather than "paying attention to its core business." He said, "All that stuff sounds good in an annual report, but they are losing money from it. Are they a sugar company, or aren't they?"

This statement reflects a deep-seated rift in the sugar industry between the advocates of diversification and those skeptical about whether any crop or product can be more profitable than sugar. The skeptics cite a long list of failed attempts that have been made in sugar-producing provinces: ramie,[8] cattle, prawns, fruit trees, bananas, flowers, milkfish, tilapia, and several kinds of light industry. They note that many entrepreneurial planters got burnt in the past by trying to produce products that either had no market (e.g., ramie) or for which they had no expertise. Inevitably, these planters went back to growing sugarcane. The advocates of diversification believe that sugar on its own has a bleak future and that farmers and mills need to invest in linked industries (e.g., particle board, candy manufacture, or cattle fed on cane tops) or else find alternatives as quickly as possible. The advocates often accuse the skeptics of being attracted to the ease of the planter's life. One planter, now also a businessman, told me, "These planters just love to watch their grass grow and play golf. It isn't that they don't want to do other things, it's just that nothing is as easy as sugar. Basically, they're allergic to work."

Perhaps the most famous diversification advocate in the industry is Daniel "Bitay" Lacson, former Governor of Negros Occidental, Ramos administration insider, and former chairman of the PNB. Lacson is also a shipping company executive, sugar planter, and producer of prawns, cut flowers, and cattle. While he was governor, he encouraged the successful craft-producing organization, the Association of Negros Producers, and he established an Agromanagement Study Center at the University of St. LaSalle in Bacolod. He frequently used the rhetoric of economics, urging sugar producers to find a "comparative advantage" in other crops, to establish "forward linkages" by establishing sugar-using industries, and to recognize that global free trade would benefit rather than harm Third World countries. He exhorted the milling companies to lead the way by becoming "diversified agro-industrial centers" that produce many related products. For the planting sector he devised a widely publicized scheme that he referred to as "60–30–10." According to this scheme, which he implemented on his own farm, 60 percent of the land remained dedicated to sugarcane cultivation, 30 percent was converted to "high value crops" (e.g., flowers, fruits, black pepper, asparagus), and 10 percent was given to the workers to produce either food crops or cash crops on their own. Of course, it was Lacson's fervent hope that those high-value crops would prove so lucrative that the planters would be gradually weaned away from sugar. But very few planters followed the governor's lead, and the entire 60–30–10 plan became the object of derision. One planter who owned ten hectares of land put it to me this way: "Prawns and flowers are for rich people. I am a sugar planter, and I am proud of it." Worker advocates and political leftists considered the 60-30-10 plan to be, in the words of one priest, "weak elite reformism," patently intended to forestall full-scale land reform.

Despite these many traumas in the industry it is still possible for a sugarcane planter to make a good living, especially compared with other farmers in the Philippines. In money value, sugar is the nation's fifth leading crop after rice, corn, coconut, and fruits and nuts (and just ahead of banana), but it is probably still the most profitable. Although its total money value in 1991 was 24 percent that of rice, its crop area was less than 8 percent that devoted to rice. For corn, a crop generally associated with poor farmers, the figures are 57 percent money value and 7 percent hectarage. Given that the average cost of production of sugar is $0.13 to 0.15 per pound—not counting the cost of money—and the average domestic price is $0.16 to 0.18, sugar continues to be a profitable crop, albeit nowhere near as lucrative as in the glory days prior to 1974.

I had many frank conversations with planters about their costs and profits. One estimated that the average cost of planting sugar in his district in 1993 was about P15,000–20,000 per hectare, including labor costs. He had only spent P10,000 and was quite certain that, had he spent more, he could have increased his yield well beyond the 80 piculs per hectare that he realized. Still, averaging the composite price of sugar throughout that year to P530 per picul, that planter's land netted P32,400 per hectare. Factoring in the mill's 35 percent share, however, reduces the planter's portion to P21,060 per hectare. Since he owns about eighty hectares, he earned P1,684,800 in that year, or approximately $60,171 at the 1993 exchange rate. He did not receive a crop loan, so the cost of money was not a factor. At that income he was able to maintain a household in Bacolod with fourteen servants for himself, his wife, his five children, and his wife's aged grandmother. His household payroll was about P30,000 a month. Moreover, he owned a condominium apartment in Manila.

Another planter is well-known in Negros as being among the province's most knowledgable and innovative farm owners. He is also a politician and a notable breeder of fighting cocks. In that same year his average costs were high, at P30,000, but his yield was 150 piculs per hectare. Factoring in the 65 percent planters' share, he netted about P32,175 per hectare. So the higher input costs did yield greater profits, assuming the average quality of the second planter's land and cane varietals were the same as that of the first. That second planter owns nearly 400 hectares, giving him an annual income in that year of approximately P12,870,000, or $459,643. In other words, a planter with large land holdings can still make quite a lot of money from sugar, but nowhere near as much as, say, a real estate mogul, a major industrialist, or even a big-time sugar trader. A small planter who owns, say, five hectares, has costs of P15,000 and a yield of 100 piculs per hectare, would only make P123,500 ($4,411) assuming a composite sugar price of P530 per picul. That income is higher than the Philippine average, but it hardly qualifies one for the status of "sugar baron."

The costs of planting sugarcane include fertilizer, pesticides, machine and physical plant maintenance, cane points, thirteen-month pay for workers (a legal requirement of the Department of Labor and Employment), social security payments, medicines, the per-picul liens imposed for "social amelioration," security, and lobbying, and, of course, for wages. The plainspoken planter who owns 400 hectares admitted to me that most planters view wages as one of the variable costs of planting. "At twelve-cents-per-pound or higher cost of production, a planter would have to starve his workers to make decent money in most years." Despite the government insistence that "86 percent of planters today conform to the minimum wage law" (Region VI Director, DOLE, pers. com., 1992), that planter's view reflects a widespread perception about the wage component of production costs. Most planters say that wages generally amount to about 50 percent of production costs.

There is considerable debate about what percentage of sugar planters actually pay the minimum wage, which varies by region and in 1993 averaged 103 pesos per day for sugarcane workers. It seems clear that larger planters are more likely to pay it than smaller ones. But since no one is paid when he or she does not work, and sugarcane farming is characterized by long periods of idleness, this wage remains below reasonable family subsistence needs. The SRA administrator told me that, in 1986, 90 percent of planters short-changed their workers. But by 1992, thanks to a campaign by the SRA, DOLE, Social Security, and Governor Lacson, compliance was up to 86 percent. A different SRA official warned me that the figures on wage-law compliance are notoriously suspect because "Big planters never let anyone see their *real* books." An NFSW (union) official claimed that most workers make only P35–65 per day, and only average two to three working days per week.

Another major cost is cane hauling. Larger planters tend to own their own trucks to transport cane from farm to mill, but most planters either rent trucks from the burgeoning trucking companies or rely on the mill to provide them. Many mills give hauling allowances to planters, but these generally do not cover the entire cost of transporting the cane. Several planters explained to me that because ten-wheeler trucks are not produced in the Philippines they can be purchased duty-free. Six-wheelers, however, are made there and so the tariff on imported ones is prohibitive. But Philippine-made six-wheelers are "not tough enough" to haul cane, and sugar planters are reluctant to buy them.[9] Because of the tariff difference, it is cheaper to purchase a ten-wheeler than an imported six-wheeler. But while the larger trucks are more convenient for carrying cane on the decent roads between transloading stations and mills, only the smaller trucks can negotiate the inaccessible, poorly maintained, and narrow roads leading to many cane fields. Near one field for which the planter had to pay P150 per ton to haul his cane, I could barely walk on the boulder-strewn, muddy road, let alone imagine a large, fully laden truck driving on it. Government officials at all levels also complain that the larger trucks that constantly ply the roads in sugar-producing areas during milling season greatly damage the good roads, making their maintenance impossible. The combination of falling cane, the lack of reflectors or functioning lights, the narrowness of the roads, and the rather reckless driving habits of the truck drivers and those forced to drive behind them also take an extremely high human cost in traffic fatalities.

A 1987 World Bank study estimated that there were 30,000 growers of sugarcane in the Philippines. Of them, 77 percent owned less than ten hectares (small); 18 percent between ten and fifty hectares (medium); and 5 percent more than fifty hectares (large). The small farms accounted for about 22 percent of all the sugar hectarage, the medium farms for 35 percent, and the large farms for 43 percent.

Although there are still large sugar plantations in the Philippines, such as the giant Hacienda Luisita in Tarlac (owned by the Cojuangco family, whose most famous scion is Corazon Aquino), the trend in recent years is toward smaller holdings. Among the main reasons for this is "natural land reform," which is how landowners refer to the process of sequential partitioning through inheritance. Many landowners have legally incorporated in an effort to forestall further partitioning and to protect themselves from personal liability for crop loans, but others have been deterred from this strategy by the 30 percent corporate tax rate. Many who have incorporated readily admit that these are really "paper corporations" that remain decidedly in the hands of senior family members.

Banking and Finance

Although financial institutions are not part of the sugar industry, per se, their impact upon it is so great that it is necessary at this point to discuss them briefly. Recall that when the sugar industry was initially established in the Visayas, planters relied upon loans provided by foreign trading companies and banks. The bank-provided crop loan remains common in Negros and Panay, but less so in other sugar-growing areas, up to the present. One indirect indicator of the decline in the importance of the sugar industry relative to urban industry and commerce is the intensity of bank lending by region. As late as the 1950s, fully 25 percent of all bank loans in the nation went to the Western Visayas, mostly to the Negros sugar industry. By 1991, the Western Visayas was the fourth most active region for lending (after the National Capital Region, Central Luzon, and Central Visayas), but it had only 2.8 percent of all loans from commercial banks. The National Capital Region (Metro Manila) had 82.4 percent of all loans. This even though the peso amount of bank loans to the sugar industry was higher in absolute terms in 1991 than it had ever been (figures from Central Bank 1992).

A planter receives a loan from the bank before planting and repays with interest once his *quedan*s—the coupons representing ownership of physical sugar in a central's warehouse (see chapter 4)—are sold. But because of the ten-month growing cycle and the lag in selling *quedan*s, the planter typically receives his loan for the next crop year before he has repaid the loan for the previous year. For many decades, sugar planters were among the most credit-worthy people in the nation, and banks solicited their patronage. In the aftermath of the crisis, however, the institution of the crop loan has become far more problematic. In the mid-1980s many planters defaulted on loans while many of the more solvent ones are still repaying restructured debts. While the PNB and other government banks were driven to insolvency by being forced to make imprudent loans during the Marcos years, today the PNB has been privatized and all banks must operate with an eye on the bottom line, and within Central Bank regulations. Under these circumstances, banks today will lend amply to sugar *traders*, but planters are considered a more substantial risk. While the PNB and a few other banks still give crop loans on a selective basis, most private commercial banks have ceased doing so.

The combination of *quedan* financing and crop loans gives rise to some abuses, the most common of which is "pole vaulting." If a planter has not repaid his crop loan by the end of the year, the central must remit all of that planter's outstanding *quedan*s to the bank. Pole vaulting is simply having some of one's *quedan*s made out to relatives, workers, or servants in order to hold on to all of one's *que-*

dans and delay repayment. Most often, a planter will mill with more than one central in order to hide *quedans* from the bank and the tax collector. Banks were not strict about this practice until 1983 when the Central Bank closed down its rediscounting window, through which the government covered 80 percent of bank losses. But since individual banks now must bear the full burden of any bad debts they incur, they have joined the Bureau of Internal Revenue in trying to stamp out this practice. It is still true that many planters do not use their crop loans for the purpose for which they are given; some buy cars, improve their homes, take trips, or pay off other debts with money intended for the purchase of cane points, fertilizer, fuel, and farm machinery.

In 1991 the Victorias Milling Company decided that giving ample, collateral-free crop loans could help increase the supply of cane being brought to its under-capacity mill. An official with the central recounted to me how, despite the high sugar prices during that year, many planters defaulted on the loans, and Victorias took huge losses. Some planters took advantage of the easy credit by diverting their loans into the building of capital-intensive prawn ponds. But while sugar prices were high, prawn prices hit a new low, and many of the planters themselves incurred huge losses. The company decided to get out of the financing business and encourage the planters in their district to establish credit cooperatives to become self-financing. Of course, Victorias had no legal right or, for that matter, any desire to foreclose on planter property. Although the idea of establishing planter cooperatives is widely discussed in sugar growing areas (in part because of government tax and credit incentives), these discussions rarely result in any action. Most often, they break down over the issue of whether the coop will be organized according to one person, one vote, as advocated by smaller planters, or voting rights and power will be apportioned according to hectarage, as insisted upon by larger planters.

Perhaps the greatest impediment to diversification out of sugar has been interest rates. In 1991, prevailing annual rates on bank loans had declined to 24 to 29 percent, down from 36 to 42 percent in 1990. In contrast, interest rates on passbook savings accounts ranged from 4 to 8 percent, and those on time deposits ranged from 13 to 16.5 percent. No wonder then that so many businessmen, traders, and planters seemed obsessed by the "cost of money." The reasons for high interest rates include the continued servicing of the enormous debt accrued during the Marcos years, persistent government deficits, inadequate tax collection, a large trade imbalance, tight money policies of the Central Bank (including one of the highest reserve requirements in the world), and the policy of intervening in foreign exchange markets to bolster the value of the peso. The effects of high interest rates on the sugar industry are varied and important: centrals are reluctant to borrow to make the capital improvements necessary to enhance efficiency; traders who borrow to buy *quedans* must sell and move sugar almost immediately; most planters who want to diversify out of sugar cannot afford to borrow, and if they can they must invest in businesses that will quickly yield high profits. Some planters allege that "Chinese" traders have the unfair advantage of borrowing money from banks in Hong Kong and Taiwan at far lower interest rates than "Filipinos" can get from domestic banks. Although many molasses traders admit that they are financed by the Japanese companies for whom they provide molasses, almost every sugar trader with whom I spoke told me that they were financed entirely by Philippine banks, but at lower interest rates than pertain to crop loans owing to the traders' greater credit-worthiness and better repayment histories. One trader quipped, "The few banks that still give crop loans to sugar planters lend at prime plus, plus, plus."

In addition to interest rates, a related factor that affects business decisions is the policy of issuing high-interest "T-bills" (by the government treasury) and "CB-bills" (by the Central Bank) in order to draw in excess money to tighten supply and to secure funds to prop up the peso and cover the national debt. When people buy these bills rather than depositing in banks less money is available for lending, which tends to drive up interest rates. When banks have excess supplies of cash, the Central Bank encourages them to purchase T-bills or CB-bills rather than stimulating lending demand by allowing interests rates to fall. Such a policy reins in inflation and helps the government pay its debts, but it discourages productive investment and diversification. Most important, when the return on T-bills averages 19–22 percent, as they did in 1992, this becomes the baseline acceptable return on any new investment. Businessmen and sugar planters ask (in the words of one): "Why risk my money starting a business when I can make 19 percent with T-bills?" The strategy of starting out with small margins in order to build up market share is deemed fine for the Japanese, but imprudent in the Philippines. The

Ramos administration did take important steps to reduce interest rates, such as lowering the bank reserve requirement and easing restrictions on foreign currency transactions. Unfortunately, by allowing Philippine currency to find its more "natural" exchange value, the peso has gone from 28 to the U.S. dollar in 1994 to over 51 to the dollar in early-2002, thereby causing inflation and upward pressure on interest rates.

CARP

Another factor that has forced credit to dry up for sugar planters is the Comprehensive Agrarian Reform Program (CARP). Since the limited efforts at land reform during the Marcos years were aimed at redistributing tenanted lands, sugar and coconut farms were exempted. This had the unfortunate effect of encouraging many rice farmers to convert to sugar and coconut. Although sugar lands are not exempt under CARP, they are treated as low priority except for the few remaining tenanted farms in Luzon. One of the biggest problems with the current approach to agrarian reform is that the program was created with urgency, and announced with fanfare, but is being implemented at a glacial and uneven pace. Unlike land reform in Taiwan and Japan, the CARP program—passed by the elite-dominated Philippine Congress during the Aquino administration—requires the government to *pay* landowners for their properties and for beneficiaries in turn to purchase the land from the government over a long amortization period. In fact, the post-Marcos Philippine Constitution states that agrarian reform will entail "just compensation" for land owners, although one congressman from Negros sought to amend that phrase to "full compensation." One planter told me: "When it comes to CARP, most planters are members of the OMDB club—over my dead body."

But while it is all being sorted out, the uncertainty surrounding land holdings has had profound effects on the economies of rural provinces. Many younger, better-educated members of sugar planting families would like to sell their land so they might concentrate on their professions or pursue business plans. Others want to use their holdings as collateral in order to invest or start businesses. Unfortunately, CARP has caused a crash in the price of farmland, and those few banks that continue to accept sugar land as collateral do so at a fraction of its productive value. Planters also complain that the bonds being offered as payment for land when an owner offers a

Voluntary Offer for Sale (VOS) prevent meaningful diversification because they cannot readily be converted into usable capital (Billig 1991). In other words, the possibility that CARP will one day be implemented and that sugar land will be targeted has made it very difficult for some planters to sell land that they otherwise would have and could have sold. One trader who had recently purchased a mill told me that he would love to further integrate by purchasing farmland, but that he, "of course, will have to wait until all this CARP business is decided one way or another." A milling company executive explained to me that he had "noticed a definite decline in agricultural practices since CARP. Planters just aren't putting as much into the land as they used to, and it shows in the quality of the cane we're getting." A milling association official estimated that 70 percent of the planters in Negros would—and should—sell out were it not for CARP. He pointed to the irony that the agrarian reform program had the unintended consequence of causing non-farmers to hold on to inherited land rather than sell it to those who still wanted to farm.

There has been some effort to encourage sugar planters to give VOSs. To date, however, very few have been offered, and most of those that have been are stalled by bureaucratic obstacles. With the exception of some highly publicized transfers—for example, much of the land owned by Danding Cojuangco and Roberto Benedicto—little sugar land has been transferred to workers. Most people who know the sugar industry, no matter what their political persuasion, assert that a simple redistribution of land without education, agricultural extension, credit services, marketing assistance, and reasonable amortization terms, would not only decimate sugar production, but would do little to help the workers. Land reform recipients most often continue to grow sugar themselves rather than to diversify or grow subsistence crops (Billig 1992), but many have ended up reselling the land after concluding that they could not farm it economically. Time and again I was told that agrarian reform requires much more than simple redistribution, but few express confidence that the Philippine government has the will and the resources to do it successfully. Many people in the Philippines go so far as to assert that successful land reform cannot take place in a democracy where wealthy people continue to be elected to office. In the meantime, sugar planters have spent the last several years bickering with the Department of Agrarian Reform (DAR) and the Land Bank over the various valuation schemes for sugar land, and in some cases they have organized efforts to thwart CARP by not registering with DAR. The president of the Land Bank admitted that over 90 percent of the valuations for VOSS in Negros had been rejected by the owners, who have the right to do so. Many assert that foreclosed, abandoned, and public land should be distributed before productive land is touched. But others point out that only a small amount of good sugar land was ever actually foreclosed, and there is no abandoned or public land upon which people do not live, if only as squatters. One congressman from a sugar-producing area of Mindanao appropriated the rhetoric of environmentalism by frequently referring to CARP as "unsustainable."

A major controversy took place in the summer of 1992 when DAR redistributed "foreclosed" land to worker/beneficiaries on Hacienda Asia in southern Negros. The Pfleider family was able to obtain a court order declaring that they, rather than the PNB, were still the rightful owners of the hacienda. Two people died and several were injured when the Pfleiders attempted to evict the workers from the land. This incident illustrates how amorphous the concept of "foreclosure" is when applied to sugar land and crop loans. The SRA administrator told me "The days of the Sugar Baron are over, but the kids of the Barons often still live in luxury. But their power is gone. In fact, most 'rich' planters today are forecloseable if the banks decided ever to crack down. It's a good thing they now have a friend in Bitay Lacson at PNB."

The governor of Negros Occidental in the mid-1990s, Rafael "Lito" Coscolluela, told me in an interview that he thought the Hacienda Asia incident set the worst possible precedent, causing "the whole (agrarian reform) program to lose credibility by undermining its moral basis. Farmer beneficiaries who already have certificates of ownership are now being told that those certificates might be worthless because some court decided to act on the petition of a land owner." The governor, who was sharply critical of the way CARP had been implemented, also said it was ironic that CARP itself had deterred many planters from pursuing his predecessor's excellent 60–30–10 plan. "People are reluctant to start growing high-value crops under such insecurity." Although Coscolluela was a proponent of agrarian reform, he believed that CARP was a failure because it did nothing to encourage diversification and provided little aid to land recipients. As the governor of a province dependent upon agriculture he was particularly angry at the deleterious impact that CARP had on rural economies.

I interviewed one planter who had offered a VOS to the DAR after he decided he wanted to concentrate all his efforts on his more lucrative trading business. Unlike the majority of planters, he was willing to accept the Land Bank's P25,000 per hectare valuation rather than holding out for P50,000–60,000 that most planters think the land is worth. He was even willing to accept interest-bearing bonds rather than insist on cash up front. He had already set up a cooperative among his workers so that the land would not be broken up into many tiny holdings. The workers themselves, he asserted, disliked the DAR officials with whom they dealt, and felt that the DAR people were just interested in getting the transfer accomplished rather than helping the workers make their enterprise successful. The DAR people seemed poorly acquainted with their own procedures, and knew nothing about sugar farming. The beneficiaries had to pay for the land over twenty-five years at 6 percent annual interest. Since workers would more likely be able to make these payments as cooperatives rather than as individuals, the planter wondered why the DAR seemed so stumped by questions about how cooperatives should work. How would shares be managed? What if someone wanted out of the cooperative? Would he be bought out, or lose his equity? Would the members be accruing equity as individuals, families, or as a whole cooperative unit? The bureaucrats who administer CARP could not answer these or most other questions.

Another older planter with whom I spoke was "sick of the sugar business," so he put 477 of his 511 hectares up for VOS. His workers really wanted the land, but he was still waiting to hear about the valuation. He was quite sure that his workers would continue to plant sugarcane, and he hoped that "someone would take the initiative" to organize them into a well-managed cooperative, because "that would be the only hope" for them to be able to afford the land. He also said, "The Land Bank is unbelievably stupid; they let these workers' cooperatives get away with a lot of pole vaulting." But even without a cooperative, "a person can still make money with one hectare and a carabao." He had no problem accepting bonds for 70 percent of his payment (the other 30 percent would be cash), since "Chinese traders will buy the bonds at 90 percent value." "Most Negrenses," he said, "inherited land and are too attached to it. I myself would like to go to heaven, so let my workers eat." He thought that the valuation for his district would be around P70,000 for sugar land and P50,000 for rice land.[11] But if one does not like one's valuation, one can reject it and go to an adjudication board. One planter he knew got a valuation of P4–5 million for 280 hectares, but the adjudication board gave her P24 million. The workers appealed, and it then went to the courts. "This is what happens. The justice system is so slow, CARP can't be implemented. Due process and land reform just don't go together." I was amazed when he told me that, "Frankly, if I were in government, I would just take it away from us planters and give them [the workers] the land. This country could use a more equitable distribution of wealth." He thought that the valuations being offered to planters were *too high*. Obviously, his opinion was quite rare among planters. Still, in my presence he warned his younger nephew that he would be crazy to give a VOS. "If my kids had wanted the land, and if I weren't seventy-four, I would have held on and put it in my will."

Given the peculiar nature of the crop loan, planters have more leverage with the banks than they would normally have. Since this year's crop must be planted before last year's loan is fully repaid, planters argue that they will not be able to repay last year's loan *unless* they get a new one to finance this year's crop. Banks reluctantly go along with this because the collateral consists of agricultural land—if they ever actually foreclosed they would be holding property worth less than the value of the loan. This is one of the ironies of CARP. If government-owned banks and the DAR cooperated, the bank would foreclose after default and the land could be made available for redistribution. But since these agencies worked at cross-purposes, it was CARP itself that rendered the collateral worthless and the bank reluctant to foreclose. Government-owned banks prefer to keep the loans performing so that they do not have to write off losses and look bad to Congress, the President, and the IMF. One banker told me that although the PNB looked reasonably healthy on paper, it was actually in deep trouble because so many of its loans were just barely performing. Another factor that sustains the crop-loan system is the long-standing personal and kin ties between planters and bankers. On Negros, for instance, bankers tend to be members of the elite class and are inevitably related to one or more prominent sugar-planting families. No wonder only small, non-elite planters ever get foreclosed.

One banking official whose bank still gave crop loans told me that his company had never foreclosed on a sugar planter for nonrepayment, though they had cut off loans to many planters. Generally, the planters who got "taken out" would borrow money from another bank to repay the outstanding loan within three years. Since the passage of CARP his bank had insisted that no more than 70 percent of collateral for crop loans be agricultural land. At least 30 percent had to be put up in the form of residential and/or commercial property, something many planters were reluctant to do. Still, he reckoned that half of all sugarcane planters, at least in Negros, still relied on crop loans, a far higher percentage than for any other agricultural commodity. Although credit was far tighter for smaller planters, even they tended to be financed, most often by rural banks or moneylenders at high interest rates.

One issue that has caused much debate over CARP concerns the extent to which there are significant economies of scale in sugarcane farming. Although most large planters assert that it would obviously be crazy to break up large holdings to create many more, less productive smaller ones, the actual evidence for this is ambiguous. Some studies even suggest that small farms tend to have higher sugarcane yields as long as one compares farms with the same level of technological inputs. In other words, when inputs and machinery are held equal—carabaos are used to plow and human labor is used to plant, weed, fertilize, and harvest—there is no great advantage *per hectare* to large holdings, and there may even be a slight disadvantage. But it is undeniably the case that larger farms do tend to use more tractors and modern inputs, and do tend to have higher yields per hectare once the above *ceteris paribus* assumption is relaxed. In a pro-land reform speech the governor of the BOI reminded an audience of planters of the need to differentiate the "mode of ownership from the mode of production." In other words, it is still possible to have decentralized ownership of land that is organized into larger productive units that preserve the economies of scale. Of course, such a mode of production would entail cooperatives, which do not have an encouraging history in Philippine agriculture.

Not surprisingly, a spokesperson for the National Federation of Sugarcane Workers (NFSW), often considered the most radical (or "red") of the several unions that try to organize sugar workers, praised the CARP law but strongly criticized its execution. Most of the land that had been given to beneficiaries, she argued, belonged to small planters on the verge of foreclosure, while the land of large planters had hardly moved at all. "Even foreclosed and abandoned land," she stated, "was not moving rapidly." While the government offered planters P25,000–30,000 per hectare for a VOS on class A land, it expected the beneficiaries to pay much more than that amount per hectare. So most land that was redistributed ended up being re-appropriated by the Land Bank for non-payment. Her union was attempting to interest foreign NGOs and aid organizations in helping to finance land recipients, but this was proving slow going. She said that much of the land leasing that took place in sugar provinces was basically intended to hide the true extent of land holdings in order to foil CARP and the minimum-wage provisions. The Sugar Restitution Law—in which the government vowed to compensate planters for their Marcos-era losses—was a particular disaster in that it prevented many properties that should have been foreclosed from actually being appropriated for land reform. She cited one instance of land that was slated for redistribution to workers that was instead turned into a residential subdivision for wealthy people. Her particular union—unlike most of the others—had incurred the wrath of planters by advocating agrarian reform *without* compensation to previous owners and *without* payment from the beneficiaries. But she admitted that "such a thing could not happen in the Philippines." Whereas most of the other unions (the "yellow" ones) stuck to wage and benefit issues and had not pressed questions of land ownership, the NFSW was proud to be the one that did all it could to "transfer the land to its rightful owners—the tillers of the soil." She was sure that when the tillers owned the land there would be higher agricultural production and greater "sustainability." The most important task for her union, in her view, was to continue establishing worker cooperatives so that land reform would not necessarily result in extreme fractionation of holdings. Because of NFSW's establishing of cooperatives, she said, planters frequently referred to them as "communists." Several planters with whom I spoke did exactly that.

The U.S. Quota

The U.S. sugar quota is one of the most important determinants of the worldwide market in sugar. Philippine producers appear quite obsessed with American sugar production and consumption, and they follow avidly the ups-and-downs of their position within the quota system. A lien that supports an extensive lobbying effort in Washington is placed on every picul of sugar produced in the Philippines. Philippine producers constantly try to interpret and decipher small changes in their U.S. quota, convinced that each minor blip contains significant information about the regard with which the Philippines is held by the U.S. government.

What happened in 1998 was fairly typical of recent years. In midyear the Philippine Association of Sugar Refiners, Inc. (PASRI) issued a press statement asking the National Food Authority to authorize the importation of 200,000 m.t. of sugar. Although the millers' association, PSMA, urged caution and the two planters' confederations, CONFED and NFSP, expressed outright disapproval, few disputed that flagging domestic supply was unable to meet growing domestic demand. By June, refiners were closing down for lack of raw sugar, wholesale sugar prices were very high and climbing, and consumers and food manufacturers were beginning to feel the crunch (*Balita-L listserve*, 9 July 1998). Ultimately, the Philippines imported 258,215 m.t. of sugar in 1998 (FAO statistic). And yet, the SRA remained firmly committed to fulfilling the country's U.S. import quota even though the price received at the time in the U.S. market was *lower* than the price in the domestic market. The Philippines exported 185,226 m.t. of raw sugar to the United States in the same year it was importing a far larger amount. In other words, exporting sugar to the United States under the quota system continues despite high prices and short supplies in the Philippines. This illustrates the profound effect the U.S. quota has on the worldwide market for sugar, and the utmost importance that most members of the Philippine sugar industry place on the industry's position in the U.S. quota system. In addition to the quota's economic value, the symbolic value of the Philippine status within the quota system, what it signifies about the special relationship between the two countries, is a potent and sensitive fact for those in the sugar industry.

Even though 75–92 percent of all sugar produced in the Philippines today is consumed domestically, most of the sugar the Philippines does export goes to the United States. Most Filipinos (including most journalists) do not understand the byzantine U.S. sugar quota system, and some believe that it is profoundly disadvantageous to the Philippines. But in fact the quota has been disproportionately generous to the Philippines relative to other exporting countries. The Philippines is nowhere near the third most prolific producer of sugar in the world, or even among the forty countries with U.S. import quotas, yet it has the third largest quota.

Due to the extremely high world prices in the mid-1970s, the U.S. government removed the country-by-country quotas and permitted virtually free trade in sugar (Skully 1998: 17). That the United States allowed the Laurel-Langley Agreement to expire in 1974 (see chapter 2) was part of that free-trade policy. As prices declined through the 1970s, however, politically influential U.S. sugar producers increasingly demanded stricter controls on cheaper imports. After a system of import fees proved ineffective, the quota system was instituted in May 1982. The explicit objective of this system is to keep the producer price of this highly regulated commodity above the minimum price set in U.S. farm legislation (Skully 1998: 17). The USDA tries to keep the producer price of raw sugar stable at about $0.21 to 0.24 per pound, and it *guarantees* producers at least 0.18 per pound by excusing the low-interest crop loans given by the Commodity Credit Corporation (CCC) when the price drops below that level.[12] The former system of direct, sliding-scale subsidies to sugar producers no longer exists. Today the high producer price is maintained by CCC stock-financing loans and precise import controls.

Not surprisingly, the quota system has been used as an instrument of foreign trade policy to reward favored nations and to punish disfavored ones. While the crop estimates and annual allowable quota amounts are administered by the USDA, the actual percentage allocation granted to each country is determined by the Office of the U.S. Trade Representative and is subject to a considerable amount of lobbying, diplomacy, and congressional pressure. Although the initial percentages given to each country in 1982 were based upon each country's imports during the period 1975–1981, the changes made to those percentages since 1982 reflect many factors, some of which are decidedly political. South Africa and Nicaragua, for example, had their quotas suspended and later restored based upon foreign policy considerations. Haiti's quota was suspended in 1992 and restored only after the United States was satisfied with that country's political situation. No wonder many countries with shares fear the demise of the communist regime in Cuba. With the strong Cuban lobby in the United States advocating for "redevelopment," it is likely that Cuba would be granted a large share that would be expropriated from the shares of other countries.

From 1982 until 1990 the system worked according to absolute national quotas. Each country was legally entitled to a set percentage of the total yearly importation. But in May of 1989 a panel of the General Agreement on Tariffs and Trade (GATT), responding to a formal complaint by Australia, found the U.S. sugar quota to be in violation of international trade rules. The 96–0 vote against the United States in the GATT Council caused considerable consternation among U.S. sugar producers and sugar-friendly legislators. But the sugar interests found a way to circumvent the GATT ruling. In October 1990 the sugar quota officially became the "tariff-rate quota" (called TRQ) (Suarez 1997: 15). Although this new system may be in literal compliance with GATT rules, the change is purely cosmetic. Rather than an absolute import quota, the TRQ allows each country to import its given percentage of sugar into the United States *at the most favorable tariff rate*. While it is no longer explicitly illegal for a country to import over-quota sugar into the United States, the tariff rate applied to such sugar is prohibitive even for the most efficient producer (e.g., Australia). A country without any quota share is no longer legally prohibited from importing sugar into the United States, but none could afford actually to do so. In fiscal 1998, the over-quota tariff was 16.72 cents per pound (stabilizing at 15.36 cents by fiscal 2000). In contrast, the tariff for in-quota sugar is .625 cents per pound for most countries, but even that amount is waived for countries covered by the Generalized System of Preferences (GSP), the Caribbean Basin Initiative, and the Andean Preference (Skully 1998: 19).[13] The sugar quota has lost none of its teeth since the GATT ruling. There are, in addition to the TRQ program, other, smaller import programs that apply to specific countries or to specific American businesses. These include the special arrangement with Mexico and Canada under NAFTA, the Refined Sugar Re-export Program (which allows U.S. food-producing exporters to import world-market priced sugar), the Sugar-Containing Products Re-export Program, the small Refined Sugar TRQ, and the Polyhydric Program (which allows producers of polyhydric alcohol to purchase world-market raw sugar).

Every year, beginning on October 1, USDA gauges annual domestic sugar production. Based upon that estimate, it informs those countries from which it imports how much sugar they are entitled to send to the United States in that year, usually underestimating at first and then increasing the importation amount as the year progresses. As of the 1996 Farm Bill, the Philippines has been entitled to supply 13 percent of all TRQ sugar entering the United States (down from 13.5 percent in the previous three Farm Bills). But when American sugar growers have a productive year, the total amount of imports is less than it would be for a bad or average year; hence, 13 percent would be a smaller absolute amount. The initial total TRQ raw-sugar allocation for fiscal 1997, for example, was 2.10 million m.t. (which rose to 2.32 million by the end of the fiscal year), but a 9 percent increase in U.S. domestic production in fiscal 1998 lowered it to 1.80 million, thus reducing Philippine imports by about 68,000 m.t. from one year to the next (*Sugar and Sweetener,* Economic Research Service, USDA, May 1998: 37).[14] Since many Philippine producers and journalists believe, incorrectly, that the U.S. quota is an absolute *amount* of sugar rather than a percentage of the total authorized importation, some commonly perceive such a reduction as a punishment or a sign of American disfavor. That the total importation was much less the year after the U.S. military bases were asked to leave the Philippines (1992) than the year before was of course perceived by many as such a punishment. But the Philippines received the same *percentage* of the total importation in both years. Most Philippine sugar producers, especially planters, do not understand how the U.S. TRQ system works, and they tend to imagine the conspiratorial worst.

Sugar consumption in the United States in 1997–1998 was 9.95 million tons (*Sugar and Sweeteners Yearbook,* 13 Jan. 1998); 1998 domestic production was 7.37 million tons (FAO), leaving a shortfall of about 2.6 million tons made up through the various import quotas.[15] From that total, 1.8 million tons was reserved for the TRQ program, at least in the beginning of the crop year. The nearly ten million tons of sugar consumed by Americans, incidentally, is mostly in the form of processed food ingredients, candy, and baked goods. In contrast, most of the two million tons of sugar consumed in the Philippines is contained in sweetened beverages; the great majority of U.S. beverages are sweetened with high-fructose corn syrup rather than sugar. In 1997 the United States produced 8.6 million tons of this syrup, mostly for domestic consumption.

Although the Philippines is not one of the world's biggest sugar producers, it had the third-highest absolute quota under the 1982 scheme and still has the third-highest tariff-rate quota (after the Dominican Republic and Brazil).[16] But when its percentage declined in 1996 from 13.5 percent to 13.0 percent many Filipino producers regarded this as a political affront and a signal that without the military bases the Philippines was no longer considered an important U.S. ally. And yet, of the top ten quota countries, only one (South Africa) experienced a slight rise in its quota (from 2.1 to 2.2 percent) with the 1996 Farm Bill; the other nine all were reduced. The reason for this is simply that there were several nations added to the quota system for the first time, and the shares for these new quotas were mainly taken from the largest importers. Given that total Philippine production no longer warrants such a high quota, that there have been years in which the Philippines could not fulfill all its quota, and that Philippine raw sugar has a poor record of meeting quality standards relative to other quota countries, the reduction of 0.5 percent seems entirely reasonable.

Another illustration of Philippine misunderstanding of the U.S. quota concerns the restoration of South Africa's quota following years of embargo. In 1986, the United States divided South Africa's quota among the other exporters, granting the Philippines an additional 2.3 percent. In 1992, those portions were given back to South Africa, causing the Philippines to "lose" 48,758 tons of exports worth $22,300,000. Many Filipinos believed that this too was a punitive action directed against their country because of the military bases, even though the other exporting nations also lost their additional portions. SRA Administrator Yulo flew to Washington to try to prevent this 2.3 percent loss, arguing that the Philippines was never apprised of its temporary nature and that the restoration should be equally allocated among all exporters, even though the Philippines had been given the largest share of South Africa's quota in 1986 in the wake of the EDSA Revolution.

The United States has a special tariff-rate quota for *refined* sugar that is far smaller than that for raw sugar. Only NAFTA partner Mexico is allowed to export an appreciable quantity of refined sugar to the United States. Most other quota countries are only allowed to export *raw* sugar to the United States. This, too, is a protectionist measure designed to support the interests of the giant American sugar companies. Other importing countries such as Japan and Singapore also insist upon refining all their sugar domestically, thereby capturing the substantial value added from the most capital-intensive phase of sugar production. Sugar refiners test every shipment of raw sugar for such properties as color, molasses content, bacteria, and polarization. In fact, many Philippine refiners have emulated the contracts of large U.S. importers (such as Amstar) that include penalties and premiums based on such quality parameters. They will even refuse to purchase sugars that do not meet their exacting standards. That several Philippine shipments have been sent back in recent years has caused considerable anguish among Filipino producers, and I have even heard this interpreted as a political act intended to undermine Philippine pride and punish the Philippines for purported slights.

Although the producer price of sugar in the United States is kept at a level far above the world-market price, there are many countries in which sugar is considerably more expensive than it is in the United States, owing to inefficiency, high costs, and protectionism. The cost difference between the lowest- and highest-cost producers is astonishing. For 1994–1995, the average cost of producing raw cane sugar in five low-cost countries was 8.93 cents per pound (LMC International 1997). These countries (which include Australia, Brazil, and Swaziland) make large profits when they sell sugar to the United States. The average cost in seven high-cost countries (which include Barbados, Taiwan, and Papua New Guinea) was 51.78 cents per pound (LMC International 1997)! Such countries regularly fail to fulfill their quotas, often sending no sugar at all to the United States. Since the average cost of production among countries that export cane sugar to the United States is about 15 cents per pound (LMC International 1997), and the producer price is generally 21–24 cents per pound, the profit margins are small (or even negative) for some countries. These numbers also underline the contention that there are very few sugar-producing countries that can profit by selling on the world market, where sugar generally sells for between 10 and 14 cents per pound. (In mid-1998 it dropped to 6.48 cents owing to a worldwide glut. *Sugar and Sweeteners Yearbook,* 24 May 2000).

A growing number of voices argue that the Philippines should reduce its dependency on the United States by pulling out of the sugar-quota system. They point out that in recent years the price of sugar on the domestic market has been almost as high—sometimes even higher—than the U.S. price, and so the Philippines would lose nothing by ceasing its exports. In response, SRA officials (who are responsible for reserving the portion destined for the U.S. market) argue that, in purely economic terms, if the 10–20 percent of total sugar production currently set aside for export to the United States would enter the domestic market, the composite price of sugar would be considerably lower than the current domestic price, and producers would suffer. In addition, they note that the domestic market is volatile whereas the U.S. market has relatively stable pricing. Finally, they asserted that even if U.S. prices would drop below Philippine production costs, it would be important to retain a foothold in the U.S. market as a hedge against future worldwide market instability.

Most Philippine sugar producers, however, do not apply such purely economic reasoning to the matter. They regard possessing a share of the quota as an important entitlement and a sign of their nation's high regard in the eyes of the United States. Having the third-largest quota in the world and the largest outside the Western Hemisphere is a source of pride to participants in an industry long vilified in the West and at home. Fulfilling that quota assiduously is considered a matter of honor. As is the case with many of the topics I will discuss related to the sugar industry, there is more at stake here than a matter of the bottom line or a need for greater efficiency. There are many economists both in the United States and the Philippines who regard the quota system as inefficient madness. They argue that an auction system would ensure that the more efficient producers displace less efficient ones, and that this would be a boon to both producers and consumers. They do not understand the *meaning* that the quota has taken on in the Philippines and in other sugar exporting countries.

American sugar producers have been widely criticized in the United States for being protectionist, powerful, and polluting. There have been countless news stories about how sugarcane producers have polluted the Everglades and bayous, and depleted the Lake Okeechobee water table. Other stories focus on the plight of the largely migrant (chiefly Mexican and Haitian) cane cutters who live under poor conditions and make low wages. Still others focus on how many millions of dollars sugar producers give to the congressional delegations of sugar-producing states, and how those delegations in turn fight hard to protect the interests of "Big Sugar" (Wilkinson 1989). In 1993 the pending NAFTA legislation was nearly scuttled by the Florida, Texas, and Louisiana delegations who argued that the "free-trade" bill had too few protections for U.S. sugar producers. In particular, they expressed concern that Mexico would switch to high-fructose corn syrup for beverage production in order to create an artificial surplus of sugar that would, under the legislation, automatically allow them to export that surplus to the United States. Mexico is already a major sugar producer, in most years producing around five million tons. Although Mexico and Canada are allowed special entry quotas separate from the TRQ system, the bill that finally passed came far from providing "free trade" in sugar among the three NAFTA partners. American sugar (and citrus) producers were given special protection in the NAFTA agreement that was finally enacted, and corn sweeteners were ultimately counted as part of the Mexican quota.

Needless to say, Philippine sugar producers were as nervous about NAFTA and the impact of Mexican sugar as were U.S. producers. Many expressed concern that Cuban sugar would inevitably enter the U.S. market through Mexico. The Philippine industry used its per-picul lien to lobby hard with Senators Inouye and Breaux, as well as Congressional representatives from sugar-producing states, to meliorate the impact of NAFTA on Philippine sugar imports. They regarded the special protections afforded to sugar in the final bill as being their victory as much as a victory of U.S. producers. That senators from Hawai'i and Louisiana are regarded as champions of Philippine sugar says something important about the common cause between U.S. producers and those in the TRQ countries.

In 2000, several media outlets aired or printed stories about a General Accounting Office audit estimating that the sugar program costs U.S. consumers $2 billion per year, and also stories about the U.S. government plan to prop up sugar prices in a year of record-high domestic production. In addition to (the usual) forgiving of hundreds of CCC loans and keeping a strong hand on import quotas, the CCC actually purchased outright 150,000 tons of sugar valued at $70 million. According to a report by Lisa Meyers that aired on the NBC Nightly News (16 June 2000): ". . . those taxpayer dollars are in addition to the inflated prices the public already pays for sugar and don't even know it. 'This is one of the most serious outrages on the agricultural side,' said Sen. Richard Lugar, R-Ind. 'Clearly, consumers have never understood that they're paying a tax every time they get a pound of sugar.' And also every time they buy a candy bar or cereal or even a canned ham. It's all because of the sugar program. Here's how it works: The government uses import restrictions and price supports to drive up sugar prices. Today, the world price of sugar is about eight cents per pound. But U.S. growers get about 22 cents" (MSNBC On-line). The story went on to discuss two brothers who gave $1,800,000 to both the Democratic and Republican parties over four years, and who make $65 million per year from the sugar program.

Five weeks later another news item stated that, as a result of lower prices caused by overproduction, thousands of sugar farmers were threatening to forfeit their crops rather than repay their CCC loans. To avoid mass forfeiture and impossible storage problems, the USDA was devising a plan to pay farmers to destroy standing crops. The estimated cost of implementing this plan was $1 billion. A USDA undersecretary claimed that USDA was trying to help "struggling sugar producers through a very difficult period, deal responsibly with forfeited sugar, and implement existing law." One reason for the overproduction, the article stated, is that many farmers had switched to sugarbeets in previous years because of low prices for corn and other crops. Once again, Senator Lugar was cited as the leading opponent of the sugar program, and this plan in particular (*Associated Press,* 27 July 2000). TRQ countries feared that the Office of the U.S. Trade Representative would set the total sugar importation at a level *lower than* the commitment the United States had made to GATT-WTO.

Organizations such as the Sugar Association, and the American Sugarbeet Growers' Association not only lobby on behalf of American sugar producers, but they also issue press releases and public relations pieces to counter the negative image that these news stories engender about the sugar industry. The lobbying and counter-lobbying gets especially intense around the U.S. Farm Bill renewals —every five years. In 1996, there were many stories emerging from the sugar industry about how the sugar program makes sense and actually saves the taxpayers money. These tended to stress that the program works by import controls and guaranteed loans rather than outright subsidies, and therefore does not (by law) cost the taxpayers any money (the CCC purchase in 2000 and the USDA payment to destroy standing crops, notwithstanding). The American producers frequently debunk the concept of the "world market" in which sugar is freely traded in order to disabuse American citizens of the idea that it is fair to compare U.S. prices to world-market prices. Here, for example, is an excerpt from the American Sugarbeet Growers' Association website congratulating Congress for preserving the sugar program in the 1996 Farm Bill. It is titled "U.S. Sugar Policy

Makes Sense." "Sugar, an essential ingredient in our food, is natural, abundant, and reasonably priced in the United States. For that, thanks are due to the efficient U.S. sugar farmers and to the Congress for establishing and maintaining a no-cost sugar policy. Without such a policy, U.S. consumers would be at the mercy of the highly volatile 'world dump market,' with all of its wild gyrations and unreliable supply. Also, efficient U.S. sugar farmers could be driven out of business by unfair competition from highly subsidized foreign producers." The phrase "dump market" is also a favorite of former SRA Administrator Rodolfo Gamboa. He used it in every conversation we had and in every speech I heard him give.

On the other side, conservative free-market organizations (such as the Heritage Foundation) have allied with consumer-oriented organizations (such as the Coalition for Sugar Reform) to argue that while the sugar programs do not cost *taxpayers* a great deal of money, they cost *consumers* billions of dollars each year. According to a Heritage Foundation publication: "The current sugar program operates as a cartel in which a handful of wealthy processors determine who has the right to produce sugar in this country.... The result is a U.S. price nearly twice as high as the world price ... Because there is no cost to the taxpayers, defenders of the sugar program argue that it should be preserved. However, this program—which controls sugar prices, limits imports to keep prices high, and then dictates how much domestically produced sugar can be sold—does impose a cost of $1.4 billion annually on U.S. consumers. . . . The sugar program is big government and corporate welfare at their worst. Almost half of its $1.4 billion in benefits goes to one percent of sugar growers (Frydenlund 1995)." The article goes on to argue in favor of the (ultimately unsuccessful) "market oriented and internationally competitive" Sugar Reform Act of 1995, which would have dismantled the sugar program. Such a piece could easily have been written about the Philippine sugar industry by the Philippine Food Exporters' Association. I count more than fifty advocacy websites that address the U.S. sugar programs surrounding the 1996 Farm Bill, divided approximately equally between the opponents and critics of renewing the sugar program.

Since the Philippines is not a Lomé Convention country—i.e., one of the African, Caribbean, and Pacific (ACP) nations entitled to import sugar to the European Union under quota—there is little point in detailing how the complex EU sugar-support system works.

But that system does have profound implications for the worldwide production of sugar and world-market prices. If U.S. producer prices for raw sugar are generally in the $0.22–0.24 per-pound range, EU producer prices are generally 0.32 to 0.36. Most European countries were net importers as late as the early 1970s, but since the support system was put into place in 1968 European production has increased about 70 percent, and nations of western and northern Europe have been among the world's largest producers and exporters of sugar (Roney 1991).[17] In 1999, for instance, the EU produced 18.4 million m.t. of sugar (more than any country in the world except Brazil), imported 4.3 million almost all by preferential agreement, and exported 7.8 million. France alone produced 4.9 million m.t. (the world's seventh leading producer) (FAO). Even the densely populated Benelux nations produced 2.4 million m.t. In contrast, in 1968 the EC produced 10.4 million m.t., France produced 2.4 million, and the Benelux countries produced 1.3 million. The European system is less circuitous than the American system. Sugar producers there are directly subsidized through an elaborate system of price supports. Without such subsidies it would be impossible for them to export sugar without losing a great deal of money. Virtually no sugar outside of the Lomé Convention is imported into Europe due to prohibitive import levies.

When Philippine sugar producers argue that the "world market" is an artificial surplus market in which only subsidized producers earn a profit, rather than a "free market" that reflects the true underlying worldwide supply of and demand for sugar, the main culprits they cite are the Europeans. No wonder the former SRA Administrator Rodolfo Gamboa once told me that while he does not like the idea of Thai or Australian sugar entering the Philippines, the prospect that he hates more than anything is for "highly subsidized European sugar" to be imported into any ASEAN country. As one planter said, "That EC [soon to be EU] subsidy is absurd. How can anyone expect people in poor countries to compete with that? They need to liberalize; not force us to." A milling association official called the EU sugar system, "the most salient fact in the world sugar industry today. . . . And it really hurts tropical countries more than anything." One planter, knowing that I was an American, asked, "Isn't it ironic that all the money the United States spends to defend Europe allows them to afford such rich subsidies for their sugarbeet farmers?" Many food processors argue that if other countries subsidize their sugar production, then Filipino businesses should take advantage of those subsidies by buying cheap world-market sugar and exporting value-added processed food. Obviously, such an argument drives Philippine sugar producers apoplectic.

The world sugar market has changed drastically in the last thirty years. Whereas in 1970 both the United States and Europe had to import large quantities of sugar in order to satisfy domestic demand, today both are among the world's largest sugar producers, and Europe exports far more than it imports. One German-born, American international sugar consultant told me, "In the past, sugar was *made* in poor countries, and imported by rich countries. Now many developed countries are exporting subsidized sugar. How can the poor countries hope to compete?" Now that so much of the sugar that crosses borders does so by preferential agreement and quota, the world market has become a minor feature of the world sugar trade. In fact, the major reason that many countries sell sugar on the world market at all is to eliminate surpluses in order to keep their domestic sugar prices high. In this sense the phrase "dump market" is not far off the mark. The same consultant expressed hope that international trade agreements would give the advantage back to the poorer countries, but he did not believe those agreements would extract significant sacrifices from American or European producers for at least fifteen years. "But still," he said, as free-trade becomes increasingly accepted as the worldwide norm "the world market [will be] the future of the sugar business." Then he paused and said, almost in a whisper, that he was not at all convinced that the Philippine sugar industry could hang on for the fifteen years it would take for the world sugar business to change.

Property Rights, *Quedans*, and the SRA

In the aftermath of the EDSA Revolution, a brief historical opportunity existed. The new democratic government of the Philippines could at that moment have taken a strong hand to restructure, reorganize, and (perhaps) revitalize the sugar industry. The method of apportioning property rights could have been revamped, extensive land reform enacted, and an incentive structure to encourage investment and reduce transaction costs put into place. But none of that transpired. Instead, the government created an agency that appreciably restored the old system and sanctioned the old property-rights allocation and "perverse" incentives. While many in the government employed the rhetoric of agrarian reform, and Congress passed agrarian reform legislation, inaction was virtually assured by the bureaucratic machinery created to enact reform and the lack of clear purpose among the bureaucrats. The culture of sectoral conflict, "groupism," natural prerogative, planter autonomy, and political machination proved stronger than the best intentions of politicians, technocrats, and even forward-thinking elements in the sugar industry. Although the worldwide sugar economy and Philippine society were changing rapidly in the 1980s and 1990s, the Philippine sugar industry was for the most part reestablishing the pre-Marcos institutional order.

That policies pertaining to rice and corn tend to foster low prices to benefit consumers, whereas policies pertaining to sugar foster high prices to benefit producers, may be partly explained by the "luxury" nature of sugar as compared to the subsistence necessity of rice and corn. But in large measure the difference can also be related to rice and corn farmers tending to be poorly organized, geographically dispersed, small-scale farmers with little political clout, while sugar producers—both agricultural and industrial—still retain considerable political influence.[1] Agencies of the Philippine Department of Agriculture are charged with the task of closely monitoring the supplies of, demand for, and prices of rice and corn in order to keep prices stable and low for the benefit of consumers (Billig 1991; David

1989). Upward pressure on the price of rice often leads to demonstrations, even riots, in Manila, and government officials try to forestall such occurrences. It is also true that industrial interests lobby for cheap rice in order to restrain upward pressure on urban wages. But rice farmers complain frequently that when supplies are ample, prices are low, but when supplies are tight and there is upward pressure on prices, the government authorizes massive rice imports from Vietnam and Thailand, thereby increasing supplies and dampening prices. This policy insures that rice farmers will never be able to make a decent living planting rice, and thus insures that the Philippines will remain dependent on imports for the foreseeable future. Even though the Green Revolution in rice was born in the Philippines—at the International Rice Research Institute (IRRI) in Los Baños—Philippine government policy continues to place the nation in the embarrassing position of not being self-sufficient in that all-important staple grain.

The main method of insuring high sugar prices, aside from import control and tariffs, is the action of another agriculture department agency: The Sugar Regulatory Administration (SRA). There is, of course, nothing unusual about having a government agency oversee the marketing and trading of sugar. As discussed in chapter 3, few sugar-producing nations can afford to allow a "free market" in sugar to exist given the way it is bought and sold internationally. Government agencies in sugar-producing nations all over the world monitor and regulate the import and export of sugar to insure steady domestic supplies and to guarantee that its international quotas are serviced. These agencies also represent their countries in international sugar organizations and lobby foreign governments to maintain and improve their quota statuses. In a game in which every player is "cheating," playing "honestly" would guarantee that one would lose.

Unlike the defunct PHILSUCOM, the SRA (which was created in 1986) does not buy and sell sugar, nor does it set prices. Aside from regulating the many facets of the industry, the agency is charged with coordinating research and development, maintaining extension services, issuing licenses to traders, monitoring mills, lobbying governments in importing countries, representing the Philippines in world sugar organizations, serving as a liaison between the industry and the government, and acting as public-relations agent for Philippine sugar. It does not involve itself actively in labor relations, wage issues, land reform, social welfare, or the "peace and order" problem that is endemic to the industry.

Perhaps the most important function of the SRA—certainly its most controversial—is to administer the share-classification system. This system serves the dual purpose of apportioning sugar to different markets and maintaining price stability within and between crop years. It is through this system that the SRA acts to balance the interests of producers, traders, and consumers, and it is the nature of this balance that generates most of the conflict, especially when producers feel that the agency is failing to protect their interests. Underlying the share-classification system is a method and morality of apportioning property rights to and responsibilities for the raw materials and finished products of the sugar industry. Although most people in the Philippine industry regard this underlying property allocation as self-evident and legitimate, the fact is that sugar industries in most other countries apportion property differently, using different mechanisms. Institutions that specify the allocation of property influence the structure of incentives, the relative efficiency of various sectors, and the ways that different actors choose to spend their time and efforts. More important, since these institutions have moral implications for what groups and individuals in different sectors regard as rightfully "theirs," they profoundly influence what those groups and individuals consider to be in the public as opposed to private interest. Despite the constant debates that take place over the particulars of the SRA apportionments throughout any milling season, there is surprisingly little discussion of the relative merits of truly alternative property schemes that might have positive effects on the overall health of the industry. Not only do people frame their interests within the given scheme, but that scheme is widely considered just, correct, and entirely reasonable. In other words, it is fully institutionalized and grounded in taken-for-granted assumptions that have little to do with economic considerations. Still, in the last few years there was one noteworthy—though largely unsuccessful—attempt at institutional innovation in the property-rights regime. The responses to, implications of, and debates about this innovation will be discussed at length presently.

In late August or early September of each crop year, the SRA issues Sugar Order No. 1. This is the first apportionment of milled sugar into five categories: A-sugar, destined for export to the United States as determined by that year's U.S. quota; B-sugar, immediately sellable in the Philippine domestic market; C-sugar, the reserve portion which will be gradually converted to other classes by subsequent sugar orders; D-sugar, destined for the world market and used to unload surplus sugar to prevent supply from exceeding demand; and E-sugar, a special lower-priced category intended for export-oriented food processors.

These categories are the overall norms. Since this system took effect in 1986, however, there has been much experimentation and political wrangling over the categories. E-sugar was a controversial innovation and has only been used once, in 1992. In 1993 there was no C-sugar. Instead, B was divided into immediately marketable B and gradually marketable B1. In 1996 there was B1 sugar again, but rather than being gradually marketable domestic sugar it was simply the erstwhile, now discredited, E-sugar under a different name; that is, sugar allocated exclusively for food exporters sold at world-market prices. C-sugar has always been the most controversial and politicized category because it must be "converted" to usable sugar throughout the year. Increasingly, D-sugar never reaches the world market because of shortfalls in domestic supply, although, as we shall see in the next chapter, the D portion may still be allocated to satisfy the food-producing exporters. In surplus years in which Philippine D-sugar does get sold on the world market, the majority of it is purchased by the Japanese (*Manila Star*, 21 Oct. 1993). Since 1997 and the subsequent El Niño shortfalls, only the A and B categories have been allocated. In 1997–1998, for example, Sugar Order No. 1 specified A = 12 percent and B = 88 percent. Clearly, the very categories themselves are the subjects of negotiation, and the SRA seems never able to make every constituency happy with its classification scheme and sugar orders.

When a planter delivers his cane to a central by truck, the cane is milled as rapidly as possible to avoid sucrose loss. But prior to milling, the sugarcane is weighed and sampled for purity and sweetness in order to estimate how much sugar will be yielded from a unit of that particular shipment (which is a function of cane age, moisture content, cane varietal, skill of cutting, and many other variables). The sampling of "first expressed juice" is supervised by a chemist from the central as well as a representative of a planters' association that operates in that mill. Based upon a formula that estimates the amount of sugar and molasses that will be milled from a given cane shipment, the central issues *quedan*s to both the planter and to itself.

These *quedans*, which must be issued in the proportions of the different categories of sugar determined by the extant sugar order, are warehouse receipts or coupons representing ownership of a certain amount of sugar stored in the central's *bodega*, or warehouse. For example (making up fairly typical figures), after the central takes its 35 percent share a planter retains ownership of 1,000 piculs of sugar. *Quedans* will be issued for 150 piculs of A-sugar (15 percent), 600 piculs of B-sugar (60 percent), 200 piculs of C-sugar (20 percent), 50 piculs of D-sugar (5 percent), and 50 piculs of E-sugar (5 percent). The planters will also be issued *quedans* for the molasses, a by-product of the milling process. For its effort the central also issues *quedans* to itself in the same proportions for the 25 to 40 percent of the sugar it owns, depending upon the share agreement that pertains at that particular central. No money changes hands between the central and the planter.

Of course, the price of sugar in each category differs. On 11 November 1993, for example, the trader-price quotes for sugar milled at the BISCOM central in Negros were as follows, per 50-kilogram bag: A *quedans* = P578 (P731 per picul); B *quedans* = P438 (P554 per picul); C *quedans* = P394 (P498 per picul); and D *quedans* = P316 (P400 per picul). Applying the above percentages and combining the D and E categories (since there was no E in 1993), one gets a composite price of sugar on that day of P444.10 per bag, or P561.65 per picul. Applying the conversion rate of 28 pesos to the dollar, that composite price translates to 14.4 U.S. cents per pound. By contrast, note that the price of the world-market component (D *quedans*) was 10.2 cents per pound, the U.S.-bound sugar (A *quedans*) was 18.8 cents per pound, and the immediately marketable domestic sugar (B *quedans*) was 14.2 cents per pound. Since the United States only buys raw sugar, the price quotes for A *quedans* from every mill were exactly the same. But since the Victorias Milling Company—the nation's largest central and refiner—gives a premium for Victorias *quedan* holders to have their sugar refined there, traders were offering 4 to 5 percent more for B, C, and D *quedans* from Victorias than for BISCOM or La Carlota *quedans*.

Ever since the breakup of the fixed milling districts, centrals have been forced to compete for cane. Aside from negotiating the share (i.e., the planter-miller distribution of the finished sugar and molasses), centrals must give various other incentives, such as hauling allowances, longer storage without fees, and access to favored traders. Of course, some mills simply produce better quality sugar more efficiently, and planters tend to gravitate toward these centrals. And, as the above example illustrates, the *quedan*s for sugar milled at one central may be sold for more money than those for sugar at a different central.

This *quedan* (or share) system in which both planter and miller retain rights to the finished sugar is a distinctive part of the industrial structure of sugar production in the Philippines, and it long predates the SRA. In fact, administering and supervising "an orderly system of *quedan*ning" is one of the functions explicitly mentioned in the Executive Order No. 18 that created the SRA. The share-*quedan* was established during the American colonial period partly because provincial areas such as Negros had insufficient cash in circulation. But more importantly it was a way to persuade powerful *hacenderos* —who had previously both grown sugarcane and milled sugar on their farms—to bring their sugarcane and cede the milling function to the new factory centrals.[2] By issuing *quedan*s and allowing the planters to retain ownership rights to the sugar in the centrals' warehouses, the colonial government succeeded in making the rapid transformation from inefficient on-the-farm milling of low-grade sugar to centrifugal milling in modern industrial factories. And the *hacenderos* continued to experience the sense of autonomy that they associated with the ownership of physical sugar.

In many sugar-producing nations farm and mill operations are fully or cooperatively integrated. The apportionment of property rights to sugar between those who grow cane and those who mill the sugar under such circumstances is not an issue. In most other nations in which production is not integrated, the cane-purchase system prevails. The mill receives the cane from the farmer, weighs it, assesses its conformity to standards, often takes a core sample to test for quality (which is more direct and accurate than the first expressed-juice method), then purchases the cane from the planter based upon a weight-quality formula. Once the mill has purchased the cane, it owns all of the sugar and molasses that is produced. The farmer has no ownership rights to the finished product once he sells his sugarcane. Again, this is not how the system works in the Philippines, where the mill and the planter each retain property rights in certain proportions to the finished products (sugar, molasses, and, at least theoretically, all by-products).[3] The only circumstance in which raw cane is purchased in the Philippines is when a planter (or mill) buys cane directly from a smaller, marginal planter and then has all the *quedan*s issued in his (or its) own name. For example, Victorias purchases cane from small farmers on Panay in order to keep its mill operating during Negros' off-milling season. Several entrepreneurial truckers have recently begun to purchase cane from small planters and sell it at a profit to centrals. Small planters often prefer to have the cash up-front rather than wait to sell their *quedan*s to traders. Mills, all of which operate under capacity, are happy to buy additional cane and issue all of the *quedan*s to themselves.

A mill, planters' association, or individual planter can present *quedan*s at the *bodega* and haul off the physical sugar that they own. But this is not what typically happens. With a few notable exceptions, centrals and planters have resisted going into trading, transport, and marketing. These functions are carried out by a complex web of traders and brokers. Many planters talk about traders with hostility and seem to think that all they do is shuffle paper *quedan*s. but it is traders—at least the larger ones—who actually move the physical sugar from the *bodega*s to the trucks, the barges, the ships, and the consumers.[4] It is true, however, that there is a substantial secondary and tertiary market for *quedan*s, wherein traders or brokers purchase *quedan*s from producers and sell them later to other traders at a profit. Producers want to sell their *quedan*s as quickly as possible, but trading is competitive. If a planter can afford the storage fees and has some cash on hand, he can wait for a better offer before selling. There is also much speculation involved in sugar trading, especially surrounding the timing of "conversions" from one category of sugar to another—another highly controversial part of the SRA's function.

During the course of the year, the SRA board will periodically issue sugar orders that convert one class of sugar to another. Theoretically, any class of sugar may be converted to any other, but in practice it is almost always the reserve (C) sugar that is converted to A or B. If there were no reserve, all sugar would be immediately marketable and the price would be high at the beginning of the milling season, thus encouraging planters to mill early, flooding the centrals with more cane than they could handle. By setting aside a reserve and converting it slowly to marketable sugar, the price is kept reasonably constant throughout the year and the supply to the mill is kept more steady within milling season. But, of course, C-sugar is relatively cheap compared to A or B. A planter could hold on to his C *quedan*s and wait for a conversion, but this is a risky strategy, especially given the storage fees he incurs by leaving his sugar in the *bodega*. A trader could buy C *quedan*s, wait for a conversion, and make a windfall when the cheap reserve sugar he bought becomes more expensive marketable sugar. But he also incurs storage fees and, most importantly, if he used bank credit to purchase *quedan*s (as most do given the large quantities they buy), he will be losing money to the high Philippine interest rates. Traders assert that the "cost of money" makes it essential to turn over one's sugar as soon as possible after purchasing the *quedan*s. But if a trader could know the timing of a conversion beforehand, he could reap a large profit while minimizing the time in which he is paying interest. Traders say that they speculate on conversions based upon their knowledge of the dynamics of the market, but there are, nevertheless, well-documented instances of hoarding, collusion, and other forms of price manipulation by traders.

Although most traders deny that anyone in their sector receives inside information on the timing of conversions, smaller traders admit that they suspect that the "Big Five" trading families—all of whom are "Chinese"—do have some sort of special access to the SRA.[5] No one denies that *quedan*s for C-sugar trade most actively just before conversions are announced, and that this looks like insider trading. But most aver that traders monitor the supply and demand for sugar much as the SRA does, and this leads them to predict when conversions need to occur. Many traders also state that they follow the lead of the Big Five, so their (inside) information is only secondhand.

Most planters are completely convinced that the SRA leaks information on the timing of conversions to favorite traders, depriving planters of their just profits. They are equally convinced that traders collude amongst themselves to set prices. Virtually all planters and many smaller traders believe that the pattern of *quedan* buying and selling could only be explained by collusion among the major traders, and that this has gotten more obvious since traders began to purchase so many centrals. Several people cited the joint purchase of the BUSCO central in Mindanao by a consortium of Big Five traders —supposedly arch competitors. Big Five traders, in turn, state that the proliferation of smaller traders makes it impossible for them to control prices as large traders did in the past, and that competition in some enterprises does not preclude cooperation in others. In fact,

Big Five traders state that the entire notion of a "Big Five" is more mythical than real. Few deny that trading has become more competitive in recent years as the SRA has loosened its licensing requirements and the number of traders has proliferated.

The SRA is frequently accused of being in the pocket of large traders. A preeminent accuser has been Romeo Guanzon, formerly congressman from Bacolod (the capital and main city on Negros), the President of the National Federation of Sugarcane Planters (NFSP —one of the two main planters' federations), and a politician who prides himself on being "sugar's congressman." Although SRA officials deny that information on conversions is leaked or that Big Five traders get any special consideration, Guanzon is certain that high SRA officials are in league with powerful traders and that they conspire to profit at the expense of planters. Guanzon and other producers argue that the entire system of conversions leads to lower prices for planters and windfalls for unproductive traders, that it fosters corruption, and that it should therefore be completely scrapped. He advocates having only two categories—A and B—the former pro-rated among planters, and the latter steadily released to the market throughout the year.

Officials of the SRA counter that it is necessary to maintain the reserve and world-market categories in order to achieve price stability, and that the SRA is not charged only with ensuring that planters receive the highest possible prices but also with protecting consumers from excessively high prices. Administrator Rodolfo Gamboa asserted that if the SRA operated only in the planters' interests, industrial consumers would be encouraged to import sugar and the entire industry would suffer.[6] He also argued that without A, B, C, and D categories, there would be "a free-wheeling market" in which no one would make money. The former president of a national organization of food exporters confirmed this assessment but drew an entirely different implication from it when he told me that if there were no A, B, C, and D *quedans* (i.e., if all sugar were made immediately available for whatever usage commanded the best price), the price of Philippine sugar would be considerably lower, and food processors would have less incentive to buy imported sugar. Of course, Gamboa believed that such a "free-wheeling market" with lower sugar prices would be a disaster, whereas the food exporter thought it would be a step in the right direction for his industry. As I will discuss at length in chapter 5, disputes between sugar producers and food processors have become highly acrimonious and have been followed avidly by politicians and the national media.

Guanzon also asserts that the D category—sugar destined for the world market—should be eliminated. He argues, first, that the price of D-sugar is often less than half that of B and almost always below the cost of production. Second, if D-sugar is converted to A or B, as has happened in the past, the traders again profit at the expense of producers. Third, he cites anecdotal evidence that some large industrial sugar users in the Philippines manage to procure D-sugar for their own use, and thus avoid paying for higher priced B-sugar. And lastly, he says that the Philippines does not need to divert any sugar to the world market, which functions mostly as a low price surplus market. There is enough domestic demand for sugar to make participation in the world market unnecessary.

The SRA (in this case, Yulo) responded that D-sugar was converted upward only once: in 1986, the first year of the SRA's operation. That was due to a faulty estimate of the sources of demand and was a mistake that will not be repeated. Furthermore, he argues that if D-sugar were eliminated, the domestic market would be flooded with 8 to 12 percent more sugar in a typical year, thereby lowering the price of B-sugar. An analysis conducted by SRA economists suggests that the composite price of all sugar would be lower if D-sugar were diverted to the domestic market. Yulo further asserts that it is necessary for the Philippines to retain a foothold in the world market in the event that those prices rise rapidly due to some future instability.

Despite Yulo's argument, no D-sugar is set aside in years in which Philippine production falls short of the amount needed to satisfy both the U.S. quota and domestic demand, as has happened in every year since 1997. In 1992, the SRA came close to trying out Guanzon's suggestion, with rather negative results. The only categories allotted were A, B, and B1, the latter being a new category of domestic sugar that could only enter the market 120 days after the *quedan* was written. In other words, rather than converting from a reserve through sugar orders, the conversion took place automatically, reducing the possibility of speculation and insider information. No sugar was designated for the world market. This created problems. Domestic consumption that year was 1.6 million m.t. and the U.S. quota export was 178,000 m.t. But since production was 2.1 million m.t., there was a surplus of 300,000 tons by the end of the milling year. By August, prices of domestic sugar began to drop sharply (to P525 per picul), leading to a fear that the sugar remaining in the *bodega*s would cause prices to be low at the beginning of the next milling season, the time when prices are traditionally highest. The SRA tried to encourage traders to sell the surplus sugar on the world market, even though they had purchased the *quedan*s at the far higher domestic price. To encourage them to incur such losses the SRA devised an "advance swap," by which any *quedan*-holder who sold domestic sugar on the world market would be compensated by having an equal quantity of the following year's D-sugar specially converted to B. Unfortunately, there were few takers because most traders believed that the next year's B price would be closer to the world-market price. The automatic conversion innovation has not been used since.

The 1991 advent of the new category, E-sugar, stirred up another controversy over SRA policy. The E category was another reflection of the growing clout of urban industrial interests at the expense of landed rural ones. E-sugar was meant to be solely for export-oriented food processors, enabling them to buy lower-price sugar (about P300 cheaper per picul than B) in order to remain competitive with food companies in Thailand, Indonesia, Malaysia, and Singapore. As will be discussed in detail, industrial consumers complained that the sugar they were forced to buy was priced so much higher than world-market sugar that it posed an unfair cost to them, and their complaints were beginning to be heard in government and in the press. After several notable instances in which industrial users surreptitiously imported cheaper foreign sugar, as well as a great deal of lobbying by the food industry, the SRA agreed to set up the special category and to require the issuing of E *quedan*s for 5 percent of all milled sugar. Although many producers initially objected to E-sugar, the SRA made a strong case that it was needed to keep imports out, and most planters fear imports more than anything else. It did not take long for rumors of corruption, conspiracy, and collusion to swirl about. As usual, the reputed villains were the traders, who were said to be buying up all the E *quedan*s but hoarding the sugar in hope of forcing the SRA to convert it upward. Others believed that traders were diverting E-sugar illegally into the domestic market at huge mark-ups. There were, in any case, indications that food processors were continuing their quiet efforts to import sugar (Sa-onoy and Delfin columns in *Today*, 25 July 1991).

Many food processors complained bitterly that no matter how hard they tried to obtain sugar at E prices, none of it was ever actually available for purchase, and the sugar took more than a month to be delivered when one was lucky enough to find *quedan*s to purchase. Planters complained that they were often left holding their E *quedan*s because many traders thought that this sugar was not profitable enough to handle. There was even a widespread rumor among planters and several newspaper articles suggesting that "large amounts of E-sugar was left rotting in warehouses" (*Visayan Daily Star,* 23 July 1992), which was absurd given that sugar is stored in *bodega*s without classification. All sugar in the warehouse is equal; only the *quedan* possesses the classification. An SRA official with whom I discussed that rumor had a good laugh imagining a big pile of sugar labeled "E" rotting in some corner of a *bodega.* But he used the episode to point out a surprising and serious fact, one consistent with my own research findings: most planters do not have a firm understanding of the institutional organization of their own industry.

By 1993, the experiment in E-sugar had been declared a failure. Instead, the SRA authorized specified amounts of D-sugar to be released to certified food processors and exporters at world-market prices, one sugar order at a time. One company that availed itself of this D-sugar was San Miguel, the nation's largest and most high-profile corporation, and one of the leading consumers of sugar.[7] Needless to say, the NFSP sensed yet another rip-off and complained bitterly that the SRA was in league with the processors and exporters to depress producer prices. Many food processors, for their part, complained that when world-market prices are low—as is most often the case—traders and planters withhold D *quedan*s, and it becomes impossible for the food processors to find any to purchase at that price. Whereas San Miguel has the volume and clout to insure that its needs are satisfied, most food processors feel that their sugar supplies are far more dependent upon the unpredictable movements of the domestic sugar trade. So while sugar at world-market prices is theoretically available to the processors, in practice they must continue to buy the far more expensive B *quedan*s (sugar at the domestic price) in order to stay in business.

The A-sugar category, the portion destined for the United States as determined by the annual USDA import quota, has also come under scrutiny. Since Sugar Order No. 1 comes out before the U.S.

quota is established in October, the SRA tends to allocate a fairly low portion to A-sugar and convert upward later on. Even during bad years, A-sugar is given highest priority; not only is it usually the highest priced category, but it is paid for in dollars rather than pesos, earning valuable foreign exchange. So even at the risk of a shortfall in the domestic market and having to import to satisfy domestic demand, the Philippines meets its U.S. quota. Occasionally, because of low production and a fairly high U.S. quota, the price of B-sugar actually exceeds that of A-sugar. Predictably, when this happens some planters advocate the temporary or even permanent elimination of A-sugar. Since domestic sugar now earns more than U.S.-bound sugar, they reason, why not concentrate solely on satisfying the Philippines' own demand? Of course, if the 15 to 25 percent portion of A-sugar were diverted into the domestic market, the price of B-sugar would plummet to well below that of A-sugar. Plus it is still the case that in most years A-sugar is priced considerably higher than B-sugar, and the U.S. sugar market is far less volatile than the domestic one. The SRA continues to do all it can to service its U.S. quota. They realize, as many planters seem not to, that the U.S. government and sugar interests would be all too willing to penalize a country that only met its quota when American prices were higher than domestic prices. Such a country would easily lose all or part of that quota in the next U.S. Farm Bill. Since the U.S. military bases were asked to leave the Philippines, the strategic importance of that nation to the United States has lessened, and such "special favors" as a high sugar quota may truly be in jeopardy.

As should be obvious by now, decisions by the SRA are made in a highly charged political atmosphere. One debate, which in some ways underlies many of the others, concerns the make-up of the three-person SRA board: one representative of the planters, one of the millers, and one of government. Most planters' associations throughout the Philippines are affiliated with one or the other of the two arch-rival planters' federations: CONFED or NFSP (see my discussion of "groupism" in chapter 6). Since the majority of associations are members of CONFED, the planters' representative on the board has always been a CONFED partisan. But since Congressman Guanzon is president of the NFSP, he has always insisted that his group be represented on the board.[8] This has led to a situation in which the NFSP perceives itself as the opposition, taking exception to *any* action taken by the SRA, and publicly blaming the SRA for any problem that befalls the industry. Guanzon's position, however, was weakened after the 1992 election. According to SRA Administrator Rodolfo Gamboa, "Guanzon felt left out when the SRA was organized. He thought Cory should have rewarded him, so anything Yulo did he [Guanzon] criticized. But since he supported Mitra [the former speaker of the house who ran unsuccessfully against Fidel Ramos], he [Guanzon] has no reason to expect any of the spoils." CONFED and NFSP constantly manipulate events and information to gain advantage over one another. Whereas "the planters" could once function with impressive unity, nowadays the internecine struggles seem more rancorous than those between sectors. In 1992, for instance, a planned meeting of planters to plot strategy for preventing the liberalization of sugar imports had to be cancelled due to lack of agreement between the two federations on controlling the meeting's agenda.

There are also other factions who would like to see the make-up of the SRA board changed or expanded. People in the labor sector, for example, complain bitterly that there is no labor representation. Some decry that no one on the board represents the interests of consumers or food processors. Others cite the obvious conflict inherent in the fact that the "government" representative (i.e., the SRA administrator himself) has always been a sugar planter allied with the biggest planters' federation. This certainly gives the appearance of the SRA being an advocate for the producers rather than a balanced, independent overseer of all facets of the industry. While Administrator Gamboa told me that *he*, the government representative on the board, is the one who represents the interests of consumers, people in the food processing industry scoff at that presumption. Gamboa also reiterated that labor conditions in the industry are decidedly not the responsibility of the SRA, but rather that of the Department of Labor and Employment (DOLE).

The tendency to blame the SRA as a proxy for political jockeying was apparent during the scandal that rocked the industry in the middle of 1992. Two of the least efficient centrals in Negros (Bacolod-Murcia and Talisay) had been leased by a family of sugar traders in 1991. When these mills proved unprofitable, forcing the family to incur large debts, they were in turn sub-leased to a different group of traders, among whom was a creditor of the first trading family. At the end of the milling season it became clear that there was not enough sugar in those centrals' *bodega*s to cover the *quedan*s they had written. In other words, sugar had been removed from the *bodegas*, and presumably sold illegally, without *quedans* being presented. Although it is still not known how much sugar was involved, planters (including Congressman Guanzon) instigated dozens of court cases, claiming they had been stung. The mill manager implicated in the scam fled the country. Aside from the economic losses suffered by some planters, many in the industry worried that such a scandal threatened to undermine the entire *quedan* system, which is fundamentally based upon the trust of all parties that *quedans* can be redeemed for sugar. Needless to say, NFSP officials took the SRA to task for this debacle, threatening to sue the agency for insufficient and dishonest oversight of the movement of sugar. They argued that this episode demonstrated that the SRA was incompetent and hopelessly corrupt. The SRA, for its part, responded that nothing in its charter or its budget allows it to supervise *bodegas* twenty-four hours a day. If owners of mills are intent on pirating sugar from their own *bodegas*, there is little the SRA can do to stop them. The act that chartered the SRA deliberately gave the agency minimal clout, coming as it did in the aftermath of the PHILSUCOM experience. Several planters told me in confidence that the SRA was not culpable in this incident, and that the attack upon it in the wake of the scandal was only the NFSP taking the opportunity to score political points at the expense of the CONFED-dominated agency.

Another function of the SRA is to administer the liens placed upon each *quedan*. The central that issues the *quedan* must extract a certain amount per picul for a number of special functions. These include (in 1993–1994): P5 for the Sugar Development Foundation, which supports both lobbying the U.S. government and "safety and security" (i.e., CAFGU security forces) on sugar farms; P2.54 for the Sugar Industry Foundation, Inc. (SIFI), which supports programs to uplift sugar workers;[9] and P1.75 for the Social Amelioration Fund. The remaining liens are for Social Security and the DOLE Working Fund. Although these liens amount only to about P11 per picul, there are disputes over them that mirror the political battles over other issues in the industry. At one conference I attended, a planter from Mindanao received a loud ovation when he argued that the liens represented an illegal taking of planter property without consent. Several planters averred that they would fight any attempt to increase the liens.

The Share-*Quedan* System and the Structure of Incentives

The share-*quedan* system is an idiosyncratic institution with profound implications for the structure of incentives within the industry. In served several purposes in the past: It was an efficient mechanism for administering the U.S. quota in the 1930s because it tied planters to single centrals while preserving the illusion of independence. This was needed to persuade planters to give up the autonomy that came with on-the-farm milling in order modernize the industry with centrifugal mills. It served to elicit an enormous increase in cane production during the period in which the centrals were being built and capacity was expanding. It enabled planters to remain aloof from marketing while still feeling in control of their product. It provided an effective balance of power between planters and millers. It established the idiom for negotiating changing economic and political clout between the two sectors. And finally it enabled transactions to occur with minimal accounting of cash and credit.

But today this system is promoting inefficiency, low investment, institutional stasis, and high transaction costs. Yet attempts to change it are met with strong resistance by planters and traders, and one is frequently told that the alternatives to the share-*quedan* system are politically and morally unacceptable. What follows are some examples of the purely economic consequences of this system of property allocation.

- The proliferation of *quedan*s and the diffuse ownership of milled sugar promotes unproductive secondary and tertiary trading (i.e., high transaction costs). Although a few of the larger mills have begun to market their sugar directly to large industrial consumers (beverage companies, candy makers, fruit canneries, etc.), these consumers still complain that not even the biggest traders can guarantee reliable supplies of sugar. The commodities-purchasing manager of the Philippines' largest ice cream manufacturer told me that he greatly prefers to buy sugar in large quantities directly from mills, but because of low supply and the fact that traders can often sell at lower prices than mills, he must purchase from traders as well. Sometimes he has to buy *quedan*s from planters' associations, but that is the most inefficient of all sources since one must then deal with "a bag full of *quedan*s" instead of only a few, and one must arrange transport of the physical sugar separately. Planters' associations, unlike large traders, do not have the wherewithal to move sugar from *bodega* to consumer. The manager related that he receives many phone calls every day from sugar traders trying to peddle *quedans*.[10]

Traders likewise complain that they can rarely garner enough supply to satisfy major consumers. There are thousands of *quedan* holders (in other words, thousands of owners of sugar) who run the gamut from the farmer who has less than one hectare to the giant Victorias Milling Company. Thus the movement of *quedans* typically winds its way through multiple steps of brokers, small traders, medium-sized traders, and the large traders who sell sugar to consumers. The SRA has issued sugar trading licenses to over 500 individuals and companies. At each stage, there is speculation and the hope of selling one's *quedans* down the line at a profit. Whereas in most countries the mills own sugar and market that sugar to customers, the trading frenzy in the Philippines adds appreciably to the final cost of the product.

Planters bitterly complain about mill inefficiency, millers complain about the decrepit state of sugarcane agriculture, and millers, planters, and consumers all complain about being cheated by the much-reviled traders. But virtually everyone takes for granted the separation of miller, trader, and planter into separate, contentious "sectors." Such a separation does not exist in all sugar-producing countries and is the result of the particular history and institutional organization of the Philippine industry. Many other countries have developed cooperatives that integrate the farming, milling, and trading functions into single, coordinated institutional entities, often worker-owned.[11]

• Philippine sugar tends to be expensive, far more expensive than world-market sugar, and this has created an enormous controversy between the food processors and the sugar producers, with the government trying to forge some sort of mutually agreeable middle ground. The food exporters, in particular, have managed to gain public relations points by arguing that the high cost of sugar—which only benefits the "pampered," politically powerful, wasteful, "feudal," sugar barons—makes it difficult for their "modern," value-added products to compete in foreign markets against other tropical food producers. And as much as the price of sugar is an issue for food processors, so are the transaction costs and supply difficulties. Food processing executives frequently decry the fact that under the current system traders are often incapable of supplying their companies' needs in a timely and efficient manner because it is so difficult for traders to purchase large numbers of *quedans* and coordinate transport and delivery. The food processors scoff at the "generous" offer of the SRA to allow them to purchase E-sugar (especially for food exporters) and later D-sugar (at world-market prices). What is the point of jumping through all the bureaucratic hoops necessary to receive SRA authorization to buy these *quedans* if that sugar is seldom available to be bought, if no trader is capable of supplying it in quantity, and if (after paying the Value-Added Tax and the refining and transport fees) it costs more than world-market sugar that can be bought from other countries? Many say it is cheaper and easier for food processors to buy sugar from companies in Thailand, Singapore, or Hong Kong than to rely on domestic suppliers.

- The system creates a disincentive for the improvement of mills. Although a few mills have received infusions of capital in the last decade or so, most of those have been upgraded after being purchased by large-scale traders. The majority of Philippine mills are aging and inefficient, and many are being abandoned as lost causes. A 1989 report on the sugar industry by the Asian Development Bank suggested that at least ten Philippine mills should close immediately, and sixteen have done so since 1993. Since planters own as much as 75 percent of the sugar in a central's *bodega*, any capital expenditure by the milling company that improves efficiency (i.e., more sugar per unit of sugarcane) accrues mainly to planters who did not pay for it. Several millers told me that they would love to reach agreement with planters' associations in which the mill and the planters share the cost of the upgrade, but such an arrangement has never come to fruition (with the exception of the two mills actually owned by planters' groups). Planters scoff at the idea of paying to improve mills. They often cite the history of acrimony between the sectors and the prevailing sense that milling companies make large profits by exploiting and cheating the planters. The very idea of planters *paying* to upgrade a sugar central is regarded as offensive, if not comical. Millers, for their part, frequently say that they cannot afford to upgrade given that they own only 25 to 40 percent of the sugar. It would take too long to amortize such capital investments and would make it very difficult for the mill to service its debts. If the mill owned all of the sugar in its *bodega*, however, and was able to "capture" all of the improvement in efficiency that came with the capital investment, most millers agree that such an investment would make sense. With greater extraction efficiency they could, in turn, attract more planters to their mill.

- Mills in Brazil, Cuba, India, and other countries proudly proclaim that they produce dozens of products from the sugarcane plant in addition to sugar and molasses. Philippine mills are among the worst in the world at pursuing the common linkages, and this is directly related to the property-sharing institution. The failure to exploit the potential uses of *bagasse* is perhaps the most classic illustration. Most sugar mills in the world—and all in the Philippines—are powered by boilers fueled by *bagasse*, the straw-like residue of sugarcane after all the juice has been pressed out.[12] In many sugar-producing countries, the supply of *bagasse* is so great and the boilers are so efficient that mills make considerable money selling excess power to the local power grid. In addition, *bagasse* is frequently used to make construction-grade particleboard, fiberboard, cement-bonded board, low-grade paper, and other commercially viable ancillary products that could be profitable in a country experiencing a severe shortage of lumber owing to deforestation and a legal ban on tree cutting. But no Philippine mill cogenerates and sells electricity and none produces ancillary products from *bagasse*.

Many millers have explained to me that they would certainly upgrade their boilers to make them more efficient if they had any incentive to do so. Under the current system, planters give the *bagasse* to the mill for free, because it is perceived as having no commercial value. But if a mill upgraded its boilers (using its own capital) and sold power to the grid or marketed manufactured by-products, the planters would immediately claim their rightful shares of *bagasse* (i.e., it would have to be *quedan*ed like sugar and molasses) and demand some of the profit from the collateral business. So Philippine millers claim that it is actually *better* to have inefficient boilers using low-pressure steam because it allows them to incinerate the "useless" *bagasse*. One miller complained to me that it was imperative to get rid of this excess *bagasse* because it "causes fires during the summer." Even under the current system some planters complain about the "huge windfall" for the mills because they "appropriate *bagasse* for free." Some argue that all mills should be *quedan*ning *bagasse* or at least paying for it, even though mills only use it as fuel.

- Food processors and large consumers require a consistent, reliable, and predictable supply of sugar. Executives of these companies complain that under the current system of diffuse ownership of sugar it is impossible to sign advance contracts with traders or mills for the provision of sugar. Since the allocation of sugar in the different categories changes in every year depending upon that year's supply, the U.S. quota, and conditions of the world market, companies that require large amounts of sugar always fear that they will not be able to garner an adequate number of *quedan*s to meet their anticipated needs. For companies that produce such sugar-dependent products as sweetened beverages or canned fruit, such uncertainty and the lack of advance contracts can be worrisome, indeed. This uncertainty is even more pronounced for food-exporting companies who are theoretically entitled to purchase D- or E-sugar, the allocations of which may be zero in any given year and which are difficult to find even in better years. Japanese food and commodity-importing companies—potentially lucrative destinations for Philippine sugar and processed food—are particularly deterred by the uncertainty of supply that results from the share-*quedan* system. Many food processors point out that under a cane-purchase system there would be fewer sellers of sugar in the market and each would have a larger, more reliable supply that could be contracted in advance.

The difficulty in garnering large, reliable quantities of sugar under the share-*quedan* system is one reason that several wealthy traders purchased sugar centrals during the last decade. Rather than build a new central, a trader will typically purchase and refit an older or idled one. A trader who owns a mill will theoretically have a steady supply of sugar without needing to borrow money to buy other producers' *quedan*s. Large industrial consumers prefer to deal with such consolidated suppliers because they are less likely to experience shortages.

There have also been a few instances of millers buying up farm acreage to provide steady supply, but these have not been extensive enough to be considered true consolidation. The top-down consolidation represented by traders purchasing mills is, in the view of many planters, a regrettable trend, signifying the erosion of their own bargaining power relative to that of traders. Although traders in the past have frequently purchased or leased farm property to gain social respectability, their purchasing mills is a relatively new phenomenon. Many planters grudgingly acknowledge that this trend may ultimately be good for business, but most regard it as socially and morally inappropriate for so much of the industry's power and wealth to rest in the hands of the most despised and mistrusted sector. As one miller told me, "You know how it is; traders will be traders, and someone needs to make sure that they start acting like real millers." Of course, much of the animosity is ethnic. The "Chinese"—as defined by the vague and shifting criteria of "chineseness" employed in the Philippines and much of Southeast Asia—are still perceived as a sort of cabal out to cheat the real Filipinos. In fact, the binary opposite of Chinese in Filipino discourse about ethnicity is "Filipino," implying that one can be either Chinese or Filipino, but not both.

Some planters and millers applaud these new trader–millers bringing large infusions of capital into a sector that desperately needs investment. One sugar technologist with whom I spoke, however, echoed the widely espoused belief (with obvious ethnic undertones) that "traders lack the technical knowledge and management ability to run such large and technologically complicated organizations." He wondered why *every* trader suddenly felt that the only way to gain respectability was to become a miller, in contrast to the past when buying land and becoming a planter was the only path to respectability. From 1993 to 2000 the milling industry became increasingly dominated by trader-owned mills, not only because so many more centrals were purchased by traders, but because the sixteen mills that closed down during that period were disproportionately not trader-owned.

No one in the industry today believes that consolidation can proceed from the bottom up; that is, from the planters. Even large planters simply cannot afford to buy centrals anymore, and few of them have the liquidity or credit-worthiness to enter trading on a significant scale. A few Philippine planters have attempted to consolidate in the past. For example, a consortium of planters created the First Farmers mill in Negros, and a group of very small planters under the guidance of church officials purchased the tiny Daconcogon mill in undeveloped southern Negros. However, most of these attempts were small and highly localized. First Farmers is a reasonably good mill, but many planters consider it a failure as a planters' cooperative. One disgruntled planter told me that elections to the First Farmers' board of directors "are about how many Lizareses, Ledesmas, Villanuevas, and Montinolas" are on the board rather than about who would be most competent. The one major exception—the most integrated operation in the nation—is Hacienda Luisita in

Tarlac. It is owned by the Cojuangco family and consists of a 6,000-hectare farm, an associated mill (Central Azucarera de Tarlac), a refinery that produces most of the supermarket sugar sold in Luzon, and a trading operation. Nonetheless, today only traders and end-users, most of whom are based in Manila, have the cash, collateral, and clout to consolidate the industry, and they are using these assets in ample measure.[13] Many of the anti-trader tirades of Romeo Guanzon and his followers can be understood as attempts to forestall the ceding of dominance from the planters to the traders and consumers, refusing to recognize that it is a *fait accompli.*

- The share-*quedan* system also fosters seemingly perpetual acrimony over the terms of each mill's contract with its planters. Although SRA and legal guidelines (specific to the different mill capacities) detail the acceptable shares, mills remain free to negotiate planter and miller shares on their own. More controversially, many continue to cut special deals with favored or larger-scale planters in order to attract cane supply or to do favors for those with close relationships. Smaller planters—the ones who need a greater share of the sugar—most often receive lower shares than the major producers. Millers defend this practice, arguing that milling cane for small-scale producers is simply not cost-effective. Disputes over the difference between, say, a 70-30 split and a 65-35 split remain among the most ubiquitous in the industry.

- Theoretically, the amount of sugar in any central's *bodega* is exactly equal to the amount represented by that central's outstanding *quedan*s possessed by planters, traders, and the central itself. Not infrequently, however, when a trader who possesses *quedan*s comes to redeem the physical sugar, none remains. Such "sugarless *quedan* scams" typically cause headlines in newspapers and are the subjects of lawsuits. Sometimes, such as in a celebrated 1992 case, an unscrupulous mill official will receive a pay-off from an even less scrupulous trader allowing that trader to smuggle sugar out of the mill's *bodega* under cover of darkness. In that particular case, many members of an influential planters' association were the victims. One notable planter-politician told me that this scam had "undermined the sacredness of the *quedan*." But since the *quedan*s issued are, in fact, *estimates* of sugar a given weight of cane will yield, some instances of sugarless *quedan*s result simply from mills overstating their extraction efficiencies to mollify their own investors, banks, and the SRA. One seldom-discussed result of such overstatements is that mills issue *quedan*s for amounts of sugar that they are not always able to produce, and *quedan*-holders who try to claim sugar toward the end of the milling season may be left holding the bag, so to speak. There is a legal stipulation that a planters' association can penalize a mill if its efficiency falls below the reported levels, but the data and formulae used to compute this are sufficiently complex as to make the burden of proof quite difficult. Moreover, mills often contribute money to planters' associations to insure continued smooth relations. Not surprisingly, planters blame the SRA for ineffectual oversight of mill operations, but the SRA responds that it is not legally empowered and does not possess the resources to monitor mills round the clock. One trader-owned mill in Negros actually bars SRA employees from entering the mill's property! Any mill intent on cheating its planters and traders by not covering its *quedan*s with sugar must be dealt with through the notoriously slow and corrupt legal system. Under a cane-purchase system, a mill that overestimated expected sugar yield would only hurt itself since it would own all the sugar in the *bodega*.

- One agency of the Philippine government that strongly supports perpetuation of the share-*quedan* system is the Bureau of Internal Revenue (BIR). BIR officials claim that sugar is among the easiest agricultural industries in the nation from which to collect taxes. Since the mills must keep precise records of *quedan*s issued, the BIR has a seemingly fool-proof way of checking planter and mill incomes, at least after agents make certain assumptions about the prices offered for those *quedan*s by traders. Planters do in fact complain that they are "forced" to pay taxes more honestly than just about any other businesspeople in the country. But a few with whom I am particularly friendly confided that tax honesty is often overstated for effect, and there are still many ways for a planter to avoid paying his full tax burden. I was impressed at the ingeniousness of some of these methods, but it would not be ethical to divulge them.

- One recent consequence of the property-rights-allocation system has been the construction of new sugar refineries. As discussed in the last chapter, industrial and even domestic consumers increasingly demand high-quality refined sugar, and large industrial consumers such as beverage companies have imposed stringent quality standards on refineries. Many milling companies have erected refineries—availing themselves of tax incentives—in order to fill this demand.

Another important reason to build a sugar refinery, in the midst of all the uncertainty surrounding the fate of the sugar industry, is that almost all the significant profit from the value added from raw to refined sugar goes to the milling company rather than the planter. Mills know that they cannot survive on their 25 to 40 percent share of the profits from raw sugar, and they know that the market increasingly demands refined sugar. So, traders will now buy *quedan*s for raw sugar from planters, pay the refining fees to refineries that profit from those fees (most of which are connected to mills and owned by milling companies), and sell the refined sugar at a large mark-up to consumers. Some milling companies themselves have started marketing their own refined sugar. Not surprisingly, I have heard planters grumble that they need to find a way to capture some of that value-added mark-up, that it is somehow unfair that mills and traders are cheating them out of the planters' rightful profits. Of course, most struggling Philippine mills cannot afford to erect refineries. Traders who have purchased mills in recent years typically have erected (or intend to erect) refineries, because in the future only those traders with refineries will be able to service the demand of industrial consumers. Only a few years ago virtually all the final product was raw sugar, but today more and more of the final product is white refined sugar. And increasingly, the refineries that produce that final product are owned by people who were until recently traders.

In 1992 I interviewed an eminent Indian sugar technologist serving as a consultant to a few Philippine centrals. Since the Indian industry is organized quite differently, he was able to provide a fascinating contrast. In India, planters cooperatively own most mills, mills pool their supply of *bagasse* to sell electricity, the cane-purchase system of property allocation is used, and cooperatives are constantly devising new spin-off products. During a period in which the price of sugar remained relatively stable, the price of a ton of sugarcane increased from $17 to $27, mostly owing to the diversification of the mills' products. The mills in India also cooperate to fund the world-class research and development facility at Coimbatore, which now produces cane varieties grown in the United States and Australia and is on the cutting edge of research into sugar-based products for commercial use. The Coimbatore facility is a stark contrast to the La Granja research station in Negros discussed in chapter 3. The technologist referred to the share-*quedan* system of property allocation as "idiotic," and the result of "cultural inertia," and he pointed out many additional institutional reasons that Philippine sugar is becoming less efficient and competitive. He believes that unless the Philippine industry can achieve large-scale institutional reorganization, particularly by changing to a cane-purchase system of property allocation, it will collapse within a decade or so.

For these reasons, several key figures in the industry have advocated replacing the share-*quedan* system of property allocation with a straight cane purchase in which the central owns all the sugar, molasses, and *bagasse* in its *bodega* once it has paid the planter for his sugarcane. Under such a system, any improvement in extraction efficiency would accrue entirely to the mill, thereby increasing the mill's incentive to make capital improvements. Centrals would compete for supplies of cane by offering different prices by tonnage,[14] and planters could continue to decide freely with whom to mill without regard for the anachronistic milling districts or railroad links. If a central that was relatively far away was offering a good price in a given week, a planter might choose to mill there despite the higher transport costs. The signals from the market to the planter would be summarized by one set of figures: the prices that different centrals were offering for cane. Even today, there is fierce competition among the centrals for cane. Under the cane purchase, those mills that can produce the most sugar from a given unit of cane would be able to offer the best prices, and would attract the most planters. Inefficient mills would either have to improve or close.

A 1986 World Bank study of Philippine sugar recommended that the industry needed to "Improve efficiency through measures including the introduction of a direct-cane-purchase system" (World Bank 1986: 31). In 1991 the SRA convened a committee to study alternative cane/sugar payment systems, consisting of millers, economists, and SRA technologists. It produced a persuasive report describing how the cane purchase works in other sugar-producing countries and calling for the implementation of such a system in the Philippines. The report, *Towards an Alternative Cane/Sugar Payment System (APS)*, was presented at the 1993 PHILSUTECH (Philippine Sugar Technologists) convention, which gave it overwhelming support. But the very few planters in attendance were clearly not persuaded. An SRA official who was instrumental in preparing the report was discouraged. "We have been working on this issue one way or another for nearly ten years now. The SRA barely funded our study, so it could not be as comprehensive as we would have liked. And this is the third time we have presented the idea in public. No one takes it seriously, because the planters see it as a millers' initiative. CONFED and NFSP didn't even reply to us. The planters just will not let this happen."

Most planters with whom I spoke were convinced that the centrals would use such a system to deprive the planters of their just due. Several expressed genuine fear of such competition, though one savvy planter stated that such sentiments were nothing more than the result of a century of protection and quota, on top of the "crab mentality" that is common in the Philippines. More than one planter told me that he would readily accept cane purchase if it were accompanied by a return to fixed milling districts and government-set prices. In other words, all planters would be able to mill with the closest central because all centrals would offer exactly the same price, without regard for differences in efficiency. Such a fear of competition remains characteristic of the sugar industry. Given recent history, it is remarkable that so many planters retain their faith in the government's ability to allocate resources fairly and efficiently. Perhaps they simply trust the government more than they trust each other.

The Cane-purchase Alternative and Planter Culture

For more than twenty years there have been advocates of switching to the cane-purchase system; for example, Arsenio Yulo, the first administrator of the SRA. Every study that has been commissioned —and there have been many—has concluded that the share-*quedan* system is a major reason for the continued decline of the industry. It is almost universally agreed upon that the cane purchase would result in a widespread shakeout of traders, particularly those without the ability to transport and market sugar, and in an overall reduction of transaction costs. The larger traders, however, would prosper since there would be fewer but higher-volume suppliers of raw sugar. This would enable traders and mills to garner the large supplies of sugar demanded by both foreign and domestic consumers without having to purchase thousands of *quedans* from hundreds of *quedan* holders. Many of the less efficient and unproductive centrals would close because they would rapidly lose the competition for cane supply. More efficient mills would have greater incentive to make capital improvements, to upgrade their machinery and technology, to enhance their boilers, to finance research and development, and to diversify their products. Mills would likely take over many of the transport and marketing functions currently accomplished by traders, and they would become more versatile and integrated businesses. Planters, in turn, would have greater incentive to make improvements in their cane yields and cane quality and to concentrate on agriculture rather than speculating on when to sell their *quedan*s. From a strictly economic perspective, there is little doubt that the cane purchase would be a great improvement for the industry's well-being relative to the extant share-*quedan* system. But as we are about to see, few people in the industry think about property allocation from a strictly economic perspective.

I asked people from many different sectors of the industry what they think of switching to cane purchase and whether they thought it could ever actually happen. Most workers were indifferent to my questions about how property rights to sugar are allocated; not surprising giving that they are not directly affected by who owns the sugar. A few suggested, though, that it would be a good thing if planters came back to the farms and learned a thing or two about growing sugar, which the cane purchase might encourage. Some workers told me that if they themselves owned the land and grew sugar, they would prefer to sell the cane for cash rather than to wait weeks or months to sell the *quedan*s to traders. Most asserted that they would do a better job of growing sugarcane than the farms on which they worked. Only two said that if they owned the land they would not grow sugarcane at all.

Needless to say, most traders were vehemently opposed to such a switch. Many bluntly said that it would be bad because it would put them out of business. Larger traders—the ones who would likely survive the switch—expressed great skepticism about the ability of the notoriously cumbersome bureaucracies that own and operate the centrals to market sugar and to serve consumers, especially the large food processors whose demands for sugar and molasses must be met on precise schedules. Traders argue that the high transaction costs that come with the constant movement of *quedan*s are more than offset by the highly competitive nature of trading, which tends to keep prices as low as they can be. Under a cane purchase, I was told by several traders, mills would own all the sugar and would certainly collude with one another to insure that prices stayed high —no doubt higher than under the extant *quedan* system. A few major traders, however—those who own and operate mills—expressed unqualified enthusiasm for the cane purchase. Under such a system, they would own all the sugar in their *bodega*s, and that would greatly enhance their abilities to serve their large industrial customers. These trader-millers doubted whether a cane purchase could ever be accomplished because of strong planter opposition. Interestingly, while the planters contend that power increasingly rests with the big traders who, with the purchase of centrals, have come to control the industry, those same traders continue to perceive the industry as being dominated by the planters.

Millers are generally the most receptive to cane purchase, but they are also skeptical about whether it can ever be instituted. Some expressed fear that under such a system planters would figure out ways of cheating by offering burnt, old canes with high trash content. Others said that offering cash incentives for planters to provide trash-free cane could obviate that problem. Some worried about the expense of buying core sampling machines to test for cane quality. Others admitted that core sampling was "the wave of the future," and they would probably have to buy the machines anyway. Some admitted frankly that the centrals they manage could never survive the switch because they were already "beyond hope," and it would not be possible or prudent to make the enormous capital expenditure required to render them competitive again. Several of these millers worried that switching to a cane purchase would require greater cash liquidity than their centrals currently possess. Managers of better mills, not surprisingly, suggested that the fact that "only the fittest (mills) would survive" under a cane purchase was a good thing for the industry. Most millers expressed enthusiasm, some great enthusiasm, for the idea of switching to a cane purchase. One manager of a large Negros central even told me that under a cane purchase his mill would have such an ample supply of sugar that it would be able to export for the first time. Under the current system, that central cannot even satisfy the needs of its domestic customers. A manager of one Luzon central told me, "The share system is a fossil. It absolutely prevents productive investment in mills. The mills *need* the cane purchase. The industry needs it. But the farmers are tradition-bound and insecure. They fear it would be competitive, would take pricing out of their hands, and they could not control it. The government needs to step in and impose the cane purchase." The managers of larger and more efficient mills all said that they would likely invest more to upgrade their mills under a cane purchase, and would especially upgrade their boilers in order to cogenerate electricity. A few said that they would consider building refineries or increasing the capacity of extant refineries if they had a more reliable supply of raw sugar. Despite this enthusiasm, most millers stated very clearly that while the cane purchase would definitely be in the interest of mills and consumers, the planters would simply never agree to it, and no one believed that the switch would happen in the foreseeable future. It surprised me how frequently millers used the English word "culture" (specifically, "planter culture") to explain why the planters would never accept a cane purchase.

Planters, for their part, understand intellectually why a cane purchase would be better for the industry in some ways. Several took pleasure at the thought that the Chinese traders would be most negatively affected by the change. But very few with whom I spoke could overcome their cultural values, perceptions, and self-images enough to actually advocate such a switch. Most, in fact, strongly opposed it, and a few became uncharacteristically agitated even discussing it. There were many and diverse reasons cited for this opposition and discomfort. One of the most prominent is the distrust of the millers. Indeed, the single most common response I received to the initial question was: "They [the millers] will cheat us." The idea that mills would weigh the cane, own and operate the core sampling machines that test for quality, and determine the prices they pay for cane struck planters as giving the mills far too much power. There is a strong perception that when planters own most of the sugar in the mills' *bodegas* the planters somehow wield far more clout over the mills. ("When you own sugar, the mill respects you.") When asked whether enhanced competition among mills for cane supply might serve to keep them honest and influence them to offer higher prices, the planters frequently brought up the prospect of collusion and price-fixing among mills. Planters expressed little trust in either the SRA or the Philippine government to oversee weighing and quality determination, and some even suspected that the planters' association officials who would supervise these processes could easily be bribed or otherwise co-opted. When I asked whether planters or planters' associations would be willing to contribute money to upgrade mill efficiency (since under the current system they would benefit even more than the mills), a frequent response was nervous laughter. Several planters dismissed the suggestion as preposterous since they do not own the mills; no one thought it reasonable.

Some of the more conspiratorially minded planters suggested

that the traders "would never allow" the cane purchase to be enacted. They tended to view traders as a well-organized cabal of Chinese businessmen, each knowing and related to all the others, and all acting to insure themselves the lion's share of the sugar industry's profits. The traders, in turn, always stress how competitive, even cutthroat, their business is, and that Chinese ethnicity provides no particular advantage or even common bond.

Another frequently heard argument against the cane purchase concerns the way banks handle crop loans to planters. *Quedan*s are most often used as collateral for crop loans; the loans are given in advance of the year's crop, and the *quedan*s can be legally forfeited if a planter fails to repay the loan. Without *quedan*s representing ownership of sugar, planters fear they would have to risk their houses as collateral. But since most larger planters have legally incorporated their enterprises so as to avoid personal liability, this is more rhetorical device than real possibility.

Many planters suggest that bankers would never give crop loans were it not for the share-*quedan* system, but every banker I spoke to suggested otherwise. Though some were skeptical about the entire institution of crop loans, most said that it would be possible to make loans on advance of crops even within a cane-purchase system as long as mills were willing to enforce liens. Likewise, a high official at the BIR told me that while the *quedan* facilitates collection of taxes from sugar producers, switching to a cane purchase would not likely make things much more difficult so long as the mills were legally bound to record and declare all their purchases honestly. In fact, one BIR official claimed that with fewer owners of sugar under the cane purchase, it might become easier to tax the sugar industry. One banker thought doing away with the *quedan*s would be a positive step in that it would eliminate the possibility of "pole vaulting"— the illegal titling of *quedan*s in the names of relatives, friends, and servants to avoid having them repossessed for non-repayment.

In the end, however, the most heartfelt and deeply rooted response given by planters has to do with what it actually means to be a "planter." Unlike in the past, planters in the contemporary Philippines almost never use the word *hacendero* to refer to themselves or those of their class. That word—frequently pejorative—is more typically used by those who want to portray them as indolent, self-indulgent sugar barons, and that implication is now widespread. But the word "planter" has certainly taken on connotations beyond that of someone who grows sugar or who owns land upon which sugar is grown. The distinction is well-illustrated in the following quote regarding the possibility of switching to the cane purchase: "If I do not own sugar, if I do not sell *quedan*s to traders, if I am not a businessman, then what am I? Just a farmer?" It is the ownership of sugar and the haggling and bargaining over the *quedan*s representing real sugar that defines for most planters exactly what it is they do for a living. Although some consider themselves first and foremost to be agriculturists, and sharply rebuke others for failing to keep up with modern methods and technology of sugar agriculture, they are a small minority. Farming is considered by most to be appropriate work for hired hands, much as is cooking or doing laundry. Making phone calls, receiving price quotes, applying for bank loans, deciding when to sell one's *quedan*s and when to hang on, speculating about the timing of conversions, and staying abreast of the politics of sugar are the real roles and responsibilities of a modern "planter." Without the *quedan* and the right of ownership of sugar, a planter is just someone who produces and sells sugarcane—a farmer. And such a role has decidedly low status in the hierarchical sensibilities of the planter class. The ownership of sugar gives the planter his sense of self-respect and control over his own destiny. In the words of one planter, "The *quedan* system is more *democratic* than the cane purchase. With the *quedan*, I am in control. I can hold onto sugar as long as I like. With the cane purchase, I am at their [the mills'] mercy."

Planters often use an idiom of masculinity when discussing the ownership of sugar. Perhaps the bluntest assertion of this was a response to a miller who tried to institute a cane purchase unilaterally (discussed below). One planter who usually brought his cane to that mill said: "He [the mill owner] is trying to cut our balls off." There are frequent suggestions that farming is a rather effeminate as well as servile activity as compared to wheeling and dealing over *quedan*s. The cane purchase, by depriving the planter of the ownership of physical sugar, would deprive him of much of what makes him a man, and much of what makes his life worth living. Whether this would foster greater efficiency in the industry is beside the point.[15]

The share system was codified by law in 1953 (Republic Act No. 809, that mandated share ratios based on mill capacity in the absence of specific milling contracts), and therefore abrogating it would actually require legislative action. Many planters told me that any attempt at repealing the Act, or even a hint at such an attempt, would elicit a fierce response from the two planters' federations and from every planters' association in the country. The congressmen from sugar-producing areas would fight such a repeal with every weapon at their disposal.[16] Some planters told me that the only condition under which they would accept a cane purchase would be if the government stepped in strongly, enforced fixed milling districts again, and set cane prices across the board; in other words, they would not accept a cane purchase in a competitive environment in which information was scarce and transaction costs high. Their fear stems from an idea that the current system is the most just and the most beneficial for planters; any change would necessarily result in empowering other sectors, and the planters would inevitably be cheated out of their rightful profits. Planters further hate the thought that under a new system that they do not well understand other planters would be able to play the system successfully and do better than they themselves. Most people agree that a switch to cane purchase could only be accomplished one milling contract at a time, but planters say that any mill that tried to impose a cane purchase would soon find itself without sugarcane to mill since planters would send their canes to mills that continued to issue *quedan*s. That is precisely what happened during the great cane-purchase experiment of 1993.

The Cane Purchase Experiment

Alejandro "Andoy" Go is a prosperous sugar trader, and owner of the Lucky Two trading company based in Manila. When I interviewed him in 1993 and 1994 he was sixty-three-years old. Mr. Go is Chinese in the literal sense of having been born in China and speaking Hokkien as his first and most proficient language. He also speaks Tagalog and some Ilonggo, but very little English. In 1990 Mr. Go acquired from the Ledesma family and the Jardine-Davies Company (which also owns the Hawaiian-Philippine Central in Negros) one-hundred percent of the mill in San Carlos, Negros Occidental—the nation's oldest continuously-operating sugar central (*Manila Bulletin* 29 June 1992). According to one of Mr. Go's sons, Mr. Go had always dreamed of being a sugar producer in addition to a trader. He already owned minority shares in two other mills: 22.5 percent of the BUSCO central in Mindanao (which he owned with other Big Five traders), and 9 percent of the HIDECO mill on the island of Leyte. He had little to do with those centrals' operations, however, and after buying the San Carlos mill he handed over most of the trading arm of the business to his daughter Mary so that he could concentrate his efforts on running his newly purchased mill. In addition to his desire to become a miller, another motivation for buying the San Carlos central was that mill's easy access to the growing and industrializing city of Cebu (often called "Ce-boom"). San Carlos is on the eastern, Cebuano-speaking side of Negros, only a short distance across the Tañon Strait from Cebu.

But the main motivation for the purchase was Mr. Go's inability to provide his larger customers with sufficient quantities of *refined* sugar in a market that increasingly demands both reliable supply and high quality. Although Mr. Go bought the San Carlos mill itself for a low price, he built what he and his sons described as a world-class refinery, at considerable expense. In fact, Mr. Go frequently refers to the mill as existing only to provide a steady supply of raw sugar for the refinery. Proudly boasting that their new Thai-designed refinery had already passed the stringent Coca-Cola quality control tests ("it's even better than Victorias'"), the Gos felt that their advantages over other refiners—trading contacts, barges, warehousing facilities, and business acumen—would insure that their sales of high-quality sugar to major industrial consumers would grow rapidly. Mr. Go was so eager to get his new refinery operating that he neglected to register for the time-consuming Board of Investment tax-incentive program for which he qualified. He also had a new, more efficient boiler and power system built so that the available *bagasse* could fuel both the mill and the refinery, and he built a conveyer from the mill's wharf to the mill to facilitate efficient transport of cane from out-of-district planters.

Also to attract out-of-district planters, Mr. Go erected eight transloading stations, purchased sixty trucks, and paid for the repair of the virtually impassable road from the western coast of Negros through the mountains to San Carlos. Without that road, large trucks must approach San Carlos from the north coastal route, quadrupling the mileage. In addition, Mr. Go expanded the capacity of the mill from 4,000 to 6000 tons of cane per day, and he planned to add three full months to the milling season by beginning in October instead of January. However, since the milling season in the San Carlos district is the shortest in Negros (January to June, because the rainy season arrives later on the eastern side of the island), adding those three months was contingent upon being able to garner an adequate supply of cane from out of the district.

One immediate problem the Gos faced was the disparity between the mill's production capacity (1.8 million 50-kilogram bags per year, even after the expansion) and the refinery's capacity (nearly 3 million bags per year). Even more problematic was that the mill had been operating significantly under capacity, typically producing less than a million bags of raw sugar each year. So the immediate task was to attract as many planters to the San Carlos mill as possible so as to keep the refinery working near its capacity. But since San Carlos is a relatively isolated place in which the narrow coastal plain turns abruptly into high mountains, the immediate milling district would not provide an adequate supply of cane to service the refinery, especially considering the short milling season in the San Carlos district. (The district is relatively small, but it has larger-than-average size land holdings.) Moreover, since planters in the district could sell their *quedan*s to any trader they wished, much of the raw sugar in the San Carlos *bodega* might not end up in the Go refinery. And, of course, according to the San Carlos milling contract, the mill owned only 32 percent of the product, while the planters owned 68 percent.

One solution Mr. Go contemplated was to purchase raw sugar from other centrals. But this would not solve the *bagasse* shortage—the refinery was being fueled by expensive bunker oil most of the time—and it would defeat the purpose of buying the mill in the first place. So Mr. Go devised a bold course of action that would—if successful—allow him to increase the mill's volume *and* own the lion's share of the raw sugar in the mill's *bodega*. The plan was to institute a cane-purchase system that would attract out-of-district planters and insure that in-district raw sugar would end up in the San Carlos refinery. Mr. Go's idea was to encourage truck haulers to purchase cane from small farmers and sell the cane at a profit to San Carlos after traveling on the newly repaired mountain road. He made it known to planters in the more southerly districts of Negros Oriental that he was offering good prices and cash up-front, and he had the canes transloaded onto barges for shipment up to San Carlos. He also induced one of Negros' largest planters, Eduardo "Danding" Cojuangco—himself an ardent advocate of sugar industry "rationalization"—to truck a large amount of his sugarcane to San Carlos. Planters in the circumscribed San Carlos milling district were given the option of either taking their share (i.e., being issued *quedan*s for 68 percent of the sugar and molasses, along with a P2.50 per ton of cane "*bagasse* rebate") or selling their cane outright. Mr. Go strongly encouraged the latter option, although he realized that only smaller planters and those having cash flow problems would generally prefer the cane purchase.

It was a radical plan, and many in the sugar industry turned their attention to San Carlos to see whether it would work. Most planters I spoke to were rooting against it, and strongly. Many millers expressed resentment that Mr. Go was violating the gentlemen's agreement not to be overly aggressive in pursuit of sugarcane from other districts. For although the milling districts were no longer official entities, and planters were now free to send their canes to any central, most millers and planters still value the concept of the natural milling district for maintaining greater order and less competition than would prevail in a truly free market.

By mid-1993 the plan was already being declared a massive failure, although the Go family did not yet acknowledge this. While canes were coming in from outside of the district, the major planters' association of the San Carlos Central had declared a boycott, and a significant proportion of the district's planters were sending their canes to the URSUMCO, Danao, and Victorias mills. Since San Carlos is remote, the out-of-district supply did not come close to compensating for the in-district boycott, and the mill was running at extremely low volume. A Go son admitted to me that the volume of raw sugar being produced was so low that it was having a deleterious effect on the efficiency of the refinery and the quality of the refined sugar. Unless the mill and the refinery could act in tandem and at high volume to save on fuel, the entire plan would likely fail.

Many people in the industry suggested that the Gos were being too generous and too lenient with out-of-district planters by offering excessively high prices for the cane. The Gos justified the high cane prices both by the need to increase the mill's volume and by the fact that they, unlike virtually every other mill, refused to offer any special "incentives" to large and influential planters. They assumed that the requisite supply of cane would be elicited by price alone. Although shipments of cane could officially be rejected for having a high trash content or for containing burnt canes, and the Gos had plans for instituting a quality-sampling procedure, no shipment had yet been turned down by the mill. The cane was being bought strictly by weight, regardless of quality. Several people intimated that planters were selling their worst canes to San Carlos—canes that no other mill would have accepted. In mid-1993, the Gos were pressed for cash and had to reduce the price of cane from P500 to P480 and then to P460 per ton, but they instituted a P20 per ton bonus for low trash content. Although they insisted that every planter received the same price and privileges, many believed that Danding Cojuangco was given a "special deal" and got a higher price.

In addition to offering high prices, the Gos were using their new fleet of trucks and new transloading stations to haul cane at no cost to the planters. In some mills planters themselves must pay the hauling and trucking fees—as high as P150 per ton depending on distance and road conditions—to transport their cane to the mill. Other mills offer hauling allowances at least to some planters. BISCOM, for example, offers its planters P60 per ton, Hawaiian-Philippines offers P80, and Ma-ao offers P90 to induce planters to stick with that inefficient mill. But completely free hauling was virtually unheard of, and other millers expressed anger at the precedent that the Gos were setting.

According to the Gos, the planters in the district had become used to being coddled by the previous owners of the central. The planters had virtually dictated the terms and conditions of the share contract, the mill was expected to lend heavy farm equipment to its planters, storage fees were regularly waived, large planters' canes were given special priority in the timing of milling, and planters would frequently "request" that the central hire any number of the planters' relatives. Further, the mill had financed (some say "financed," some say "gave incentives to," others say "bribed") the planters' association to assure peaceful and cooperative relations. The San Carlos Planters' Association was dominated by the district's largest single planter, Jose Villanueva,[17] whose 1,600 hectares abut the mill's property. Mr. Villanueva decided that he would not sign any milling contract with Andoy Go, that he would boycott the San Carlos mill, and that he would revoke the right-of-way of the central's rail line that passed through his property and by which most of the in-district cane reached the mill. To add insult to injury, the Mayor of the town of Canlaon, in the mountains along the path of the access road, refused to allow the road repair crews to work within his town's borders, thus scuttling the effort to alleviate the mill's isolation.

The Gos argued that these disputes occurred only because they insisted upon running the central as a "rational" business—*their* business—and that they simply refused to be pushed around by planters and politicians who demanded a piece of the action and had gotten used to controlling the action. Given that they (the Gos) were offering high prices to buy cane, why expect them also to act against their own interests and to compromise their autonomy by providing all these other "incentives"? Mr. Go had purchased the central and built the refinery with his money, but the planters still acted as if the mill belonged to *them*. Mr. Go admitted freely that his ultimate goal was to own *all* the sugar in his *bodega,* and to make his mill attractive enough to planters that they would be eager to send their cane to San Carlos.

Mr. Go's sons acknowledged that their father relishes the idea of doing things in novel ways, and that he makes fast and firm decisions, but they insisted that being the center of the increasingly public controversy was bad for business. They praised their father's hard-working, fast, decisive style as the kind of "Chinese" way of doing business that makes "Filipinos" envious. They admitted that they were hoping that the inefficient and struggling Danao Central, the closest mill to San Carlos in the north, would close down soon and that the planters who mill with Danao would gravitate to San Carlos. They realized that making such an admission was a clear violation of the gentlemen's agreement among millers, and they seemed to take some pleasure in that realization. They stated that their relationship with Jerome Paras, a congressman from Negros Oriental and the new president of the San Carlos Planters' Association, was much better than it was with Mr. Villanueva, and they saw signs that planters in the district would soon be returning to the fold. Since planters in the district were losing money because of the transportation expenses they incurred by sending their canes out of the district, there was considerable financial pressure to mill at San Carlos. Even Mr. Villanueva appeared to be softening. They acknowledged that San Carlos was perceived as a place to dump low-quality cane, but vowed to become stricter in enforcing quality standards and to establish a reputation as a mill that emphasized quality from top to bottom. When asked whether their new system was in violation of Republic Act No. 809 (as several planters charged), they responded that the Act was vague, unenforceable, and difficult to understand, and that they hadn't actually read it. They understood that planters would probably continue to insist that their good cane be *quedan*ed and try to sell only their poor cane, and that such an outcome would undermine the entire plan.

They talked of expanding the mill's capacity from 6,500 to 8,000 tons of cane per day in order to make the refinery more efficient, but they admitted that they were only actually milling around 2,500 tons per day. They said that Jardine-Davies had "trashed the mill," "run it into the ground," and "used it as a cash cow," but that they, the Gos, had brought it back to quality. They stated that their father was interested in integrating his business even further by buying sugar land and entering the agricultural sector, but that he would not do so as long as CARP was in effect. The Gos, especially the sons, were extremely adept at portraying their new system as being a "free market," and "rational" solution that represented the wave of the future in the Philippines and the salvation of the sugar industry if only the reactionary forces would pay attention. They frequently depicted their father as a visionary entrepreneur and a Horatio Alger-like capitalist hero. As Alex Go said: "My dad is a really great guy. You know, he didn't go to school. There are some things that Harvard can't teach you. He has no vices and is a really innovative businessman."

Not surprisingly, the perspective of those within the Planters' Association was different. Several people in the Association spoke candidly with me about their relations with Mr. Go and the central. No one agreed with the sons' suggestion that there were any appreciable signs that the rift was healing and the boycott was easing. They complained that "the Chinese guys refuse to consult with us about all the changes they're making." "They insist on acting as if it were their mill only." "Millers are supposed to seek advice and ask permission before making *any* changes, especially radical ones." Although most of the planters faulted Mr. Go for not treating everyone the same (in particular for striking a special deal with Danding Cojuangco, not a San Carlos district planter and not a member of their Association), others complained that Mr. Go failed to treat large, influential planters within the district—the ones who dominate the Association—with "the deference they deserve" and failed to "provide special favors" to them. Although planters admitted that the mill does legally belong to Mr. Go, they also felt that Mr. Go's persistent claim that it is *his* mill clearly violated their sensibilities about planter-miller relations. They felt that Mr. Go's openly stated desire to own all the sugar in the mill's *bodega* was emblematic of his arrogance. The Planters' Association members were used to owning 68 percent of the sugar in the mill's *bodega,* and this, they felt, gave them the right to exercise considerable influence over the mill's operations. Once again, I was told that he was trying "to turn us into farmers only." The planters complained that Mr. Go himself was inaccessible, and that his sons (whom he relies upon to manage day-by-day operations) "are mere boys who are in way over their heads."

Planters complained bitterly that out-of-district planters were allowed to mill at San Carlos without first joining and paying dues to the San Carlos Planters' Association, which is very much contrary to the traditional practice at other centrals. Many planters said that the mill had been run far more efficiently by Jardine-Davies, and that under the Gos there are constant breakdowns, delays, and long queues that caused cane deterioration and low productivity. Some members of the association admitted that a part of that problem stemmed from Mr. Villanueva's denying the railroad right of way, and a few even praised the Gos for the speed with which they instituted a truck hauling and hydraulic conveyor system to substitute for railroad hauling. One planter said, "Like typical Chinese, they are strong on ideas, but weak on management." Whereas Jardine-Davies provided free storage of sugar, Mr. Go imposed a storage fee of P0.65 per bag, which pressured the planters to sell their *quedan*s quickly—presumably to Mr. Go. Even more draconian was the doubling of the stevedoring charge to P3 per bag, again pressuring the planters to sell their *quedan*s to Mr. Go. So, not only did Mr. Go *say* that he wanted to own all the sugar in the *bodega*, he was actually penalizing those planters who sold their *quedan*s to other traders. Planters hate feeling pressured and disempowered; they much prefer feeling coddled.

Mr. Go's reputation in the wider sugar industry was mixed, and he tended to evoke strong opinions. Most planters came to think of him as the devil incarnate and hoped that his experiment would fail. One particularly colorful planter told me, "Andoy Go is a bastard. But Jose Villanueva is a bastard too. They should go screw each other. But I will never trust those Chinese guys." An official in one of the planters' federations told me that Mr. Go's cane purchase was in direct violation of Republic Act 809, and that he should be prosecuted. An official in the other federation told me that Mr. Go had caused serious problems with the San Carlos Planters' Association by disavowing promises to planters made by his sons. Many millers admired what Mr. Go was trying to accomplish but did not approve of his "unorthodox" style. An official at another mill said that the San Carlos refinery was in fact producing high-quality sugar, but this official was exceedingly angry at Mr. Go for ratcheting up the competition among mills, for being so aggressive in the pursuit of cane from other mills' districts, and for poisoning the relationship between millers and planters. He accused Mr. Go of not fitting in with the "culture of milling." One official in the largest Millers' Association told me: "Andoy Go still thinks and acts like a trader. Some other Chinese mill owners really are welcome additions to the family of millers. I hope Andoy's sons will become *real* millers."

A sugar purchaser for a major multinational beverage company scoffed that the San Carlos refinery was producing unacceptably low quality sugar and that Mr. Go was an illiterate cheater who made his money selling adulterated, repacked sugar in Manila's Divisoria district. A rival miller told me that Mr. Go had "really benefited from the Marcos era," was "a known smuggler," and could not be trusted. A miller-trader told me that most of Mr. Go's trucks were being used to haul sugarcane to *other* mills, and that Mr. Go was now making most of his money in the trucking business. One official at the SRA spoke admiringly of Mr. Go, but said definitively that "the numbers just don't add up" for his experiment to succeed. A different SRA official admitted that he was hoping that Mr. Go would succeed and that other mills would emulate his system. A major sugar trader told me that he was impressed at Mr. Go's "guts," but he wished that he would be less independent and stubborn because he was tarnishing the reputation of all mill-owning traders. The Governor of Negros Occidental, Rafael "Lito" Coscolluela, opined that Mr. Go's operation seemed "highly professional," and that he personally hoped the cane-purchase experiment would succeed, but that he felt that planters were too suspicious of millers to accept the cane purchase. The Governor—who is from a prominent planting family—repeated the oft-heard assertion that the cane purchase could give millers more opportunity to cheat. For better or for ill, Andoy Go had stirred things up considerably, and had become the focus of attention within the industry.

About three months after I conducted my last interviews with Mr. Go, his sons, and several members of the San Carlos Planters' Association I received a phone call from Alex Go, the manager of the San Carlos Central. He invited me to come back to San Carlos to spend some time with him and his brothers as well as other mill employees. Since I was still living in Negros at the time, and I had become very interested in the cane-purchase experiment, I immediately agreed to make the six-hour bus ride to the other side of the island. My curiosity had also been piqued because it was not often that informants requested to speak with *me*.

I had in the interim learned that the rift between the Planters' Association and the Gos had not abated and that the Gos were financially strapped. The Planters' Association was filing a legal case against the mill for breach of the milling contract. Since the mill had a lower recovery rate than that guaranteed by the contract, the planters argued that the mill was legally bound to reimburse them the difference between their actual *quedan*s and the amount of sugar that should have been milled from the planters' cane. Several people repeated rumors that Mr. Go was looking to sell his 22.5 percent share in the BUSCO mill (something the Go sons denied). An official at the Hawaiian-Philippines mill admitted to me that the Jardine-Davies Company was interested in buying the San Carlos central back from Mr. Go if (when) Mr. Go failed. Given all this, it seemed an odd time for the managers of the hard-pressed San Carlos mill to volunteer to provide additional information to a foreign anthropologist.

After an excellent lunch in which the brothers insisted (in the presence of mill foremen and supervisors) that all was going according to plan, I was bade back into the mill's executive office for more conversation with Alex Go and another high-level San Carlos manager. Here I was told the reason I had been invited. The mill was doing terribly. They were not getting anywhere near the volume of cane they needed to recover their large investment, and the all-important refinery was operating badly and far below capacity. They did not know what to do. Since so many people in the sugar industry were against them, and they were reluctant to admit that they were failing to people inside the industry, they were seeking *my* assistance. Did I have any advice to give them that would help them turn the operation around? I was, after all, a sugar expert, and since I was a foreigner and not a member of the industry, asking advice from me spared them embarrassment. How were other mills managing to prosper in such a competitive environment? Where had they (the Gos) gone wrong, and how could they fix it?

I must admit I was flattered. Of course, the Gos knew that I had spoken to many people in the industry and that I had followed their cane-purchase experiment avidly. A large part of their request to me was to provide them with an independent assessment of their repulation, and information about what other people in the industry were saying about them. The idea that I was some sort of a sugar expert who could help turn around a struggling mill certainly made me feel as if I had become "a player." For a brief moment I considered trying to help them out. I did feel sympathy for them, both for the business predicament they were in and for the sense of shame they felt that had inspired them to ask me for help. Fortunately, I was able to resist the temptation that such a moment provides. I am *not* a sugar expert; I am an anthropologist trying to understand how a particular industry works and how the people in it think. My advice was worth very little, and my offering advice would almost certainly compromise my reputation for neutrality that had afforded me wide access to every sector of the industry. Even had I had an opinion about how the Gos should proceed—which, frankly, I did not—I felt that it was unethical for me to become so deeply involved in the affairs of the industry I was trying to understand. So, for both ethical and practical reasons I demurred and suggested to the Gos that they really should hire an independent Filipino consultant with a strong background in sugar. This was the first time I was asked to use what I had learned in the course of my research to become involved in the affairs of the industry. But as you will see in the next chapter, it would not be the last.

An article in an on-line Philippine news service in early 1999 made it quite clear that the Go cane-purchase experiment had been a failure over the long term as well as the short. Five years after the initial episode, relations with the Planters' Association had not improved. The association was, in fact, suing the San Carlos central for being unable to cover the planters' *quedan*s with physical sugar (i.e., another "sugarless *quedan* scam"). At first the association had asked the SRA to file suit on the association's behalf, but the SRA had no legal standing to do so. Although SRA Administrator Nicolas Alonso was negotiating with the central's management—still the Go family—about whether the central would be allowed to mill in the upcoming crop year, it was clear that the majority of the Planters' Association members had already signed contracts to mill with other centrals. "So that, even if the mill were to rescue operations, it is questionable whether there could be sufficient cane supply to make such a move viable financially" (*Balita-L listserve,* 27 Jan. 1999). The mill, purchased to insure a steady supply of sugar for the Gos' trading customers, had become an albatross around their necks.

Culture and the "Supply and Demand" of Institutions

Classical economists, business historians, and new institutional economists frequently write about how the "supply of institutions" tends to follow and fulfill the demand for them. In this economistic view, the institutional organization of industries, firms, and enterprises tends toward ever-more-efficient forms while maladaptive structures and ways of operating are weeded out by evolutionary competition. The alternative view—with roots in Marx and especially Weber—sees the institutional organization of industries, firms, and enterprises as resulting more from the interplay of differential power, culture, and the path dependency of history. Often those institutions represent the unintended consequences of social and cultural developments that were initially unrelated to business or economic organization. In this non-linear, contextual view, the path toward greater efficiency—if it exists at all—is episodic, unpredictable, and frequently unsuccessful.

The share-*quedan* system—begun in the 1920s as a way to encourage sugar planters to enter the modern colonial economy—is one property-rights institution that has persisted despite the widespread knowledge that it is inefficient and may *inter alia* be propelling the industry to its demise. Originally an informal innovation, today it has been legally and contractually rigidified. More important, it represents in concrete form a principle or value held dear by sugar planters: the ownership of physical sugar, and the autonomy that comes with the ability to sell that sugar to whomever one pleases. That this method of apportioning property rights is inefficient for the industry as a whole and works against the interests of other powerful sectors within the industry has spawned experimentation with at least one alternative—institutional stasis has led to attempted institutional innovation. But the "supply" of that innovation in no way guarantees, or even predisposes that the alternative will drive out the inefficient institution. Indeed, the cane-purchase experiment has failed. Despite its obvious advantages, the cane purchase appears no closer to implementation today than in did in the early 1990s.

Perhaps in stressing immediate historical contingency, I am overlooking the *longue durée*. Perhaps I am being misled by the short timespan of anthropological research. Perhaps my analysis is too synchronic to notice the inexorable progress toward greater efficiency. Perhaps as more traders purchase and upgrade mills and more inefficient mills close down, the power in the industry will shift to the large trader-millers and the cane purchase will be adopted because it serves their interests most apparently. Less likely, perhaps a future Philippine government will decide actually to implement CARP or some new agrarian reform program. If this results in an agricultural sector in which all sugar planters have small land holdings, then perhaps the cane purchase will have to be adopted. Maybe over a longer period the sugar industry will either adopt the cane purchase or disappear. And if it disappears, it could be used as more (albeit negative) evidence for the proposition that enterprises must either adopt more efficient forms of organization or be driven to "extinction." But the sugar industry has survived with the share-*quedan* system for eighty years, since the advent of centrifugal milling. It has done so largely due to protectionism, quotas, and the wielding of political influence. One might argue that in a truly "free market" efficient institutions always drive out inefficient ones over the long term, but that is a mere theoretical abstraction divorced from the way economic life is actually lived, even—some would say especially—under that economic system we vaguely call "capitalism." No one could accuse the sugar industry of being non-capitalist, yet all over the world the production of and commerce in sugar bears no relation whatsoever to any abstract "free market." I suspect this is the case with most commodities that one would choose to study, and that the persistence of inefficient institutional forms is the rule rather than the exception.

One could, I suppose, interpret Mr. Go's cane-purchase experiment as a positive first step in the fits-or-starts movement toward a more efficient institutional form. But the truth is that the experiment *was* a failure. It demonstrated that a new form of property rights allocation—even one that could save the industry from catastrophe—cannot survive if enough people with power and influence perceive it to be antithetical to their interests, broadly—and culturally—construed. Institutional forms do not arise *sui generis,* and they do not thrive simply because they are "better" on average for everyone concerned in the narrowly economic sense. They must emerge from previous forms and within cultural contexts. The uni-directional view of the flow of power and interest—some group or class imposing its will on others—may be relevant to analyses of the interaction between elites and subalterns, but it is less relevant to the interaction among competing elites within industries, firms, or other social formations. The idea that industries or other social formations function as unified corporate bodies driven by consensus is also belied by the persistence of the share-*quedan* system and the many conflicts that that system generates. No external, a priori conception of "interests" or "power" is capable of understanding the rise, fall, or persistence of institutional forms. For such an understanding we must situate those forms within history and must contextualize them within the moral, emotional, and subjective understandings of those to whom the institutions belong.

The *balance* of elite power and the conflicts among elites in the Philippine sugar industry are not clearly defined by sector. Most traders, for example, are vehemently opposed to switching to a cane-purchase system because it would eliminate the function they currently fill. Large-scale traders who have purchased mills, however, like Mr. Go, for example, are the most forceful advocates for the switch. They purchase mills in order to have a captive supply of sugar, and they would relish the opportunity to own all the sugar that they mill.

Millers tend to favor switching to a cane purchase, but many worry that it would harm their relationships with planters; and those millers who run old, inefficient mills oppose the switch because they realize it would put their mills out of business.

Planters frequently express strong opposition to the cane purchase because it would rob them of the autonomy that comes with owning sugar, and turn them into "mere farmers." But there are numerically more small farmers than there are large ones, and although small farmers have less influence, they tend to favor the ready cash provided by the cane purchase. For small farmers, the *quedan* is more of an encumbrance than a deep-seated cultural value. Even among large planters, there are some for whom the ownership of sugar is not a cherished value. Danding Cojuangco, for example, is a diversified businessman and one of the biggest planters in the country, and yet he advocates sugar industry "rationalization" and sent much of his cane to San Carlos; he would just as soon the *quedan* went the way of the dinosaur.

Bankers admit that the *quedan* is a convenient form of collateral for crop loans. But, despite what many planters and a few SRA officials think, all the bankers with whom I spoke said that they would be willing to work out an alternative if the cane purchase were implemented.

Large industrial consumers of sugar are generally highly enthusiastic about the cane purchase because it would entail dealing with fewer, better-equipped suppliers. A few purchasing managers in these companies, however, expressed concern that those suppliers could gain too much political clout and might collude to bar imports and raise the price of sugar.

So the competition among elites on this subject is fluid, and positions are not easily predictable based on exogenous understandings of "objective" economic gain. And it is the balance of culturally defined interests among complex alliances of elites, as well as the moral sanctity of a long-cherished institutional form, that will keep the share-*quedan* system alive into the foreseeable future, efficiency notwithstanding.

Interestingly, two groups reputed to be increasingly the most powerful forces in the industry—mill-owning large traders and major industrial consumers of sugar—both tend to favor switching to the cane purchase. If one took the simplistic view that those with the greatest economic and political power should be able to impose institutional forms that serve their interests, one would conclude that it is only a matter of time before the cane purchase wins the day. But, once again, the balance among the competing groups is more critical than a hopelessly ambiguous ranking on some imaginary power scale. Although the planters are extremely disorganized and disunited, sugarcane is still grown on land that they own, and no miller or consumer can acquire Philippine-grown sugar without them. Although planters can no longer command votes and wield political influence the way they used to—much to the glee of their countrymen—the opposition of large planters to cane purchase and their strong attachment to owning sugar will continue to keep the share-*quedan* operative for some time. That the government's main agency for making and enforcing sugar policy is still dominated by large planters is another key element to the balance of power.

While conducting this research I was asked by a milling executive which of the two property rights allocation systems—share-*quedan* or cane-purchase—did I think was more "modern," in the sense that it fit better with the free-market normative preference for more "privatized" property rights. Since the rhetoric of the "free market" had gained prestige, especially during the Ramos years, the executive who asked me this was trying to evaluate which system would fit better with that new orientation. I did not and do not know how to answer such a question. Certainly, the economic efficiency of the industry as a whole would be improved by switching to the cane purchase. But if more "privatized" property rights are the higher value, then just as certainly, there are more private owners of sugar under the share-*quedan* system than there would be under the cane purchase. Such a question underlines how misguided it is to employ one's own reified normative preferences when attempting to understand complex human institutions. The controversy over the cane-purchase experiment illustrates clearly how much more heterogeneous such institutions are than is conveyed by simple, overarching dichotomies and dualisms such as "communal" versus "private" property. The share-*quedan* and cane-purchase property rights allocations are different, and they have significantly different implications for the distribution of power, for the way individuals perceive themselves in relation to others, and for the economic well-being of the industry to which they belong. Understanding those implications is the role of the outside scholar. Preaching the superiority of some overarching system of property rights or another is best left to the politicians, advocates, and ideologues. In my role as a scholar of a country not my own, I try to take a dispassionate, disinterested view of competing values. That the cane purchase *would* lead to greater economic efficiency and productivity in the industry as a whole I have no doubt, as I believe I have made quite clear in this chapter. Using Weber's neo-Kantian language, such an assertion is a matter of what "is." That the pursuit of greater efficiency and productivity in the making of sugar, however, is a superior value to the other values deeply felt and passionately expressed by those inside of the industry, I am not prepared to say. For such an assertion is a matter of what "ought" to be, and I strongly believe that it is not my place to make judgments like these about other people's lives and livelihoods. In our role as concerned citizens we are often obligated to make such choices about competing values. In our role as foreign scholars we are obligated to leave the "oughts" to those whose lives are directly affected.

The Great Importation War

On 30 June 1992 Fidel Ramos was inaugurated President of the Philippines for a single six-year term. Ramos was the nation's first Protestant president, a West Point graduate, a former general, and a hero of the EDSA revolution. As Cory Aquino's Minister of Defense, he remained steadfastly loyal to the reborn, post-Marcos democracy in putting down multiple coup attempts by right-wing officers. He won a plurality of votes over seven other candidates whose ranks included Imelda Marcos and Danding Cojuangco. Just before the election an article about Ramos appeared in the *Far Eastern Economic Review* (28 May 1992: 14–15) entitled "Man of the Makati Club: Corporate Lobby Fills Ramos' Vote-bank" portraying his association with, and indebtedness to corporate, financial, and industrial interests rather than rural and agrarian ones.[1] Unlike his predecessor, Mrs. Aquino, the Pangasinan-born Ramos had no personal association with the sugar industry. Soon after his election it became clear that Ramos was interested in attracting foreign investment and encouraging exports, and that his administration would be dominated by free-market, free-trade, neo-liberal technocrats rather than the *trapos* of old.[2]

By early July of 1992, the issue of free trade versus protectionism became the most widely discussed topic in the sugar industry. Within one week of the inauguration, the Monetary Board (the policy-making body of the Central Bank) issued a list of commodities targeted for import liberalization under IMF guidelines. Much to the surprise and consternation of those in the industry, sugar appeared on that list. Although it took several days for the potential impact of this move to sink in, soon there was a widespread furor in sugar-producing areas. This furor has not abated since. Once again, positions and alliances are far from straightforward and difficult to predict, but for the most part the sugar producers and the SRA stand on the protectionist side. On the free-trade side stand food processors, especially exporters of processed food, the Department of Finance, the Monetary Board, the National Economic Development Authority (NEDA), and even some influential figures in the Department of Agriculture, to which the SRA is an attached agency.

Prior to this move to liberalize importation, it was not explicitly illegal for a company to import sugar into the Philippines; it was merely very difficult. Until the early 1990s, banks were required to sell their dollars and other foreign currency to the Central Bank. Commercial banks acted as agents of the Central Bank in foreign exchange transactions, but they did not possess independent supplies of exchange. While a bank could issue an international letter of credit, all such letters were guaranteed by the Central Bank and had to be approved by it. Without such a letter, a Philippine company would only be able to pay a foreign supplier in pesos, unacceptable in an international transaction. A letter of credit enabled the Philippine company to pay the Central Bank in pesos, while the Bank remitted payment to the supplier in dollars. This was one method by which the Philippine government retained control over imports and managed its foreign exchange.

If a Philippine food company decided to take advantage of the cheaper world-market prices by importing sugar, it would have to go to a bank to obtain a letter of credit. Since sugar appeared on the list of restricted imports, the bank would have to ask the Central Bank for permission. The Central Bank, in turn, would normally ask the SRA whether to allow the importation. If the SRA felt that domestic supply was insufficient and that the processor had a compelling need for the sugar, it would authorize the Central Bank to issue the letter. Usually such requests were rejected because domestic supplies were deemed adequate. In 1988, however, sugar production was so low that the government itself imported 100,000 m.t. of sugar to arrest rapidly rising prices. Predictably, this elicited demonstrations by planters and millers in front of the SRA offices.

Theoretically, a multinational firm with an independent supply of dollars could import sugar without a letter of credit. They would be reluctant to do so, however, for three reasons: the SRA would also inform Customs to prevent the sugar from entering the country (though Customs is considered one of the government's most corrupt agencies); planters' organizations would likely publicize such an "anti-national" act and the company would lose good will; and, the company would still have to pay the 50-percent tariff which, after transport costs are factored in, might be enough to make the imported sugar in the end more expensive than the domestic product.

In 1991, for example, there was much concern in sugar-producing areas that multinationals were in fact "opening the gates to importation" in response to the high domestic prices (Sa-onoy column in *Today,* 25 July 1991), and there were suggestions of boycotts being organized against such firms as Kraft, Del Monte, and Franklin Baker. In 1990, Congressman Guanzon led a Congressional inquiry into a much-publicized incident in which the Shemberg Manufacturing Co. had a large shipment of imported sugar impounded at port by Customs. The SRA contended that it was asked for authorization only after the letter of credit was already issued to Shemberg, and that the agency pressed Customs to impound the shipment as soon as they got wind of it. Although many producers are critical of the SRA's performance in monitoring imports, the agency points out that its legal clout and enforcement capabilities are severely limited. Certainly there are problems of coordination and communication between the SRA, the Central Bank, and Customs, and there are allegations of corruption at every step in the process. Not surprisingly, in the wake of the Shemberg incident, CONFED leaders pressed the government to make sugar importation explicitly illegal and to crack down on what they perceived to be rampant smuggling of foreign sugar into the Philippines. Not only was this request never acted upon, but there was even a move, ultimately unsuccessful, to reduce the tariff on imported sugar to 30 percent.[3] Conflict about sugar importation and smuggling was smoldering even before the Monetary Board recommendation fanned a flame.

There was much reaction to the Board's recommendation. Rather than responding to the substance of the move, many reacted to what they thought the term "import liberalization" meant. In fact, the initial 1992 import-liberalization recommendation had no effect on tariff rates, and was merely part of a larger program of easing bureaucratic obstacles to international trade. As the government was moving to decentralize foreign currency holdings, deregulate banks, and simplify licensing requirements, the Central Bank was trying to ease the process by which letters of credit were authorized and negotiated. The "import liberalization" consisted of little more than removing sugar from the list of products placed under quantitative restriction. The Central Bank was saying in effect that a company that wanted to import sugar would be able to obtain letters and customs clearance without having to justify the import by proving a domestic shortage. The importer would still have to pay the tariff, and it remained illegal for a trader to sell world-market sugar on the domestic market without specific SRA authorization.

Perhaps the most distressing fact of all, so far as the sugar industry was concerned, was the special treatment being afforded to the food-exporting companies. The Aquino administration had already reoriented the main economic policy thrust from import substitution to export-led growth, and the Ramos administration would do all it could to facilitate exports. The food exporters had long claimed that the high price of Philippine sugar was a major reason that they could not be cost-competitive with food producers in other countries, and this argument held sway with the executive branch of the government. Although some of those exporting companies are large multinationals (Dole, Del Monte, Nestle) with independent supplies of foreign exchange, many of them are small Filipino producers of products like banana chips, dried mangos, and nata de coco, barely surviving in a highly competitive business.[4] In 1989, the SRA first began to give allocations of D-sugar, at world-market prices, to authorized food exporters. Then, when the exporters complained that traders could not or would not provide adequate amounts of D-sugar, the government extended the "bonded warehouse" system to food exporters. This system would become the focus of enormous controversy in subsequent years.

The bonded warehouse system is widely used internationally as a way to allow value-added exporters to import their raw materials duty-free. In the Philippines, this system is tremendously important for the production of the nation's two leading exports, electronics and garments, for which about 80 percent of the raw materials are imported. Exporters claim that it is expensive to maintain a bonded warehouse because companies must pay fees to the Customs Bureau to defray the cost of salaries to the Customs officers who are required to supervise operations very closely. If a company uses any part of the imported raw materials for its domestic products, then it must pay the duty for that portion of the import. If imported sugar, for example, is not liquidated within six months, the company is assessed the equivalent of a 150 percent tariff. Although it is not very difficult to set up a bonded warehouse, it does entail a great deal of paperwork and documentation to maintain one. Some claim that the entire system is rife with corruption and that bonded warehouses are mostly established for the purpose of smuggling cheap imports into the domestic market. In any case, by 1992 many food exporters had already begun to import refined sugar into bonded warehouses. The sugar industry feared that the Monetary Board's import-liberalization policy and the easing up of currency controls would greatly increase such imports of foreign sugar.

Initially, there was talk of a boycott and much rhetoric about the "back-stabbing" action of the Monetary Board. But in a dramatic meeting held at the SRA's Bacolod headquarters, cooler heads prevailed. As is often the case, the eloquent voice of moderation belonged to Daniel "Bitay" Lacson. He argued that if industry representatives went to the president asking for special protection out of sheer patriotism or economic nationalism, their appeal would fail. The president's economic advisers favored liberalized trade and looked askance at industries whose inefficiency caused them to burden consumers. Even President Aquino, herself from a prominent sugar planting family, had been dismayed that domestic sugar prices had become so much higher than those of the world market. Lacson recommended that the industry own up to its failures, admit that its inefficiencies harmed the consumer, and ask for five years of additional tariff protection in order to get its house in order. But industry leaders had to realize that the clock was ticking. If they could not make the industry more competitive, or if its efforts broke down because of continued political bickering, then the industry must expect to bear the ultimate consequence after those five years.

Industry leaders at first took Lacson's advice. CONFED, NFSP, the SRA, and representatives of the milling and labor sectors all presented requests for temporary increases in tariffs to offset the import liberalization. The documents prepared by the planters' organizations stressed the subsidies that other countries give to their sugar industries, the residual, surplus nature of the world market, and—as usual—the profound impact that import liberalization would have upon sugar workers if it were instituted before the industry became competitive. The document by CONFED echoed an opinion widely held in the industry, suggesting that the government was partly to blame for the high costs of production. Whereas other countries subsidized the purchase of imported farm inputs, the Philippines placed tariffs on them. They asked the president to eliminate tariffs on fertilizers (the most costly input), tractors and trucks, and to provide tax incentives for mill rehabilitation and refinery construction.[5] The president responded first by deferring the import liberalization until October 1992, then by increasing the tariff on unrefined sugar from 50 to 75 percent for a period of three years. This was in direct repudiation of another Monetary Board recommendation. Soon thereafter, the president also increased the tariffs on refined sugar, molasses, and caloric sugar substitutes to 75 percent, and on non-caloric substitutes from 10 to 100 percent. For a brief time the government overlooked fructose in its new tariff structure, motivating a few food processors to switch to that sweetener until the oversight was corrected.

Although Lacson's clout was able to help keep imports at bay temporarily, his main agenda vis-à-vis the sugar industry was to advocate "globalization" and "rationalization" and to get people in the industry to change their attitudes. He argued that sugar producers should look for opportunities to diversify out of their low-value crop, that they should sell their products aggressively and seek out new markets, and, most of all, that they must reject the legacy of quotas, protection, and conspicuous consumption and learn how to compete in global markets without special privilege. He stressed that the GATT (now WTO) process would ultimately benefit the Philippines by enabling it to sell more of the labor-intensive manufactured goods that earn large amounts of foreign exchange. He pointed out that one unfortunate result of banning the importation of agricultural commodities, for example, would be if developed countries placed further quantitative restrictions on garments, the Philippines' leading export and dollar earner. Rather than resisting open trade, Filipinos needed to learn how to succeed in the new competitive global environment. Lacson was highly respected,[6] but he had become one of the industry's most blunt and outspoken critics, and (at least in private) he was an unabashed pessimist regarding the future of sugar. Despite his prominent attempts to protect the sugar industry, he frequently asserted that sugarcane farming was no longer a viable way to make money and that only the most efficient and knowledgable agriculturists should keep growing it. He was certain that if the industry did not improve the efficiency of mills, the productivity of farms, the "stewardship of the land," and the treatment of workers, it would virtually collapse within a decade.

There is no doubt that if the Philippines were to allow unrestricted imports of sugar into the country the domestic industry would be plunged into a crisis that would dwarf that of the mid-

1980s, and from which it would likely never recover. Many argued that the Philippines was not the only country that protected its domestic sugar industry, that virtually every sugar-producing country in the world did so, including the United States and the European Union. The plethora of preferential agreements, quotas, and price manipulations had rendered sugar notoriously insulated from, "the response of production and consumption to market signals" (Brown 1987: vii). The difference between the Philippines and other producing countries, however, was that protectionism had not deterred most other countries from investing to improve the yields of their farms and the efficiency of their mills. The Philippines was losing ground in both these areas, and had consequently lost its comparative advantage in sugar production.

Dueling Voices

The import-liberalization debate of 1992 set the stage for what would become a long-running, highly acrimonious battle between sugar producers and food processors. As the government increasingly employed the rhetoric of free trade and export stimulation, the food processors became emboldened to press their claims with government and in the media. They argued that the sugar producers were using their political clout to aggrandize themselves while bilking the Philippine consumer. And since the price of sugar in the Philippines was so much higher than the world-market price, the "value-added," "modern," "export-oriented" food processing industry was unable to compete with companies in countries where sugar was efficiently produced and cheaper (e.g., Thailand), or countries that produced no sugar at all but bought all their supplies on the world market (e.g., Singapore). The exporters argued that the sugar industry's proud claim that it had made world-market priced sugar (D and E *quedan*s) available to food exporters was a mere public-relations ploy since few traders would buy or sell those *quedan*s and little sugar was ever available at that price. And besides, they noted, D- and E-sugar was still more expensive than imports after factoring in refining costs (often called "tolling fees" in the Philippines), taxes, and transportation. It was irrational, given new international economic realities, to favor "feudal," "fat cat," "sugar barons" over industries with such growth potential as food processing.

The sugar producers, for their part, insisted that the food processors were "anti-national," so intent on obtaining cheap raw materials that they were willing to crush the millions of their countrymen employed in the sugar industry. Food processors, they claimed, were deluded by the term "world market" into believing that there really was such a place in which sugar was freely and openly traded at prices that reflected the underlying supply and demand for the commodity. The idea that one small sugar-producing country such as the Philippines should suddenly live according to free-market principles while the rest of the world's sugar producers practiced protectionism, import quotas, and price supports was absurd. And besides, the sugar producers *had* made nearly world-market priced sugar available to export-oriented food processors, but few of the food processors had availed themselves of it. Some planters claimed that they still held D and E *quedan*s from the previous year for which there were no buyers. According to them, the sugar industry had bent over backwards, only to be blamed and scorned by uncompromising ideologues in government and the food industry. The food processors were "full of crap" and should be boycotted if they insisted upon importing foreign sugar onto Philippine shores. One planter told me that the SRA should buy its own submarine and torpedo any ships carrying foreign sugar to the Philippines.

As this battle heated up, there were, once again, attempts made to co-opt the anthropologist (me) to use my "expertise" to make the case for one side or the other. The final attempt to get me to declare my allegiance publicly and fight for one set of interests would mark the rather abrupt end of my field research in Negros. But I will tell that story later.

As is often the case, many sugar planters blamed the Philippine government for their plight and used that argument as justification for continued protection. In addition to the aforementioned tariffs on imported agricultural inputs, many point out that the value-added tax (VAT) on both raw sugar *and* refined sugar is double-dipping, and is the main reason that Philippine refined is more expensive than imported refined. Many cite high interest rates and the issuing of high-yield treasury bills as creating disincentives for investment in farm and mill improvement. Sugar planters frequently rail about how Customs, the Central Bank, and the SRA tacitly allow traders to smuggle in foreign sugar and sell it at a huge profit on the domestic market. They fault the government for the poor physical infrastructure, expensive and unreliable shipping, failure to make good on the promise of restitution for the Marcos-Benedicto swindling, and for the much-hated CARP agrarian reform program. And, of course, they complain about the SRA's failures in research and development, in overseeing the *quedan* system, and in monitoring mill productivity and honesty. A spokesman for the NFSP chided the SRA for its "weak performance" in "pressing our need to stop imports at all costs," and he took the opportunity to assail CONFED (the rival planters' federation) for taking a similarly weak stand. Despite the reputation of the "sugar barons" for having great political influence, one would think by talking to planters that they are the much-beleaguered objects of a government conspiracy to undermine them in every possible way.

Several sugar planters told me that the multinational food-processing companies were not their enemies, but rather it was the small, well-organized food exporters that were leading the anti-sugar campaign. I found this to be true to some extent, but things were far more complex than most planters knew. Companies like Coke, Pepsi, and Nestle, whose Philippine subsidiaries sold most of their products on the domestic market, were in fact extremely tactful when discussing issues pertaining to sugar price and availability, as were large domestic companies such as San Miguel. But companies whose Philippine operations were geared toward export (e.g., Dole, Del Monte, Ajinomoto) tended to be more blunt in stating their negative opinions about the domestic sugar industry. Although the leadership and spokespersons for PHILFOODEX (Philippine Food Exporters) and other such organizations tended to be from smaller, Philippine-owned companies, the extent to which multinationals funded and supported their operations was the source of much speculation and was treated with (as the Filipinos say) *delicadeza*. Although most of these big companies stated that they remained detached from Philippine political debates, many planters expressed fear that these major consumers of sugar would exercise their considerable influence on the side of the free-trade advocates. One planter said that it would be dangerous to "wake the sleeping bears" (meaning Coke, Pepsi, and San Miguel—all major sugar consumers whose products could be produced with sugar substitutes); but unbeknownst to most planters those companies were already awake and subtly making their opinions known in the halls of power.

One encountered a great deal of confusion and contradictory beliefs about what various international agreements and agencies did or did not say about sugar. Some sugar producers thought that it would be perfectly in line with the GATT Uruguay Round, for instance, to make sugar importation technically legal, but to place a 100 percent tariff on it.[7] In fact, the 100 percent tariff became a widely repeated slogan among planters for more than a year. Others believed that because the United States and the European Union had highly protectionist quota and price-support policies to bolster their domestic sugar industries, then GATT, WTO, and the IMF could hardly deprive third-world countries of similar policies. It is true that neither U.S. nor EU sugar policies would pass muster with the IMF should those governments be in positions to request loans. But, of course, they are not likely to be in such positions any time soon. Some planters asserted that it was simply not possible that major international organizations could force on a poor country policies that would do such obvious damage to thousands of struggling workers. Obviously, these planters had little experience or knowledge concerning how the IMF has operated in poor countries. Most people in the industry advocated a system in which imports of sugar would be totally banned unless there was a demonstrated shortage of domestic supply, much as is done with rice. In other words, they wanted the government to step in and "rationalize" the supply of sugar, to move further away from the "free-market" being touted by "the smart boys" of NEDA and the Monetary Board.

The leading advocate in the Philippine Senate for the anti-import position was Senator Gloria Macapagal Arroyo (now president of the Philippines). Although she has a Ph.D. in economics and a generally pro-business reputation, she also used the term "rationalization" to mean prohibiting imports unless there was a domestic shortage. Most people explained the seeming contradiction by the fact that the senator's husband is a sugar planter. She explicitly contrasted "rationalization" with "liberalization," thereby co-opting the technocratic voice in the service of anti-neo-liberal policy. One owner of a food exporting company exclaimed to me (referring to Senator Arroyo), "What kind of economist is that?!"

At a strategy meeting of planters in September 1992, Bitay Lacson explained that membership in GATT and a loan requested from the IMF[8] did necessitate trade liberalization, but that sugar was a low priority given the protectionist policies of the developed countries. Still, planters should welcome liberalization as a chance to rededicate themselves to efficiency, competitiveness, diversification, and globalization. If the Thais could make money exporting sugar all over Asia, so too could the Filipinos if only they would buckle down and get with the new world economic order of borderless markets, free-flowing comparative advantage, and consumer sovereignty. "Never forget," Lacson told the planters, "that Third World countries benefit *more* from free trade than rich countries. It gives us the chance to sell our products more cheaply to them. It is wrong to resist the GATT process for short-term self-interest." He vowed to carry the sugar industry's plan to the president but only if they would be able to produce a "rational," unified plan that owned up to the industry's failures and spelled out the path the industry would take to yank itself into modernity. Lacson is so articulate and well respected that he nearly persuaded a few sugar planters, imbued as they were with the ethic of rent seeking, protectionism, and natural privilege, to accept the neo-liberal paradigm that he espouses. Nearly, and only for a short moment.

An official of Philippine Sugar Millers Association (PSMA), the largest millers' association, told me that the executive branch of government listens to Lacson because he speaks the language of modern economics. Lacson's "quoting of economic research and talk of globalization and the free market" touches a nerve because he sounds so attuned to world trends. But "when he uses the price of sugar in Singapore as the benchmark instead of the average price in producing countries," he creates a wrong impression that must be disputed. "Look at the United States," said the official. "The world-market price is eleven cents per pound, the U.S. government guarantees eighteen cents, and U.S. prices are typically twenty-two to twenty-four cents. Is *that* globalization? And look at Japan. They are global, but they are also nationalistic. That should be our model."

Arsenio Yulo, the administrator of the SRA from its 1986 inception until 1993, told me that the CONFED-led boycott of food processors had been an abysmal failure. In his view, the idea that Filipinos would boycott such companies as Coke, Pepsi, and San Miguel to protect the sugar industry was just silly. If the sugar industry wants to make the case that it is in the national interest for consumers to pay a higher price for sugar, then the industry must project a more conciliatory image. "Never, never antagonize consumers, especially with the current government in place. They [the consumers] will import sugar and squash you if you burn them. Consumers must be courted and coddled. When I cajole these big companies not to import to help the Philippine people, they respond, 'As long as there is adequate supply, we will buy domestic.'" Yulo defended the right of food-processing *exporters* to import world-market sugar to use in their products. "Why should Philippine exporters be forced to pay sixteen cents per pound (the domestic price at the time) when their competition only pays eleven cents? The food-exporting industry is up-and-coming, and the nation needs to help them. Even though some of them are very noisy opponents of the sugar industry, they too should be coddled, not antagonized." Whether some of the bonded warehouses had been involved in smuggling (as alleged by planters), Yulo did not know or would not say. His conciliatory approach earned the wrath of some members of the sugar industry, particularly the NFSP leadership who viewed him as a CONFED partisan and a lackey of food companies. When the previously mentioned NFSP official faulted the SRA for its "weak performance" in "pressing our need to stop imports at all costs," he was talking about Yulo.

By mid-1993 the debate entered a new phase with the introduction of House Bill No. 9252 (and later House Bill No. 628), the "import-rationalization" bill brought before Congress by representatives from sugar-producing areas led by Romeo Guanzon of Bacolod (and NFSP). This bill would have made it illegal to import sugar into the Philippines unless there was a demonstrated shortfall in supply. In the event of an import authorization, only millers and planters would be authorized to purchase that sugar, and *quedan*s representing that sugar could then be sold to traders and consumers as if it were domestic sugar (after giving ten percent of the profits to the workers—a clause added to make the bill more palatable). I attended a strategy meeting of sugar industry leaders with the "sugar bloc" congressional delegation in August 1993 in Manila. Negros Occidental Governor Rafael Coscolluela gave the keynote address. Coscolluela told the leaders and representatives that their never-ending search for a single charismatic leader to serve as the voice and public persona of Philippine sugar was misguided, and that neither he nor his predecessor and mentor Bitay Lacson had any interest in being that leader. He held up a box of sugar cubes—made in Hawai'i—which he had purchased in a local market, and said, "This must stop." He decried the double VAT and the "lack of sympathy" in the Department of Finance, and he asserted that the VAT must be rectified through legislative action since the bureaucrats had failed to correct it. Although he expressed strong support for agrarian reform, he said that CARP had been a disaster because it prevented land from being sold or used as collateral, and it contained no provisions encouraging diversification, industrialization, or aid to poor farmers. Following Coscolluela, three congressmen (from Negros, Bukidnon in Mindanao, and Pampanga) spoke out against CARP and for the import-rationalization bill. As usual, each one mentioned that the industry must always think of its workers, and use the plight of the workers in its public relations efforts. Another congressman, who happens to be a molasses trader, said that he would propose a bill exempting molasses from the VAT. Finally, just as the meeting seemed to be winding down, in came Speaker of the House Jose de Venecia, a close protégé of the president. De Venecia spoke about how interest and treasury-bill rates had been lowered during the current administration, and he asked for the sugar industry to support the pending "high-value-crops" bill which encouraged all farmers to put aside a proportion of land to plant crops such as asparagus, black pepper, fruits, and flowers. He said (much to the consternation of several planters in the audience), "Sugar, rice, and corn—no matter who owns the land—are prescriptions for poverty."

I was struck by a number of things at this "strategy meeting." First, attendance was poor; only about ten of the forty members of the "sugar bloc" were there. Second, rather than being a dialogue, it was completely dominated by the congressmen, most of whom were clearly posturing. Third, topics covered included the VAT, interest rates, diversification (cattle, flowers, particle board, MSG, asparagus, and fertilizer production were all mentioned), local government taxation, industrialization, U.S. and EU sugar policies, and, especially, CARP. Fourth, there was virtually no discussion of the import bill that was the ostensible reason for the meeting. Fifth, the most influential politician who spoke, Speaker de Venecia, was tactfully telling the members of the sugar industry to stop planting sugar! One CONFED official I know was clearly becoming more and more uncomfortable and frustrated while sitting there. He told me later that the congressmen and the millers were being far too timid. He said the sugar industry still has a great deal of political clout if they would only stand up and *use* it. They might not win this particular fight, but at least they should go down trying. It seemed to him as if the congressmen were dissembling about the bill, but were trying to portray themselves as sugar supporters nonetheless. Once again, one came away from this strategy meeting feeling that the political might of the "sugar barons" was no longer all it was cracked up to be.

A CONFED official later tried to explain the subtext to me: The prevailing opinion was that the import-rationalization bill looked to be in trouble in the House and might be "amended to death." More important, however, there were signals from Malacañang Palace that, citing IMF and GATT, the president would probably veto the bill should it pass both houses. Unlike in the United States, when the Philippine president signals that he intends to veto a bill, especially when it is clear that the veto cannot be over-ridden, congress usually opts to table the legislation so as to avoid a protracted fight and to spare all parties embarrassment.[9] The true blame for the president's position, according to the CONFED official, goes to "the executive branch's economic managers," but it seemed that the majority of the Cabinet was also against the bill. "The industry must be ready to accept relief through tariffs rather than legislation," he asserted. There was just so much the congressmen could do under such conditions, and they did not want to lose face if they failed to get the bill enacted, as seemed likely. This CONFED official also faulted PSMA, the millers' organization, for its relative indifference to the political activity surrounding the import ban. The millers, he said, were so intent on conveying an image of being modern industrialists that they failed to press the interests of their own industry. In fact, one PSMA official did tell me "a law restricting imports of sugar would give the industry a bad image." The CONFED official reserved his greatest antipathy, however, for PHILFOODEX for their public relations campaign vilifying the sugar industry. "What do those people want? What is wrong with buying our D-sugar, anyway?" He said that he had no doubt that some of the imported sugar and many of the confection products made from imported sugar ended up entering domestic markets illegally. "While they and their columnists make us out to be some kind of feudal lords, they are a bunch of smugglers and cheaters."

Just after the meeting broke up I interviewed a congresswoman from Negros closely associated with the sugar industry. She told me that the so-called sugar bloc in congress was only united insofar as they represented sugar-producing districts; they had few other common issues or interests. Some of the members were not even particularly strong supporters of sugar, and most were not participants in the industry. Although she described herself as being strongly committed to protecting sugar, she was also an ardent advocate of diversification. She did not believe that Philippine sugar had much of a future, and she was skeptical about whether Congress should be involved in this issue at all, suggesting that the Philippines already had too many laws and regulations that interfered with markets. "Even the sugar industry needs to be freed up—once it is ready to compete," she claimed. But for the time being, she stated, as long as the United States and European Union protected their sugar so heavily, so must the Philippines.

Once it became widely known that the executive branch was opposed to the import ban, some industry leaders decided to take another tack. There was an extant piece of pending legislation, Memorandum Order 95, the implementing order for the "Magna Carta of Small Farmers" designed to protect agricultural commodities produced by the rural poor. This legislation stated, among other things, that imports of commodities produced domestically in sufficient quantities should be regulated. The SRA tried to get sugar listed as one of the commodities covered, arguing that most sugar planters were in fact small farmers, but met considerable resistance from within its own parent agency, the Department of Agriculture. Sugar producers were clearly angry with the Department for its reluctance to protect the interests of the sugar industry. But the image of the "sugar barons" had made it highly impolitic for government officials to be seen as doing sugar's bidding. As several of the politicians had pointed out at the strategy meeting, the sugar industry did indeed have a serious public relations problem.

During this period, Rodolfo Gamboa, Yulo's successor as SRA administrator, made many speeches and gave several interviews in an effort to sway public opinion toward the import ban. I heard three of those speeches and conducted two lengthy private interviews with Gamboa. The world market, to use a phrase that Gamboa made famous in the Philippines, was a "dump market" for surplus sugar. He said it was meaningless to compare Philippine prices to those unrealistic prices, and foolish to be deceived by the seemingly innocuous sound of the term "world market." Sugar was "the most corrupt commodity market in the world." The Philippines found itself squeezed between the pressure to break down trade barriers (through GATT, etc.) and the agricultural-protection policies of the developed countries. The solution, he argued, was for the Philippines to protect sugar *more* rather than less. ASEAN needed to create a strong trading bloc in sugar to counter the American quota system and the European Lomé Convention. In addition, the Philippines had to seek "counter-trade" agreements, such as one with Russia in which Philippine sugar and tobacco were exchanged for Russian military hardware. "The food processors have a point when they say that Philippine sugar is not as efficiently produced as it could be, but no one can be competitive in a dump market." He gave the example of other countries which had far lower interest rates and actual subsidies (instead of taxes) on agricultural inputs. According to Executive Order 8, the 75 percent tariff on imported sugar would, if it went through, only last for three years. Then it would be automatically reduced to 50 percent. So the sugar industry had to get its house in order fast. He argued that the *quedan* classification system was essential for efficient apportionment of sugar into categories. "Without it, composite prices would be lower and would wildly fluctuate. Without *quedan*s, the banks would have no collateral with which to give crop loans." The planters, he noted, did not understand the importance of the SRA at all. "They think we could just do away with C- and D-sugar, and prices would be higher. They are very mistaken." He faulted his predecessor, Yulo, for being too consumer-oriented, while he, Gamboa, was more explicitly pro-producer.[10] If the executive branch insisted on a "free market" in sugar, then the industry would die, something he vowed to prevent at all costs. Gamboa felt that the importation issue had become too shrill and emotional. PHILFOODEX imported only a small amount of sugar, but they were "very vocal and unreasonable." Without the tariff increase (to 75 percent), "any Tom, Dick, or Harry would import sugar." While the industry advocated a total import ban (i.e., the import-rationalization bill), he said with a wink that he would not state his own opinion about this. He thought that some people in the government were using GATT and the IMF as excuses. "If their trade liberalization goes through, even San Miguel and Coke would import. And why shouldn't they? Prices would be so low, we could not compete." He said every time sugar prices went up, he got a stern call from the Department of Trade and Industry—sometimes from the president himself. "What is wrong," Gamboa asked me, "with a system in which food exporters have to buy D-sugar if it is available; and if it is not available they are given authorization to import?" This seemed reasonable to him. The political debate over importation, he predicted, would determine the fate of the sugar industry for all time. "We are entering a critical period."

Every planter with whom I spoke about the import bill brought up the issue of smuggling. In their view, the food exporters had no legitimate reason to import sugar, since D-sugar costs the same as imports. The only reason exporters insisted on being allowed to import sugar was because they were in league with unscrupulous traders who leaked imported sugar and food made with imported sugar into the domestic market, making huge windfalls. Everyone mentioned the well-publicized Shemberg incident in which that Philippine-owned multinational was alleged to have allowed some sugar from its bonded warehouse to be sold domestically. With the exception of one planter who asserted that "a Chinese trader" had illegally imported 18,000 m.t. of molasses and sold it at a huge profit, no one was able to cite any other specific instance of smuggling. One leader of a planters' confederation told me, "We realize that this [the import ban] is a rash solution to smuggling, but unfortunately that is the reality in the Philippines. If you give people a crack, they'll make it a gaping hole." Most agreed that the sugar industry needed to become more efficient, but they asserted that the only way to facilitate increased efficiency was for the government to shield the industry from competition while they rebuilt and rededicated themselves to upgrading. Many asserted that it was too soon after Marcos to expect the industry to be able to compete on its own.

So far, I have been presenting some of the not-particularly-unified voices from within the sugar industry. But now it is time to hear from the other side, the food processing industry.

PHILFOODEX and Its Allies

I spent a fair bit of time in 1993 and 1994 with a woman who owned a company that produces prepared food mixes for both the domestic and export markets. Her company's packet mixes for such Filipino favorites as *sinigang, adobo,* and *karikari* can even be found in oriental markets in Lancaster, Pennsylvania. She was the founder and past president of PHILFOODEX, and was widely considered that organization's most radical and visible member. Her grandfather had been a sugar planter in Pampanga, but she had come to believe that the sugar industry was pampered and was the cause of much distress to Philippine consumers and food processors. One of her company's products, nata de coco, had been pioneered by Filipinos; but the Japanese were satisfying most of their large demand by buying from Taiwan, mostly because the Taiwanese produced no sugar and obtained their sugar from the world market. E-sugar had been very difficult to find, she related, and it took a month to receive delivery if one were lucky enough to find any. She said that she would rather buy D-sugar than import, but if the final cost of refined D-sugar was so much more expensive than imports, it would hurt her business to buy the domestic sugar. The paperwork that was required to receive import authorization or even a D allocation was "absolutely nuts," and had to be reduced. If D-sugar or imported sugar was leaking into the domestic market, she argued, the government should prosecute the unscrupulous traders who were responsible. "Food processors are not in the sugar-trading business," so she doubted that anyone in her industry was smuggling sugar. The Shemberg Company may well have leaked imported sugar from its bonded warehouse, but she insisted that was an isolated incident. And besides, Shemberg was not a member of PHILFOODEX.

She recounted how Nestle—the Swiss-based multinational that not-so-secretly supported PHILFOODEX—had recently written a letter to the Department of Trade and Industry stating that the price of sugar would be a major consideration in Nestle's decisions about where to build new plants, and asking what was the government plan to keep sugar prices under control. The agency had assured Nestle that import liberalization was the new order of the day, and that the government would do all it could to keep the cost of raw materials competitive.

I accompanied her to a meeting of a sugar industry organization called Sugar 2000 at which she stood up and spoke passionately of the need to provide ample supplies of world-market-priced sugar for food exporters—or allow freer importation. The resounding chorus of boos that this speech elicited was something I had never heard before in the Philippines, especially directed at a woman. When I commented on this to someone sitting near me he said, "We are learning from you Americans." This founder of PHILFOODEX asked me whether I would be willing to write an advocacy article supporting her organization's position, but I politely declined, pleading the need to maintain scholarly neutrality.

I met with the incumbent president of PHILFOODEX at his office in his small food-processing company. He told me that his industry stood for global competitiveness and modern economic realities. The sugar producers, on the other hand, stood for monopoly, protectionism, and self-interest. The millers were somewhat more reasonable than the planters, but he said they "seem to have a sincerity problem." Even if a food exporter could find D- or E-sugar—which was difficult—it ended up being considerably more expensive than imported sugar after one paid the VAT, tolling (i.e., refining) fees, and transport costs.[11] The president said that the system of dealing with so many traders in the Philippines was madness. Traders did not want to sell D-sugar, because it was such low-margin business. "They withhold D *quedan*s from the market until the price goes up, so we [i.e., food processors] never get this sugar at the price and the amount that we need." And since the allocation of D-sugar changed every year depending upon domestic production, no trader would ever sign a long-term contract for its provision either to Philippine food exporters or foreign buyers. He said that the members of PHILFOODEX, mostly small food companies, shared a bonded warehouse and imported sugar to use in their exported food products (actually, only seventeen of the seventy-four members imported sugar). He complained that the paperwork and oversight was very onerous, especially if a company exported more than one product and had to do all the paperwork for each. The accusation that sugar was leaking out of the PHILFOODEX warehouse he declared absolutely scurrilous. "We are not in the business of selling sugar, let alone smuggling it. Some vindictive, political members of the sugar industry plant the accusations with the journalists that they control." PHILFOODEX, on the other hand, "never pays off journalists. Even if we wanted to, we couldn't afford it. The sugar barons think it is cheaper to pay off journalists and politicians than to modernize." The 75 percent tariff had only deterred the non-exporting members of PHILFOODEX from importing, because exporters were legally exempt from the tariff if they followed all the bonded warehouse rules. But PHILFOODEX represented only a tiny fraction of sugar sales, he reminded me, since they were all small producers. His company itself imported only 200 tons per year, mostly Australian raw sugar refined in Singapore. Food exporters in the United States and Europe were also legally allowed to buy world-market priced sugar, but those countries made it far easier than the Philippines. He asked, "What possibly could be the rationale to make things even more difficult for food exporters by banning imports altogether, unless there is demonstrated shortage? What do the sugar producers have to gain from smothering the food-exporting industry?" Under the pending bill, he asserted, imported sugar would cost as much as B-sugar by the time it got to the consumer. Since consumers, even food exporters, would be prohibited from importing directly, the traders, millers, and planters would buy at world-market prices, then all take their cuts. In his view, all this talk about doing it in this way to prevent smuggling was just subterfuge. If smuggling was the problem, then the government should prosecute the smugglers; not take it out on legitimate businesses. "Isn't it obvious," he asked me, "that the traders are the ones who smuggle sugar?" The sugar producers were saying that other countries subsidize their sugar industries, and so we must protect ours. "We say that if other countries subsidize sugar, then why shouldn't we take advantage of their subsidies and buy from them?" Maybe it was time, he proposed, that the Philippines' old, inefficient sugar industry diversify and "stop producing the stuff."

The president told me that the SRA was purely a sugar industry arm without any interest in protecting consumers. The non-exporting sugar consumers (Coke, Pepsi, etc.) did not really care much about the import ban issue, because they passed their costs on to the consumers, and they did not want to antagonize the sugar industry. But privately, they all agreed with PHILFOODEX's position and some were paying members of the organization. There were forty-five congressmen directly identified with the sugar planters. His people (i.e., the food processors) had none. So they were fortunate that the executive branch had been willing to listen to them. "We speak the same language of modern economics that they do." The sugar producers always said to them, "What do you want?; we sell you D *quedan*s." But that was just not good enough. The taxes, the inefficiency, the traders, the many fees—all this made sugar too expensive, and that was the problem. "When I meet with these sugar producers to negotiate, I always come away feeling sorry for our country."

One prominent and outspoken member of PHILFOODEX is not a native-born Filipino. He is a European, married to a Filipina (who ran unsuccessfully for the Senate in 1992), and has lived in Manila for many years. He owns a small company that produces and exports banana chips, the manufacture of which is labor-intensive but uses only three raw materials: bananas, coconut oil, and sugar. When I spoke to him he excoriated the sugar industry for using their workers as an excuse for government protection: "Our sugar workers in the Philippines are treated much worse than in other countries. They [planters] say that this is 'a private matter,' but the workers are virtually slaves." He claimed that if he were forced to buy sugar at domestic prices, he simply could not stay in business. "The Thais, Malays, and Indonesians would beat me every time." He needed the continuation of the bonded warehouse system allowing for the duty-free purchase of imported sugar in order to remain competitive. If that system were eliminated and if exporters were forced to pay high tariffs he would definitely consider opening a new plant in another country, probably Vietnam. He did buy D-sugar when it was made available, but he regarded that as totally unsatisfactory. "When the world-market price fluctuates, they [Philippine traders] withhold from us. They hate to sell us D-sugar. Plus, we have to pay to refine it and transport it. When I buy from a trader in Hong Kong or Taiwan, I get what I want when I want it. That's a big difference. It is cheaper and more convenient to buy overseas." The great flaw in the import-rationalization bill, he said, was that *they* [the sugar producers] would decide when there was a shortage, and they would reap the windfall from importation. Congressmen and Senators were just interested in winning the most votes, not doing what is morally right. Very few people in Congress really favored "the sugar mafia," but legislators were afraid of denouncing them publicly. He understood that Marcos hurt the "sugar mafia," but long before that they were lazy and inefficient. He asked, "Why must the consumer always pay for their mistakes? Why must we pay to keep the sugar mafia in business?" "I was called in to Senator Macapagal Arroyo's office. She's a free trader until it comes to sugar because of her husband's family. I was met by a bunch of sugar-industry officials intent on 'working out an arrangement' for making us buy D-sugar instead of importing. Their price quote to me was a joke. I wrote back later telling them all to screw." "How dare the sugar industry be proud of letting us have D-sugar?" The sugar producers agreed to all the food processors' requests, but domestic traders still could not match the prices of Hong Kong traders. Other Southeast Asian food exporters, he noted, were booming. In the Philippines they talked a good game, but they put up every obstacle to exporting. In his assessment, the Department of Finance and NEDA really were pro-export, but the politics were very difficult for them. Filipinos were afraid of competition because they thought they would always lose. He said the big companies who served the domestic market did not really care much about cutting costs; it was only the exporters who needed to be competitive. He wondered whether the Philippines would be better off if it did not grow any sugar. The sugar industry did not care much about the small exporters, but they were really afraid of Dole and Del Monte; after that, they feared Coke, Pepsi, and San Miguel. PHILFOODEX, he told me, was meeting extensively with senators to try to scuttle the import ban, which he regarded as a major step backwards. "We need to insure that the exporters are totally protected, and that the sugar industry cannot control our fate. The bonded warehouse system is working fine, so why destroy it now?" He said even if the bill did pass in the House he doubted that it could get through the Senate.

PHILFOODEX is not the only organization of food producers lobbying against the import ban. I also spoke with the president of the Philippine Chamber of Food Manufacturers (PCFM), an organization that was "less confrontational than PHILFOODEX" and consisted of larger, "more mature" companies. Dole and Del Monte (examined in the next section) were members of PCFM, but both also actively financed PHILFOODEX as well. Although these companies generally put on a more conciliatory face, they had actively lobbied behind the scenes to prevent the import ban. He stated that he himself was in a rather sensitive position because some influential members of his organization "benefit from sugar protectionism" and were in favor of the ban. Also, he claimed some PCFM members had no principles one way or another about protectionism and were willing to live with the import ban as long as their products (e.g., ice cream) were also protected from outside competition. He told me that the soft drink companies, despite their purported low profile, had been more active in lobbying against the ban than they would admit publicly. The domestic soft drink industry was so competitive that none of the companies could afford to offend any potential customers, but they definitely wanted the option of importing if the domestic price of sugar got too high. "The sugar producers fear the soft drink companies more than anything," he asserted. He was sharply critical of the sugar industry for its lack of concern with quality and efficiency. He decried the lack of an umbrella organization protecting consumer interests in the Philippines. Instead there was a plethora of small, uncoordinated, single-issue organizations. The growing image of the food manufacturers as a well-organized political powerhouse was nothing but sugar-industry hype. The reality was that their political action was rather disorganized, under-funded, and ineffective. He said he would not be averse to a compromise that entailed a phased-out tariff on imported sugar to give the sugar industry some time to "readjust their investments," but he thought the import ban bill was very destructive. The sugar industry was highly effective at lobbying Congress, but the food industry was counting on its friends in the executive branch.

Two officers of the North Negros Marketing Corporation—the trading arm of Victorias Milling—discussed with me the issue of selling D-sugar to food exporters. They asserted that the world-market price at which D-sugar was sold applied only to *raw* sugar, as it did everywhere in the world. "If exporters expect to buy *refined* sugar at that price, they are crazy." Of course, food exporters had to pay tolling fees, freight fees, and the VAT, just like everyone else. North Negros Marketing made only a little money selling D-sugar, they said, but the exporters could not expect Victorias to lose money on the transaction. Victorias was bending over backwards for the exporters, allowing extended payments, setting prices quarterly, and delivering in two or three days. As long as Victorias had a supply of D *quedan*s and the exporters had all their SRA allocations and permissions in order, Victorias did a good job of servicing their needs. Perhaps Hong Kong traders could sell for slightly cheaper because their sugar is subsidized. Still, they said, Philippine food exporters should buy domestic D-sugar because it was the right thing to do. The Victorias Milling Company was the nation's largest mill. It employed nearly four thousand people. That, they said, was what made this an issue of nationalism. Despite the more neutral stance of the PSMA (the millers' association), Victorias definitely intended to lobby Congress in favor of the import-restriction bill.

The issue of who must pay the VAT was clearly one about which there was much misunderstanding. The division chief of the agriculture department of the Board of Investments (BOI), an arm of the Department of Trade and Industry, was shocked to learn that Victorias was asking food exporters to pay the VAT. As long as a company exported 70 percent or more of its product, it was exempted from the VAT if it sought permission from the BOI. It was, the chief asserted, an extremely simple process. If a legitimate food exporter bought refined sugar from a domestic refiner, there should have been no

VAT. This should have made the cost of domestic D-sugar approximately equal to or a little cheaper than duty-free imported refined sugar brought into a bonded warehouse, since buying foreign sugar still entailed paying refining and freight fees. If Philippine traders and millers were insisting that their food-exporter customers pay the VAT, the traders and mills were only hurting themselves by giving the customers more incentive to import sugar. The real problem, in his view, was that the *quedan*s represent raw sugar, and D *quedan*s were only sporadically available, and refiners just did not like selling it because it was unprofitable. "Sugar producers need to sell this stuff in bulk to keep the exporters happy." But because there were too many traders, it was very difficult and time-consuming to gather together large quantities of D-sugar. Given the VAT exemption, he was perplexed as to why the sugar producers and food exporters could not come to a meeting of the minds. In his view, the misinformation about the VAT within the sugar industry was a serious problem.

But perhaps more important than the incomplete and inconsistent information about who does and does not need to pay the VAT was the effect of the institutional organization of the industry. Since most refined sugar was purchased from traders rather than directly from refineries, and since traders were legally obligated to pay the VAT, those traders simply passed on the VAT cost to their customers, even food exporters who were legally exempt. The BOI official admitted that it would have been difficult to administer the VAT exemption under such a system of selling sugar even if all parties had the same information and bureaucratic access. An SRA official admitted that there was a major problem in administering the VAT to food exporters, but said that it is a problem between the food exporters and the government. "Why," he asked, "should it concern the sugar industry at all?" Exporters should be entitled not to pay the VAT at all rather than paying it and receiving a rebate. But working that out was not the business of the sugar industry.

A manager of a sugar central told me that he thought food producers *should* pay the VAT, because the VAT "is for Filipinos." He said, "PHILFOODEX should buy Filipino even if the price is higher. If they only care about price, then to hell with them. We have D-sugar and can sell it to them at a good price. If they operate in this country, they should buy their sugar here. It's that simple." He was an ardent supporter of the import ban, and he admitted that the milling company for which he worked was "lobbying hard" for its passage, even though the PSMA was officially neutral.

Corporate Sugar Purchasers

Purchasing managers of large industrial food processors, especially multinationals, are particularly difficult to interview. They prefer not to be interviewed at all, almost always request no tape recording when they do agree to be interviewed, and tend to be extremely discreet about their company's purchasing policies and, even more so, its political lobbying activities.

The senior manager for corporate materials control of Pepsi-Cola, Philippines was also a sugar planter who owned a farm in Mindanao. When I spoke to him in early 1994, he said he saw no conflict of interest whatsoever in this position. As will be examined in chapter 6, concepts such as "conflict of interest," "nepotism," and "corruption" are typically not viewed the same way in the Philippines as in, say, the United States. The purchasing manager for RFM, another large food-producing company (ice cream, soda, and flour), came from a family of Negros sugar planters. She told me her view of importation: "It makes me mad when I hear that some companies import sugar. In my role as purchaser I want sugar prices to be low, of course; but personally I want them to be high." She did not regard this as at all problematic.

The Pepsi manager explained his company's sugar procurement to me. Pepsi bought sugar from only a few major traders, and all the sugar they bought had to be refined at one of only three refineries that met their stringent quality standards. The standards for color and purity were particularly important for making of their absolutely clear 7-Up brand. Pepsi's policy—different from its rival, Coke—was spot buying. Rather than purchasing all of its supplies on a yearly, fixed-price basis, Pepsi constantly monitored trader prices and bought its sugar week-to-week, filling only its short-term needs. Because of such short-term buying in 1989, 1990, and 1991, the manager made a lot of money for Pepsi buying and selling *quedan*s. Then new management made it clear that Pepsi was not in the sugar-trading business. Each year Pepsi's eleven Philippine plants used a total of 800,000 50-pound bags of sugar (40,000 m.t.). The price of sugar seemed to be of little concern to the manager. Since Pepsi produced entirely for the Philippine market, he explained, it passed its costs directly on to consumers. In fact, when sugar prices were low people in sugar-producing areas bought less of their product, thus depressing sales. And besides, sugar prices were a relatively minor cost factor compared with water purification and shipping, both of which he told me "are in terrible shape" in the Philippines. He himself was strongly opposed to the importation of sugar, but he admitted that higher corporate management was following the debate very closely. If sugar prices went too high and supply became too constricted, Pepsi would certainly consider importing. At the time of our interview, Pepsi had no official position on the import-rationalization legislation.

About three months later, however, Macondray and Company, a business with ties to Pepsi-Cola, Philippines, did in fact order a one-time importation of 5,000 m.t. of sugar from Malaysia, and paid the requisite tariff. Although the sugar industry threatened to take legal action and to boycott Pepsi products, a spokesman for Pepsi stated, "the company would not hesitate to import if the situation warrants it" (*The Philippine Star*, 20 July 1994).

The commodities-purchasing manager of Magnolia, a subsidiary of San Miguel and the nation's largest producer of ice cream, took a similarly flexible stance on importation. In October 1993, San Miguel sold 50 percent of Magnolia to Nestle. Magnolia bought around 6,300 m.t. of sugar per year, and sold its products to other ASEAN countries and in the Middle East, in addition to selling in the Philippines. He said that they wanted to sell to the United States, but could not because the USDA banned imports of dairy products from the Philippines. Magnolia bought most of their sugar from smaller traders and had much less stringent sugar-quality standards than Pepsi. Magnolia would only buy from traders and mills that dealt in bulk. The manager told me this was so they "don't have to deal with those messy *quedans* ourselves." The company had no long-standing relationships with traders, and always bought from whomever could deliver the right amounts at the right price. In his view, corporate consumers had "a moral obligation" to try to protect Philippine farmers as much as possible. But the sugar industry had to improve, and he thought perhaps exposing it to outside competition would help it survive in the longer term. He said it was important to sustain the local supply of inputs, although Magnolia had largely failed in its efforts to stimulate large-scale production of milk. Almost all the milk they used was imported from Australia. So far, the San

Miguel corporation had remained silent concerning the sugar-importation debate. But, he noted, if San Miguel ever came out in favor of imports, "the sugar industry would quake."

The manager of the Brewing Materials and Chemicals Department of San Miguel was proud of the way his company was forcing the sugar industry to "wake up and get efficient" by imposing strict quality standards enforced by penalties and premiums. And since sugar for brewing need not be of the purest, most expensive grade, they had also encouraged mills to experiment in the production of intermediate grades of sugar, more processed than raw but not quite refined (with names such as "white sugar," "washed sugar," and *"blanco directo,"* all of which have also become popular with baking companies). Their new favorite was liquid sugar; in fact, San Miguel had just completed building its own plant in Pampanga to produce liquid sugar from low-quality raw sugar. In order to prevent chaotic spot buying and to ensure steady supply, he said, San Miguel preferred to purchase as much of its sugar supply as possible in advance. They would agree on a fixed price with traders as much as one year in advance, and traders had to guarantee that supply. Still, it was a "logistical nightmare" trying to keep every brewery supplied with sugar all the time. That as much as 80 percent of their yearly needs were guaranteed in advance made importation less pressing for San Miguel than it was for some. They preferred to buy Philippine sugar, but there was a limit to how much price advantage they were willing to cede their competitors. If the price of sugar got too high and importation too difficult, they would switch to other fermentables, which would hurt the sugar industry. San Miguel did purchase E *quedan*s and later D *quedan*s, but these could only be purchased in amounts proportional to their exports, and the bureaucracy involved was a headache. It was illegal to use E- and D-sugar for beer produced for domestic consumption. The manager was quite mindful of the clout that San Miguel possessed, both as the nation's largest industrial corporation and as one of the largest consumers of sugar. He made it clear that the company was monitoring the sugar importation debate, and would make its opinions known as its interests demanded. Still, he realized that it was tricky for San Miguel to be a forceful advocate for lowering tariffs on imported sugar since the company itself had lobbied so hard for higher tariffs on imported beer. He faulted the SRA for being blatantly pro-producer and for not sufficiently protecting the interests of consumers. His own solutions to the woes of the industry entailed greater government control—production quotas, fixed districts, and centralized marketing. "If the sugar industry were doing what it was supposed to be doing," he argued, "this importation debate never would have come about."

Nestle, Philippines was a joint venture between the Swiss multinational and San Miguel. As part of the growing ASEAN Nestle consortium, the Philippine subsidiary specialized in the production of breakfast cereals for much of the Southeast Asian market. It was the consortial nature of ASEAN Nestle—the Malaysians specialize in chocolate, the Thais in creamers—that made Nestle so cost conscious of its raw materials. They were particularly disturbed at the way tariffs on raw materials such as sugar slowed the movement of commodities among the ASEAN countries. They bought around 18,000 m.t. of sugar per year from seven major traders. Their assistant vice-president for purchasing expressed puzzlement to me that traders could sell Victorias-refined sugar for a lower price than could the marketing arm of the Victorias mill. He also stated, "It is our [Nestle's] first priority to use local materials; but we must do so within reason. With the tariff in place, we will use local sugar. But in the future, we want the right to use imports if the price is significantly lower. We are looking into the world-market price differential as a way to cut costs." Since most of their purchases were done on a monthly spot basis, they needed the flexibility that came with legal importation. When Nestle needed sugar, and local traders could not supply it, they had to have the right to import it. He admitted that the corporate affairs division of the company was "very interested" in the import debate and was quietly but forcefully making its opinions known to the government.

The manager of the sugar unit of the strategic commodities purchasing department of Coca-Cola, Philippines (another member of "the San Miguel family") also stressed his company's strict quality standards for refined sugar. Every refinery in the Philippines, he said, "knows not to mess with Coke" on quality parameters. Coke purchased 20 percent of all the refined sugar produced in the Philippines, and the unit strictly monitored the performance of the "thirty or so" traders and mills that supplied them and whom they accredited. Coke agreed to a single yearly price in advance so as to insure a steady supply and to avoid the constant haggling over *quedan*s. If the prevailing sugar price declined during the year, the suppliers reaped a bonus; but it was worth it for Coke. Sugar represented about 15 percent of the final cost of their product, with distribution by far the largest contributor to cost. It was quite a difficult job, the manager explained, getting sugar supplies in the right amounts and timing to their many plants. It was largely run according to a linear programming model. "Coke *never* imports sugar," he asserted, although the company's own magazine, *The Bottler* 12, 1, Jan.-Feb. 1993, stated that it "will keep watch on developments in commodities and look for alternative sources." The manager claimed that the company was still very dedicated to domestic producers. He said that Coke steered clear of sugar politics, but did encourage greater efficiency in many subtle ways. When invited, Coke would state its corporate opinion about how to upgrade the sugar industry, but the industry must know that the company would always source from domestic suppliers first. He made that assertion just after telling me how much the company feared having its products boycotted if it came to be perceived as anti-Filipino. Still, if cheap imported sugar did enter the domestic market, and if Coke's competitors availed themselves of it, then Coke might be forced reluctantly to buy imported sugar as well. "We don't think that will happen any time soon. It is more likely that local refiners will themselves be forced to buy imported refined sugar to keep up with domestic demand." In such a scenario, Coke would continue to buy from the local refiners, even though the sugar being sold was imported. This would be better than buying imported refined directly. He related that PSMA had twice asked Coke to support publicly the 100 percent tariff on sugar imports. Coke declined, but it did offer its opinion about the need for Philippine sugar to become more efficient. The manager's personal opinion was that the industry had to become more centrally regulated and planned. There were too many traders, managers, politicians, and inefficient mills. Mills, he argued, needed to become more streamlined, integrated corporations. The entire industry needed to be "rationalized." "Perhaps the Chinese traders buying mills is a positive sign that this will soon happen." Interestingly, he stated that no one involved in purchasing sugar for Coke had any involvement in the sugar industry. "That would be a conflict of interest, and the company would never permit it." Four suppliers provided 60 percent of Coke's sugar, while several suppliers provided less than 1 percent. Some of the latter, he related, were decidedly political. Because of Danding Cojuangco's association with San Miguel (and the possibility that he might be given back the shares that had been confiscated as "ill-gotten gains" of his Marcos association), Coke had to buy from Cojuangco's children who traded. Also, a few congressmen traded, and Coke bought from them as a "gesture of good will." This was "the way we do business in the Philippines."

The Coke manager expressed some discomfort at the end of our interview. He wished he had not told me about buying from politically connected traders. That was common practice in the Philippines, and he had little choice but to follow it, but that I was an American and Coke was an American company might create misunderstanding and embarrassment for the company. He realized that Americans viewed such practices as "corruption," but he wanted to make sure I understood that there was nothing corrupt about it when viewed by Philippine standards. He himself seemed torn between two values, wanting to defend Philippine practices but wishing that what he perceived as American values could be employed in Philippine business.

As mentioned earlier, two companies widely feared by the sugar industry were Del Monte and Dole, large American multinationals that produced canned fruit mostly for export. The manager of corporate purchasing for Del Monte, Philippines talked to me about his business. Del Monte, Philippines was 100 percent American-owned.[12] Since the closing of the company's Hawai'i plant, the Philippines had been the main source for Del Monte's canned pineapple products. Although their plant in Kenya served some of the European market, the Philippine operation was Del Monte's largest. In the previous year Del Monte used 3,600 m.t. of imported sugar (Australian raw, refined in Singapore, bought from a Singaporean trading company), 2,000 m.t. of domestic D-sugar (they had an SRA allocation of 3,000 m.t. but could not obtain that amount from traders), and 1,250 m.t. of B-sugar for its products that were sold in the Philippines. Del Monte was large enough to have its own bonded warehouse in Cagayan de Oro province, Mindanao, near its vast pineapple fields and main processing plant. In addition to sugar, Del Monte used this warehouse to import packaging materials—which many food processors complained were extremely expensive and of poor quality in the Philippines—and a few fruit products such as cherries, kiwi juice, and orange juice. The manager viewed the idea that food manufacturers leaked imported sugar from bonded warehouses into the domestic market as "preposterous." "Del Monte does not *ever* sell sugar. If smuggling exists, then it is most certainly traders doing it." Buying D-sugar is "a pain in the neck." The whole ambiguity about the VAT, the difficulty agreeing on price, and having to deal with so many traders made buying domestic sugar "hardly worth the effort." That, he explained, was why Del Monte did not even meet their SRA allocation for D; they just could not get it in the quantity and at the price they needed. Plus, he stated, Victorias was the only domestic refinery able to meet Del Monte's stringent quality standard. Del Monte was frequently asked to test sugar from other refineries, but so far only Victorias had passed. "It would be great if the BUSCO refinery [in Mindanao] met our standards, but their bacterial content is too high." The landed price of the sugar Del Monte bought from Singapore was, he asserted, definitely cheaper than domestic D-sugar, and "quality is never an issue." The freight and refining component of the cost were hard to calculate exactly since Del Monte only paid a single composite price for the commodity. They placed an order for 1,800 m.t. and received delivery of 126 m.t. every fifteen days.[13] Then they renegotiated the price. If the import price went up, they tried to obtain more D-sugar. He expressed "some concern" about the import bill, but he also said that he "trusts SRA assurance" that the system of selling D-sugar to exporters would be improved. Still, he wanted to know *when* the SRA would authorize imports, what they planned to do about closing the price disparity between D and imports, how they would force producers to sell their D *quedan*s, and how they planned to rationalize the allocation of D *quedan*s to the food exporters. Mostly, he wanted to know how the consumers' voices would be heard in the whole process. "If imports are banned, won't the price of D naturally go up?" It is important to note that the manager was using here a kind of indirectness and politeness not uncommon in Philippine discourse. He *said* that he completely trusted the SRA to manage the new system fairly and well, but he also made it abundantly clear that he was very skeptical in practice. He *said* that he did not oppose the import ban, but he made it abundantly clear that he did.

He admitted that Del Monte—one of the nation's biggest food exporters—was in fact joining PHILFOODEX in fighting the import ban legislation or at least insuring that food exporters were exempted. He explained that Del Monte's industrial relations department lobbied both the legislative and executive branches of government, and that they employed a public relations firm to protect the company's image in the Philippines. (He suggested that the sugar industry attempted to undermine the company's reputation in the press.) Still, "a multinational must be very subtle about political involvement, since we do not want to be perceived as acting like colonialists" (even though most of the managers and lobbyists are Filipinos). Del Monte's importation of sugar had already caused the company to be threatened with a boycott for "not helping the poor families in Negros." Food manufacturing must be cost-competitive or everyone would suffer. "Why restrict sugar importation when everything else is being liberalized? It makes no sense." Del Monte, he asserted, greatly resented the implication that such a law was needed because food exporters were smugglers. "The bonded warehouse system is working fine, so leave it alone." "When the SRA tells Del Monte that the import ban will give the industry the chance to modernize, they are using backwards logic. The sugar producers in the Philippines are very arrogant and selfish. They need a healthy dose of competition to make them more efficient."

I conducted a lengthy interview with both the purchasing manager and the director of industrial relations of Dole, Philippines, another large multinational, 97 percent American owned. This was one of the most frank and detailed interviews I had with any large industrial food processor, perhaps because of the presence of the high-level industrial relations director. The interview lasted nearly three hours, and included two phone calls to obtain price quotes from sugar traders. Only 3 percent of Dole's Philippine-made products were sold domestically; 97 percent were exported. The leading product by far—and the only one that used sugar—was canned pineapple, produced in South Cotabato province, Mindanao. (Dole had subsidiaries that produced bananas, seafoods, and fresh vegetables and flowers.) The Manila office mainly concentrated on accounting, purchasing, and "liaison" with government, other companies, and vendors. Most of the operation was run on-site in South Cotabato. As with Del Monte, only Victorias among the Philippine refineries met Dole's quality standards, though Dole hoped that the far closer BUSCO refinery would soon produce an acceptable product. Dole also planned to test San Carlos' refined sugar.

It was possible, the two Dole officials explained, that some small-time members of PHILFOODEX paid off Customs officials, bought more imported sugar than needed for their products, and sold the surplus to unscrupulous traders. But they doubted that it happened frequently or on a significant scale. Dole and Del Monte would get "absolutely slammed" if they ever leaked sugar into the domestic market. They never sold sugar under any circumstance, they asserted. Dole and other multinationals could not take a high profile in political debates, but Dole was a member in good standing of PHILFOODEX and PCFM, and they strongly supported those organizations' political lobbying to prevent the import ban. Dole and Nestle were the largest members of PHILFOODEX, though their employees were not permitted to become officers or active spokespersons.

In 1988 it was still illegal to import sugar and there was no D allocation yet. Dole, the officials explained, had to use expensive B-sugar in all its export products, which "is just madness." In 1989, beginning with Sugar Order No. 7, the SRA adapted the U.S. model and allowed food exporters to buy domestic sugar at the world-market price (i.e., D-sugar). "As soon as the order came out, Dole applied for an allocation." After a "huge amount of paperwork" and time-consuming verification of the sugar content of all Dole's products from the National Institute of Science and Technology labs (which Dole had to pay for), the SRA awarded Dole a D allocation of 1.35 million kilos of raw sugar. But the traders they used could not come close to obtaining enough Victorias refined sugar to meet Dole's allocation, and Dole was forced to buy a large amount of B-sugar to keep producing canned pineapple. The following year Dole entered an agreement with a private agent to purchase *quedan*s directly from planters, have it refined at Victorias, and then have it shipped to Mindanao. This, they would learn, was not a well-organized operation, and since the actual amount of refined sugar always fell short of the projected amount based on the raw sugar they purchased, the company lost money from the scheme.

"So," they asserted, "you can see that Dole has been trying for quite some time to find a way to save money on its sugar purchases to remain competitive." In 1992, they finally found an excellent solution, one that they wanted to persist into the future: other than the small amount of B-sugar purchased for its domestic products, *all* of the sugar that Dole purchased in that year was imported. They set up a bonded warehouse at their Mindanao plant, and they bought 4,788 m.t. of refined sugar from two different companies, one Australian and one Singaporean (in 1993 they added a Hong Kong subsidiary of a British trading firm). They never had any problem with quality, and the sugar was shipped without difficulty directly to

South Cotabato. Their foreign suppliers never once told them that there was no available sugar "as happens frequently in the Philippines." Unlike the Philippine traders, the foreign firms were "big, efficient, and reliable." Dole purchased on a six-month advance basis for deliveries amounting to about 500 m.t. per month (twenty-four container loads = 504 m.t.). They still had a D allocation from the SRA, but they did not avail themselves of it at all. "It just is not worth the greater effort and higher price." "D-sugar is very puzzling. If the raw sugar is sold at world-market price, then why is the landed cost so much higher than the imports?" Although they admitted that it was hard to tease the different cost components apart, it appeared to them that refining and freighting costs in the Philippines were simply higher than in other countries. "It may be true that the planter receives the world-market price for his D *quedan*s, but then the trader takes a hefty mark-up." The Dole officials knew full well that Dole was entitled to the VAT rebate for its exported products. They had done all the paperwork and submitted VAT claims to the proper agencies going as far back as 1988—and they had "never received a single peso" of VAT rebate! The government claimed to them that it had no money for this, even though it was a company's legal right. The government owed Dole P200 million in VAT rebates, but "multinationals are the last to get paid."

The Dole officials were fairly blunt about the import ban. "If the import ban passes through Congress, Dole will be very angry." Since the company started importing sugar, its export sales had increased, because its products had become more cost-competitive. They asked, "What would be the good of strangling the food exporters to protect the bloated sugar industry that has killed itself by its own incompetence?" Of course, Dole would survive, but the small food exporters would really suffer. "The sugar industry claims that 'no one can make money selling world-market sugar.' But obviously these Australian, Singaporean, and Hong Kong traders are making money doing it." The refinery in Singapore was already world-class, but they were completely refurbishing it again to make it even more efficient. "In the Philippines, no one is even looking at how to solve the problems." "The Philippine producers think that protection is the answer for them, but that just delays their inevitable demise. They need to learn that competition makes you more, not less, efficient. It is basic economics, but Filipinos can't stand it. Whenever the sugar industry feels threatened, they bring up all this sympathy stuff about the plight of the workers, even though they are hardly a good industry insofar as the treatment of workers goes."

While I was speaking with the industrial relations director, the purchasing manager made two phone calls to sugar traders. First he called North Negros Marketing, the trading arm of Victorias Milling. The price quoted was P588 per 50-kilogram bag, which included refining, freighting to South Cotabato, and the VAT. (That price translates to 18.98 cents per pound at the 28.103 pesos to the dollar that pertained on that day, 23 September 1993. The world-market price of *raw* sugar on that day was 9.98 cents per pound). The VAT component of the North Negros quote was P46, so if one subtracts the questionable VAT rebate, the final price would be P542 (or 17.50 cents per pound). Next the manager called SIS Trading in Singapore, and was given a landed price of P485 per 50-kilogram bag (or 15.66 cents per pound). And of course, since Dole had an authorized bonded warehouse, the Singaporean sugar would be duty-free without going through any rebate bureaucracy. Little wonder Dole wanted to keep importing sugar.

I interviewed a senior official of the Shemberg Company, who was also an official with an organization called the Association of Food Industries of which Shemberg was the dominant member. Shemberg is a Cebu-based multinational owned by a single Filipino-Chinese family named Dacay. Shemberg, which owned its own bonded warehouse in Cebu, used sugar to produce jellies, juices, and ice cream pops; but the company's main product was seaweed carageenan (used as an emulsifier), of which it was "the world's biggest" producer. Fully 95 percent of what Shemberg produced in the Philippines was exported. Some members of the owning family were also sugar traders, a fact that stirred up controversy. They did buy some B-sugar for domestic products, but most of the sugar they used they imported because of better quality and price. From 1992–1993, Shemberg imported 2,506 m.t. of sugar. Not surprisingly, in our interview this official tried to clear up many of the "misunderstandings" about Shemberg: (1) Shemberg never leaked imported sugar out of its bonded warehouse. That would be almost impossible to do. The sugar that the company traded was all domestic. It was true, the official admitted, that the senior Mr. Dacay had made his original fortune trading sugar, and allegations of smuggling have haunted him throughout his career. But technical smuggling by leaking sugar out of a closely supervised bonded warehouse would be "too dangerous and not all that profitable." The company did not do it, he insisted. (2) The sugar industry hated Shemberg not because of smuggling, he argued, but because it was the first company to establish a bonded warehouse to import sugar. He maintained that the accusation of smuggling against Shemberg was nothing more than "a public relations ploy" by the sugar industry. (3) PHILFOODEX did not, he insisted, reject Shemberg's application for membership. Shemberg had no interest in joining PHILFOODEX because Shemberg was not willing to pay fees for the *shared* bonded warehouse in Manila that Shemberg would never use. "A company with its own bonded warehouse has little reason to join PHILFOODEX." In addition, he claimed that Shemberg had a lot *more* political connections than PHILFOODEX, so Shemberg certainly did not need to join for that reason. In fact, they had been told by insiders in both the legislative and executive branches that the import ban would not come to a vote in the Senate. A compromise would be reached soon that would allow the food exporters to keep their bonded warehouses. It would likely involve a minor strengthening of tariff protection. Even though Shemberg was a Philippine-owned company with many friends in political office, it never received any VAT rebate from the BIR. The sugar industry in the Philippines "thinks the world revolves around it. They should be worrying about improving price and quality rather than all this politics." "Of course" he stated, "Shemberg would still buy from them if they sold better sugar at better prices."

In another conversation I had, with an executive at a sugar central in Negros, he commented on the fact that in that morning's newspaper (*Manila Times,* 22 Oct. 1993) there was an article announcing that the Victorias Milling Company was issuing a large stock offer to raise capital for the renovation and modernization of its A mill. The executive noted that a few other mills (BUSCO, San Carlos, and Don Pedro) were also beginning to upgrade. He attributed this trend to several factors: (1) the "innovativeness of the Chinese" who were buying mills; (2) the building of refineries that required a more reliable supply of better quality raw sugar; (3) the soon-to-expire Board of Investment tax holiday on sugar mills and refineries; and (4) the impact of the import liberalization. He stated that although no one in the sugar industry *liked* the idea of competition—"it is hard and expensive to have to stay lean and mean all the time"—the atmosphere of competition created by the import liberalization was forcing millers to consider ways of making their operations more efficient. He admitted that the import liberalization had in fact had a positive impact on the industry, but said that the industry would still try to shield itself from competition as much as possible through political action. "The import liberalization has been very good for the industry. But the industry hates it."

An official of a Luzon central told me that the Singaporean refined sugar so popular among food producers comes mostly from heavily subsidized European raw sugar. He was angry that GATT allowed European countries and the United States to continue to subsidize their own domestic sugar, but were pressuring Third World countries to institute free trade. Given that pressure, "one would think that the food producers here would want to buy Filipino sugar just to be patriotic." He faulted food producers for being too small, for having no economy of scale and low labor productivity, and for using sugar as an excuse for their own failures.

A member of the Senate that I interviewed around the same time told me that he thought the import ban would not pass in the Senate. "Senators realize that sugar people have a lot less political clout nowadays." He said he himself would oppose such a ban because it was protectionist and "would send the wrong message" at a time when the Philippines needed to "free up" its economy. He was quoted in a Philippine newspaper as referring to the sugar industry as "a parasite of the people" (*Manila Chronicle,* 25 July 1994).

Politics and the Anthropologist

It is a widespread practice in Philippine political life to pay journalists and scholars to help advance one's agenda. When some high-level leaders of planters' organizations decided amongst themselves that they needed a single "industry leader" to negotiate with government officials and serve as a spokesperson, they did not directly approach the person they had selected (Rafael Coscolluela, the governor of Negros Occidental).[14] Instead, they collected a sum of money—a rather modest sum, actually—and told a prominent newspaper columnist, "We respect your integrity as a writer, but we need this thing to be done." I was told by one industry leader, "You would be surprised at how cheap the press can be." After that original column was published, several other newspaper articles highlighted the sugar industry's search for a supreme leader to guide the upcoming political fight against the food producers and the free-marketeers in government. The final offensive on the governor was orchestrated during a meeting of labor sector leaders, a context in which it would be particularly difficult to refuse. The meeting turned into a brass-tacks negotiating session in which the terms of leadership—in particular, who would be included in the "secretariat" and who would be excluded—would be hammered out over the course of many hours.

It was decided at the same meeting that the import-rationalization bill was still the long-term goal for the industry, but that over the short term it was necessary to ask the president to amend Memorandum Order 95 (the implementing act of Magna Carta for Small Farmers) to include sugar. Governor Coscolluela and his secretariat would invite the secretary of agriculture to a full-day meeting to discuss the condition of the sugar industry and to sway the secretary to become a sugar ally. SRA Administrator Gamboa would not be included because "Sebastian [the Secretary] hates Dodol Gamboa." Bitay Lacson was also originally left off the team because many planters were beginning to doubt his loyalty to the industry's interests. (He was later invited, after a private meeting with Coscolluela in which he gave clear signs that he was willing to cede leadership to Coscolluela and be an advocate for the industry within the executive branch.)

Secretary Roberto S. Sebastian came to Bacolod armed with some "goodies" for the sugar industry. He promised P10 million to support research and development, in particular the SRA micro-propagation lab. He agreed to support a temporary and variable tariff increase for imported sugar, but held his ground against the import-rationalization bill. He said that the bill violated GATT commitments, would greatly displease the IMF, and would never become law so long as NEDA and the Department of Finance opposed it so adamantly. In addition, he rejected the request to include sugar under Memorandum Order 95, stating that sugar planters were not small farmers and that including sugar would therefore violate the spirit of the Magna Carta. Although the meeting was polite and friendly, industry leaders came away feeling that the executive branch was their enemy, and they vowed to continue pressing their claims to Congress.

Frankly, there was a sense in which all these political machinations, meetings, studies, and behind-the-scenes negotiating sessions seemed to me like so much play-acting. Governor Coscolluela, who had a large province to govern, confided to me that he felt the same thing about sugar politics. He laughed about the entire idea that he was now "leader of the industry," and while he recognized that some people took the informal title seriously, he said most people—including himself—knew how temporary and powerless it was. Still, he thought he could use this position as a way of pressuring planters to get on board with aspects of his agenda, such as diversification and better pay for sugar workers. (He was at the time embroiled in a fight with the head of CONFED over the Governor's plan to increase the provincial minimum wage.) He told me that, "If it appears that I am being used, rest assured that I am using it [the position] right back." He said explicitly that he would not spend much time advocating for the import ban, about which he was personally skeptical and which he thought had little chance of being signed by the president.

The posturing, the concern with who is "in" and who is "out," the search for a single supreme leader, and the co-optation of the press, all were theatrical efforts to show the Philippine nation that the sugar industry was still a force to be reckoned with. They would not be mistreated by bureaucrats, food processors, and academics. It seemed as much about nostalgia as about power and principle. Many of the planters who participated in these activities clearly loved what they were doing, and it made them feel important. One went so far as to tell me, "This is a lot more fun than playing golf every day." I would later come to understand that my perception that this activity was "play acting" stemmed more from my own ethnocentric bias than from the on-the-ground reality.

There was also some blunt talk during this period suggesting that the sugar industry desperately needed a political victory of some sort because sugar interests had been embarrassed by a steady sequence of recent political defeats. First had been the industry's failure to prevent passage of the much-hated agrarian reform program (CARP) and to gain an exemption for sugar land as it had under the Marcos-era agrarian reform. Then there was the failure to persuade the government to implement the restitution law. This was followed by import liberalization and the listing of sugar as a commodity to be liberalized. But perhaps the most embarrassing of all, and certainly the most discussed in 1993, was the industry's failure to deliver votes in the 1992 election. Not only had different sectors of the industry supported different candidates for important offices, but it became clear that millers and planters could no longer even command the votes on their own farms and mills. It was widely known, for example, that while most large planters in Negros Occidental supported Cojuangco for president (though some supported Ramos and others Mitra—so much for the vaunted planter unity), the province voted overwhelmingly for Miriam Defensor Santiago, the only native Ilonggo in the race. It was even rumored that the majority of workers on Cojuangco's own farm had voted for Defensor Santiago. One planter who had set up a cooperative and was transferring his land to his workers through CARP believed that his beneficence gave him the moral authority to tell the workers to vote for Ramos. Nonetheless, they voted overwhelmingly for Defensor Santiago. Another planter told me that he had threatened to "remove privileges" from his workers if they did not vote for his chosen candidate for mayor, but they ignored him and voted for a rival. It was widely said in Manila political circles that while there may be ten million voters in sugar-producing provinces, those votes could no longer be "delivered," or even counted on to vote in the perceived interests of the sugar industry. Whereas a planter could once guarantee 100 percent of the votes on his farm (and sometimes even more), in the post-Marcos Philippines even voters who accepted money to vote one way or another might use their secret ballots to vote for the candidates that *they* chose. Planters could no longer simply "report" the results on their farms; votes were now actually counted. One planter explained to me that the industry should use the new voting freedom to gain public relations points. That is, although planters *could* still command the votes of their workers by terrorizing them, planters now choose not to do so, because they had developed a "more mature attitude" toward politics. "We could use this to show that the image of the rich sugar baron is a thing of the past."[15]

An official with the SRA commented to me about the current politics of sugar. He said that the perception that the members of the Negros congressional delegation, for example, were obsessed with sugar issues only served to heighten their reputation for parochialism. On the national scene such a reputation was increasingly likely to mean that these representatives would "not be taken seriously." "They could probably do better at fostering sugar's interests if they developed national reputations as conscientious, intelligent, and broadly interested legislators rather than as front-men for sugar." Again, this perspective suggests that, despite the sugar industry's attempt to cloak itself in the mantle of nationalism, more and more Filipinos had come to view it as self-interested rather than nationalist, and to see its political marginalization as a positive step for Philippine democracy.

The debate over the import ban created some odd alliances that would be familiar to most Americans. Although the sugar industry is regarded as among the most right wing elements in the country, the bill was generally supported by some of the nation's most left wing columnists and academics. Although such leftists had no interest in forming any sort of alliance with the sugar industry, which they generally detest, they do favor protection for the country's raw materials, are ardent economic nationalists, and are mortally opposed to anything favored by the IMF. For them, the entire neo-liberal line being taken by the Ramos administration was nothing more than neo-colonial false consciousness, and so they supported the import ban. This is reminiscent of the alliances forged by Pat Buchanan with U.S. labor unions and anti-free-trade leftists.

It was not only the sugar industry that manipulated the media. Several journalists and columnists were allied with the food processors. While some of these in all likelihood did accept money from PHILFOODEX and like-minded organizations, it was easier for the food processors to find national (as opposed to regional) media willing to advance their cause. Journalists based in Manila were all too willing to position themselves as opposed to the old order by tweaking the sugar industry and advocating more "modern" economic policies. Two Filipino scholars I know agreed to accept grants (for which they did not apply) from the food industry to conduct "studies" of the impact of sugar protectionism on consumers. These studies were then fed to journalists and extensively cited in articles and columns in Manila newspapers.[16] Several members of the sugar industry accused PHILFOODEX of paying off members of Congress, using multinational money, but no one with whom I spoke would confirm or deny those accusations. For although people talk openly about paying journalists and scholars, paying politicians is increasingly viewed as "corruption," and such an admission could hurt that politician's electoral prospects in today's Philippines. Not surprisingly, members of PHILFOODEX frequently accused the sugar industry of paying off both politicians and journalists. Although the topic of political bribery had become quite sensitive, accusations and innuendo about accepting bribes were regularly used to besmirch politicians with opposing views. Several planters told me, for example, that one senator was opposed to the import ban because she was "on the take by PHILFOODEX," and another opposed it because he was having an affair with the first senator.

I was asked more than once, from people in both camps, to produce a "study" that would provide intellectual backing to one side. I was even asked by the director of one major sugar industry organization to write "an official history" of the industry. As much as I had proclaimed my neutrality at every opportunity, I think both the sugar industry and the food processors perceived me as a sympathizer. Certainly people on both sides were my friends as well as my informants, and I suppose they believed that I agreed with their views. I had not attempted to deceive anyone, however, and made it clear to anyone who asked that I would never become a partisan in any of their controversies. And yet, I must admit that being perceived as a "fellow traveler" did enhance my access to various people and events, and perhaps I should have been more forceful and clear about my neutrality. I began to get uncomfortable with all this, however, when scholarly articles I had written about Philippine sugar began to be cited in public speeches and newspaper columns. I took comfort in the fact that the citations were about equally divided between the opposing camps. But as the political and media fight became more and more feverish, I began to worry about my research being used in the very conflict that I was there to analyze. Not that I ever harbored the illusion that an anthropologist could be a fly on the wall, but these debates were becoming *serious,* and intimations of violence were vaguely hinted at from time to time. And, of course, I did want to come as close as possible to the ideal of the dispassionate observer whose presence in no way affects the unfolding events. That ideal seemed ever more elusive as the import bill came closer to a vote in the House.

But the pressure for me to become personally involved would only get worse. In early 1994, the import-rationalization bill passed in the House by a narrow margin, and the debate moved to the Senate where everyone agreed it would be an even tougher sell. Whereas 200 of the 250 members of the House are elected regionally, the twenty-four members of the Senate are all elected at-large.[17] In effect, this means that Senators seldom vote according to regional interests and the majority of them reside permanently in Metro Manila. Hence, there was no such thing as a "sugar bloc" in the Senate. Senator John Osmeña was a free-marketeer opponent of the bill from one of the nation's most prominent political families. He had read an article of mine and had cited it in a speech on the Senate floor to advance his argument that the sugar industry was inefficient not because of government action but because of its own organization. The bill's sponsor—Senator Gloria Macapagal Arroyo—had objected to the conclusion that her rival had drawn from the paper. She contacted a sugar industry leader and set the wheels in motion that would mark the abrupt end of my field research in Negros.

I received a phone call at 7:00 A.M. on a Sunday at the house where I was residing in Bacolod. It was from someone who had been a major informant and a friend. He was a passionate and natural teacher who had frequently instructed me about how the sugar industry worked technically, institutionally, and politically. He was the head of a sugar industry organization, a noted CONFED partisan, and a member of Governor Coscolluela's sugar secretariat. Indeed, he had been one of the people who had orchestrated pressing Coscolluela to become the leader of the industry. Although his tone was friendly, I could easily perceive that something was up. He seemed more serious than was his usual demeanor. He asked if I would meet him at his office in a few hours, and I agreed. When I got to his office, he said "There is a problem with one of your articles. Osmeña has been using it against us. We know that you are a friend of the sugar industry, and we need to ask you to do us a small favor." He explained to me that Senator Macapagal Arroyo had contacted him and asked him whether he could persuade me to go to Manila—at the industry's expense—and testify before a Senate hearing on the import-rationalization bill, "correcting the false impressions" that had been given about the results of my research and my own personal views about the industry. I did not, of course, have to mull over his "offer." I explained to him that, much as I was troubled by the use of my ideas in so charged a political context, it would be entirely inappropriate for a foreign, especially an American, anthropologist to testify before the Philippine Senate. And even if I were inclined to testify—which I was not—the Fulbright Office in Manila would never approve (an assertion that I confirmed by telephone later that day). My friend listened and thought for about a minute. Then he asked, "Then would you be willing to sit at the committee table and consult by passing notes while someone else corrected your views?" I explained that I would like very much to witness the

Senate debate as part of my research. But I would only do so from the public gallery and would in no way participate in the hearing. At that he seemed to be getting a bit perturbed. He did not say anything, but I interpreted his look and his silence to mean: I and "my group" have spent hours with you giving you information, providing hospitality, and becoming your friend. And now when we need you, you are betraying us. When we finally ask you for one small favor to return our hospitality and friendship, you refuse. Or perhaps I interpreted his gaze that way because I did feel a considerable amount of guilt. Although there was no possibility that I could testify—or so my American scholar's ethics told me—this person *was* my friend and had been among the people who made my research possible. I had taken so much from him and his colleagues. I had availed myself of their friendship and hospitality on numerous occasions, and I knew well how Filipinos kept track of reciprocal obligations. I was failing to live up to my *utang na loob*, my "debt of the inner self." I was doing "the right thing," but in so doing I felt selfish, ungrateful, and very foreign.

A few days later, I received a dinner invitation from another friend, an official at the Bacolod office of the SRA. After a nice meal, he diplomatically broached the issue that had been the real reason for the invitation. People in the industry were disappointed in me. They had hoped that I had become more of a friend to the industry, and they did not understand how I could now be "going against them." He handed me a large envelope. In it, he explained, was an article that would be appearing in a Negros newspaper the next day. The article—written by him—was basically a point-by-point discrediting of many of the things that I had written in the offending paper. The gist of the article was that Michael Billig is no "sugar expert"; in fact, he did not really know much about sugar at all. He told me that he actually *agreed* with almost everything I had written about the sugar industry, but that he had little choice but to write the article. He hoped it would not affect our friendship. The next day I read his article in the newspaper, and I did not set foot outside. I felt that Bacolod, my adopted Philippine hometown, had turned its back on me. Or perhaps I had turned my back on it and couldn't stand the thought. And yet, despite all of this, that SRA official and I have remained friends who correspond at least once a year. I will always cherish the wonderfully compassionate letter he sent me while I was being treated for cancer.

Later that week I headed back north to Manila. One weekend day I took the bus to Tagaytay and had lunch at a restaurant overlooking the Taal Volcano. By coincidence, on my way out I ran into two CONFED officials I knew and had interviewed. After a little small talk, one of them excused himself to go to the men's room. The other said to me quietly, "Listen, Mike, I think it would be a good idea for you to stay away from Negros for a while. There are plenty of people there who are pretty mad at you, and you know how some of those planters can be." Although he was not telling me anything I did not already know, hearing it that way sent a chill up my spine. I was not entirely sure whether that had been a sincere warning or an outright threat, but I took it seriously. I spent my last two months of research in Luzon interviewing food processors, millers' association officials, millers, and government officials. I never did return to Bacolod.

In retrospect, my unintended involvement in the industry's political affairs seems almost inevitable, and I learned a great deal from the episode. In the course of my research I had experienced many perspectives, ideas, and actions that had illustrated the highly "personalistic" nature of political life in the Philippines. And still, I had somehow subconsciously expected that this epic struggle between globalism, neo-liberalism, and "free-marketism" on the one hand, and economic nationalism, protectionism, and the old agrarian order on the other was important enough that it would be waged as a battle of lofty, abstract ideals, or at least the conflicting pursuit of direct personal interest. And yet when I beheld all the meetings, the endless internecine leadership struggles, the search for a supreme leader, the studies, the gossip, the "bribes" given to journalists, and the sheer enjoyment the participants seemed to experience in the fight, I wrongly interpreted it all to be more "play acting" than serious political conflict. I wrote in my field notes: "What an absurd system. So much pure politics. So little right and wrong or abstract ideas. It seems all about the fight for money, votes, perks, and privileges. It is wasteful and debilitating, especially considering the seriousness of the issue." I was applying an American standard, and a particularly naive one at that, to a context in which it did not belong; and in so doing I failed to appreciate how my own participation would be perceived and understood. This was politics Philippine-style, and once I began to ask questions and show an interest I was *in*, despite my protestations of disinterested neutrality. Either I was in the PHIL-

FOODEX "group" or I was with the sugar industry. My own personal interests—which I had defined for them as the pursuit of scholarly understanding—were expected to be defined by my choice of "group"; once I made that choice I would be just as obligated as anyone else to serve those interests faithfully. Moreover, I would be expected to consider those on the other side as my enemies and act accordingly, even if that entailed spying on them. This explained why I was frequently asked what such-and-such person on the other side had told me and what strategies I thought they would pursue. At times I was even instructed about what questions I *should* ask particular people on the other side and what information I needed to elicit. It suddenly dawned on me that people believed that my contacts with the other side were in fact in the nature of spying for their side, to which I was obviously loyal. One PHILFOODEX official heard about my rejection of the sugar industry's request that I testify before the Senate, and said to me, "I knew you were on our side all along."

Such a personalistic standard applies not only to actual food processors and sugar producers, but also to journalists, politicians, and even scholars. In fact, during my stay in Negros several planters had attempted to remove the province's most prominent social scientist, a faculty member at the University of St. LaSalle in Bacolod, on the grounds that "why should we be expected to pay to sustain the work of someone who is so obviously against us?" For several consecutive days this scholar was attacked by columnists in the Negros press. And yet, despite everything I had learned, I ethnocentrically expected them to be political in ways that *I* understood; but they expected me to be a scholar in ways that *they* understood. The scholarly ethic of dispassionate outsider was easy to understand in the abstract, and no one ever tried to disabuse me of it; but once the debate got *serious* there could be no question about my loyalty, especially considering the obligations that derived from the hospitality I had been given.

In chapter 1, I explained how the analysis of conflict affords the researcher special opportunities to view "critical points" that aid in the understanding and interpretation of institutions and cultures. It became clear to me from this episode that *personal* conflict serves a similar function in providing the researcher greater insight into the "critical points" of one's own understandings, biases, and psyche. I had tried very hard to remain neutral in the import ban debate in order to maintain access to informants and to foster scholarly objectivity. But in the process of coming to understand that many of my informants found my neutrality unacceptable and expected me to declare my allegiance, I was able to learn much more about them and about my own preconceptions.

The End of the Importation War

In 1927, the great economist Vilfredo Pareto predicted that protectionism would be difficult to fight politically because "If a certain measure A is the cause of the loss of one franc to each of a thousand persons, and of a thousand franc gain to one individual, the latter will expend a great deal of energy, while the former will resist weakly; and it is likely that, in the end, the person who is attempting to secure the thousand francs via A will be successful" (cited in Bhagwati 1988: 72). While supporting Pareto's famous analysis, Bhagwati goes on to assert that if "countervailing power exercised by the export interests that would suffer from protection" (p. 73) could be marshaled, then free-trade (which Bhagwati, of course, considers far more desirable) could win the day. While one may recognize in the import-rationalization debate the outlines of such a scenario, it should also be clear that the alliances and positions are not quite as clear-cut as the rationalist, individualist conception of interests would have it. For one thing, the economists' position fails to account for differentials of power and the way that power is manifested in particular contexts. In the days when the sugar industry could command votes, money, and the attention of politicians, no amount of riling up food exporters could have prevented protectionist legislation from being enacted. But in the current environment, in which neo-liberal policies are being pressed upon the nation (and are being willingly accepted and advocated) and the prevailing ideological tenor is to view sugar as the *sine qua non* of the crumbling pre-modern order, the food exporters have been able to advance their interests, though they command few votes and have few politicians actively associated with their industry.

But the food industry's political success is easy to overestimate, and members of the sugar industry typically do overestimate it. In their *realpolitik* view of the world, the success of import liberalization reflects not just national and global movement toward free-trade and neo-liberal policies, but the effective political tactics of a group of self-interested, Manila-based businesspeople. Just as the food exporters think of the sugar industry as a well-organized, monolithic, and effective political bloc, so too do people in the sugar industry think of PHILFOODEX and its allies as being better organized, better funded, and more powerful than they are. The food exporters have not created or even greatly influenced the current neo-liberal ideology that prevails in Philippine government and business. They have, rather, ridden the crest of that movement and positioned themselves rhetorically as among its worthy beneficiaries. As I will discuss in chapter 6, political action in the contemporary Philippines tends to be weakened by "personalistic groupism," in which organizations that seem to share common interests and purposes break down in squabbles about leadership, strategy, the right to speak on behalf of the industry, and the apportionment of benefits. Early in my research I was astonished to learn how much internal dissension and behind-the-scenes backbiting characterized virtually all political action in the sugar industry, and how much of the discussion was about who shall lead and who was allied with whom rather than defining and pursuing an agenda.

Likewise, PHILFOODEX meetings were typically sparsely attended, and the main topic of discussion almost always gravitated toward the poor performance of the organization's leaders. As "groups" formed around current, former, and prospective "leaders," the jockeying for position among these groups seemed to become more important than what I had expected would be the actual purpose of the organization. Since I was talking with many different people within the organization, I often found that I was expected to be a conduit of accusation and counter-accusation. One person asserted that the real problem was that many of the smaller companies within PHILFOODEX compete with one another in the market, despite their common interests on certain political issues. Another claimed that the problem stemmed from most PHILFOODEX members being "independent entrepreneur types" who preferred to lead rather than to follow. And yet another member claimed that it was due to the Filipino propensity to try to reap the benefits of other peoples' labor (i.e., to free-ride). A PHILFOODEX leader told me that the reason they worked through journalists so much was that it was far easier than organizing and executing grass-roots efforts and large-scale lobbying. He admitted that they were fortunate to have the executive branch on their side, since he was not confident in his organization's ability to sway undecided people about the issues, and he was sure that PHILFOODEX could never match the political strength of the sugar industry.

While I was conducting my research there was a major rift within PHILFOODEX between the moderates, who wanted to restrict the organization's lobbying to issues strictly affecting food *exporters*, and the radicals who wanted to include issues of concern to all food processors, and, in some versions, all consumers. One moderate decried the disruptive effects of "the few uncompromising radicals" in the organization, and that the former president was so much more radical and more publicly visible than the current president. The current vice-president—a self-declared radical whose company produced chocolate powders and confections—said, "If sugar is banned, they'd better also ban sugar-containing products. Why not just ban everything and go back to the horse and buggy? The sugar industry says, 'Yes,' let's ban candy and soft-drinks too. But this just shows the kind of slippery slope that is protectionism." The moderate president cautioned that a compromise being worked out to protect exporters and preserve the bonded warehouse system could be jeopardized if PHILFOODEX upped the ante and made more encompassing demands. He was right, but he was out-voted. Several senators expressed anger when informed that PHILFOODEX was now demanding sugar import liberalization for companies producing food for the *domestic* market. PHILFOODEX was not only playing defense, trying to stop the import ban legislation in order to protect exporters; it was now playing offense by trying to expand import liberalization and "the free market in sugar" to all Philippine companies. Just as the sugar industry used the rhetoric of protecting their poor workers to make its case, PHILFOODEX spokespeople portrayed themselves as the great protectors of the Philippine consumer. The PHILFOODEX vice-president stressed the need to "create a consumer ground swell" against protectionism so as to convince the common consumers that they were paying to subsidize the rich sugar producers. And yet PHILFOODEX was hardly strong enough or well-organized enough to make even a small ripple among consumers. But to underline everyone's overestimation of their opponents' power, the vice-president bemoaned that, "The sugar industry has an official and united stance. Why can't we have one position and act on it as effectively as they do?"

Although there are many people in the sugar industry who still believed that their industry was among the most potent political forces in the nation, they tended not to be those who were active in politics. Their view of sugar politics was based upon old reputation and contemporary bravado. It was the same view that might be held by, say, a typical middle-class professional in Manila who knew only what he or she read or saw in the media. Those actively engaged in sugar politics, however, readily expressed anxiety about the future. Although there was a tendency to idealize the past ("we were once the king-makers . . ."), many acknowledged that the degree of disunity, acrimony, and political ineffectiveness had never been greater in the sugar industry, and that the days in which sugar could dominate government policy and personnel were clearly over (". . . now we are the pawns"). The inability to deliver votes, the lack of money in both absolute and relative terms, the extreme contentiousness both between and within sectors, and that politicians were increasingly wary of being associated with sugar interests, had all led to a demoralization and a feeling of impotence. Moreover, several of the prominent younger leaders of the industry themselves touted neoliberal, free-trade policies and were strong advocates of diversification out of sugar. If one did not know better, one would think they shared more interests with PHILFOODEX members than with large sugar planters.

It is certainly true that in the aftermath of the sugar crisis of the 1970s and 1980s, and the post-Marcos restoration of democracy, the reputation of the sugar industry among most Filipinos was decidedly negative. Although most people still feared the industry's political clout and wealth, these tended to be both exaggerated and despised. The rhetoric of nationalism used by the sugar industry rang hollow with those who viewed the modern history of the nation as being dominated by the self-seeking interest of rich, luxury-besotted landowners in league with exploitative colonial masters. When the sugar industry trumpeted the plight of its workers for political effect, most Filipinos were skeptical, if not outright hostile. The reports in the worldwide media about the starving and oppressed cane workers struck a chord of national embarrassment in many Filipinos. In the minds of most of their countrymen, sugar planters had lost the right to position themselves as protectors of the common Filipino worker. As the president of PHILFOODEX explained it: "The truth is, we may be fighting the fight for the multinational food producers. But we are fighting against the cacique *hacenderos* who have had their way for too long. As a citizen and a consumer, sugar politics represents what is sick about the entire country. The worker treatment, the perpetuation of elites, and the abusive Chinese traders. It's all there. That is why the country is for us."

The Sugar Import Rationalization Act (Senate Bill 1088) never came to a vote in the Senate. The executive branch of the government led by the Department of Finance, the National Economic Development Authority, the Central Bank, and the Office of President made it clear that the president would not sign such a protectionist bill. Although the Department of Agriculture had opposed the import ban, it asked for a temporary increase in the tariff (from 75 to 100 percent) for imported sugar with scheduled yearly reductions.[18] Instead, in early January of 1994 the president issued Executive Order 148 *reducing* the tariff on certain imported goods—including sugar—to 65 percent. Legitimate food exporters continued to be allowed to import sugar duty-free into bonded warehouses. A scholar at a renowned Philippine think tank praised the president for increasingly "making an end run around Congress" to enforce laws, institute new regulations, and liberalize the economy. "Despite the legislative debate on the import ban, the government went right ahead and did what it had originally planned to do without much consultation. The mistake of the sugar industry is that it targeted the legislature for its action when the executive branch held all the chips. And the executive branch listens to Makati." A high official at PSMA told me: "Between independence and martial law, votes were the main currency of Philippine politics, and the planters could command more votes than anyone. But today, capital matters more, and the sugar producers are bit players who will be increasingly ignored in the halls of power. The new sugar bloc consists of bureaucrats and businessmen. In the past, millers thought of the planters as our main constituency. Now we realize that consumers are an even more essential constituency. Planters don't understand the needs of consumers, but we millers have no choice but to satisfy them. Even the SRA must do a better job at balancing the needs of consumers." That same official was quoted in the press as saying that the president's action was in direct violation of the Magna Carta of Small Farmers (*Philippine Star*, 4 Jan. 1994), even though the official knew full well that the sugar industry had never been able to persuade the government to include sugar in that document. Although some people in the sugar industry tried to minimize this defeat or even spin it as a victory, it was clear that once again the sugar "barons" had proven far less potent than their national reputation and their self-image would suggest.

Ironically, much of the importation debate would become moot through the 1990s owing to a combination of weather and increasing Philippine conformity to international trade agreements. The El Niño phenomenon caused severe droughts from 1997 to 1999 that had a debilitating effect on sugar production, and the La Niña torrential rains of the subsequent crop years were equally devastating. Philippine production has fallen significantly short of domestic demand in almost every recent year, and the government has had no choice but to allow large-scale imports, mostly by beverage companies, at the 65 percent tariff rate. In the first six months of 1999, for instance, the Philippines imported 350,000 tons of sugar from Australia, Thailand, and Brazil, all the while continuing to export sugar to the United States to satisfy its quota. Membership in the WTO also entailed a certain minimum level of sugar importation. The Philippines is obligated to import 48,000 tons of sugar at 50 percent tariff under its minimum access volume commitment to the WTO (member countries commit to importing the equivalent of 3 percent of yearly national consumption). Knowing the chronic Philippine problems in research and development, in 1999 the Australian sugar industry volunteered to help produce new cane varietals with better ratooning properties in exchange for an agreement in which Australia would be the exclusive supplier of the Philippine minimum access volume commitment component (*Philippine Headline News*, 24 Sept. 1999). So it would appear that the neo-liberal institutions have triumphed after all. Even though dependence on the IMF officially came to an end in 1997, and the Ramos administration gave way to the Estrada administration in 1998, the import-liberalization policies have continued unabated.

A five-year projection published by the Philippine Sugar Millers' Association claimed that the industry must spend P40 billion—four times the total spent between 1992 and 1997—to improve productivity between 1999 and 2004 in order to avert massive sugar importation to satisfy domestic demand. These projections were based on continued 5 percent annual production declines and 3.4 percent consumption increases, and predicted that the country will have to import P30 billion ($680 million) worth of sugar between 1999 and 2004. The association director cited five reasons for the industry's decline: CARP; trade liberalization; inadequate research and development; the "outmoded sharing system"; and the lack of credit (*Philippine Daily Inquirer*, 25 June 1999). He maintained that the government must "maintain tariff protection for the industry until the industry has modernized."

In 1999, now former congressman and still head of the NFSP Romeo Guanzon was still appealing to the executive branch to roll back the trade liberalization as it applied to sugar, and to increase the tariff rates. Guanzon argued in a letter to Agriculture Secretary William Dar that the Ramos Administration had been wrong to commit the Philippines to such drastic tariff reductions, that other WTO signatory nations had managed to keep their sugar tariffs high. "Other countries which are more cost-efficient in sugar production and, therefore, are more globally competitive, have, unlike the Philippines, committed to a very low percentage of tariff reduction. Thus, there is an influx of cheaper sugar from other countries imported into the Philippines at a lower tariff competing with our local sugar producers at a higher cost, at the prejudice of local sugar producers" (*Balita-L listserve*, 11 Jan. 1999). Guanzon went on to admit that the industry had become inefficient, had a high cost of production, outdated mills, and a "lack of adequate safety nets." But these facts, he argued, militated for higher rather than lower tariffs. As always, he cited the plight of the five million people directly affected by the vicissitudes of the sugar industry. And so, even in the wake of the sinking ship, the sugar industry wants the government to step in and protect its interests. They seem not to realize that they have already lost the importation war.

Rationalization, Groupism, and the Chinese

In this chapter I will employ a manifold, oblique approach to describing the cultures of Philippine sugar in order to "triangulate" on my subject. Early on in my research I was struck by how frequently three words—"rationalization," "group," and "Chinese"—were articulated by individuals in the sugar industry and food-processing industry, and I have come to feel that each of these in its way is capable of shedding powerful insight on how sugar producers think about their worlds and the changes therein. Separate discussions of those three terms will comprise the first sections of this chapter. In the last section I will describe the inner conflicts felt by one particular sugar planter whose "bi-culturalism" afforded him the special ability to view planter life from a comparative perspective and whose interactions with me forced him to voice some things that caused him anxiety and discomfort.

Given my affinity to the ideas of Max Weber, I was quite astonished by the frequent use of the term "rationalization," a term so intimately associated with Weber and so widely debated among social scientists since his death. It became quite clear, however, that this word as used in the Philippines bore little relation to the Weberian ideal types. In fact, it had no precise meaning, or rather, it had highly diverse, even contradictory, meanings. It is a battleground word and a key diagnostic concept, the struggle over which sheds abundant light on the different values and meanings that competing elites attach to the issues facing the sugar industry and the nation's political and economic life. I began to make specific notes about "rationalization" in my field notebooks with the intention of focusing on the different usages of that term in order to explicate some of those competing values and meanings.

My reaction to the word "group," on the other hand, had nothing to do with the diversity or ambiguity of its meaning as I heard it used in the Philippines. Its meaning seemed to me quite consistent, but it was narrower and more specifically referential than the typical American meaning; so much so that at first I could not grasp it. Later on, when sugar planters or food-processing executives talked about "my group," I was immediately able to understand the nuances of the term in its idiosyncratic Filipino sense. While an explication of that meaning does not shed light on specific conflicts or contestations, it does convey a powerful sense of the way many Filipino elites think about collective and individual action, and it provides insight into the institutional stasis that prevails in many sectors of the sugar industry.

While there is still a great deal of animosity toward "Chinese" traders and "Chinese values" within the sugar industry, it is clear that the industry is becoming increasingly dominated by "Chinese" capital and business practices. The Chinese are increasingly held up as the example of *positive* virtues—hard work, thrift, and focus on the bottom line, and the children of planters are more often being encouraged by their parents to major in commerce, start businesses, and "be more like the Chinese." The days in which the ownership of land was the only path to respectability in sugar producing areas are over. As urban industrial, commercial, and financial interests gain power and become culturally dominant, emulation of "the Chinese" becomes the way to success.

Finally, I will discuss one of my key informants who is also one of my best friends in the Philippines. That he is a sugar planter who spent much of his life in America and was particularly interested in helping me understand the views of planters created a classic "double hermeneutic" that proved useful to my own interpretations of planter culture. But at the same time it forced my friend to confront some painful contradictions that he might have been happier not having to confront.

Rationalization

The term "rationalization" implies a process of moving from a current or past "irrational" state or condition to a present or future condition that is more rational, reasonable, and modern. But, of course, the specific content of each of these terms or conditions varies according to one's values, opinions, and (dare I say) interests. For many, the term "rationalization" means that only "economic" factors should be used in making decisions, organizing industries and firms, apportioning property rights, and dealing with customers and suppliers. In this view, there is little or no role for government "interference" in economic matters, traditional forms of organization must be scuttled if they are inefficient, and competition generally results in greater efficiency. For others, rationalization means central planning, in particular government intervention to insure orderly control of supply and demand, to reduce competition, and to apportion profits fairly and equally. In this latter conception, the "free market" is too uncertain, too aggressive, and too advantageous to those able to wield greater power. Between these two positions lie a large number of intermediate ones, all flying the banner of "rationalization." As in previous discussions, it is not always possible to predict in advance the views of an individual based upon his or her sector, status, or wealth. Prior assessments of "interests" do not always gibe with an individual's position on rationalization, and people are frequently inconsistent regarding what the term means in various contexts, and what features do and do not need to be rationalized. Yet again, real life complexity belies *apriorist* simplicity.

The first conflict over rationalization concerns the condition of workers on haciendas. There are those who believe that farm labor must be rationalized in the sense that decisions about who works and for what remuneration must be made on purely economic bases. The majority of planters believe that such an innovation would be cruel, irresponsible, and dishonorable. Labor unions, for their part, are unsure whether such farm rationalization would be a good or a bad thing for the workers. In some ways, this dispute is most illustrative of the conflict of values between ascending urban elites and declining agrarian ones.

The Philippine sugar hacienda is more than just a farm. It is also a village for workers and their families, containing shops, schools, and churches. A significant proportion of workers on a given hacienda had parents and even grandparents who worked there also. Although workers are typically idled and not paid for significant periods of time, including almost everyone for the three-to-five month yearly "dead season" when sugar is not being planted, harvested, nor milled, it is uncommon for a worker to be fired in the sense of being asked to leave the hacienda. Signs of the old paternalistic system still abound: the loans from *hacendero* to workers, the expectation of assistance with education, health care, marriages, and funerals, the authority of the *encargado* (overseer), and the extreme deference with which the *hacendero* is treated when he visits the farm (e.g., Rutten 1982). But this system is breaking down. Few *hacendero*s live on their farms nowadays and many even fear visiting them. In 1992 I persuaded a planter friend of mine to take me to his farm. It was the first time in four years he had been there, because the last time he had been held at gun point for several hours by members of the New People's Army. Labor unions have made inroads among workers, and despite the efforts of the Aquino and Ramos administrations to disband private armies there is a presence of quasi-military armed "guards" (Citizens' Armed Forces Geographical Units, or CAFGUs) on many haciendas. Some planters will admit—very reluctantly—that they have been paying "taxes" for years to the New People's Army in order to "maintain peace and order" on their farms; in other words, to insure that their cane will not be burned, their animals stolen, and their machinery sabotaged.

While many on the left speak of the need to break the remaining vestiges of paternalism and dependency, many on the right—and a surprising number of workers—recall with nostalgia the old system, when benevolent *amo*s (masters) "took care of" child-like *dumaan*s. There are certainly signs of change, but an observer of a hacienda would continue to be struck by the passivity and obsequiousness that characterizes the behavior of the workers toward the planters, and by the way the planters continue to expect such behavior as their due.

An observer would also notice the poverty of the workers and the idleness they experience throughout much of the year. Although there are periods in which most able-bodied workers receive the daily wage—particularly the brief planting and harvesting times—for much of the year sugar needs little attention. Soon after planting a good deal of weeding is required; but weeding is *pakyaw* (or piece rate) work, to which the minimum daily wage does not apply. For this reason, many planters prefer to hire women and children for this drudge work, and pay them a rate that is very low indeed. In 1991 I met a grandmother of seventy-three returning from a full day of weeding for which she made all of P15 (or $0.60 at the time). Her pants were made out of sugar sacks. Planters say that if the minimum wage applied to weeding the task would not be done efficiently, and it would be impossible to spread the work around equitably. It is interesting to hear such "incentivist" reasoning applied to this kind of work because planters so often deny the potency of strict monetary incentive when they discuss their workers' motivations. Typically, planters invoke values such as loyalty and duty to explain some seemingly inexplicable habit of sugarcane workers, other such behaviors are explained by flaws such as laziness and lack of ambition, and still others by monetary incentives. I must admit that my internal reaction to this kind of reasoning ran along the lines of,

"How efficient can your workers be if they are hungry?" Be that as it may, once the cane has reached a critical height, weeding is no longer necessary and idleness sets in until the frenetic cutting season. Workers who have been given plots of land by the *hacenderos* often spend much of this idle time cultivating "their" land.

There are still many sugar planters in the Philippines who are knowledgeable and dedicated farmers. Although most no longer actually live on their farms, these planters spend much time there, know all the workers personally, and are involved in all the day-to-day management decisions. Such farms tend to be the most innovative, productive, diversified, and humane ones. But as stated earlier, the majority of planters might know about the business of selling *quedans* but know astonishingly little about agriculture and make no attempt to stay abreast of new developments. These are most typically the ones who spend little or no time on the farm, delegate all responsibility to *encargados* and *cabos*, have no personal relationships with the workers, and concern themselves only with the expenditures and income of the farm. In some cases, these planters are educated professionals who inherited haciendas but prefer to devote their time and attention to their careers. In other cases, they are people who simply do not like farming and prefer golfing, socializing, and traveling—all supported by profits from the farm. One gets the distinct impression that many of the problems in the farming sector today stem from the fact that so many landowners are "planters" in name only. They are planters because they inherited land rather than because of any interest, competence, or labor of their own. A large number of these planters *agree* that it would be better if sugarcane farming were left to the knowledgeable and engaged farmers, but they assert that CARP and the unencouraging history of attempts at economic diversification make it difficult for them to extricate themselves.

A few planters have talked about and even attempted "rationalization" of their farms. This has led to many acrimonious debates, acts of sabotage, and recriminations. The debates are highly pertinent to and symbolic of the clash between the paternalistic values that have characterized the hacienda for most of its history and the newer capitalist values of entrepreneurship, efficiency, and the "free market." There is an increasingly vocal segment of planters—many of whom take Eduardo "Danding" Cojuangco as their leading light—who argue that in order for sugar farms to be profitable they must be thoroughly rationalized. They must no longer be villages, and planters must be able to hire, fire, and allocate workers according to economic need and market signals. If no work is available, then the planter should be free to not hire anyone. The relationship between planter and worker should be entirely economic: impersonal, businesslike, and predicated on nothing more than work for pay. The workers should have no expectations of loans, schooling, plots of land, gifts, or longstanding commitments from the businessmen-planters. The planters in return should have no expectation of personal or political loyalty from the workers. If a town or a region has a shortage of available work at decent pay, then the workers should relocate and find better circumstances elsewhere. Typically, planters who invoke such farm rationalization espouse the "free market," "free trade," and economic "liberalization."

Cojuangco himself ran for president on a pro-business, rationalization platform, despite having made millions from his government connections as a Marcos crony. During the Marcos years, Cojuangco (whose wife is a Negrense) became one of the largest landholders in Negros. Although he raised fighting cocks, planted tree crops, and experimented with livestock, sugar became the mainstay of his Negros farm. During the Ramos administration, his son Charlie became the mayor of a nearby town.[1] Cojuangco decided to rationalize his farm, partly in an effort to demonstrate to his fellow planters that sugar could still be a profitable business. He built housing and even a school for displaced workers outside of the farm and forced all the workers and their families to relocate. He brought in sugar technologists to choose cane varietals and to plan the planting, growing, and harvesting based upon productivity concerns only. He paid decent wages, but hired and deployed workers only as required for the immediate needs of the farm. On the strength of his enormous land holdings and sugar tonnage he renegotiated his contracts with local mills and even entered into the cane purchase agreement with the Go-owned San Carlos mill on the other side of the island. By all accounts, he did make a good profit several years in a row. But he incurred so much animosity in the process, both from his workers—some of whom were suspected of burning cane fields and destroying standing crops—and his fellow planters, that he finally decided to give up on sugar entirely, to lease out much of his sugar land, to grow bananas and mangos on fewer hectares, and ultimately to offer a voluntary offer for sale on much of his Negros property. In fact, the Cojuangco property is considered one of the CARP program's greatest victories to date. There was a lot of talk among planters about why Cojuangco was getting out of sugar. Some thought that he had simply soured on the crop's prospects, others that he was hurt that Negros had voted against him in his presidential bid, and still others said that the tense relations with the workers was the reason. One planter, however, opined that Cojuangco was angry that his fellow planters had been so critical of his rationalization scheme even though (he thought) such a scheme was so obviously good for their profit margins.

The fact that the displaced workers refused to vote for Cojuangco in his 1992 presidential bid (in which he placed a strong third out of eight candidates) and refused even to vote for his selected local and provincial political candidates should come as no surprise given the circumstances. There were a number of jokes being told about the famous national candidate who could not even deliver the votes of his own workers. Still, many commented that it was rather unprecedented that workers would show such resistance and that this was, if anything, a positive sign of the formation of a more healthy democracy.

If the worker response was predictable, the reaction to the Cojuangco rationalization from the many planters with whom I spoke was more surprising. Certainly, several admired Cojuangco for his attempt and expressed a sort of envy at his ability actually to carry out the plan. Most admitted that they too would certainly be better off in a business sense if rationalization were an acceptable alternative. But most planters condemned Cojuangco and asserted that his incomplete understanding of Negrense values had led him to a rash and ill-conceived strategy that cast shame not only on himself, but also on sugar planters in general. Allowing workers and their families the rights to their own homes, garden plots, and villages on the farms, and insuring that they would have at least some work should they choose to remain, is perceived as a great burden, to be sure, but this is how the system works. It is felt that this is the planters' moral obligation. Several planters said that it would dishonor the memories of their fathers, grandfathers, and great-grandfathers if they would fail to meet their obligations as landowners by treating their workers as strictly economic factors. Since Cojuangco's own family had no real personal history with these workers and their forebears, he cavalierly assumed that this obligation did not apply to him. These planters asserted that Cojuangco had acted heartlessly by not "taking care of" the workers who would surely be incapable of taking care of themselves without the beneficence of a responsible landowner. Although some worried that Cojuangco's inability to deliver workers' votes was a bad omen for the future, most found it understandable that the workers felt no loyalty to such an irresponsible *amo*, and they expressed little sympathy for him.

One planter, a Cojuangco political ally, proudly touted his own farm's "rationalized production strategy," but he explicitly exempted his workers from having anything to do with that strategy. "My workers and the village nearby are totally dependent on me. If I lose money, they are hurt. If I make money, they do OK. I run a highly 'rational' farm, but my relationship with my workers is pretty traditional. What else can I do?" Another planter expressed distanced admiration for Cojuangco, but said, "Our farms could, of course, be much more efficient. But that would require laying off workers and causing social discord. Much of what looks like inefficiency is actually planter benevolence." Only one planter with whom I spoke favored Cojuangco-style rationalization, but he believed that it could only proceed after the planters had their land and dignity restored following the Marcos-Benedicto plunder. Once the Sugar Restitution Law was fully enacted, "let labor be exposed to market forces like any other players in the economy." This planter was strongly opposed to all minimum wage laws. "Labor is already more than 50 percent of our costs, and there is a population explosion on the farms. How can we be expected to take care of them all at higher wages? You can't just look at their money incomes. Remember, we give them free housing and let them grow vegetables from seeds that we give them. Despite their incomes, they are a lot better off than poor urban workers. As it is, we are their sole means of livelihood. The government needs to help us out." He failed to see the irony of advocating a government bailout for planters and pure market forces for workers in the same breath. Another planter blamed the government for making rationalization impossible. "There are squatters on the farms, and worker discipline is terrible. But workers can't be dismissed, and squatters can't be evicted. Any shred of doubt goes to the workers. Only the poor get justice in this country. Management is always subsidiary to employees."

Several planters point with pride to the efforts of planter and government organizations toward the "social amelioration" of sugarcane workers, and they see this as an acceptable substitute for rationalization. SIFI (the Sugar Industry Foundation, Inc.), for example, received (in 1993–1994) a 54-centavo per picul lien from NFSP members and a P2.54 per picul lien from CONFED members, and in return gave grants and assistance to planters' associations—almost all CONFED affiliates, and, according to some, political allies of the "SIFI group"—to set up "livelihood projects." These projects might include assistance with horticulture, fishing, poultry keeping, and (most commonly) piggeries, as well as skill training in construction trades and machine maintenance. The stated purpose is to give workers sufficient skills so that they can leave the farms and become economically independent. Although these projects are generally quite modest in scope—by SIFI's own reckoning they reach less than one percent of potential beneficiaries—they are frequently heralded for public relations purposes. One SIFI document prepared for a sugar technology conference stated, "The sugar industry has answered the challenge to alleviate (sic) our poor—and only we have done this." At another conference I attended, a sugar planter and self-styled labor advocate stated, "More funds for SIFI is the key to uplifting the little people in the sugar industry." One planter praised the livelihood projects and told me, "Only the most poorly educated, underskilled, and lazy ones stay on the farm once they reach adulthood. The ambitious and smart ones all leave to find better opportunities." Not surprisingly, he referred to this process as "rational," and considered it a natural sorting mechanism whereby in every generation only those who deserve the worst or cannot aspire to any better remain on the sugar farms.

One project I observed was Project Dunganon, modeled on Bangladesh's Grameen Bank and sponsored by the Negros Occidental provincial government with seed money from foreign development agencies. It lent small sums of money to groups of poor women entrepreneurs. In addition to government and planter-sponsored projects, many domestic and foreign NGOs and PVOs—some church-sponsored—operate in sugar-producing areas and have had some appreciable impact. Despite the planter rhetoric, one gets the impression that most of them realize that these livelihood projects, while well intentioned, have only scratched the surface of the problem of extreme dependency. Some planters argue that it would be more cost-effective to give cash bonuses rather than to work through such ineffectual and politicized organizations as SIFI, but others counter that "the workers would only fritter the money away." Many planters say up front that these projects must be supported, "if only for the public relations value." NFSW union officials scoff at the projects. They consider them cosmetic attempts intended more to make elites feel less guilty and to forestall significant institutional change than to truly break the bonds of dependency, inequality, and poverty. For the NFSW, only radical land reform, cooperative farming, and diversification will address these endemic problems. But that is not the kind of "rationalization" that planters have in mind.

One persistent theme I heard among planters is that they themselves feel as trapped by the values of dependency and patronage as do the workers who are trapped on their farms. All around them planters see traders, industrialists, and bankers making good profits in an increasingly flourishing economy. But they feel as if participation in such a "rational" system would be dishonorable under the circumstances. As one planter presented it: "Negros is not ready for this rationalization. It is just not our way." The attitude that planters need to take care of their childlike workers may be patronizing, and it may gall us to hear planters compare their burdens with those of their workers, but it is a cultural onus that the planters feel in an immediate and powerful way nonetheless.

Planters tend to deny any personal blame for the poor conditions under which their workers suffer. Many cite "our culture" or "our way of doing things"—forces beyond their own control—as the culprits, while others cite such intangibles as "seasonality," the "shrinking size of the farms," or "the population explosion on the farms." Almost no one sees the least irony in the *need* for their organizations to sponsor livelihood projects. Although planters may feel trapped within the system of dependency, and most of them wish it were otherwise, it is a system that they reproduce, and it is within their collective power to change it. There are, in fact, several planters who became so disgruntled about being *amo*s that they submitted voluntary offers for sales to the Department of Agrarian Reform. Many others have given farm plots, fishing boats, or tools to workers, or have offered them various kinds of profit sharing schemes, all to encourage them to become more independent. One trader-owned mill instituted a milling contract in which the central gets 30 percent of the sugar, the planter 67 percent, and the farm workers 3 percent. One planter told me that his workers like this profit-sharing scheme so much that they get angry whenever he sends his canes to any other mill. The owner of the mill told me that the contract costs him about P25 million per year, but it adds fully 50 percent to the incomes of many workers.[2] This miller had once been ambushed and nearly killed by the NPA, and he believed that "helping the workers helps fight communism." So there are possibilities for agency even within a system that feels oppressive and unalterable. It may not be possible or desirable to "rationalize" their farms the way Cojuangco did, but is that the only alternative to the status quo? If workers were paid better and were afforded greater independence, then there would be less need for "social amelioration" in the sense that this euphemism is currently used. But few planters feel that they can implement such changes unilaterally without being the butt of derision and scorn and without jeopardizing their own livelihoods and their children's patrimonies. One planter even admitted, "In order to maintain a planter's lifestyle, it requires that you starve your workers. The sugar industry can never really uplift the workers since we depend on keeping them at the edge of starvation." To twist the famous Weber-Geertz dictum around: the planters are trapped within a web of dependency and oppression that they themselves have spun.

The use of the "it's our culture" explanation is most interesting of all. In one sense, the planters are right. It *is* their culture, and they did not create it. On the other hand, this usage illustrates the static, even reactionary, implications of such a reified, post hoc, conception of culture. It is a usage that functions as an explanation and excuse for inaction. Former Governor Rafael Coscolluela, for example, frequently castigated planters for waiting around for others—SIFI, provincial and local governments, the church, NGOs—to provide workers with basic human needs. "I can't tell you how many times planters ask local governments to install water pumps on the farms. Why can't the planters themselves provide potable water to their own workers? Such basic needs must be second-nature, but they act as if it were someone else's responsibility."

I was at first surprised at the extent to which those on the left share the planters' pejorative image of the workers as "childlike," dependent, and "incapable of making their own decisions." I have heard the same sorts of descriptions from union officials, radical priests, and NGO workers. The main difference is that many planters think of these attributes as being immutable and inherited, while those on the left believe that they can be changed, if only over a long period of time, by altering the socioeconomic context and the workers' "culture." I had a conversation with one well-known activist priest about the work of a famous Negros artist whose paintings frequently depict sugarcane workers. "He paints them as if they were some sort of Nicaraguan revolutionaries: proud and strong. That's a totally false image. These people are all stooped over, they avert their eyes when they talk to you, and they are afraid to speak their minds. They really are like children in many ways. It will take at least two generations to teach them to stand on their own." Underlying the planters' and the unions' skepticism about "rationalization" is this view of the workers as incapable of existing and prospering without being taken care of by some benign but firm superior power. A Negros congresswoman asked me, "If sugar is so bad for labor, why do they all line up to work on the haciendas? They are afraid of owning their own land and living without wages. They would rebel if forced to accept land reform. On the farm they get retirement pay, health care, education, and plots of land. We provide them with these things. Kids get educated and leave the farm, but many come back to work. Why? Is it their 'culture'? Is it a good life? They get taken care of on the farm." A Negros planter, however, expressed a dissenting view: "I like to develop key people on the farm, to make them knowledgeable and responsible, to keep them motivated, loyal, and thinking. These people really show initiative. Most planters want to keep their workers docile and stupid, and that is not so hard to do. But farm efficiency requires that the workers think. If other planters pirate my workers, I view that as a credit to my system. But most stay on my farm, because I give them a 5 percent profit share and productivity bonuses." At least this view stresses that the docility and dependence that most people view as fixed attributes of workers are actually created and reproduced by the human-made institutions of the sugar industry. And with this realization comes the possibility of change.

The planters are not the only ones who feel trapped between the pursuit of greater efficiency and the need to take care of the dependent workers. The different labor unions that attempt to organize workers on sugar farms also exhibit conflict over the issues of dependency and paternalism. In fact, much of the acrimony among these unions, at least on the ideological level, concerns their respective positions on this issue. The unions for the most part are interested in obtaining a better deal for the workers, one way or another. But is this best achieved by moving forcefully toward greater worker independence and autonomy or by encouraging the planters to do a better job of "taking care of" the workers thereby running the risk of deepening worker dependency? Some unions, best exemplified by NACUSIP, the National Congress of Unions in the Sugar Industry of the Philippines, are often referred to as "yellow" unions by their more radical rivals. Their main strategy consists of negotiating with planters' associations to solidify guarantees of work, housing, job security, wages, and benefits within the hacienda system as it currently exists. For other unions—often called "red" unions and most famously exemplified by NFSW, the National Federation of Sugarcane Workers—the system as it now stands is so thoroughly corrupt, so detrimental to the freedom and dignity of the worker, that the only reasonable strategy is to work for its ultimate demise. This they will accomplish by advocating massive land reform, establishing workers' cooperatives, and proceeding full-throttle on land-to-the-tiller and meaningful livelihood programs. In other words, the days of the "*hacenderos*" are finished, and the union's role is to expedite their demise. It is time that the workers inherit the land, if not the nation. One NFSW spokesperson referred to her union's agenda as advocating for "rationalization," stating, "It is completely irrational that the ones who really know how to farm must take orders from absentee landlords who wouldn't know how to grow sugar if their lives depended on it." Regarding the yellow unions, this same spokesperson said, "They negotiate under the table. They are used by management to oppress workers." Needless to say, the NFSW is thoroughly despised by the majority of planters, who assume (without compelling evidence) that this union is a covert arm of the Communist Party of the Philippines. In the opinion of the "reds," the "yellows" are no more than lackeys of the planters willing to sacrifice the all-important goal of liberation for meager short-term gains. For the "yellows," the "reds" are impractical and dangerous dreamers who, in pursuing their ideological agenda, end up accomplishing nothing at all for the workers they claim to represent. In practice, the NFSW heeds that criticism, moderating its hard-line stance when actually negotiating on behalf of workers. On most of the NFSW-organized farms I visited, the main issues between the union and the owners seemed to be payment of the minimum wage, more equitable allocation of work, keeping *sacadas* out, the provisioning of benefits such as health care and retirement, allowing the workers access to plots of land for their own use, and, of course, collective bargaining agreements.

That the politics of union competition can be both fierce and dangerous is well illustrated by the tragic case of Ed Federico. Federico, a friend and informant of mine, had been an NPA commander during the Marcos years, but had accepted the amnesty during the Aquino administration and later founded DIWA, the Democratic and Independent Workers' Association. During a union conference at the University of the Philippines in 1991 Federico was assassinated, most probably by his former NPA colleagues distressed at his decision to work "within the system" before such a move was officially sanctioned. Some planters told me they thought Federico was killed because DIWA was challenging NFSW, the allies of the NPA.

The use of the term "rationalization" extends far beyond on-the-farm issues. One rather unusual usage concerns the response some producers have to the policy of servicing the U.S. quota despite the inability of the industry to satisfy domestic demand. Some planters told me that the Philippines should "rationalize" its position in the U.S. quota system by concentrating entirely on the domestic market. In most versions, such a move—ostensibly abrogating the country's TRQ share—would have to be accompanied by strict import controls (or "import rationalization") whether by legal stipulation or prohibitive tariffs. In other words, this "rationalization" would involve no exports and no imports. It is rational in the sense that the Philippine people demand sugar, the sugar industry can satisfy that demand, and all other considerations (quotas, markets, international trade commitments, etc.) lead to irrational outcomes beyond the control of the Philippine sugar producers.

When members of PHILFOODEX or officials from the Department of Finance, NEDA, or the Board of Investments use the term "rationalization" in reference to the sugar industry they generally mean "exposing the industry to market forces, making it more competitive." The government officials admit that at least some of this call for forcible exposure to "the market" is inspired by pressure from the IMF or other international agreements and agencies rather than a purely strategic or economic vision. Most of these officials did express resentment at the pressure being brought to bear on the Philippines, especially since they felt the Philippines was being held to a higher standard than the developed countries. But they also expressed firm commitment to the principles of "free trade," export-led growth, attracting foreign capital, and globalization. There was a definite sense of excitement, at times almost a messianic fervor, that after the long period of stagnation, of being the "sick man of Southeast Asia," the Philippines was poised to experience a period of rapid growth and enhanced economic vitality; in other words, to become a NIC (newly industrialized country—a Philippine buzzword in the 1990s). Part of this excitement was the sense that the forces of protectionism and class privilege, often embodied by the image of the "Sugar Barons," were finally being forced to beat a retreat. The days of the feudal lord were over, and it was now time to impose a "rational" economic and political order on the reborn nation. The ideologies espoused by the rural elites were now exposed as nothing but patent self-interest; they had contributed to the poverty of the Philippines and had played into the hands of the old colonial and neo-colonial masters. Now the nation would show that it could compete on an equal footing with any country in the world, and that competition, rather than always resulting in greater Philippine impoverishment and humiliation, could be the very ticket to Philippine success and glory. In this way, the free-marketeers were employing the rhetoric of nationalism to paint their opponents —the "old" agrarian elites—as being anti-national, self-interested, neo-colonial, and "irrational." This globalization-as-nationalism theme should be familiar to Americans who have listened to politicians of various persuasions proclaim the virtues of free trade over the last few decades.

Of course, food processors and food exporters knew full well that they too were arguing their cases out of self-interest. Importing cheap sugar and insuring adequate supplies would help them get a leg up on their competitors, both domestic and foreign. But self-interest, as Adam Smith taught, could lead to "rational" outcomes, and in their view *their* self-interest was consistent with the nation's interest. The self-interests of the sugar producers, on the other hand, were hurting the nation in order to aggrandize a dying "sunset industry." The planters were forcing Philippine consumers to pay excessive prices and were strangling the value-added businesses that were "the wave of the future." For consumers and businesses with high growth potential to be forced to subsidize "indolent slaveholders" was not rational. Sugar planters argued that since other countries protect and subsidize their sugar industries the Philippines must do likewise, but food processors countered that it was more rational for poor countries to avail themselves of that cheaper subsidized sugar in order to manufacture and sell food products more cost effectively. If rich countries wanted to spend their taxpayers' and consumers' money to subsidize rich sugar planters, then Filipino businesses could gain "comparative advantage" by exploiting their folly. In this view, the fact that international sugar competition was unfair provided more rather than less reason to allow the free-market solution to prevail. When pressed about what would become of the some 450,000 sugar workers if such rationalization were to happen, exporters often relied on the term "comparative advantage." If the Philippines had lost its comparative advantage in sugar, then the best, "most natural" thing to do was to diversify out of sugar as soon as possible, and to pursue crops or industries for which the country did possess comparative advantage in the contemporary global order. One businessman employed a 1980s American idiom, telling me that for the sugar industry to survive in the new global order it would have to become "leaner and meaner." Only competition, he said, could make that happen. Another businessman told me that, "High tariffs and protectionism do nothing but perpetuate the inefficiency that currently exists in our sugar industry." Another, "The sugar industry is so protected they are not market oriented. Today we must be competitive or perish." And another, "These sugar planters avoid competition at all costs, and the industry goes to hell."

Allowing the workers to own the land was often cited as one way to facilitate the individual decision-making that underlies the pursuit of comparative advantage. The continued control of the land by politically powerful large-scale landowners was seen as an impediment to comparative advantage and a recipe for stagnation. Small-scale landowners were perceived as being "more flexible" and less committed to perpetuating the old ways of doing business. The planters were wrong in their claim that mass layoffs and starvation would result from a free market in sugar. Rather, food processors argued, rationalization would ultimately benefit and empower the sugar workers. When I asked one processor how long he believed that process would take, he answered, "I'm not sure; maybe a generation or two."

The sugar producers, for their part, also fervently believed that theirs was the way of nationalism. As one planter said, "We have half a million workers, and five million people live in sugar-producing provinces. We produce enough sugar to supply the country. Why can't the food processors be patriotic and buy our sugar? If they insist on importing foreign sugar our workers will go hungry." Although most planters and millers realized that their position was rooted in self-interest, most truly believed that allowing free importation of sugar was irrational madness, and that it represented Philippine capitulation to the power of the IMF, GATT, the foreign multinationals, and the other forces of "liberalization." The planters had lived through the malnutrition, violence, and chaos of the 1980s, and they could not imagine why any of their countrymen—let alone their government—could conceive of policies that were so obviously opposed to proximate Philippine national interests. In their view, they were alone in fighting the good fight for Filipino sovereignty and national pride. Their concern with their own interests in no way undermined this principle of nationalism that most of them felt intensely. One businessman explained to me that, "Consumers have a moral obligation to protect farmers. It is important for our country that we keep growing sugar. Our industries need a local supply of inputs no matter what the prices."

I have previously referred to the sugar industry's use of the workers' interests as a rhetorical device to persuade people of the need for strong protectionism. But, at least in some cases, this need to protect the workers was also a deeply held belief. If sugar prices crashed or if the industry retrenched, many workers *would* suffer terrible deprivation—and no abstract argument about comparative advantage, or it being all for the best in "a generation or two" could persuade them that it was worth the wait. The "smart boys" in Manila with their free trade, globalization, and "fancy economics" had no idea what it was like to witness starvation. Sugar producers frequently cite the ubiquitous comparison that the bureaucrats and the food processors make between Philippine sugar and world-market sugar to illustrate how out of touch these "smart boys" are with the real world of sugar dumping, subsidy, fixed prices, and "competition," a world that always works to the disadvantage of poorer countries.

Virtually no one in the sugar industry believed that it was possible or desirable for the country unilaterally to allow free trade in sugar, to stop the SRA classification system, and to open the gates to imports. The slogan, "Fair competition, not free competition" became something of a cliché during my fieldwork. Although not every industry organization formally supported the import-rationalization (i.e., prevention) bill, virtually every individual wished that it would pass. But a large number of people, especially planters, took their opposition to free trade many steps further and advocated what some (though not Filipinos) would call a "neo-mercantilist" approach (De Soto 1989) and others would call "rent seeking" (Bates 1981; Klitgaard 1990, 1991). Given the way agencies and individuals of the Philippine state had manipulated and exploited the industry only a few years before, I was at first surprised at how many people earnestly hoped that the government would come back in and take a far stronger hand in planning and managing all aspects of the industry. From this perspective, the industry was suffering from far too much freedom, too much market, too many choices, too much competition, and too little organization, clarity, and unity. And the only way to put an end to this chaos was for the government to "rationalize" every facet of the industry in order to *guarantee* that producing sugar remained a profitable enterprise into the foreseeable future. Since sugar planters as a group tend to be as ardently "anti-communist" as any group of people I have ever encountered, I asked several of them whether they thought it contradictory to be advocating a strong central-planning model so soon after the demise of the Soviet experiment. The common response was that the Soviet model had been executed badly and politically, just as had the Marcos-Benedicto sugar "rationalization" scheme. Those bad examples did not necessarily discredit the effective and fair kind of rationalization that could occur in a healthy democracy. As one planter told me, "The market is OK at providing 'normal' profits, but production planning and regulation are needed to insure higher profits." I asked one sugar industry leader who or what agency he proposed to administer the quotas that he advocated. He smiled and said, "I'd be happy to be the one. Otherwise, how about Danding Cojuangco?"

The precise details of what people think this rationalization would mean vary from one person to the next, nor are they always internally consistent or well thought out. Perhaps the most widely cited element people point to is one sometimes advocated even by free-marketeers and moderates: the return to fixed milling districts. Most planters initially supported the movement toward truck hauling, transloading stations, and planters being able to mill their sugar at any central that offered the best deal, but an increasing number had come to oppose the open milling system as being disorderly, cut-throat, and difficult to sustain. Rather than seeing the system as giving greater freedom and greater opportunity for planter control, many complained that mills had used the new system to take advantage of planters by imposing new fees for hauling, storage, and handling, and that it had turned the once cordial planter-miller relationship (!) into a more strictly business one. Some complained that it was difficult to obtain the price information necessary to make open milling work effectively, that mills cut special deals with certain planters, that the planters' associations had proliferated too much, thereby diffusing planter bargaining power. Many asserted that the enormous increase in truck traffic had made living in sugar provinces more stressful. It was commonly asserted that the better mills were too far away, that some planters with easier access were benefiting while those in close proximity to poor mills were suffering, and that at least when everyone had been confined to a single district one had not had to worry about other people gaining advantage at one's expense. The oft-heard assertion that sugar planters hate competition holds pretty much true. Even more so they hate the idea that other planters in other places have advantages that they themselves do not share.

Many millers also decry open milling and want the government to re-impose fixed districts. They complain about having to provide trucking allowances and maintain transloading stations. They grumble about the pressures they are under to induce planters to mill with them, and to provide "incentives" to planters' associations. They protest that they must offer ever-better milling contracts that make it increasingly impossible to invest in mill improvement. At least, they say, if they had a guaranteed and fixed supply of cane they could plan their affairs accordingly. But under the open milling system they find it hard to predict cane supply from one year to the next. The common undercurrent in my conversations with millers about redistricting, however, concerned "civility." Millers frequently stated that relations among millers and between millers and planters had become less congenial and less civil since the advent of open milling. Many of these millers singled out Andoy Go for exacerbating the incivility by being overly aggressive in his pursuit of out-of-district sugarcane and for poisoning the relationships with planters. Some saw these social problems as the inevitable consequence of the combination of open milling and the increase in trader power. One miller said, "The Chinese don't care so much about cultivating personal relationships. Everything is strictly business for them. That is not how we are used to doing things."

Many planters also advocate precise production quotas in order to equilibrate supply with demand, such as were imposed on planters by American colonial authorities in the 1930s. Again, it surprised me to hear so many Filipinos argue that such quotas could be effectuated fairly and without political considerations. The entire modern history of their nation should suggest to them that production quotas, monopsonistic marketing, and fixed prices usually intensify the politicization of the industry and end up working mostly to the benefit of wealthier, politically connected sectors and individuals. But many still argue that it would be completely possible for a democratic government agency such as the SRA to execute these policies equitably if only it were empowered to do so. Of course, many advocate these policies because they believe that *they* would benefit from them. But as urban businesses increasingly define the nation's interests, those sugar elites who believe they would still be able to manipulate and control government sugar policy may be fooling themselves.[3]

Although the SRA is prohibited by statute from purchasing and marketing sugar, many planters would like to see that statute changed. Again, this seemed to me to indicate profound historical amnesia. Only a few years after a government trading monopsony had plundered and nearly destroyed the industry (hence, the statutory proscription), planters' animosity toward traders was so great that many thought it would be an improvement to "rationalize" the sugar trade by giving it over to another government marketing agency. For some planters the word "rationalization" was clearly a code for "get rid of the traders," even if that entailed giving over all marketing functions to the government. Some planters went so far as to suggest that the sugar refineries too should be completely nationalized so that the refined sugar mark-up could be equally shared among all producers. They seemed unfazed by the knowledge that private companies and individuals had invested large sums to construct and maintain these refineries. But that many of the newer refineries had been built with "Chinese" money was clearly a subtext here.

What follows are some of the other views on rationalization that one hears voiced by those within the industry:

- The government must impose standards for mills that include premiums and penalties, and it must provide full-time, round-the-clock SRA supervision of centrals' *bodega*s, weigh stations, and testing labs. Such surveillance would

prohibit sugarless *quedan* scams as well as other common methods of cheating used by mills.
- The government must force mills and traders to offer identical prices, and prices for sugar should be fixed by government fiat rather than allowed to fluctuate according to supply and demand.
- The government must force banks, or, some say, government-owned banks, to start giving ample crop loans again. Some bankers asserted that the crop-loan system needed to be rationalized, in the sense that crop loans should have to "perform" like any other bank loans, and that banks must have the power to foreclose any planter who does not repay. But planters do not share this perspective, and several told me that the government must guarantee the crop loans much as the American CCC does for U.S. producers. One banker stated that, "Self-financing is the only 'rational' strategy for a sugar planter." A planter told me that, "After the way those banks robbed us, they owe us crop loans at low rates."
- The government must pay for extensive research and development in the areas of cane varietals, soil management, and pest control. It is government inaction that has allowed the industry to lose its competitive edge, and the government must take the leading role in regaining that edge.
- The government must make massive improvements in infrastructure, especially roads, ports, shipping, and irrigation. Virtually everyone in the industry decries the severe transportation difficulties and costs they face in getting their products to their destinations, and everyone blames the government.
- The government must provide tax incentives for and duty-free importation of inputs so as to encourage greater investment in both agriculture and milling. The industry is currently being over-taxed and under-supported.
- The government should give subsidies to sugar planters, in emulation of the European model. Some planters understood that most governments that "subsidize" sugar production do so through price guarantees, but many believe that most other countries pay sugar producers outright.

In his speeches, SRA Administrator Gamboa—who knows well the difference between subsidy and price support—frequently obfuscated that difference in an effort to make it seem as if the Philippines was competing against countries that gave direct government payments to sugar producers.

All of these suggestions and more are referred to by different people as examples of "rationalization."

Ironically, many people assert that these and other policies should be enacted because it is the government's fault that the industry had gotten so inefficient and unproductive. It is now the government's responsibility to bail them out, even if only "until we are able to stand on our own two feet again." Once the government helps them out and rehabilitates them, it is said, they will be ready for competition, at some later date. The industry, in this view, desperately needs a break from competition in order to improve itself, and the government owes it to the industry to provide that break. And besides, they assert, if the industry continues on its current course the workers will suffer disproportionately. One planter told me, "We are incapable of rationalizing ourselves. Only the government can do it for us." I heard several people assert in the same sentence both that the SRA was incompetent *and* that it needed to be made stronger. This reminded me of the old joke where one woman in a resort says to another, "The food at this place is terrible." And the other woman replies, "Yes, and the portions are so small."

One trend in the industry that planters do not refer to as "rationalization" is the purchase of mills by traders. Although some apply the term to the hypothetical government-imposed consolidation of planting, milling, and trading, not all consolidation is considered rational. Planters generally believe that trading is the least rational and least productive activity in the industry, and that putting the mills in the service of traders bodes ill for the industry's future. Some planters do applaud the infusion of capital and greater efficiency of the mills, but many view the purchase of mills by traders with trepidation, if not disgust. One sugar-purchasing executive at a large company referred to this trend as, "moving toward a free market with a Sword of Damocles." And yet, for years planters have argued that industry consolidation would be a *positive* step toward the rationalization of the industry. Many cite the Cojuangco-owned Hacienda Luisita in Tarlac as a shining example of a successful, rationalized, integrated operation. But, of course, the planters always assumed that it would be the planters who would be doing the consolidating, and that has become a purely quixotic possibility now that they cannot afford to purchase mills. Thus planters have come to regard consolidation with fear and loathing. It seems even less likely that consolidation might come from the mills, some of which had in the past purchased large tracts of sugar land. The mills have largely had to stop buying land because of CARP and their own liquidity problems.

Andoy Go and his sons frequently referred to their cane purchase experiment and the entire way that they were running the San Carlos mill as moves toward "rationalization." They considered it irrational for the mill not to own 100 percent of the sugar in its own *bodega*, for planters to have the right to refine their raw sugar elsewhere when the mill operated a first-class refinery, and for individuals who spent millions to purchase a mill to be forced to allow planters who do not have any ownership stake in the mill to have equal decision-making authority. The fact that many mill workers were "retrenched" (i.e., fired) when the Gos took over was viewed as a simple business decision—the previous owners had allowed the workforce to become bloated and unproductive, and the new owners were intent on operating according to bottom-line principles only.[4] As one of Mr. Go's sons told me, "Dad is a real free market supporter. Business is business. There is no personal thing in it. That's why he makes planters so nervous. He makes decisions fast, and he sticks with them." Planters in the San Carlos Planters' Association were certainly among those who backed industry rationalization in ways discussed above; but they thoroughly despised the notion of rationalization that Mr. Go held. Which only goes to show that one person's rationalization is another person's road to ruin.

Daniel Lacson in some ways embodied much of the imprecision and ambiguity of the word "rationalization" as it was being used in the mid-1990s. Perhaps that was to be expected given that he is a businessman, banker, politician, diversified farmer, *and* sugar planter, and that he was known as a "progressive" force in the industry. He frequently rebuked those in the sugar industry who stood opposed to globalization and who favored greater protectionism. In one speech he said, "We stand for globalization, efficiency, local control, high-value crops, and new forms of land use. They stand for parochialism, centralization, old crops, and old land use. Some people will be hurt by the new global order, but they must adapt to it. Only the efficient will survive in this new rationalized environment.... The days of the indolent, luxury-minded planters are over. There is still time for us to rationalize if only we achieve unity of purpose." And yet, for all his globalization and free market rhetoric, Lacson constantly railed against the lack of clear planning or coordinated effort among industry "leaders." His 60-30-10 plan, for instance, was meant to be a sort of top-down master plan that would simultaneously make sugar planting more efficient, force diversification into high-value crops (and thereby pursue new comparative advantages), and break the cycle of worker dependency. Unfortunately, almost no one took the plan seriously. Lacson considers himself a supporter of the empowerment of the private sector, yet he fervently believes in the power of government to effect social change. He chided planters for their insularity and fear of competition, yet also for their ineffectiveness at convincing the government to bail the industry out. He praised innovative, individualist entrepreneurs, yet he argued that the sugar industry needed more authority, single-mindedness, and lobbying force. He was a champion of globalization, yet he lobbied the president on behalf of the industry to support the import-rationalization bill. He was a champion of the free market and competition, yet he supported "comprehensive planning" and the return to fixed milling districts. The chairman of CONFED gave a typically respectful but distanced response to Lacson's ideas when he told me, "Bitay has his own ways [wink], and he's a politician; but he can still be a valuable inside player for the industry." Lacson used the word "rationalization" freely and frequently, but it was not clear what exactly he meant by the word except 'to become more efficient,' one way or another. Perhaps such ambiguity comes with the territory of electoral politics. So, perhaps, does Lacson's remarkable ability to present this ambiguity in such a way that it seems entirely consistent and, well, rational.

Without belaboring the point, it seems obvious that these ambiguities and debates about what is rational and what constitutes the process of rationalization have implications for the neo-classical conception of the microfoundations of economic action. If people are "rational maximizers of utility," what exactly does that mean? What is the predictive or retrodictive value of such a seemingly scientific assertion? The word "rational" is so charged with cultural meaning, so impossible to separate from individual and group "interests" and relative positioning, so much a creation of the particulars of historical experience, that the idea of defining it *a priori* and in a way that all parties can agree upon for any given issue or action seems like little more than a Cartesian conceit. If certain practices and actions are to be defined as "rational," must we consider different sorts of practices or actions irrational? If some kinds of industrial organization are the results of the process of "rationalization," must we consider other sorts of organization irrational? And how are we to determine which is which? Although few Filipinos with whom I spoke ever used the words "maximize" or "utility" in their economic senses, I am quite certain that the same point about the need for contextualization and concreteness applies to those ambiguous terms as well.

Just before my first trip to the Philippines I taught an undergraduate course on the anthropology of population. Among the topics covered in this course was the doctrine of "the economic value of children," an attempt to explain both high and low fertility by invoking the neo-classical conception of human action. Rather than viewing high fertility, say, as "traditional," "premodern," "irrational," or the result of poor access to contraception, supporters of this doctrine tend to look for the rational economic reasons that people choose to have many children, for example, child substitution under conditions of high mortality, the need to deploy child labor, or old age security. One evening in Negros I had a fascinating conversation with a group of adult workers on a sugar farm. One of the topics we discussed was childbirth and the very high birth rate among sugarcane workers. When I asked why they thought this was so, I expected to hear about the income that children added to their families or about how children support their aging parents when they can no longer work. Not only did the workers not give these explanations; they denied them when I broached them as possibilities. Instead, the explanations I received were jestful and accompanied by giggles. One worker said, "No lights." Another said, "We like fucking." And yet another said, "What else is there to do?" Each person said that they thought it was probably a bad thing in the long run for them to have so many children, that it detracted rather than added to family income. And yet, this was the way things were on the farm.

What do we make of these workers' responses? Were they pulling my leg? Are they really rational maximizers in disguise, merely unwilling to articulate to me the hidden rationality in their behaviors? Am I to conclude that my prior explanation of their actions was more correct than their own? One problem with the economic conception of what constitutes rational conduct is that it reifies the mythical discrete box of "the economic" and thereby blocks out the other seamless motivations behind individual conduct: boredom ("What else is there to do?"), pleasure ("We like fucking"), bodily desires and needs, joy, emotional satisfaction, mental sustenance, and so many others that language cannot fully or clearly capture. For if economic rationality and economic motivation are really ideal types rather than universal empirical realities, then the nature of those ideal types must be clearly specified rather than taken as obvious, intuitive, or real. I must conclude—as I concluded from my encounters with "rationalization" in the sugar and food-processing industries—that the very notion of a single, unambiguous rationality divorced from cultural, political, economic, and historical context is merely the fantasy of an *apriorist*, "rationalist" philosophic dogma that has unfortunately come to form the foundation of the most prestigious Western social science.

Groupism

I have already asserted a number of times that many people in the sugar industry prefer that the government or some patron-authority take a stronger hand in managing the industry. They believe that when the situation gets dire enough the government will intervene to insure that producer profits are restored. There is a tacit assumption that government regulation, marketing, and quotas would, in fact, serve the interests of the planters and millers rather than the industrial consumers or urban food processors. As my research progressed I became increasingly puzzled by the disjuncture between this assumption and my own conclusions that government management of the industry would not happen in the foreseeable future even in the face of an imminent collapse, and that if it did happen it would generally tilt in favor of the consumers and food processors rather than the planters and millers. Some planters, especially, seemed to be still living in the world of the past, a world in which the government could always be manipulated to serve the sugar industry's interests, or at least the interests of the most powerful sectors and individuals within the industry.

But while there are some who believe that sugar power still reigns supreme, most planters and millers are not so naive. They recognize that their image is tarnished and their political influence is waning. They have seen the glittering skyscrapers of Makati, and know that wealth and power increasingly flow from urban capital. And they surely know that the Philippine state has ceased to be beholden to rural agrarian elites who are no longer capable of delivering money, votes, or even prestige. Yet despite this knowledge and the unencouraging recent history, sugar producers continue to place their faith in the state to protect and serve their interests. The more I pondered and talked to people about this apparent paradox, the more it became clear that this faith in the government was less an active sentiment about the state's ability to manage and protect than about widespread mistrust of other sectors, groups, and individuals within the industry. It was another manifestation of the same set of linked cultural "attributes" that leads to distaste for competition, suspicion of the Chinese, the desire for supreme leaders, and the preference for quotas, fixed districts, and set prices. The problem with the Marcos administration's sugar policies was that they were administered by someone from within the industry (Benedicto), and they empowered others within the industry (Gustilo, the Big Five traders), and these individuals and groups did what most people in the industry would have expected them to do: aggrandize themselves and their "groups" to the disadvantage of all others. If the machinery of the state could only be brought to bear in a fair and objective way, or better yet be put in the hands of someone from one's own group, then the possibility that one would be screwed by someone else in the industry could conceivably be diminished. In a "free market" or an institutional environment with little regulation and oversight, one's success depends upon one's ability to ally oneself with groups that are relatively effective at pressing one's interests aggressively. But since everyone else is doing the same, the chances that one's interests will prevail are slim unless the necessary money and support can be marshaled to exercise real power. And even then, the jockeying for position is difficult, and the successes achieved are likely to be only temporary. Moreover, the groups to which one belongs and with which one is allied are not open to free, individual choice. The choices are highly constrained by kin ties, generational position, personal history, and relative status.

It may at first seem contradictory that this propensity to form common interest "groups"—a propensity that has had some salubrious expression in the stimulation of Philippine "civil society"—

is grounded in the sort of "personalism" and mistrust that has been noted, albeit usually in highly essentialist form, by several commentators on Philippine culture. Perhaps the most infamous of these commentators has been James Fallows, whose "Damaged Culture" article in *The Atlantic Monthly* (1987) is almost universally scorned by Filipino intellectuals in public, but, surprisingly, is frequently praised in private. The article is classic essentialism: there is no real history, no process, no dialectic, and little context. The Philippines *possesses* a "culture that pulls many Filipinos toward their most self-destructive, self-defeating worst" (p. 52), and Fallows contends that this culture has remained relatively stable for quite a long time. His causal arrow moves only one way, from "culture" to poverty, political chaos, and pessimism about the future. ("It seems to me that the prospects for the Philippines are about as dismal as those for, say, South Korea are bright" p. 51.) Fallows focuses on a single cultural attribute. It is not specified as an ideal type but rather is viewed as an essential and static characteristic of the Filipino psyche. While he acknowledges that this attribute has some history behind it—there is brief mention that this culture is in part a legacy of Spanish and American colonialism—there is no sense that it may vary by class, region, age, ethnic association, temporal context, or individual temperament and choice.

And what is this attribute that defines the Philippines' damaged culture? It is "a failure of nationalism," "the war of every man against every man," "draw[ing] the boundaries of decent treatment much more narrowly" (than in Japan), and (in his most famous assertion) "total devotion to those within the circle, total war on those outside" (all quotes on p. 56). He continues, "Because the boundaries of decent treatment are limited to the family or tribe, they exclude at least 90 percent of the people in the country. And because of this fragmentation—this lack of nationalism—people treat each other worse in the Philippines than in any other Asian country I have seen" (pp. 56–57).

As is the case with most essentialist cultural accounts, there are some important grains of truth in Fallows' analysis. Filipinos do tend to be fiercely loyal to their kin groups, which they define bilaterally and very broadly. In many cases, loyalty to regional, ethnolinguistic, or tribal groups is far greater than their sense of loyalty to nation. The concepts of "the Filipino" and Filipino nationhood, after all, only began with the late nineteenth-century *ilustrados* and have not equally permeated all classes, regions, and ethnicities. Some groups (for example, many Muslim "tribes" in Mindanao and Sulu, and "tribal" peoples in the Luzon Cordillera) remain actively hostile to the Philippine nation, and many still regard their primary loyalties to be with more local identities. I often witnessed the Cebuano propensity, for example, to practice the subversive act of singing the "Pambansang Awit" (the national anthem) in Cebuano rather than the authorized Tagalog.[5]

But what Fallows overlooks is that this personalism does not often manifest itself in the "war of every man [sic] against every other man," but rather in the formation of multiple cross-cutting "groups" and loyalties that serve to widen the circle of those inside "the boundaries of decent treatment." These loyalties may be based upon fictive kinship (e.g., *kumpadre*), common youth experiences (e.g., *barkadas*, classmates), common interests or beliefs, political support networks, and even friendship. I have often marveled at the Filipino ability to hone in on mutual relatives, friends, or acquaintances when first meeting complete strangers, even ones from different parts of the country. I even find myself doing this when I first meet Filipinos (it being not too different from the process that my friends and I used to call "Jewish geography"). It may be true that, as Fallows points out, Filipinos do not have as fine-tuned a conscience about littering, honking car horns, or cigarette smoke as, say, the Dutch, but I do not believe this has much to do with their narrow "boundaries of decent treatment." And yet Filipinos themselves constantly decry their own "crab mentality," which is, I think, the most common way that Filipinos express the same cultural attribute that Fallows highlights in his article. The metaphor of the crab mentality is not exactly easy for non-Filipinos to understand. As it is frequently described, Filipinos are like crabs in a large barrel. As soon as one crab starts to climb the inner wall of the barrel in order to escape all the other crabs claw and nip at its legs and pull it back in. In other words, Filipinos hate to see other people getting ahead of themselves. And, as one noted Negros columnist put it, "It is in Negros that the crab mentality is the crabbiest. If there is a double superlative, I might add, the crabbiest of the crabbiest mentality is in the sugar industry" (Sa-onoy column, *Today*, 25 May 1993). One business consultant said, "In the sugar industry even labor, NGOS, SIFI, etcetera, are reduced to petty factionalism, shifting alliances, and constant politicization. This is due to our crab mentality. On one hand, it causes disunity; but on the other, it prevents the rule of dictators and czars." Anthropologists will recognize the crab mentality as a cultural "leveling mechanism."

One manifestation of the Filipino propensity to form groups concerns how they strategize over leadership. And here we come full circle and meet that other ideal type of Filipino cultural analysis: patron-client relations. Groups generally form around single leaders or small, often unstable, groups of leaders. These leaders frequently splinter off from other groups to found their own groups when certain individuals become disgruntled or think that they have become now capable of servicing "clients" with gifts, benefits, and promises of success. Followers come along for the ride because of their assessment of potential gain, or because their wives, cousins, uncles, or in-laws have asked or pressured them to do so. One individual is likely to be a leader or patron in one or more contexts and a subordinate or client in other contexts. Not all individuals, or even all wealthy ones, aspire to be leaders, and not everyone possesses the personal charisma necessary to achieve and maintain leadership.

The concept of "groupism" is an ideal typical construct defined by the frequent formation of groups and the constant jockeying for position both within and between these groups. It can help us to understand many facets of collective action in the sugar industry and in Philippine society in general. To give an example, I had a conversation with a noted politician where the subject of "corruption" came up. He said, "We Filipinos have a different idea of corruption than you Americans. If my group does not benefit from my being in office, then what was the point of running for office in the first place? This is not about me getting rich. I'm not getting rich from this. It's about helping people in my group to get jobs, go to school, get visas; you know, the things they need to have better lives. If you want to call that corrupt, that's your business. I don't; and I think most Filipinos would agree with me." Note that he did not talk about the benefits that would accrue to his constituents or the electorate in general, but rather those that would accrue to his group. And, contrary to Fallows' analysis, the politician did not specify benefits to his family, although that is certainly included under the much broader category of "my group." I think the way the politician spoke would be fully recognizable to most Filipinos. One provincial official told me, "Since the Local Government Code went into effect everyone wants to be a mayor. It used to be that being a congressman was the best way to help one's group, but now the mayors have a lot more power and get a lot more discretionary resources from Manila. But, you know, some local warlords don't like this because mayors are muscling in on their turf." Another man, an NFSP official, said, "We solve the lobbying problem here by putting people from our group into Congress to represent our interests directly. And the other groups do the same. I thinks that's a lot more efficient than the way you do it in the States, don't you?"

Many of the collective action difficulties in the sugar industry may be viewed more clearly under the light of groupism. One of the more problematic aspects of groupism is the tendency for groups to attempt to differentiate themselves by taking positions opposite those of dominant or rival groups, no matter what the principle at stake. That the NFSP views itself as being in opposition to each and every SRA policy or innovation clearly stems from the fact that both the planter and the government representatives on the SRA board have come from the rival federation, CONFED. NFSP President Romeo Guanzon and other NFSP officials frequently referred to the NFSP as "our group" or "my group" when explaining why they were disgruntled about some SRA policy or another. These leaders were usually quite explicit about the extent to which their disgruntlement was caused by personal slight, such as not being invited into the deliberation over or management of the policy, or not receiving any of the spoils. CONFED, for its part, was equally explicit about its desire to marginalize the NFSP (such as when an official told me that Guanzon "has no reason to expect any of the spoils" because he had supported the losing presidential candidate). And, as mentioned earlier, an integral part of one's group at this high level of the nested group hierarchy are the journalists who are willing to do one's bidding and make one's case in the public arena. Virtually every study, every plan, and every strategy document produced by any sugar-industry organization creates an uproar of dissent and a point-counterpoint debate among newspaper columnists. Even my own articles were much praised and much criticized in the papers.

Every time some "sugar council," meeting, or committee is convened, arguments break out about the composition, agenda, and format. Such councils, meetings, or committees frequently end in greater disharmony than when they started. For example, members of the high-level committee convened to study "alternative payment systems" (i.e., the cane purchase) were quite open about their frustration from attempting to bring their report (three times) to various sectors of the industry. "The PSMA (Philippine Sugar Millers Association) did not want us to visit mills affiliated with AIM (Association of Integrated Millers, the other, now-moribund millers' group). The planters viewed it as a millers' initiative. So the study became politicized, and no one took us seriously."

Recall that CONFED itself, to which the majority of planters' associations belong, was founded by a group of planters fed-up with the dictatorial ways of NFSP President Armando Gustilo, the "warlord of North Negros," during the Marcos era. I was astounded in 1993 to read a paid supplement in one of the Negros newspapers entitled "The Legacy of Armando C. Gustilo" (*Today*, 5 July 1993), which, although it admitted that the late president had made "a bad enemy," was considered "brutal" by some, and had been known as "Napoleon of the North," "Leader of the Black Shirt," and "Armalite" (the Philippine version of the M-16 rifle), was gushingly hagiographic: ". . . there could never be another Armin Gustilo but his memories will live forever." "That was Armin Gustilo, a compassionate, understanding, and kind leader who had demonstrated concern for the welfare of his people."[6] I could not confirm with certainty who had paid to run this piece of journalism, but there was evidence that it was sponsored by a CONFED partisan who considered himself the heir to Gustilo, and was often referred to as the "leader of the Gustilo group." He had affiliated with CONFED when the NFSP was taken over by the Guanzon group after the EDSA Revolution. This man had become so much of a gadfly within the CONFED ranks that during my fieldwork the CONFED leaders were discussing ways of marginalizing him and even stripping him of his position within the leadership. He was a particular enemy of the "SIFI group" within CONFED. SIFI was the organization with the ostensible purpose of channeling funds to planters' associations to help them establish "livelihood projects" for workers, and had been a Gustilo patronage front that employed hundreds of workers with no responsibilities. SIFI was making an effort to purge itself of the Gustilo influence, and the current "SIFI group" within CONFED had become major players in planter politics. As a result, the head of the Gustilo group—who himself aspired to become executive director of SIFI—positioned himself as their bitter foe. The newspaper supplement was a strategic effort to bolster his leadership status among a certain group of former Gustilo acolytes and to energize that group to struggle against the SIFI leadership. As discussed earlier, the NFSP also detested the CONFED-associated SIFI group and only allowed its member associations to pay the legally mandated 54-centavo lien to support SIFI's "social amelioration" efforts, rather than the "voluntary" P2.54 lien paid by CONFED associations. At first I found it odd that SIFI, an organization supposedly dedicated to "social amelioration," was the focus of so much political intrigue and animosity, but I soon learned that any kind of organization was fair game to become a "group" (as in 'political player') if its leaders chose to take it in that direction. The nature of the power base does not have to be directly related to the way power is exercised.

The process by which the SIFI group convinced Governor Coscolluela to take over as the "leader of the sugar industry" and became his "secretariat" was fascinating to witness. One SIFI official described it in stark terms:

> Even though most of the SIFI group supported Cojuangco, we knew that the Ramos people had the upper hand. We also knew that this could be political suicide for Lito [Coscolluela]. On June 5th [1993] we met with our media people on the issue of picking a sugar leader. We had five names originally: Joe Marie Montinola [national chair of CONFED]; Dodol Gamboa [SRA administrator]; Roming Guanzon [congressman and NFSP president]; Bernard Trebol [millers' representative on SRA board]; and Buc-An Yulo [former SRA administrator]. We dropped Gamboa straight off. He's too pro-consumer.... Montinola is too ambitious and has a lot of enemies.... Buc-An's star faded after his big Senate loss, and he was funded by trader money. Trebol is a miller and not ready yet to be the leader. Roming is too old, lacks initiative, and works through his henchmen. Besides, he's a *trapo*. We thought about Danding Cojuangco, but that would close more doors than it would open. And he's too pessimistic about sugar. Bitay was not sending the right signals. We didn't know which side he's on. This diversification crusade is anti-sugar. But he is close to the President. We decided to leave him out in the cold and force him to ask us to be a player. Now Lito, he lacks charisma and has no national audience. He is perceived as a Bitay flunky. But he is our highest elected official, and we know him to be a fair player. So we issued the call to him through our columnists.... What really convinced him is when NACUSIP made the official resolution for Lito to be leader of the industry [at a labor

sector meeting]. Even NFSW went along. We knew he couldn't say no to the unions. . . .

His performance has been good so far, as long as he's fed the right information—by us. Of course, we [the SIFI group] became his secretariat to advise, provide information, and do legwork. We use funds from the chairman of the SIFI board's discretionary budget. We know Lito has his own agenda, but we can work with that. . . . He gave us five or six names that he wanted excluded [first on the list was the aforementioned Gustilo protégé], which was no problem. He wants all the emotional people stifled. We told those people, "You want to be invited in, then shut up" . . . Then the fun began. Many people who were not invited started calling the governor. Bitay asked us to a meeting to say that he's not against the industry, that he wants to be a player. We scolded him for creating the image of being against sugar. After Bitay met privately with Lito, he [Bitay] became a valuable Cabinet insider. . . . There is still plenty of opposition to Lito in the industry, and some people just won't toe the line. But he's a good consensus builder.

This account is fascinating on so many levels: the bluntness, the calculations of people's qualities and reputations, the failure to mention the actual issues about which the governor would lead, the characterization of Gamboa as "pro-consumer," the use of labor unions and journalists to do the bidding of planters, the image of Bitay Lacson being "scolded" by the SIFI group, the idea that being "funded by trader money" makes one a potential enemy, and the patent attempt to boost the fortunes of one group through a "leader" not ostensibly affiliated with that group. In the end, the Coscolluela leadership did not last very long; it collapsed after the failure of the import-rationalization bill in the Senate. From the beginning, the NFSP and even CONFED distanced themselves from the SIFI group's bald attempt at self-aggrandizement. Administrator Gamboa, whom the SIFI leaders said "remains a free actor," and whom they characterized as being "obstructive and obnoxious," was not about to appear subservient to Governor Coscolluela and his secretariat where sugar matters were concerned. Only two weeks after I interviewed the SIFI official, a different SIFI official told me, "Right now, there are still too many spokesmen and misinformed loose cannons." A high CONFED official explained to me, "This business of Lito being the leader is just a sham perpetrated by the SIFI group.

Lito is too busy for this. Why has SIFI become a player at all? What ever happened to its livelihood mission? These guys are a bunch of ambitious know-it-alls." A Millers' Association official smiled broadly when I asked about the new leader of the industry, and responded that, "This is the kind of old-fashioned game that some planters still like to play. These are the games they play instead of focusing on their farms. I think millers got over this sort of thing a long time ago. It's pretty silly, isn't it? You'll get used to it after a while." It is not surprising, then, that this attempt at achieving unity was a short-lived failure.

Sugar industry leaders themselves frequently rail about how factionalism and groupism hurt the industry and work against its interests. In one 1992 speech I heard, Bitay Lacson thundered, "Factionalism is killing you. The elections are over, now get on with business." In the question-and-answer session that followed he scolded further: "In this industry everyone is pathologically afraid of being screwed by everyone else. That's why the SRA needs more clout. They need to establish trust." Lito Coscolluela told me that, "The 'groups' in the sugar industry really weaken it. The lack of unity and the crab mentality make it very hard to coordinate or accomplish anything. There is way too much backbiting." SRA Administrator Arsenio Yulo had a similarly negative appraisal: ". . . every planters' association is trying to show every other one that they can be more hard-line and aggressive than the rest. That will backfire every time. I don't know what would make them act together."

In previous sections I have discussed how attempts at establishing planter cooperatives, planter-run mills, and other forms of integrated organizations have met with little success because of leadership struggles. Wealthy planters with large land holdings, for example, are generally quite reluctant to join organizations in which their superior wealth and power do not lead to their being acknowledged as the natural leaders. As an SRA official put it to me, "Wealthy planters won't stand for one man, one vote. They insist that voting on all issues be proportional to hectarage." But those organizations that are dominated by these natural leaders tend not to function as true cooperatives, or in the interests of the majority of *individuals*. In other words, such organizations become typical "groups" within the industry, in which the struggle for leadership and the eternal infighting become more important than the substance. The charters of most planters' associations, for example, specify that voting will take place according to the number of piculs each member mills with that particular central, a principle that always leads to the dominance of the larger, wealthier planters and very often to fissioning and proliferating of the associations when some planters become convinced that the leadership is mainly serving their own or their group's interests rather than those of some other individual or group. This is a criticism that many smaller planters level against, say, the First Farmers central in Negros; and it is also cited as a major reason that Victorias Milling's attempt to establish self-financing planters' cooperatives failed. I witnessed the first board election of a newly established (ultimately failed) planters' cooperative. All sixteen members of the coop were elected to some position, but it was quite clear that the important positions were reserved for the larger planters, who, while using considerable tact, made it manifest that the success of the coop depended upon their good graces.

This principle applies even at higher levels of the group hierarchy. I witnessed an election for the board of SIFI in which it was clear that each planters' association received votes proportional to its production rather than its membership. When it became clear that the aforementioned Gustilo protégé would lose the election he brought up several objections to the by-laws and election procedures, threatened lawsuits, and nearly threw the meeting into chaos. The meeting chair railed, "Why did you not object to the by-laws in the year when *you* were elected to the board?" Not only did the disgruntled protégé stay at the meeting, he even nominated members of his "group" for every single board position. In an interview the following day, the protégé (who is also president of a planters' association) asked me, "Did I put up a gallant fight?" He explained that he thought SIFI had become overly politicized, and he wanted to *de*politicize it and make its projects more equitably distributed. He added, rather ominously, "Everyone in my group feels the same way." He admitted that he resented that "This SIFI group has the ear of the Governor. Lito is good and honest, but he's being manipulated by a bunch of crooks." In discussing Gustilo ("a fine gentleman and a talented politician") he used some of the exact same language that had appeared in the previously discussed newspaper supplement. One month after this interview he was summarily ousted from his leadership position with CONFED and replaced by a member of the SIFI group.

Planters who mill at Victorias must join one of the sanctioned planters' associations. In 1994 there were twelve of them, and so a planter has plenty of choice. A mill manager told me where he thought problems had started: "During martial law there was only one big association. After martial law all the 'groups' were given freedom, and they went wild. Everyone wants to be a big shot. This industry is the very definition of the crab mentality. It's crazy. Fortunately, the milling sector is the most united of all right now, and also the least overtly political. Since the planters can't lead, maybe it's time the millers take over." It often seems that the main adversary of these associations is each other rather than the mill. There are some good reasons for that to be the case. First of all, many of these associations spun off from other extant associations, usually under acrimonious circumstances (several did so to escape the on-going influence of the "Gustilo group" at Victorias). Second, it is no secret that the mill *pays* for the good will of its associations. One Victorias official confided to me that these "subsidies" each year include one million pesos in molasses overages, 650 thousand in sugar overages, four million per contract in signing bonuses, and two million in service fees. He admitted that most of the money goes to the larger planters who control the associations, and in exchange it is expected that the association will "rarely speak ill of the central." More than one planter told me that the main reason for Andoy Go's difficulties with the San Carlos Planters' Association is that, "he [Go] doesn't pay off the Association." Obviously, this practice is not restricted to Victorias; it is virtually universal, and Go was flouting it.

Of course, the very fact that many mills experienced such a proliferation of associations greatly undermined planter bargaining power. One influential planter and high CONFED official who mills with BISCOM in southern Negros told me proudly about the circumstances that led to his founding of PASON (Planters' Association of Southern Negros) out of the larger, more established BIPA (Binalbagan-Isabela Planters' Association). He said the latter had become "corrupt" and dominated by one family (which figures prominently in Berlow 1996). But only a few years later BISCOM had five associations, and the new owner of the mill was practicing a "divide and conquer" strategy, encouraging influential planters to start their own associations based upon their own "groups," and this further undermined planter bargaining power. One member of the BIPA board said that the mill owner was "brilliant" at this strategy and was "able to do just about anything he wants since the associations don't cooperate to press planters' rights." The PASON founder confided that the mill owner frequently begs him to accept low-interest loans from the mill owner as a way for the owner to exercise influence over the planters' association. One planter with whom I spoke joined PASON for a short time and thought that it operated fairly and effectively; but since he was related by marriage to the family that dominated BIPA, he felt considerable pressure to return to that association, which he admitted had become "stagnant and idle." An official at a different mill told me that it was "a mixed blessing" that his mill had only three planters' associations. On the one hand, having only three associations meant spending less time, effort, and money negotiating; on the other hand, planter power was relatively more concentrated in that particular mill.

Lest I give the impression that this propensity toward "groupism" characterizes only the sugar planters, let me say that I witnessed much the same phenomenon among labor unions, traders, and the food processors. There were six competing labor unions attempting to organize sugar workers in Negros alone. They seemed to spend about as much time discrediting each other as they did organizing workers. Similarly, PHILFOODEX competes with the PCFM (Philippine Chamber of Food Manufacturers) and numerous other industry organizations. Several important members of PHILFOODEX would not admit publicly that they were members of that controversial organization, but would acknowledge membership in other, less-confrontational food-producer organizations. A high PHILFOODEX official claimed, "PHILFOODEX is sensitive to this, and tries to keep the smaller companies in the limelight. Filipinos like to support small underdogs, anyway." Within PHILFOODEX there were several competing groups partly organized according to the moderate/radical distinction, but mostly grouped by loyalties to specific leaders. Within only a few months I witnessed the elections of two new PHILFOODEX presidents, both of which appeared more as "palace coups" than orderly transitions.

There were three millers' associations, but two of those had become relatively moribund by 1993. That the PSMA was considered the most effective, peaceful, and well-organized association in the industry was both a cause and an effect of the relative lack of groupism in that sector. Of course, the constituent members of PSMA are not free-standing *individuals* but rather large industrial companies with professional managers, and this militates against the groupism that affects the planters. One PSMA official told me, "Mills hire professionals; they have technical and management savvy. Planters' associations are too political. In the past, they talked farming. Now they talk lawyerese. Maybe it's time the planters step aside and let the millers lead the industry. Actually, I think this is happening by default, since planters have much less wealth and control fewer votes nowadays. Under our new constitutional order, the planters are finished as major power brokers. Up to today, leadership in the sugar industry was perceived as a matter of inheritance. In the milling sector, competence always reigned because we employ professionals. That is the way of the future."

Several traders admitted to me that traders do group together and collude for particular projects and purposes (such as the common ownership of the BUSCO central by the Big Five). But they then went on to assert that trading had become so much more competitive since the fall of Marcos that no single trader or group of traders had the power to fix prices and terms anymore. In the current cutthroat trading environment, someone or some group will always act to undermine any bloc or agreement, and competitors have no choice but to follow the pack. Acts of collusion and groupism, in other words, were constrained by competition and fated to be unstable and fleeting. Planters often give contradictory opinions concerning trader groupism. On one hand, planters decry trader collusion, price fixing, and conspiracy; on the other, they admit that traders compete fiercely with one another and are each others' worst enemies. As one planter asserted, "The Chinese don't work well together with people outside their own families." It is the case that traders have generally remained aloof of traditional sugar politics and had less reason to form groups because they commanded no blocks of votes and had no reason to retain large numbers of loyal acolytes outside of their own enterprises.

Fallows and like-minded essentialists would take the personalism and groupism that characterizes Philippine culture to indicate that the Philippines is a "low-trust society" characterized by "weak civil society." The problem, as they see it, is not the inability to form non-market, non-state groups but rather the paucity of the right kind of groups to accomplish charitable purposes, stimulate civic engagement and nationalist fervor, and become Tocqueville's "crucible of democracy." In this view, hierarchical groups that foster private interests or particular political or economic agendas do not qualify as building blocks of healthy civil society and may, in fact, work at cross-purposes to civil society. Such an *a priori* approach to what is and what is not a good kind civil society is simplistic and devoid of cultural context. It is true that Filipinos tend to form personal interest groups in which jockeying for leadership tends to be the main activity, but it is also true that many Filipinos are active in their children's' schools, that the NGO movement is extraordinarily strong and vibrant, that youth sports organizations are taken seriously and are almost entirely run by volunteers, and that more people participate in religious organizations than in any society I have ever seen. Not only do most Filipinos attend church regularly, but many become involved in the smaller, more focused organizations such as Couples For Christ, El Shaddai, or Opus Dei. The spirit of volunteerism and charity is, in many ways, talked about more openly and ardently than in the United States, and discussions of "values" and "civic responsibility" are rarely met with cynicism or derision. Nonetheless, it does appear that Philippine voluntary organizations, though quite active, rarely transcend class boundaries. For example, the aforementioned Couples For Christ serves middle-class professionals, and El Shaddai serves the impoverished masses. It is obvious too that most NGOs and PVOs are created so that middle-class and wealthy people can become involved in helping their poor countrymen, and that those poor rarely have much of a voice in how they are helped. But none of that detracts from the good work that some of these organizations do or from the civic engagement that they engender. It is the case that many NGOs and PVOs come to act like typical Filipino groups, replete with leadership struggles and the propensity toward fissioning, but the success that many of these organizations have had at promoting their stated agendas and getting people involved is undeniable. The simplistic approach notwithstanding, the contemporary Philippines is a country in which personalism, groupism, and civil society are flourishing side-by-side. They are not mutually exclusive, essential attributes, at least in this particular time and place.

One PHILFOODEX member summarized the dilemma of Philippine groupism well: "There is a lot of free-riding in our organization. We need to get more people really interested in our issues. Some say, 'Make it worth their whiles'; others say, 'They should do it out of commitment.' Some feel that the mission of the organization does not conform to their own particular interests. The key problem is that we are an organization in which members are also competitors with one another. But we need to cooperate to achieve common purposes. We in the Philippines really have not worked out a good method of setting up rules of cooperation between competitive individuals and factions. There doesn't seem to be a group in the country that doesn't have this same problem." The development of institutional forms to facilitate the formation of different kinds of groups is a perpetual work in progress, and different sectors, classes, and categories develop such forms at different rates and in different ways depending on their traditions and interests, and the actions of their individual agents. Whole societies are always imprecise units from which to make generalizations about civil society.[7]

"Chinese"

I admit that the Filipino use of the word "Chinese" resonated with my own Jewishness and knowledge about European Jewry. At one point a planter even referred to two traders he disliked as "real Jews," meaning devious, conniving, dishonest power-brokers, although he admitted that I was the first actual Jew he had ever met. Much of what Filipinos say about "the Chinese" sounds to me vaguely familiar—the outsider pariah group that had succeeded economically, but only by exploiting the disadvantaged and vulnerable majority. "The Chinese" are typically spoken of as an ethnically pure, conspiratorial cabal who make money by out-maneuvering the naive, trusting Filipino. They dominate retail sales and the trading sectors of many industries, including sugar, and are thought to act in concert to fix prices to the detriment of the "Filipino" planters, many of whose grandparents or great-grandparents were Chinese mestizos.

That many mills have been purchased by traders in the last decade has caused anguish among planters who perceive the balance of sectoral power shifting away from the planters to the traders, and the industry becoming increasingly dominated by the Chinese who, they say, have no sense of the "traditions and values" of the sugar industry. And yet, there is a growing sense that at least some of the entrepreneurial and managerial ways of "the Chinese trader" have won the day in the Philippines, and that these ways are the wave of the future. The prevailing image has shifted from the modest but tough, tee-shirt wearing, small-scale trader with a deceptively crude storefront to the urban, well-connected tycoon who runs a global enterprise, albeit a family-dominated one. Increasingly one hears such phrases as, "We need to be more like the Chinese," or that the Chinese "had it right all along," and one sees the children of sugar planters being encouraged by their parents to pursue careers in business, commerce, banking, and industry. With the growth of "Chinese" economic power has come greater social respectability. At one time such terms as "trader" and "commerce" were seen as déclassé, and land was the *sine qua non* of acceptable status. But now that planters are no longer quite so rich and powerful, the line between the Chinese and the Filipino is becoming ever-more blurred as the former becomes the reference group for the latter.[8]

Of course, the Philippine sugar industry is not unique in this regard. Commercial activity is largely a Chinese affair in many Southeast Asian nations, and this fact has spawned a substantial descriptive and explanatory literature (e.g., Wickberg 1965; McBeath 1973; Omohundro 1981; Cheong 1983; Tan 1984; Cariño 1998; Mackie 1992, 1998; Szanton 1998). Curiously, many Filipinos echo the culturological school in asserting that there is some aspect of Filipino culture that makes Filipinos constitutionally averse to commerce, sales, and marketing. The Chinese, on the other hand, are said to be naturally good at commerce.[9] A related "explanation" is that Chinese learn to live frugally, to plough profits back into their businesses, to plan more for the long-term, and to sacrifice profit today for market share in the future; Filipinos, on the other hand, are said to want to spend as soon as they earn, or even before. Others dismiss such cultural explanations and focus instead on the reputed ease with which Chinese can obtain credit from "Chinese banks" while Filipinos need collateral. The "clannish" Chinese are said to "take care of their own" by facilitating contacts, allowing easy credit, and doing special favors for wide networks of kin. Still others counter that it is not merely being Chinese that makes one a good credit risk, but rather a solid history of timely repayment, which most Chinese pride themselves in maintaining. But even some of these people admit that being Chinese can help in initially establishing a credit history and that personal contacts are essential if one wants to get started in business, especially one such as sugar trading that requires a good deal of cash up front. Some believe that Chinese traders conspire to drive non-Chinese out of business, but others assert that competition among Chinese traders is far fiercer than that between Chinese and non-Chinese.

One fascinating recent development regarding the position of the Chinese further supports my point about the rise of the industrial and commercial classes at the expense of the landed elites. In

Negros, only a few years back, sugar planters were the most highly respected segment of society, and it was not considered respectable to enter other businesses or professions. Chinese were rarely seen in organizations such as Rotary Clubs, and commercial activities were not respectable. If Chinese were "clannish" it was because they were not fully accepted by the dominant class, although a few became wealthy enough to achieve respect in the typical Negros way: by buying sugar land. After the crisis of the 1980s, however, this state of affairs changed dramatically. While planters were going broke, many traders and businessmen were prospering. Today, the young scions of the planter class are pursuing higher education, entering professions, and priding themselves on their entrepreneurial drive (Billig 1994). Many say that those who continue to rely on sugar planting as their sole source of income are no longer respected, and that the disciplined, savvy, risk-taking Chinese businessman should serve as a model for upwardly-mobile Filipinos.

While there is still plenty of hostility toward the Chinese, and many planters decry the growth of trader power in the sugar industry, most planters admit that the "values" they associate with the Chinese—frugality, "rationality," and hard work—are winning the day, for better or for worse. One milling executive explained why he felt this trend should not worry people in the sugar industry: "Most of the Chinese who are buying mills are becoming real millers. They are learning how to be professional managers, and are doing a better job of it than most of the previous owners. We could use a healthy dose of the efficient thinking they bring, and, God knows, we could use their money." As is true of most sectors of Philippine society, the line between "Chinese" and "Filipino" in the sugar industry becomes more blurred each generation as so many of the descendents of Chinese immigrants intermarry, convert to Catholicism, and never learn to speak the language of their ancestors. So as "the Chinese" gain power and respectability, their distinctive identity changes, assimilates, and becomes increasingly unrecognizable to those who know only the old ways and attitudes.

The "American" Planter

One of my most interesting and important informants was more able than most to articulate for me many of the cultural attributes of sugar planters. The reason for his insights was that he himself had spent much of his youth in the United States, and he brought a comparative perspective to bear on his fellow planters. While his bi-culturalism certainly helped me in my research, I often felt that it was a mixed blessing for him. There were many instances in which he seemed torn and pained over aspects of his life and the way he was expected to live it. Many of the taken-for-granted things that are the day-by-day stuff of culture he could not take for granted and instead regarded with a distanced skepticism, and sometimes disdain. He seemed to feel powerless and constrained in ways that other planters rarely did. I often felt guilty that my presence and his ardent desire to help me understand his life—one American to another—forced him to more deeply confront practices and ideas that made him uncomfortable about his own way of life. And, of course, I learned much from his discomfort.

This man is a member of two prominent Negros families, and he spent his early childhood in Negros. When he was a teenager, his father, a physician, moved the family to the suburbs of a large Midwestern U.S. city. He graduated from an American high school and then attended a well-known Jesuit university from which he graduated as a political science major. After college he returned to the Philippines and married a Negrense woman from two sugar families even more prominent than his own. Because she was a sole heiress, they inherited several large holdings of sugar land and an enormous house in Bacolod—my friend became a sugar planter. He and his wife have five children, a household of fourteen servants, seven vehicles, a lovely vacation retreat at the base of Mount Canlaon, and a condominium apartment in Manila. His wife opened a boutique that sold women's clothing that she designed herself. They visit the United States occasionally but can no longer afford to bring the entire family. I suspect that his semi-retired father pays for most of these trips. My friend is proud of his American "roots," and he often manifests that pride by disparaging the Philippines and things Filipino, at least to me. He thinks of himself as being more cosmopolitan than most of his fellow planters and fellow Negrenses.

My planter friend knows little about sugar agriculture and does not care a great deal about it. He seldom visits his sugar farms (which are mainly in southern Negros), but he does spend a fair bit of time at his one property (in northern Negros) where he keeps his fighting cocks. Breeding and raising cocks is one of his main avocations, though by Negros standards he is a small-time cock raiser. Sometimes I get the sense that his affinity for the sport is more a way to bond with his uncle—with whom he is very close and who is a major figure in Philippine cockfighting—than a true passion. He does not spend a great deal of time watching cockfighting.[10] He spends some time every week working out his payroll, which he transmits to his workers through the farm supervisors (*encargado*s) that he employs. He frequently makes phone calls to traders in order to sell *quedan*s, and he took me to several *quedan* auctions. He enjoys the wheeling-and-dealing aspect of *quedan* ownership, and is, for that reason, an opponent of the cane purchase. He plays golf (at his country club), swims, and was the provincial head of a national youth soccer league. He is extremely active in his Rotary Club and even rose to the rank of District Governor for the Western Visayas and western Mindanao.

Nevertheless, he frequently appears to be unsatisfied with the ways he spends his time. In fact, it would be fair to say that he found the planter's life to be unfulfilling and morally bankrupt, though he would never say so quite that openly. He felt that he was making a living—a rather good living—without really *working* for it, and this rankled him. For a time he took law school courses in search of "a real profession." He obtained a real estate license with the intention of becoming a broker. He devised a scheme to build and rent low-cost housing. He tried to sell securities. He has been involved in numerous business schemes, none of which took off. He loves the idea of entrepreneurism, but he has little knowledge or experience of starting a business, and he dislikes the idea of going too far into debt. He is partly proud, but partly embarrassed, about the success of his wife's business and the discipline and determination that she brings to bear on it. He seems to be perpetually seeking a career or a purpose befitting a person of his economic standing, lifestyle, and level of education. Since he *was* (and still is) a sugar planter, at one point he decided to try to become more involved in agriculture, but that bored him very quickly. His involvement in Rotary and the soccer league were both highly satisfying, but such activities were not substitutes for a productive career. Although these were time-consuming activities that precluded him from doing much else, they were not the answers that he was seeking. He frequently conveyed the sense that he himself thought that he was cheating his way through life, and he found this very disturbing. He considered selling much of his land to start a business, and indeed he did lease the majority of it at one point, but his wife would not permit the sale of her family legacy, and he could not find any buyers willing to pay anywhere near what he felt the land was worth (owing to CARP, at least in his account to me). He considered moving his whole family to the United States, but was understandably afraid of the uncertainty that such a move would entail. One way or another, he was stuck being a sugar planter, but now the trick was finding a real "grown-up" way to occupy his time and attention.

Although he had been a political science major, his political affinities were largely defined by the "groups" to which he belonged, and they were largely defined by his extensive and cross-cutting family connections. Once again, both he and his wife belonged to several prominent families—they were related in some way to most of the notables in Negros sugar—and my friend could not afford the luxury of allowing abstract principles and ideas to take precedence over family ties. At one point he and his wife each had to campaign for different candidates for governor because their consanguineal connections had to trump their affinal ones. I frequently got the sense that being politically defined by his family loyalties drove him quite crazy, and he was an avid fan of American politics which he followed much the same way he did American baseball and basketball. He watched CNN religiously, read several American news magazines, and loved discussing American politics with me. On the American scene, he expressed clear ideological preferences, which he would almost never do about Philippine politics. The planters' associations to which he belonged were chosen entirely based upon family connections, and he always voted for association leaders in predictable ways. He frequently was called upon to campaign for one relative or another. This was an activity he seemed to detest, but what could he do?

One moment of real tension between us occurred when I probed a bit too hard about some of his more notorious relatives. One branch of his wife's family was known as the "warlords of the south," and my friend was rather touchy about that. Even more sensitive was his relationship to his uncle, the infamous former sugar-czar and Marcos crony, Roberto S. Benedicto. My friend told me, almost jokingly, about how while in college he would receive large sums of money from his uncle to come home to the Philippines for vacations. He would fly first-class, be met by a limo at the Hong Kong airport, have a spree (shopping and otherwise), then fly to the Philippines where he would be met by another limo in Manila. It was obvious to me that my friend was pained by the widespread talk about the evil things that Benedicto had done—the court cases, the hard feelings. This was during the period when Benedicto, "RSB," was negotiating restitution and return to the Philippines. In a casual conversation I asked him what *he* thought of what had happened to the sugar industry during the Marcos period. He became visibly upset: "Look, I know you want me to say something negative about RSB, but I won't. I never will. He is a great person, and there are a lot of lies being spread about him. But I am not going to repeat any of them. And I am definitely not going to listen to any of them. He is not a thief; he helped a lot of people; he was good for sugar and the province. What kind of person would I be if I said bad things about my relative? A lot of bad stuff happened during Marcos. Why not blame Marcos and Imelda and leave it at that?" That other relatives of his were among those who disparaged—and were swindled by—Benedicto was inevitable given the intricate, complex webs of Negros kinship. Some of those same relatives could suggest to my friend that Benedicto was indeed a thief, and one even did so in my presence. ("Face it, RSB is a brutal and corrupt bastard, and he deserves whatever is coming to him.") But the subject was simply too embarrassing for my friend to discuss with me, and we never did so again.

When I first met my friend in January 1990, he was not particularly religious, considerably less so than his wife. By 1994, however, he had become something of religious seeker. He had attended several meetings of Opus Dei with a relative, but he found them too dour. He began attending Couples for Christ meetings to satisfy his wife's desire that he do so, but then found himself increasingly enamored of the message and the people. Many of his relatives were becoming active in Couples for Christ, and one even rose to prominence in the national organization. My friend tried to convey to me that he did not really take the singing, the praying, and the hierarchy all that seriously—I was, after all, in some way, a like-minded secular American—but it was clear to me from his words and actions, as well as those of his friends that I knew, that he was gaining a greater sense of purpose and belonging from his new religious engagement. I felt bad that he was sheepish about admitting this on my account.

I had several conversations with my friend about his servants and his workers. Although much of what he had to say might have been said by any American liberal, these "progressive" sentiments were frequently tinged with paternalism, even disdain. He seemed mostly unaware of the contradictions in his views. "These people really are more like children than you think," he once said. "If I don't tell them who to vote for, how will they know?" said the former political science major. "I have so many responsibilities to take care of my people. What would happen to them if I sold out? . . . These people in my household, I can't fire any of them. I pay for their school and other expenses, and some of them have been with this family since I was a boy. It used to be a lot cheaper to maintain a large household, but now these people all make decent wages." Although he admitted that he did not know much about farming, he once said, "If these people owned the land, if I was not here, how would they support themselves?" He was one of those planters who expressed a fervent wish to be able to "rationalize" his farm the way Danding Cojuangco, whom he greatly admired, had tried to, but who also criticized Cojuangco for acting dishonorably and failing to "take care of his people." He was also one of those planters who frequently attempted to use me to provide them with information, to convey messages to certain people, and to have me act as an intermediary because of the contacts that my research had opened up to me. Sometimes these requests would be so subtle that at first I did not really understand them. Other times they would be quite frank ("Ask ___ when he plans to pay me").

On a few occasions my friend accompanied me to interviews, mostly to meet people to whom he was introducing me. Perhaps the two most memorable such interviews were with a labor leader and a milling executive. The labor leader was Ed Federico, the founder of DIWA, who would be assassinated only four months later. Since Federico was a former NPA guerilla who was now involved in organizing sugar workers, my friend anticipated that he would feel hostility or even hatred toward Federico. However, Federico was extremely gracious, and he and my friend got along well. Federico spoke eloquently about egalitarianism, empowerment, and democracy, all sentiments with which my friend strongly agreed, at least in the abstract. My friend appeared to be extremely disconcerted to find himself coming away from the meeting so favorably impressed by someone he had, going into the meeting, regarded as a class enemy. He was truly moved and disturbed when he heard about Federico's murder.

The miller was an executive at a large central to which my friend never sent his own cane. My friend came away impressed at how "businesslike" and "rational" was the operation of the central, and how technically knowledgeable and competent was the executive. These attributes seemed to defy his stereotype of millers, and it made him think, "planters really have a lot to learn about modern business." My friend greatly enjoyed "talking the talk" of business, and this made him regretful about missed opportunities and his own lack of initiative.

My friend enjoys having me around in many ways. He loves to talk with an American of his own age about New York City, American sports and politics, and fatherhood (we have daughters almost exactly the same age). We are truly dear friends. But there is no doubt that my presence forces him to confront many of the self-contradictions that remain safely in the background when I am not there. His egalitarian ideology coupled with his paternalistic reality; his sense of his own cosmopolitanism coupled with the self-perceived provinciality of his life; his wealth coupled with his self-perceived idleness; his love of cockfighting coupled with his attitude that the sport is barbaric; his admiration for swaggering, "tough-guy," macho planters coupled with his own gentleness and generosity; these and many more are contradictions that he cannot articulate well, but that obviously cause him anxiety exacerbated by my presence and his desire to help me understand. My friend was interpreting sugar planter culture, but he was also trying very hard to understand it for himself so that he might live in it comfortably. His knowledge of one particular alternative that he greatly admired was not making that process any easier, and my presence both stimulated his efforts at interpretation and made him feel less well-adapted to the choices that he himself had made, but which felt to him like constraints.

The fact that my friend spent so much time outside of the Philippines makes him somewhat different from most sugar planters. But the difference is more one of degree than kind. Most middle to large planters watch American television, follow American politics, and admire what they consider to be American values. Most of them have traveled to the United States and Europe, would send their children to American universities if they could afford it, and consider themselves relatively sophisticated and cosmopolitan. Most of them express surprisingly "liberal" sentiments about democracy, voting, corruption, and political life, at least when conversing with an American anthropologist. The extent to which they talk about their *own* social milieu as if from an external perspective is surprising. Nevertheless, they view that social milieu as a given fact that is impervious to change or to their own agency. The dependency, the paternalism, the lack of "rationality," the familism, the groupism, the rent-seeking are all "the facts of life" in the Philippine sugar industry, and while individual planters may decry these facts of life they generally take no personal responsibility for reproducing them. Most feel as if they have no choice but to adapt to circumstances as they are, though they would never have designed such circumstances themselves. After reading about sugar planters as evil Simon Legrees on black horses before I ever came to the Philippines, I was at first somewhat surprised at the widespread sentiment among planters who despise "the system" under which they operate, but who nonetheless are willing to defend it because it is the way they make their livings and because they cannot imagine a process of moving to an alternative system. This is not to say that they do not acknowledge the changes that are taking place. The majority do acknowledge them, but fear that they may upset what is already a precarious balance. The free market, globalization, import liberalization, are all happening much too quickly, and the people who benefit from them are no less self-interested than are sugar planters. Thus it becomes necessary to keep fighting the good fight for one's own interests. They are greatly pained by the extent to which the cosmopolitan liberals in their own country and in the United States seem to despise them. One told me, "You know, I guess if I were an intellectual in Manila I would hate sugar planters myself. But we didn't make this system, and I don't see what they expect us to do about it short of cutting our own throats." They tend to be liberals of an extremely conservative bent, and most of them are well aware that the traditional sugar planter lifestyle has a very limited future. I met only one or two who would encourage their children to become sugar planters.

Conclusion: The Institutions and Cultures of Philippine Sugar

The Aranetas. The Lopezes. The Elizaldes. Most Filipinos have heard these names and know them to be among the most prominent and wealthy families in the country. But fewer know that these families were once major players in the sugar industry, owning vast tracts of sugar land and some of the oldest centrifugal mills. Today, the Araneta and Elizalde mills, kept operating for sentimental reasons well past their useful lives, have closed, and the Lopez mill continues now as only a minor operation. Most Filipinos know these families for their diversified, mighty urban enterprises and their powerful political connections. The "sugar elites" that continue to dominate the nation's economic and political lives no longer have much to do with sugar. Most prominent and powerful families and individuals in today's Philippines *never* had anything to do with sugar. And some of the names that increasingly dominate sugar—Sy, Gokongwei, Chan—are newcomers to sugar production and have entered in order to service the diversified urban industrial and commercial enterprises that made them wealthy enough to buy sugar centrals.

The title of this book refers to the "cultures" of Philippine sugar rather than the "culture." It should by now be abundantly clear why that is so. Culture is an analyst's ideal type, and its boundaries must be specified if the term is to have any social referent or frame of comparison. Terms like "sub-culture" or "sub-sub-culture" have some heuristic value but imply that these cultural boundaries are natural units, things of nature. Most Filipinos think of "the sugar industry" as a monolithic, unified, natural entity, and the prevailing image they hold of it is that of the large planters. But while planters share many "cultural" attributes with their fellow Filipinos—the millers, traders, food processors, sugarcane workers—it is the *differences* in meanings, morals, and interests that constitute the engines of change in any society, particularly one experiencing such rapid change as the contemporary Philippines. In the social sciences, the "consensus tradition's" views of culture and society have focused mainly on the commonalties that allow societies to solve the "problem of order." But such a model simply will not do if we are interested in tracking, explaining, and interpreting social change. In that sense, this work is very much in the "conflict tradition" of social scientific theory and practice (Collins 1994). The very fact that I can argue for the need to separate individuals raised in planter families, but no longer embedded in the social and economic milieu of sugarcane planting, from planters still involved with planter culture and institutions is but another symptom of the movement, mixing, and borderlessness so characteristic of our contemporary world. But it is possible, and common, to exaggerate the absence of borders. We can still isolate and study planter culture and contrast it to, say, banker or miller culture if that is the relevant and useful contrast we seek to make. To do so is not to imply fixed and permanent boundaries between the two ideal typical entities. In Geertz's unparalleled wording:

> Anthropology, one of whose vocations, at least, is to locate such demarcations, to discriminate such breaks and describe such continuities, has fumbled with the issue from the beginning, and fumbles with it still. But it is, nonetheless, not to be evaded with dim banalities about the humanness of humankind or underlying factors of likeness and commonality, if only because, "in nature," as the positivists used to like to say, people themselves make such contrasts and draw such lines: regard themselves, at some times, for some purposes, as French not English, Hindu not Buddhist, Hutu not Tutsi, Latino not Indio, Shi'i not Sunni, Hopi not Navajo, Black not White, Orange not Green. Whatever we might wish, or regard as enlightenment, the severalty of culture abides and proliferates, even amidst, indeed in response to, the powerfully connecting forces of modern manufacture, finance, travel, and trade. The more things come together, the more they remain apart: the uniform world is not much closer than the classless society (2000: 248).

I would add that cultural difference not only persists *despite* the homogenizing effects of "modern manufacture, finance, travel, and trade" but that these differences—such as those among the different sectors of the Philippine sugar industry and the different classes, occupations, regions, and "groups" of Philippine society—in part generate the movements of such "modern" economic and social trends. As with Geertz's Indonesia, "the cultural variousness . . . (which, so far as I can see, is as vast as ever, despite the supposedly homogenizing effects of television, rock, and high late capitalism) finds expression in the form of struggles over the nature of this whole. . . . It is less a consensus that is at issue than a viable way of doing without it" (2000: 255). The struggle among competing elites that in my view is so important a part of social and economic change is largely a struggle among competing values, morals, and meanings as much as among competing objective interests. And, of course, in the real world there are no objective interests above and apart from those values, morals, and meanings. At the end of the day anthropologists must *impose* those demarcations on the social forms that we study as much as we must "locate" them; and we must take responsibility for the choices that we make.

Culture is not static, and it does not loom over our minds causing us to do and think things like so many marionettes. Although sugar planters live in a web of culture—no more nor less than we all do—many of them (or their children) become millers or traders or physicians or real estate developers (as they remain parents, spouses, church-goers, members of "groups," ethnics, etc.). They are able to become those things, to fit in to those cultures (or sub-cultures, if you prefer), not because they take on new objective interests or utility functions in their new lines of work, but because their reference groups, those culturally dominant groups or individuals whom they emulate, are changing. They are able to fit because they exist within new institutional environments and have to play by new sets of rules. Of course, these dominant reference groups and institutional environments had long histories and developed gradually. In a sense these newcomers "jumped into" historical streams that they did not create nor even influence. But once they made the leap, they could and often did become among the most innovative actors within their new social milieus. The Aranetas were planters (and soldiers), some of whom became millers. And as millers they were among those whom the planters—their erstwhile colleagues and class equals—fought against most acrimoniously. (In the words of one milling executive, "The planters never hated anyone more than they hated Amading Araneta.") But over time the mills that they owned and operated became a small sideline of the family's main business interest, and the Aranetas today are best known as fabulously wealthy developers of commercial real estate in Metro Manila. Likewise, most millers today marvel at the extent to which the majority of "Chinese" traders who have purchased mills in the last decade or so have *become* millers. They decry the one or two who "still act like traders," and there is enormous cultural and institutional pressure on those few to conform to the standards and rules of the milling profession, and to perceive their interests in the same ways that millers do. Millers, even ones who themselves came to the profession from non-miller backgrounds, seem utterly surprised at how easy it was for these traders to change their values and ways of conducting business, to adopt "miller culture." They expected and feared that the milling profession would become more trader-like, more Chinese, and less "professional" as it became more infused with "Chinese money." This reminds me of the fear that so many Americans —even ones whose parents or grandparents immigrated to the United States—have that immigrants somehow change the essential values of American culture and therefore must be forced to assimilate as quickly as possible lest they affect fragile American culture with their alien ways. In both cases, there is a naturalization or essentialization of "the culture" that views it as coterminous with the individuals who "possess" it.

The problem with "restoration of planter power" thinking is that it takes the group of individuals—the planters—and their culture as being fixed, static entities. It may be that some "planters, "or the members of families that made their fortunes in sugar, have done much better economically since the fall of Marcos and have managed to reassert their positions in local politics. But I think those are the minority. Most of the planters who have gained wealth and power in the last decade and a half are those who have diversified out of sugar, or given up sugar entirely. Some degree of planter power may have been restored, but not as planter power, per se. Those who have obstinately stuck with sugar have, for the most part, witnessed one set-back or defeat after another. They have had to hear and read that they are part of a "sunset industry," that they represent the "old colonial/feudal order" and that "their day is over." Planter power has blended into the already extant business power, trader power, banking power, management power, and professional power, though there is considerable overlap of the families or even individuals who represent these avenues of power. The children of planters who pursue these new professions and pathways to success, while still retaining their connections to sugar-producing families and provinces, *are no longer planters* in any meaningful sense of the term. And rather than bringing planters' values and perceptions to the worlds of business, politics, and the professions, they adopt the cultural expectations and play by the institutional rules of these new spheres. As newcomers with little "baggage," they innovate, or at least a small minority do, but they do not typically do so in ways that one would recognize as "planter." The idea that planter power *qua* planter power has been restored, that sugarcane planters remain among the most powerful and wealthy "players" in the nation, has been discredited by events of the past two decades. Many planters have yet to catch on and continue to insist that it would be a mistake to underestimate their considerable (but admittedly, rusty) political clout, but most clearly understand that sugar power is no longer very potent in today's globalized, Makati-dominated Philippines. In fact, most realize that not only are they no longer the predominant players in the nation, they are no longer even the predominant players in the sugar industry! Most industry commentators, for example, would readily admit that the most effective organization in the industry today is the millers' association, PSMA, rather than the feuding and disorganized planters' federations, CONFED and NFSP. That trader power is on the ascendance is clearly the most important trend in the industry today.

And yet, as planter *power* continues to wane, the remnants of planter culture and the cultural legacy of planter domination remain unstably intact. The profound inegalitarianism and paternalism of Philippine elite sensibilities, the idea that government exists to do the bidding of the rich and powerful, the notion that people in positions of power should use that power to help members of their families or groups, have all been transposed into elite urban sectors. It remains to be seen whether these and related values will be transmuted into other sorts of values that somehow better reflect the new power alignments. Or perhaps they will persist and adapt in recognizable forms into the foreseeable future. Most likely, change will be complex, uneven, and episodic. When one hears the elders of planter families counseling their children to "be more like the Chinese," one suspects that one is witnessing profound cultural change with serious implications for the future of this rapidly changing nation.

I do not want to leave readers with the impression that what is occurring in the Philippines is the replacement of one culture by another. It is not an abrupt transition from the rent-seeking, vote-commanding, power-grabbing, "corrupt" dominance of the landed elites toward the fair-minded, rule-abiding, honest, and decent reign of the business elites. Such a conclusion would be an absurd distortion of the complex and gradual changes taking place. The decline of the rural agrarian elites will not signify the end overnight of rent-seeking, neo-mercantilism, or the patrimonial state, and what will ultimately come about is impossible to predict. It is fair to say that rent-seeking, neo-mercantilism, and patrimonialism exist in some degree and in wide variety in all capitalist countries, and in many non-capitalist ones as well. To some extent the conclusion of one noted Philippine columnist, Calixto V. Chikiamco, remains and will continue to remain painfully true of most Filipino elites, no matter what their sector or their way of making money: "The source of wealth of the Philippine elite is primarily that of privileges (land ownership, political connections, favors, grants, licenses, etc.). There is no responsibility and accountability attached to this wealth. Legitimate capitalists, at least, are accountable and responsible to the market: they must earn their keep daily by producing quality goods for their customers, or else their businesses will 'die.' Not so with the privileged elite of Philippine society. . . . The Philippine elite have no concept of 'shared fate' with the rest of the nation. . . ." ("Politics of Reform," *Manila Standard*, 22 Aug. 1993).

Still, the institutional matrices of global and local capitalism are changing, and radically so. One part of that change is that capitalists in at least some increasingly important sectors—legitimate and otherwise—are less and less able to ignore accountability and responsibility to the market. As these businessmen and women seek to become more competitive in the face of new realities, the effects on values, meanings, and institutions will cascade in roughly predictable yet particularistic ways. The kinds of businesses likely to dominate the Philippine future are no longer those producing primary agricultural commodities, so the ways of doing business that have sustained those agrarian elites will increasingly fall by the wayside in response to new needs and new ways of thinking. We cannot predict the details of how Philippine culture will change with political and economic developments such as the growth of urban enterprise and the massively increased transnational capital flow. Nevertheless, it would be foolhardy to ignore these developments, or to argue that the values of Philippine capitalism or Philippine elites taken as a single, homogeneous entity are somehow so deeply ingrained that they will resist the juggernaut of global forces. The "patrimonial state" dominated by wealthy elite families might persist into the foreseeable future; but when those elite families are urban-based corporate executives rather than rural landowners, the values, perceptions, and principles upon which the patrimonial state is based will be different. That difference will feed back upon the society at large, the cultures of future elites, and the institutions and assumptions upon which the state—patrimonial or otherwise—will be based in the years to come. To phrase it plainly and perhaps simplistically: A patrimonial state "controlled" by urban businessmen pursues a different agenda and follows a different developmental trajectory than one "controlled" by rural landlords and producers of basic commodities. Which or what *kind* of elites dominate the state is at least as important as the relatively unexceptional fact that elites *do* dominate the state, much as the policies pursued in the Caribbean by the nineteenth-century British state changed radically once control was wrested from the planters and agrarian aristocrats by the rising bourgeoisie and advocates of "free trade" (Mintz 1985). Thereafter, British politics and society changed radically. In America the decline of plantation power occurred far more traumatically, but the effects of rising Northern, industrial dominance were equally widespread. Chikiamco and other commentators focus on the elements of elite culture and power that appear to apply generally to all Philippine elites; that is, for them the fact of elitehood is the most salient fact. My argument diverges from theirs in foregrounding the *differences* among elites and the *conflicts* engendered by those differences, and in its claim that these are the driving forces of cultural and institutional change.

During the 1998 presidential campaign, front-running Vice-President (now disgraced ex-President) Joseph "Erap" Estrada came to Bacolod to tout his "market-based" master plan for the sugar industry. As reported on *Balita-L* (24 May 1998) his plan was a mixed bag that must have confused and dismayed sugar planters. The plan was intended both to "save the sugar industry" and to "clear the way for cheap sugar for Filipino consumers." It entailed "rais[ing] sugar output, lower[ing] production costs, and overhaul[ing] the tariff and *quedan* systems that have penalized consumers and food processors" and the "calibrated removal of protectionist barriers that have barred Filipino consumers from enjoying cheap sugar despite the global glut and soft prices." "But," the plan stated, "the lowering of tariffs must be done at a *rational* pace and not beyond those undertaken by neighbor nations and others committed to the World Trade Organization that had replaced the General Agreement on Tariffs and Trade." Further, "The tariff cut schedule must be made contingent on the adoption of a *rationalization* program to allow sugar mills to retool their facilities and the stitching on of a 'safety nets' package especially for sugar workers who will be adversely affected by market *liberalization*" (italics mine). And to top it all off, the report warned that "High tariffs and historical access to the U.S. sugar quota have served to penalize both sugar consumers and our food processors."

That Estrada would come to Negros Occidental to announce this plan, and pitch it as a bailout of the sugar industry, suggests once again that the sugar planter's version of rationalization is losing ground to the "market-based," trade-liberalization, globalization, neo-liberal version that is coming to dominate Philippine economic and political life. Even eight or ten years ago, no major national politician would have had the temerity to make such an "in-your-face" presentation in Negros, especially one that declared that the sugar industry had lost its battle with the hated food processors. In mentioning import liberalization, high production costs, the (penalizing) *quedan* system, the high cost of sugar for consumers and food processors, and the need to rationalize the industry, Estrada inadvertently summed up most of the major defeats that the sugar industry has suffered in the last decade or so and—as in the case of the *quedan* system—may continue to suffer in the years ahead. Again, this speech is a useful illustration of the error in viewing the Philippines as still dominated by landed "Sugar Barons."

One scholar whose work affirms the salience of this "capitalist transformation" is anthropologist Michael Pinches (1996, 1997, 1999). In three articles based on extensive interviews conducted in Manila and Cebu, Pinches documents the rapid growth of the "bourgeoisie and middle class" in the Philippines. More important, he discusses how these new rich "pose a considerable cultural challenge" (1999: 277) to the old elite, and how many of the younger generation of the old elite have reoriented their economic strategies and cultural values in order to maintain their wealth and prestige. Simply put, many of "the feudal aristocrats . . . known for their high living and political prowess . . . became urban capitalists through investments in manufacture, banking, real estate, and agribusiness" (pp. 277–278).

"While members of the old elite continue to dominate much of the Philippine economy, they have done so only by reorienting themselves to the changing economic environment. Those who have relied solely on old forms and areas of wealth accumulation have generally suffered downward mobility" (p. 278). But, of course, most of the new rich and new middle class (which Pinches plausibly argues should be linked, owing to shared cultural precepts) did not come from the old elite, but rather from the pursuit of the new "meritocratic ethos" (p. 288) that appears to have spread rapidly throughout most of the nation. The pejorative connotation attached to the very term "new rich" has given way to the image of the "meritorious entrepreneur" (p. 281), widely celebrated as the new Philippine hero. So too, as we have seen, the image of "the Chinese" has undergone a rapid transformation from scheming, exploitative traders to industrious, frugal, and commercially astute models for Filipinos to emulate. The pariahs have become the paragons! State policies stressing "privatization, liberalization, and level playing fields" (281) have reinforced and reproduced these cultural and structural changes. To a significant extent, the old elite's sensibilities about "taste" and "refinement" persist, and many regard the new rich as tasteless upstarts without proper "breeding." But these judgments appear to be losing force as broader-based conspicuous consumption and more complex cultural criteria of stratification take hold. Although many of the new rich continue to imitate the tastes of the old elite, the new rich increasingly look outside of the Philippines for their consumption and lifestyle referents. As noted earlier, the new rich no longer perceive the ownership of agricultural land as a criterion of status or class. In an argument similar to that which I am putting forth in this work, Pinches regards this capitalist transformation as a dialectical, mutually constituting interplay of economy, politics, structure, and culture, and he regards it as the most important trend in the Philippines today.

The transition from the domination by rural agrarian elites to domination by urban-industrial, commercial, and financial elites is a typical, if not universal feature of capitalist development, the *sine qua non* of "modernity." In the Philippines, this process is hardly autochthonous, as indeed it was in only a few nations in world history. But the Philippine transition—episodic and non-linear as it is —is happening *today;* it is here for us to witness and study. Certainly, there are aspects of contemporary Philippine life that seem to indicate that the rural agrarian elites are hanging on, reasserting their power, and fighting against the new order. It would be foolish to deny this. But to assert that these indicate that the country remains or will remain in the thrall of landed interests is to miss the larger picture, and most of the smaller ones to boot. The signs of the increasing dominance of urban capital and culture are everywhere. It should not surprise us that the ideal typical "spheres" of law, politics, finance, values, and perceptions appear to be disarticulated and imperfectly coordinated during this time of transition. Although social life is a seamless whole in many ways, the forces of change do not affect all things simultaneously or with the same magnitude.

As Philippine exports continue to move toward value-added products and away from raw materials, the industries that produce these manufactured products, and the bankers who support them, will have to compete with similar industries in countries such as Thailand, Malaysia, Indonesia, and Taiwan. If the raw materials available to these industries are too costly owing to artificially high prices, they will be less competitive and the nation will lose out on foreign exchange, employment, and tax revenue. Moreover, a perception of the Philippines as a protectionist nation could result in tariffs and other prejudicial practices by those countries that are the biggest markets for its industrial products such as electronics and garments. Philippine industries and banks will not allow minor interest groups such as sugar planters to hurt them in these ways. Much as with other countries' transitions to capitalism, when wealth is predominantly in the form of land, agrarian interests exercise considerable dominance over political and economic life. But as agriculture gives way to industry, trade, and finance, urban-based interests achieve their ascendancy at the expense of the once-preeminent landed elites. This transition is on-going in the Philippines right now, and the sugar industry must recognize it and adapt to it before it is too late.

The Philippine sugar industry has been almost completely insulated from market forces for over half a century, and the result is inefficiency, uncompetitiveness, labor problems, and a crumbling infrastructure. Sugar producers today know that their industry is in trouble, that their products are too costly, and that their productivity too low. Everyone says they are in favor of modernization and "rationalization" so that the Philippines can once again take pride in its world-class sugar industry. And yet many producers assert that the solution is to become more rather than less isolated from international competition and the "discipline of the market." Such people typically advocate a return to fixed milling districts, production quotas and set prices, precluding land reform from ever affecting sugar holdings, permanently high tariffs, making sugar importation illegal, and having the SRA function solely to insure higher prices. The attitude seems to be that planters prospered when those things pertained, so why not go back to them? These self-styled defenders of the industry seem to believe that planters and millers can still exercise sufficient power to accomplish their immediate aims, and that they will be able to do so well into the future, even if their actions work to the detriment of consumers, workers, bankers, and industrialists.

Perhaps the clearest indicator of the transition is that the Philippine state so frequently and predictably tilts toward consumers and food processors—constituencies incapable of commanding large blocks of votes—to the perceived detriment of the once-mighty sugar planters—who themselves have lost the ability to command votes effectively. Candidates favored by planters have lost the last two presidential elections to "men of the Makati club," and such sugar-associated people as Buc-An Yulo have been routed in their attempts to get elected to the Philippine Senate. The era in which Philippine producers can "use political clout as a substitute for painful but necessary adjustments" (Brown 1987: 13) has ended. The colonial and neo-colonial status of sugar and the power and prestige the planters once held make this transition all the more gut-wrenching for them, and motivates them to fight for the preservation of the old order that much harder. And many do fight. But far more employ an "If you can't beat 'em, join 'em" strategy so that they, and especially their children, will not be left behind mired in the ways of the past. I personally know many planters who fight to preserve the industry and want it to reclaim its past glory, and yet strongly encourage their own children to pursue alternate careers and opportunities. The planters may have lost the war to retain the old order; but as individuals and families they are still among the best placed to be "winners," owing to their superior resources, connections, and access to modern education. In fact, in today's Philippines the only way they can preserve their power and wealth, and even their dignity, is to play by the rules and take on the values of the new order.

Although it is likely that efficient planters will continue to grow sugar into the foreseeable future, we have already witnessed the pressure of CARP, the shakeout and consolidation in the milling sector, the progress of import liberalization, the massive urban bias in finance, and the vilification of the "Sugar Barons" in the Philippine media. Provinces near Manila such as Cavite and Laguna have virtually stopped producing sugar in the last decade owing to the press of urban industry and rising land prices. Bacolod, that capital and largest city in Negros Occidental, the very heart of sugarland, has witnessed an economic boom since 1990 that astonishes even its residents. Whereas once the fortunes of that city entirely tracked the ups and downs of the sugar economy, today its new housing developments, several excellent hotels, good restaurants, fast food chains, and thriving up-scale shops seem to have spun free of the city's sugar moorings. Many sugar planters account for this boom by invoking "Chinese money," that *deus ex machina* of all nefarious trends, but it is increasingly apparent that sugar provinces are diversifying out of the monocrop, monoeconomies that once dominated them, and they are doing so without much help from the sugar industry.

While the rapid growth and expanding influence of the urban middle class will enhance Philippine prosperity and improve the prospects for democracy, it does not bode well for the sugar industry. One result of the crisis of the 1980s was that the image of the industry was severely tarnished among the middle class. Not only do urban consumers resent the high prices they must pay "to keep the sugar barons happy," but there is a growing sentiment that the sugar industry represents a "feudal" atavism that is an embarrassment to a modern nation. Many people within the industry say, with considerable justification, that their reputation is exaggerated and unfair. Some blame the "left wing press" and "nationalist intellectuals" for turning the urban professionals against them. But most acknowledge that the industry has a serious public relations problem.

Although demand for sugar continues to grow in many developing countries, those with the largest markets (e.g., India and China) have been able to satisfy much of their demand through expanded domestic production. With the exception of Japan, demand in the huge hard-currency markets of the developed world is softening. In the United States this is due to an anti-sugar health consciousness, the advent and wide acceptance of palatable low-calorie substitutes (which make Philippine sugar producers apoplectic), and the increasing use of grain-based sweeteners that exploit the comparative advantage of American agriculture. Demand for sugar in the United States in 1987 was only 60 percent of what it had been in 1970; while in Western Europe it was 83 percent (Brown 1987: 10–11). Whereas in 1960 the ratio of U.S. consumption of sugar to corn syrup was 10-to-1, by 1985 it was 1-to-1 (Brown 1987: 16).

But many Philippine producers state that demand in the rest of the world is of little consequence as long as demand at home continues to grow. It is true that the Philippine population continues to grow at 2 percent per year and that there is great room for improvement in per capita GDP that tends to lead to higher sugar consumption. But in the summer of 1991 (March through May in the Philippines), the nation experienced a surprising 15 to 20 percent dip in the consumption of sugar-based products (soft drinks, ice cream and fruit juices) despite a nationwide drought and severe problems with water supply in Metro Manila (*SRA Newsletter,* March–April 1991). The most plausible explanation for this decrease was the sharply higher prices for these products because of the record price of domestic sugar. This underlines a simple economic reality that too many sugar producers seem to ignore: demand is partly a function of price. The demand for imported sugar by the food-processing industry and the slackening of consumer demand in the face of high prices illustrate clearly that in an interconnected world one cannot close a market so completely as to suspend the principles of supply and demand. That the great importation debate has been "solved" by several consecutive years in which Philippine production fell considerably short of domestic demand suggest how dire the industry's situation may now be.

In the Philippines, virtually all domestic sugar is used in ingestible products such as candy, sweets, soft drinks, table sugar, and rum. That is not the case in some other sugar-producing countries. In Brazil, for example, a significant proportion of the automobiles are fueled by ethanol or other alcohol compounds produced from sugar at costs that are competitive with petroleum. While most ethanol produced in developed countries is made from grain, virtually all of it produced in tropical countries comes from sugar cane. There have been many tentative initiatives in the Philippines to produce alternative products and develop various spin-offs from cane. SRA officials and others in the sugar industry speak with admiration of the accomplishments of the Brazilians and Cubans in developing and marketing over one hundred viable products from sugar cane. Aside from ethanol, at various times people have discussed paperboard, furfural, cattle fed with canetops, and innumerable other possible uses, but the Philippines continues to lag behind these countries in investment and product development. It is fair to say that the institutional incentive structure of the Philippine sugar industry is such that there is little hope of recreating Brazilian and Cuban styles of diversification in the foreseeable future. It is also possible that diversification within sugar is not a practicable development strategy. One would be reluctant to hold Cuba up as a case to be emulated.

Another widely discussed possibility for sugar-growing areas is agricultural diversification, either linked with sugar or out of sugar entirely. On Negros, one hears many accounts of past and present diversification schemes. Usually they are tales of woe. During the crisis there was a rush to plant crops or raise livestock that would allow farmers to make their loan payments, feed their families, and stay solvent. These included ramie, corn, sorghum, pineapples, flowers, black pepper, coffee, hogs, poultry, and cattle. Although an influential group continues to make a case for the potential profitability of cattle on Negros (fed on cane tops and molasses), virtually all of these experiments ended in failure, and most of the acreage has reverted to sugar. One farmer told me that during the crisis he planted thirty hectares of corn and was making some money at it, but then the agriculture secretary announced a large corn importation and the price dropped precipitously. The farmer went back to sugar.

Of course, the Philippine sugar industry does not exist in a vacuum and cannot be understood apart from the broader national and global systems within which it functions. Nationally, numerous economic policies and factors directly affect the sugar industry, including currency valuation, interest rates, taxation, capital flight from rural areas, disincentives for economic diversification and investment, infrastructure development, wage rates, agrarian reform, and pricing policies for food staples. Internationally, no sugar producer can avoid the impact of preferential agreements, quotas, subsidies, tariffs, and trade competition. It seems unlikely that protectionism in sugar will soon disappear, that countries will stop coddling their high-cost, labor-exploiting, non-competitive sugar industries. Since the United States and the European Union are large producers as well as consumers, and since they are among the most protective of their politically influential sugar industries, it is doubtful that the WTO process will force them to dismantle their sugar quota systems any time soon. It may be that even if the planters had managed to retain more of their political clout after the fall of Marcos, the Philippine sugar industry would have declined anyway due to global forces.

Although the Philippine sugar industry is desperately threatened, it is not yet moribund. What will destroy it irredeemably, however, is if its current institutional structure remains intact. This structure was perfectly suited to mitigating the sectoral disputes of a bygone era, to managing a now-defunct production quota that penalized rather than rewarded efficiency and innovation, and to promoting the immediate profits of sugar producers. But these interests are now diametrically opposed to the long-term well-being of the industry, and unless this discordance is faced squarely and honestly, the industry is in mortal danger of imminent collapse. Too many people within the industry act as if its institutional structure is sacrosanct and inviolable, and that any changes that take place must therefore be accommodated within that structure. They seem to believe that exhorting people to do what is right will provide them with sufficient incentive to do it, even if the institutional structure provides strong disincentive. They suppose that returning to the conditions of a halcyon past will solve the very modern problems that beset the industry today. But institutional organizations are human constructs and can therefore be altered by concerted human action. It will be sad if the century-old Philippine sugar industry dies because of its own inertia and shortsightedness. The organization of an industry, much as all institutions, can be changed if the people involved are able to summon up the will to do the right thing, even if they must sacrifice some short-term gain.

The main example of institutional stasis discussed in this book has been the share-*quedan* method of allocating rights to sugar. This method was instituted during the American colonial period as a way to persuade sugar planters to deliver their cane to the new industrial, centrifugal mills by allowing the planters to retain property rights over the largest portion of the milled sugar. It succeeded at that task admirably, and within a short time the Philippines saw the full institutionalization of the sectoral division between planter and miller. With this, however, came other, dismal effects: acrimony over share contracts, "sugarless *quedan* scams," and accusations of short-weighing, insider trading, and delivering trashy cane.

Whereas in most sugar-producing countries share systems have given way to straight-cane purchases, in the Philippines the share-*quedan* system persists even though most people in the industry realize that it leads to high transaction costs and disincentives to capital investment and product development. It is likely that primary sugar traders would exist in the Philippines even if mills owned all the sugar produced. The share-*quedan* system, however, is responsible for the enormous proliferation of the secondary and tertiary trading sector because there are thousands of sugar owners (i.e., *quedan*-holders) ready to sell their *quedan*s as quickly as possible for the best short-term price. The majority of traders and brokers do nothing but buy *quedan*s and sell them to other traders; that is, they do not have the wherewithal to transport sugar and deliver it to consumers. Mills, for their part, complain with justification that since they own only 25 to 40 percent of the sugar in their own warehouses it is difficult to make the capital investments necessary to upgrade their mills and keep them running efficiently. The planters will not contribute to mill rehabilitation since they seldom have any equity stakes in the mills themselves. In particular, mills want to retain their inefficient boilers in order to burn as much *bagasse* as possible. While in other countries mills cogenerate and sell power and produce many profitable products from *bagasse*, Philippine millers fear that if they began to profit from *bagasse* they would have no choice but to *quedan* it and remit most of those profits to the planters, who made no investment in the technology that allowed the new products to be produced. Thus, this useful by-product of sugar milling goes up in smoke, pouring soot into the air wherever sugar is milled.

Most millers favor a transition to the cane-purchase system, as do most large traders and government sugar technocrats. Of course, smaller traders rightfully worry that the cane purchase would put them out of business, so they bitterly oppose it. It is planter opposition to the switch, however, that has led to the preservation of the anachronistic share-*quedan* system. Planters greatly fear that the more technically and financially sophisticated millers will cheat them under the new method of apportioning property rights. They also bristle at the thought that selling sugarcane rather than owning sugar would make them nothing but "farmers." Despite the common implication of the word "planter," most Philippine sugar planters are no longer serious agriculturists, and they leave the farming side in the hands of professional foremen. Planters perceive their main function to be transacting *quedan*s, and, although planters rarely *see* the actual physical sugar that they own, that key function is entirely predicated on *owning* sugar. It is the ownership of sugar and the selling of *quedan*s that makes planters businessmen rather than simple farmers, and this is a role that most of them relish and are unwilling to relinquish.

Earlier in this book I described one attempt by an institutional innovator to institute unilaterally a cane-purchase system at his central. He was a large trader who had purchased a mill and erected a refinery in order to service his industrial customers. He perceived the share-*quedan* system as "irrational madness" that defeated the entire purpose of owning a mill. Since planters could decide not to have their sugar processed in his refinery, and since they insisted on being consulted about all changes in the way the mill operated, this trader learned that even the owner of a mill could not amass enough sugar to provide a ready and predictable supply for beverage companies. He also learned that he could not succeed if he was the only one to impose the cane purchase while all other mills stuck with the share-*quedan* system. This was true even though his had been one of the most self-contained districts in the country. His attempt at innovation failed because the planters rejected it and the other mills used his experiment to portray themselves as being all the more planter-friendly. And so, the older institutional form, underlain by and interacting with deep-seated cultural values, easily survived this attempt at institutional innovation.

This is not to say that such ingrained institutional forms are destined to persist no matter what the prevailing trends in the industry or the larger society. In an industry increasingly dominated by large traders who have purchased mills (just the people who would benefit most from a switch to the cane purchase), in a country increasingly dominated by urban businessmen, the planters' aversion to becoming farmers will look increasingly quaint and irrelevant. That speech in Negros by presidential candidate Estrada, in which he decried "the tariff and *quedan* systems that have penalized consumers and food processors," suggests that the sensitivities of the sugar planters are no longer afforded the same respect and deference as in the past. Perhaps such an institutional change would help convince more planters that they are, in fact, farmers and stewards of the land, that they need to start playing those roles diligently and well. Some will, no doubt, take that message and learn a thing or two about agriculture. A few may even decide that there are better crops for them to grow or products for them to produce. It will certainly drive many current planters away from sugar planting and toward other sorts of enterprises. Also, it will further propel the process of industry domination by the millers, large traders, and industrial sugar consumers. Perhaps as planter *qua* planter power continues to erode, the opposition to CARP or some future agrarian reform proposal will also erode, and the Philippines will be able to pursue land reform without its being watered down and delayed to the point of complete impotence. Or perhaps not.

The narrative of the genesis, persistence, and (potential) decline of the share-*quedan* system serves as my best micro-level parable of the way cultures and institutional forms interact. Rather than viewing culture as, on the one hand, an essentialized, reified, "800-pound gorilla" that looms oppressively over our thoughts, perceptions, and values, or as, on the other, a fleeting reflection of individual strategizing, "rationality," or praxis, the view proffered here takes culture as an ideal type that we can describe, and that has real effects on individual thought and conduct, but which is always subject to change, negotiation, and co-optation. Especially so as it influences and is influenced by the institutional forms and power relations which are themselves entirely human, negotiable artifacts. The institution of the share-*quedan* system was created entirely for pragmatic purposes, in the interest of a particular colonial agenda. It interacted with an already deep-seated value—the ownership of sugar—that planters held by virtue of the pre-central haciendas being integrated farms and factories. During the period in which planter power reigned supreme, planters increasingly defined themselves as businessmen, power brokers, and socialites. The colonial quotas and fixed districts guaranteed their wealth, and this only enhanced their self-perception as landed gentry, including their strong aversion to actual farm labor. In such a protected, uncompetitive environment the institutional flaws in the share-*quedan* system were hardly manifest. Only as global forces and local power relations shifted did those flaws come to the fore. The fact that planters strongly valued their positions as landed gentry was enough to preserve the old institutional order as long as they were able to exert their influence over the other sectors of the industry, or at least convince the others that the way of the planter was in everyone's best interests. There is no inevitable human drive to greater efficiency, and innovations do not necessarily succeed simply because they facilitate efficiency in the abstract. But once other sectors and other individual players felt themselves constrained by the old institutional order, and could see and examine other models in other places that could further their own interests, institutional innovation was likely to occur so long as those other sectors and individuals had the clout to pull it off. As planter power has waned, planter desires, values, and interests look increasingly old-fashioned and inefficient to those in the industry who now have the money and resources to influence ways of doing business, and who have the attention of the state. The institutional forms drive the culture, which in turn drives the institutional forms. Power—the ability to influence and change the institutional forms—is the driving engine of both institutional change and institutional stasis. It is a perpetual, mutually constitutive and influencing, dialectical process. Therefore, the point at which we, the analysts, decide to enter this stream of history is an arbitrary choice, one that we must make without suggesting that such a point was inevitable or natural. The advantage of thinking of culture, power, and institutions as ideal types rather than as things of nature is that it forces us to take responsibility for our own choices and perspectives, and for the roles that we play in the creation of the ideal types.

"Rational," "efficient," "liberal," "interests," "civil society." These are all terms that we think we understand, that conjure up mental images, and that facilitate discussion of "economic" life. Although there is plenty of room for disagreement in any society, we have our own ideal types of positive, modern, liberal, and productive economic policies and strategies, of how rational actors should pursue their interests, of what efficient organizations and institutions look like, and of what constitutes good as opposed to bad forms of civil society. If there is a major methodological argument in this work it is in opposition to the *apriorist*, formalist, rationalist, nomothetic, universalistic approach to economic life that has come to dominate the discipline of economics in the last half century and that, in the guise of "economic imperialism" and rational choice theory, has made significant inroads into other social sciences. For economic anthropologists, particularly those of the neo-Weberian bent, all these terms, concepts, values, and perceptions, in every kind of society, are embedded so deeply in their cultural and institutional contexts as to be virtually meaningless and certainly ethnocentric outside of those contexts.

If this kind of economic anthropology represents in any of its parts another legacy of the Enlightenment—and we must also own up to our important Romantic heritage as well—it is Hume's empirically oriented version rather than Descartes' rationalist one. It asserts that the only way to learn about and study economic life is to go forth into the world and talk to people, live with them, try to understand how they think and what motivates them to act as they do, and to produce a narrative that, to the best of one's ability, gives a fair and honest interpretation of their worlds. How is economic life structured? How did it come to be *this* way and not alternative ways? What values and meanings underlie and are, in turn, affected by the ways people make their livings and exchange goods and symbols? What are the incentives to change or not to change? What individuals or groups are able to advance their ideas and agendas? Where are the opportunities for innovation, and whose ox will be gored? What are the points of conflict and what compromises have been worked out? How does the industry (or village, or city, or union, or company) relate to other industries and to national and global political and economic forces?

As soon as one takes on the task of studying economies empirically, one realizes very quickly that the discrete box we call "the economy" is itself an ideal type, an artificial mental construct, out of which we must wander if we are to have any hope of understanding the world as it is. Cutting culture down to size and staying inside of that discrete, equally artificial, box will not do as a solution for economic anthropology. Economic anthropology must retain its holistic vision or lose its soul. And holism is hard. It requires that we, the analysts, constantly make choices about what to consider, what to ignore, what to privilege, and what to downplay. These choices are not *there* in the world itself for us to behold and grasp. We must impose this order on the world in order to make any sense of it. But, still, we must let the social world be our guide and not allow ourselves to become enthralled with any pre-ordained grand dogma, political ideology, or axe to grind. The ideal types that we impose must themselves remain rather close to the ground and open to modification and recontextualization.

The key concept of "rationalization" provides a useful illustration of the need for empirically based economic anthropology. That some individuals and groups tend to use that word to mean movement toward a more "free market," "competitive," and "globalized" economic order, while others use exactly the same term to refer to the greater use of quotas, protectionism, government price setting, and reduced competition should indicate to us that this is a term that can shed important light on certain conflicts in the industry. Asking which usage of the term is more "correct," which conforms better to the technical usage in economics or business, and which do we prefer are all thoroughly useless questions, either without meaningful answers or whose answers do nothing to facilitate understanding of the Philippine sugar industry. It is the very ambiguity and the contestation over the meaning of the term that allows us to use the term as a tool to advance our understanding. The fixed meanings that come with *apriorism* close the window on the ambiguities that are the keys to grasping the stuff of social life. The content of "rationalization" is not knowable *a priori* for this time, this place, and these people. There is no substitute for an active engagement with "insiders" willing to explain and interpret their worlds to an uninformed outsider.

One additional problem with the rationalist approach is its tendency to mix its normative prescriptions with its empirical research (when rationalists actually *do* empirical research). After all, if some actions and institutions are "rational," others must be "irrational," and pursuing irrational actions and preserving irrational institutions leads to bad economic policies and decisions. In the case of neo-classical economics such normative prescriptions most typically take the form of favoring "free markets," "free trade," and economic policies vaguely identified today as "neo-liberal." Ironically, economics shares this predilection toward normative prescriptiveness with various forms of leftist social science, including "advocacy" or "action" anthropology. Obviously, the content of these leftist prescriptions tends to be entirely different from that of the neo-classical economists' prescriptions, but the tone of moral superiority and greater access to the right, the good, and the reasonable are much the same.

In contrast to most works on Philippine sugar, in this book the planters are not the villains. Indeed there are no villains here, only actors, groups, and informants. Likewise, the food processors, traders, or even the workers are not the heroes. The conflicts of the sugar industry are not *my* conflicts in the sense that I feel an abiding responsibility to help "solve" them. Whether or not I personally consider the preservation of the old neo-mercantilist order to be a gain or a loss is neither relevant to my study nor particularly interesting. As an anthropologist, I am not rooting for any particular outcome, sector, or even individual, except for my fervent hope that the sugar workers will never again experience the malnutrition, displacement, and violence that characterized the crisis of the 1980s. I have no normative preference for Western-style "bourgeois virtues" (McCloskey 1996).

This is not to imply that I am somehow gifted with the ability to be "objective" in the sense of detached, magisterial, and outside, or that I am not dependent upon my own culturally and personally constructed interpretations. There is no high rock from which the anthropologist makes his or her pronouncements about social reality. What it means is simply that I have made a decent effort to keep my own political ideals and beliefs out of other peoples' business. When dealing with competing elites, one must make every effort to position oneself as a neutral and disinterested observer in order to gain and retain access to as wide an array of people and opinions as possible. In the case of studying Philippine sugar, a perception that I was a biased observer with an agenda would not only have limited my access, but it may have been outright dangerous. But more important, when social scientists imply that they possess special moral insight or deeper moral "knowledge" by virtue of being social scientists, they are deceiving themselves and their informants. I am as culturally embedded as any other person. Some might take that simple fact as implying a license to permit moral and political preaching, to afford my ideology equal status to that of my informants. I take it to imply the need for greater caution when writing about other peoples' societies and lives. Much as many of the things I saw and heard in my fieldwork rankled me personally, I have tried hard to remain as dispassionate as possible in my work as an anthropologist. I still have not encountered a better source for sorting through this distinction than Weber's essay, "Science as a Vocation" (Gerth and Mills 1946).

This work tells the story of the declining influence and power of one group of elites and the concomitant rise in the fortunes of other elites, even when the actual people who comprise those new elites considerably overlap with those who comprised the old. I can honestly state that I have not rooted for any of them and have certainly not rooted against any of them. To be sure, I have liked some of my informants better than others as people and as informants. Some of them remain close friends; others not at all. I have tried to assess whether there is any significant sectoral correlation to these preferences, whether, for example, I have tended to like planters, or food exporters, or millers, or union leaders better in general than I have liked others. I can discern no such correlation. Still, it would be disingenuous for me not to admit that my field notes are replete with expressions of annoyance, even disgust, that mostly occur after spending time on sugar farms. The conditions under which sugar workers live and work remain appalling to me personally, and it was not easy to leave that sentiment behind in my field notes. But my relative ease has little to do with what I take to be the serious moral obligation of an anthropologist not to allow one's personal, culturally constructed moral and political sentiments to overwhelm or greatly color one's empirical analyses. Though I am sure some anthropologists will criticize me for failing to express sufficient indignation at many aspects of the institutions and cultures of the Philippine sugar industry, I only hope I succeeded in leaving my indignation and disgust in my field notes.

The story of modern Philippine history and society has an epic quality to it, and I can understand why so many commentators have chosen to stress the tragic, static, and unsettling aspects of this epic story. But for better or for worse, the Philippines is a nation undergoing enormous social change right now. It is a nation in which people still seriously debate what kind of constitution should be enacted, whether the federal government should be run according to a presidential or parliamentary system, how best to impose the rule of law, what is the meaning of private property, how best to teach values and civic virtue to young people, and what should be the role of the nation in the community of nations. It is a country in which the roles of government, business, labor, the military, the church, the landlords, and the poor masses are all up for grabs and contested. It is a nation unsure of its identity, its commonality, and its sources of pride. It is a nation of one culture and of many. And it will be such a nation in the years to come. The epic continues.

Notes

Chapter 1 Introduction
1. Much of the non-journalistic scholarship was from three authors: a Filipina anthropologist (Violeta B. Lopez-Gonzaga), an American historian of Southeast Asia (Alfred McCoy), and an Irish Columban activist priest (Niall O'Brien). See the bibliography for references. I first learned about the crisis in Negros from a 1988 report by journalist Alan Berlow on National Public Radio (see Berlow 1996).
2. Three very different anthropological works that focus on elite culture are Cohen (1981), Marcus (1992), and Janelli (1993).
3. Other scholars of modern Asian societies raise similar points about the relevance of Weber (Geertz 1963b; Wertheim 1995; Vandergeest and Buttel 1988; Biggart 1991). Berger also discusses Asian cultures and societies at considerable length (e.g., Berger and Hsiao 1988). The flexible notion of "economic culture" as developed by Berger (1986) from Weberian influences has influenced my own views. One outstanding work in my discipline that comes close to my own theoretical perspective is Hefner (1990). He refers to his perspective as simultaneously "interpretive and circumstantial" (p. xii), seeking to "bring a hermeneutically informed approach to bear on the complex realities of economic and political life" (p. xvii).
4. One of my favorite statements about objectivity comes from Geertz but is attributed to Robert Solow: " . . . as complete objectivity is impossible . . . , one might as well let one's sentiments run loose. . . . That is like saying that as a perfectly aseptic environment is impossible, one might as well conduct surgery in a sewer" (Geertz 1973: 30).
5. Some economists, political scientists, and sociologists explicitly recognize and analyze the persistence of inefficient institutions and forms of organization (e.g., Akerlof 1976; Bates 1981; Matthews 1986; North 1990). In the literature on industrial organization, however, a teleological and functionalist logic typically prevails which implies a drive toward greater efficiency (e.g., Chandler 1977, 1984, 1990; Williamson 1985).
6. The familiar word "monopoly" refers to a market with a single seller. The less familiar "monopsony" refers to a market with a single buyer, such as an exclusive government trading agency.

7. Some of the founding literature of this perspective includes Hollnsteiner (1963), Lynch (1964), Landé (1965), and Eisenstadt and Roniger (1984). An (increasingly) critical literature on the topic includes Kerkvliet (1990, 1995), Sidel (1989, 1997), Cannell (1999), and several articles in McCoy (1993).
8. Pinches (1996, 1997, 1999) is one scholar who has focused on the rise of an urban-based "new rich" and has criticized characterizations of the Philippines as having changed little since the 1960s. His work, based upon many interviews with business elites and entrepreneurs in Manila and Cebu, stresses both the structural and cultural changes associated with the transition. I discuss Pinches more fully in chapter 7.
9. The old sociological notion of "reference groups" (Eisenstadt 1954; Merton 1957; Berger 1963) is still, in my mind, a useful tool for understanding the culture-changing power of competition among elite groups and the replacement of one dominant group by another. There are recent indications that this notion is too powerful not to be revived (e.g., Schor 1998).
10. Based upon extensive comparative research, Eisenstadt (1986) concurs that conflict among elites with competing interests is a far more important and ubiquitous cause of change in complex societies than is conflict between those with and without access to the means of production.
11. Although I will henceforth dispense with the quotation marks around the word "Chinese," it must be stated that this classification is an imprecise one that requires considerable experience to understand. There are, to be sure, some important sugar traders (for example) who are first-generation immigrants from southern China, who continue to use the Hokkien dialect in their business dealings, who support Chinese temples, and whose self-identification is "Chinese." But most Chinese traders are the children or grandchildren of immigrants, speak little or no Chinese, are Roman Catholic, and consider themselves decidedly Filipino. They are regarded as Chinese mainly because they have Chinese surnames and engage in businesses traditionally regarded as Chinese. The irony here is that most of the founders of the prominent Negros sugar families were themselves Chinese mestizos who came over from the neighboring island of Panay in the nineteenth century (McCoy 1982).

Chapter 2 The Legacy of Colonialism and Neo-colonialism

1. This section merely scratches the surface of a long and complex history. For greater detail about the general history of the sugar industry readers may see Larkin (1993) and Quirino (1974). Discussions of the industry under martial law may be found in Hawes (1987) and McCoy

(1983). Some sources for the history and development of sugar on Negros are Genova (1988), Cuesta (1980), McCoy (1982, 1984, 1991), O'Brien (1987), Sa-onoy (1984, 1992), Aguilar (1984, 1994, 1998, 2000), Lopez-Gonzaga (1983, 1984, 1985, 1986, 1987a, 1987b, 1989, 1991), Lopez-Gonzaga, Aguilar, and Demegilio (1988), Lopez-Gonzaga and Decena (1990), Ledesma and Montinola (1988), Jagan and Cunnington (1987), and Billig (1991, 1992a, 1993, 1994). Aguilar (1998) is a culturally rich, theoretically sophisticated, somewhat revisionist history that I strongly recommend.

2. Magellan landed (and later died) in Cebu in 1521 and "claimed" the islands for Spain, but actual colonization did not begin until 1565 when Philip II—for whom the islands were named (and who was not yet born when Magellan landed)—sent Legazpi to establish the first Spanish settlement. The colony was "acquired" by the United States during the Spanish-American War, though it took another seven years to subdue the Philippine revolutionaries. They had at first greeted the Americans as liberators but they soon realized that their revolution would be double-crossed under the guise of making the Philippines ready for democratic self-government. Now *there* is Philippine history in a nutshell!

3. Today, one picul equals 63.25 kilos, but traditionally it equaled 140 pounds. In the 1991–1992 crop year, the Philippines officially switched from the picul to the 50-kilogram bag as the official measure of unrefined sugar. But since virtually everyone in the industry still thinks in piculs, I use that unit in this work.

4. Interest in pre-1855 and even pre-Hispanic Negros history has recently intensified (e.g., Sa-onoy 1992; Scott 1992; Aguilar 1998). We have learned, for example, that the tribal economy and technology on the island were more advanced and thriving than the Spanish friars and soldiers portrayed them. The prevailing notion among Negros elites, that their ancestors claimed land in an untouched "frontier," has recently come under considerable scrutiny. The archaeological investigations of Junker (1994, 1996, 1999) have gone a long way toward confirming that Negros was not a primitive backwater even in pre-Hispanic times.

5. The surnames Montilla, Luzuriaga, Locsin (and its variant, Lacson), and Gaston are still prominent among the Negros elite.

6. Aguilar (1994) discusses the forces leading to this opening.

7. Aguilar (1998) argues that McCoy and others have overstated Loney's role in the transformation of the Western Visayas economy. In Aguilar's account, Chinese-born merchants who were agents for or partners of Manila-based Chinese were more responsible for the demise of the mestizo textile industry. It is the Iloilo mestizos themselves who

should receive the credit (or the blame) for refashioning themselves as the sugar-planter class on Negros.
8. Saravia is an infamous figure in Negros history for having led a brutal massacre against a group of tribal people who resisted colonial control. The twenty-four-year-old officer became the first provincial governor in 1855. In 1857 he was removed from office, charged with serious misconduct, and exiled to Africa for life. The town in Negros that was once called "Saravia" has been renamed E. B. Magalona (Sa-onoy 1992: 73–78).
9. The subject of the cash advances given by *hacenderos* to workers is an area of interpretive debate among historians. McCoy (1982) and Lopez-Gonzaga (1991) generally consider this practice to be "debt bondage" while Aguilar interprets it as resulting from the relatively strong market position of the laborers who could only be enticed to migrate by cash up front. Aguilar also argues that the coercive mechanisms of keeping the workers on the hacienda were largely ineffective, and that planters were compelled to offer "fair treatment" to workers in order to keep them (1998: 131–135).
10. Aguilar (1998: 79–80) points out a remarkable linguistic difference in the framing of tenancy relations in Tagalog-speaking areas (such as Pampanga) versus Ilonggo-speaking areas (such as Negros Occidental). In Tagalog the term for a tenant on the land is *kasama*, which means "partner." The word *agsa*, used for a tenant in Ilonggo, comes from the Hokkien (Chinese) word *acsa*, which is similar in meaning to the English word "shit."
11. The United States had already become the leading destination for Philippine sugar by the mid-1870s, supplanting the United Kingdom. By the late 1890s the low quality of Philippine sugar had become a major impediment in the American and European markets whose consumers increasingly demanded refined white sugar. In 1901, 90.8 percent of Philippine sugar exports went to China and Japan (Aguilar 1998: 124).
12. Aguilar (1998) presents an extended discussion of the importance of spirits and spirit worship in Negros, and the use of spirit beliefs as a form of resistance against capitalist incursion. Most fascinating of all is his discussion of the way Spanish friars used and co-opted spirit beliefs in the process of *conquista espiritual* (p. 33).
13. In Negros the *pacto de retro* served more as a means by which the wealthy acquired land from the poor, thus giving it its reputation as an exploitative institution. Larkin (1993: 87) points out that it functioned as a sort of incipient mortgage system in Pampanga and was an important source of informal credit there.
14. Moscovado sugar is produced by crushing the cane with a carabao-driven crusher, then boiling the juice in large cauldrons, pouring the

boiling juice into clay pots called *pilones*, and allowing the molasses to drain out through a hole in the pot. The sugar remaining in the *pilon* develops a hard outer crust with softer, dark grains of sugar inside. It is still produced on farms in very undeveloped areas of the Visayas (e.g., Antique), and it is delicious. Ruins of moscovado mills can still be seen on farms in Negros and Pampanga.

15. Larkin discusses a few attempts to circumvent the provisions of the 1902 Public Land Act, the 1902 Homestead Act, and the 1914 revised Public Land Law. These attempts, which led to the creation of integrated sugar estates in Mindoro (which failed due to unfavorable conditions and difficulty attracting labor), Pampanga, and Laguna, exploited a loophole in the initial version of the Act concerning the disposition of former friar holdings (1993: 57–58).

16. The first such contract—at the (still existing) San Carlos central on Negros—lasted for thirty years and guaranteed the mill 40 percent of the sugar manufactured (Larkin 1993: 58). It is interesting that anomalous San Carlos—built in 1913 by American-Hawaiian investors who owned none of the surrounding land—would become the prototype for property rights apportionment for the whole industry. The mill district is a natural unit for San Carlos since the town is located on a thin coastal plain on the eastern side of Negros and is rather self-contained. Even today, access from the major towns on the island's western side is virtually impossible across the mountains and requires a long coastal trip. Whereas most people in Negros Occidental speak Ilonggo—facing west toward Iloilo, San Carlos residents speak Cebuano—facing east toward Cebu. A second sizable mill, Canlubang on Luzon, built in 1914 and recently closed, also opted for the share system. The rest is history, so to speak.

17. The PNB was founded in 1916 at the instigation of American Governor General Francis B. Harrison, who was disappointed at the increasing foreign domination of the Philippine economy (including the sugar centrals). The primary purpose of the PNB, which replaced the aforementioned Agricultural Bank, was to make loans to native agricultural producers, and the sugar industry quickly became its leading lendee. Six of the centrals built over the next decade—five in Negros, one in Pampanga—were referred to as "bank centrals" since they were built with PNB money and run by Filipinos rather than foreigners. During the Commonwealth period, the Philippine government would exercise considerable control over the operation of these.

18. The United States instituted the Torrens system in 1902, which encouraged landowners to obtain legal title to their holdings. The results proved disappointing, and the colonial government began a cadastral survey of the entire Philippines in 1913. By 1922 most of Negros' best farmland was legally titled. There is much evidence that the process of

titling led to the displacement of many small farmers by larger, more powerful landowners, often by nefarious means (McCoy 1982: 320–322).
19. Hofileña (1996) provides a fascinating account of the war in Negros from the perspective of one sugar planter.
20. There has, nonetheless, been a tendency to exaggerate the ability of the industry to function as an effective political bloc. The disparate interests among the different sectors and among powerful individuals within sectors has ensured that coordination and consensus within the industry were never as great as the omnipotent image suggests. There has never been a president from Negros.
21. The aforementioned Araneta family, a powerful milling conglomerate, tried to dictate the terms of milling contracts and keep planters from encroaching upon their sector, thus creating an acrimonious legal battle between millers and planters. The planters won this fight by exercising their political clout in the most coordinated display to date.
22. Including the now-ubiquitous transloading stations where trucks from far away centrals receive cane from planters.
23. All currencies marked with a dollar sign ($) are in U.S. dollars and cents.
24. PHILSUCOM had been created in 1974 by Presidential Decree No. 388, but was not activated until 1977. Benedicto, a prominent member of a Negros sugar family and a former resistance fighter, had been Marcos' fraternity brother. While ambassador to Japan he had been instrumental in arranging for the construction of the new Philippine centrals by Japanese firms. For more complete discussions of PHILEX and PHILSUCOM see Hawes (1987) and Sa-onoy (1984).
25. Benedicto left the Philippines on the same plane as Marcos. After that he resided comfortably in Venezuela, Hong Kong, and other places, until returning to the Philippines in 1993. Negotiations are currently under way for him to return a portion of his ill-gotten gains in exchange for limited amnesty from prosecution. Many sugar planters would like nothing better than to have their day in court with "RSB."

Benedicto was not the only crony involved in pillaging the sugar industry. Among others were Armando Gustilo, the president of the National Federation of Sugarcane Planters and the "warlord" of North Negros (now deceased), and Eduardo (Danding) Cojuangco, of the powerful Tarlac landowning family and a cousin of Corazon Aquino. Cojuangco became the nation's largest owner of sugar land and finished third in the 1992 presidential election.
26. See O'Brien (1987), McCoy (1984), and Berlow (1996). A gripping fictional treatment is found in Peter Finch's 1991 mystery novel, *Sugarland*.

Chapter 3 Production, Financing, CARP, and the U.S. Quota

1. Some 2000 production numbers for comparison: India 18.94 million m.t., Cuba 4.13 million m.t., Thailand 5.72 million m.t., Australia 5.78 million m.t., Brazil 14.50 million m.t. (down from 21.06 the previous year), and the United States 7.72 million m.t. (FAO). Up to 1987, world supply exceeded demand in twenty out of twenty-five years (Brown 1987: 6), including most of the 1980s. Since then, sugar consumption has more often exceeded production largely owing to a rapid rise in Asian demand. About 25 to 30 percent of the world's sugar is traded internationally, with the remainder being consumed in the countries that produce it.
2. In the Philippines, piculs sugar per hectare (PS/HA) is a more common measure of farm productivity than tons per hectare. Philippine PS/HA generally ranges from 70 to 85. Australian PS/HA generally ranges from 175–200.
3. PSTC varies widely among centrals. In 1990–1991, the worst in the nation (Golden Front on Panay) had a PSTC of 1.13, while that of the best (Davao on Mindanao) was 1.76 (final production CY 1990 to 1991: SRA). One SRA official admitted to me in an interview that *all* Philippine mill performance data are overstated due to "cooked numbers," and he advised me not to take these data seriously.

    Some representative figures for overall sucrose recovery (in 1988) were: Philippines (80.08 percent), Hawai'i (84.80 percent), South Africa (85.65 percent), Mauritius (87.70 percent), and Australia (89.74 percent) (Covar 1990). Former SRA administrator Arsenio Yulo confided to me in 1994 that Australia had exceeded 92 percent overall recovery.
4. Ratooning does not necessarily entail large decreases in productivity if the cane varietal is genetically selected for its ratooning properties. Some cane varietals in Australia, for example, can yield as many as seven ratoons without appreciable deterioration.
5. The Philippines exports no refined sugar. Many developed countries protect domestic refiners by accepting only raw sugar from foreign suppliers. The United States accepts only a small amount of refined sugar from countries other than its NAFTA partners, Canada and Mexico. In 1998, Australia was the world's second leading exporter (behind Brazil), and Thailand was fourth (behind Cuba).
6. The current average turn-around time in the Philippines is nine years, far above other cane producing countries. In 1992 only about one hundred breeding crosses were made, compared with seven hundred the previous year. Since the preponderance of crosses do not possess the requisite properties, it is likely that no new varietals were produced from the one hundred crosses (B. Zaragoza, pers. com.).
7. Aside from high yields on Australian farms and world-leading extrac-

tion rates in their smaller, more efficient, less polluting mills, the Australians use the fewest workers in both farm and mill, harvest largely by machine, and use a straight cane-purchase-property allocation facilitated by state-of-the-art core sampling machines.

8. Ramie is a fiber crop produced mainly in China. It has gained only limited acceptance for use in textiles but is commonly used for placemats and other decorative objects.

9. I am not sure whether Philippine-made trucks are really of poorer quality or whether this reputation is a symptom of the notorious Filipino inferiority complex about domestic products. This complex is famously illustrated by a joke known to every Filipino: A surgeon tells his patient, "Don't worry, I'll be able to use a local anesthetic for this procedure." The patient hesitates, then says, "Please, doctor, couldn't you use an imported one?"

10. See Pandan (1991), De los Reyes and Jopillo (1991), and, Ledesma and Montinola (1988) for how CARP relates to sugar land; see Joven (1990) for a primer on CARP. The definitive study on Philippine land reform is Riedinger (1995). The Ramos administration clearly never considered CARP implementation to be a major priority. Amazingly, the chairman of the Senate Committee on Agrarian Reform was Gregorio Honasan, the right-wing former army officer who led the coup attempts against Mrs. Aquino's government. While President Estrada advocated more aggressive land reform, little actually happened in his administration.

11. Under the 1989 Schedule of Current and Fair Market Values, first-class sugar land was valued at P25,000 per hectare. A 1994 revision increased the value of all classes of land, but, of course, the cost of the higher valuation would simply be passed on to the proposed beneficiaries. Governor Rafael Coscolluela told me of an incident in which a planter's land was valued at a high P60,000 per hectare, but the planter rejected the valuation insisting the land was worth P200,000 per hectare. The governor said, "Such a failure of minds to meet is the very thing that will make land reform impossible."

12. People in the sugar business often refer to the U.S. producer price of raw sugar as the "New York Contract no. 14" price and the world market price as the "New York Contract no. 11" price, reflecting the sugar futures trading on the New York Coffee, Sugar, and Cocoa Exchange. I see no good reason to use that jargon in this book. If the producer price of sugar exceeds $0.18 per pound—and it is usually 0.22–0.24—the producer must repay his CCC loan. But if the price is less than $0.18, the producer forfeits his sugar and the loan is liquidated. That is why it is referred to as a "stock financing" loan.

13. In 1994, as the new U.S. Farm Bill was being debated in Congress, the Philippines was actively lobbying to be renewed for Generalized Sys-

tem of Preference coverage to save the additional tariff. SRA Administrator Rodolfo Gamboa blamed Philippine labor unions for besmirching the reputation of Philippine sugar in the United States and for actively lobbying to get the Philippines omitted in the first place because of the poor treatment of sugarcane workers. (*Philippine Star*, 20 Mar. 1994). The Philippines was, nevertheless, renewed.

14. Under the Uruguay Round of GATT, the United States pledged not to allow total importation to go below 1.23 million tons (Skully 1998: 18), and the USDA proudly asserts that the typical total importation is approximately double that amount. Later in the 1998 fiscal year the USDA increased the overall importation and added 27,411 metric tons to the Philippine allocation (Sandique 1998).

15. Less than 50 percent of U.S. sugar comes from cane, produced in Florida, Texas, Louisiana, Hawai'i, and Puerto Rico. The remainder comes from beets, produced mostly in the upper Midwest. Beets yield less sugar per ton and per acre than cane, and therefore have a higher cost of production. But the United States has approximately 53 percent more acreage in beets than in cane (*Sugar and Sweeteners Yearbook*, 24 May 2000).

16. The 1982 quotas and the 1997 TRQs for the top five importers are as follows: (1) Dominican Republic—17.6 percent/17.0 percent; (2) Brazil—14.5 percent/14.0 percent; (3) Philippines—13.5 percent/13.0 percent; (4) Australia—8.3 percent/8.0 percent; (5) Guatemala—4.8 percent/4.6 percent (Skully 1998: 19).

17. Despite the importance of cane cultivation in Madeira and the Canary Islands in the history of European sugar production (Mintz 1985), nearly all of the EU's production today comes from beets.

Chapter 4 Property Rights, *Quedans*, and the SRA

1. Bates (1981 and 1988) discusses similar disparities in price policies in Africa.
2. Such a share system is by no means rare historically. In economies that are not fully monetized it is common for millers of grain to take a share of the final product as payment for milling. As I was writing this chapter, I spent an afternoon at a state park in Maryland only one hour from my home which contains a still-functioning gristmill dating from 1794. The brochure describes how the miller would "tak[e] his 'pottle' from each bushel of grain, about 1/8th of the bushel" (Susquehanna State Park, Rock Run Grist Mill, Historic Walking Tour).
3. The sugar industry of Mauritius continues to use a type of share system, but it has been greatly modified by adding incentives for the mills to improve efficiency. Planters' shares are calculated based upon a formula that relates the mill's performance to the nationwide average. A mill that falls below the average must subsidize the planters for the

mill's shortcomings. This formula also applies a cane-quality factor that requires the use of core sampling. The sugar industry in Colombia uses a share system similar to that in the Philippines.

4. Since Negros Occidental has no deep-water port, sugar is loaded onto barges and transshipped to neighboring islands. From there most of it is shipped to Metro Manila where most industrial end-users and exporters are located. Needless to say, getting sugar to market is complicated in an island nation.

   Another cost incurred by traders is paying to have the milled sugar refined and working out the logistics for this terminal phase of milling. Although several centrals have purchased the expensive refinery equipment in the last few years, only about 50 percent of all Philippine sugar gets refined. In Negros, for example, only three of the eighteen centrals in 1993 had refineries, and only one of those (the giant Victorias Milling Co.) was refining on a commercial scale. About 25 percent of internationally traded sugar is refined in the producing country. The remainder is exported raw and refined at the destination. The Japanese purchase only raw sugar, which gets refined in Japan. Singapore, one of Asia's major exporters of refined sugar, produces no raw sugar. The Singaporeans buy cheap world-market sugar, refine it, and then export it at very competitive prices, even to some food processing companies in the Philippines.

5. The existence of the current Big Five is a fairly recent phenomenon, dating only from the martial law period. Some of the older trading families were undermined by NASUTRA by being given smaller allocations of sugar. The current Big Five and a few other traders benefited from their closeness to Marcos and his cronies, receiving disproportionately large allocations.

6. Arsenio Yulo was administrator from the SRA's inception until 1992. In July of that year Rodolfo Gamboa, who had previously been the planters' representative on the SRA board and was an official of one of the major planters' federations, was appointed administrator, thus illustrating the loose nature of the sectoral representation. In 1997, Miguel Suarez, an official with the Negros Occidental provincial government and a strong planters' advocate, replaced Gamboa. The current administrator is Nicolas Alonso.

7. Whereas the alcohol in most American-brewed beer is fermented from corn and German beer (by law) fermented from barley malt, most San Miguel beer is fermented from sugar. But if alternative fermentables (e.g., cassava, rice) are cheaper than sugar in any given year San Miguel will use those alternatives. The manager of the Brewing Materials and Chemicals Department of San Miguel excoriated the sugar industry for its inefficiency and called for strong government action to solve the

industry's woes, including production quotas and forced modernization.
8. CONFED was begun as a spin-off from the NFSP during the later Marcos years as a rebellion against Armando Gustilo, the powerful president of NFSP and a Marcos crony who dominated the sugar industry in northern Negros. Although Guanzon was an ally of Mrs. Aquino, he became NFSP president after Gustilo's death and has remained loyal to that organization, which now represents about 17 percent of production. Planters' associations rather than individual planters are members of one or the other federation. Since a planter might belong to more than one association, especially if he sends his cane to more than one mill, it is not uncommon for an individual to be with both CONFED and NFSP at the same time. But most planters do identify themselves as partisans of one or the other.
9. Actually, only CONFED members pay the P2.54 lien for SIFI. Following a dispute over how that organization was managed, NFSP pulled out and only required its members to pay the legally mandated 54-centavo lien for SIFI. Nonetheless, several planters' associations and centrals either contribute voluntarily or support their own livelihood projects. I was told proudly by a high SIFI official that the number of employees at SIFI headquarters had been reduced to sixty-four, and that the portion of its budget spent on projects was up to 30 percent (i.e., 70 percent is spent on salaries, overhead, etc.). These numbers seem wasteful, but it should be noted that SIFI once served as an instrument of patronage for Gustilo, who packed the staff with relatives and supporters. The SIFI "group" are major power brokers among the planters.
10. Molasses trading tends to be somewhat more orderly. Molasses, mostly used for rum distilling, producing monosodium glutamate (MSG), and animal feed, has fewer traders but greater transportation difficulties than sugar. Large purchasers of molasses typically deal with only three to five traders, and payment is often in advance of receiving the molasses. This keeps costs down by enabling those traders to avoid borrowing from banks to buy up molasses *quedan*s. Many of the larger molasses traders own barges to move molasses to end-users. A significant proportion of Philippine molasses is loaded onto Japanese ships in Manila and shipped to Japan, provided it can meet the rigorous Japanese quality and purity standards.
11. See Attwood (1989, 1992), Baru (1990), and Baviskar (1980) for the case of India, Mazumdar (1998) for China, and Pérez-López (1991) for Cuba.
12. Most Philippine mills are initially fired up with more expensive bunker oil at the beginning of the milling season, and then change over to *bagasse* as soon as there is sufficient supply.
13. One example of this trend is the Sy family, the owners of Makati Agro,

one of the Big Five trading companies. Not only do the Sys own part of three centrals, but they have erected a giant distillery in Negros (in partnership with La Tondeña, the rum-making subsidiary of San Miguel). They hope to garner a significant portion of the molasses produced by the Negros centrals and become the largest alcohol producer in the Philippines.

14. Many point out, however, that since cane quality is as important as quantity in determining yield, a shift to a cane purchase would require investing in core sampling machinery to assess quality prior to milling. Such technology is available from other countries; in fact, Victorias already owns three samplers. Given the lack of trust between planters and millers, it is probable that a regulatory agent would have to supervise the weighing and sampling at each purchase point. This would entail a new role for the SRA or a successor agency.
15. According to Aguilar, this predilection toward selling and speculating instead of farming precedes the advent of the share-*quedan* system by at least several decades. In discussing planters at the turn of the twentieth century he states: "Thus, the *hacendero*s dabbled in the market; and not surprisingly, as prices constituted the aspect of the industry best known to most *hacendero*s who, as a rule, were hardly conversant with the technical or financial intricacies of sugar production. As former textile traders, playing with prices was what they knew" (1998: 108).
16. Republic Act 809 is an ambiguous law that few people in the industry understand. It applies theoretically only to those situations in which mills and planters are unable to forge a milling contract, but it also sets guidelines about milling contracts based upon mill capacity. Whether a mill could legally establish a contract based upon cane purchase is debatable. One CONFED official told me that the Act unambiguously states that all sugar must be *quedan*ed. Some argue that the law clearly implies that the sharing must be in kind (i.e., in sugar) and not in the income from sugar (cash). I myself do not read that implication in the law nor do I take the law to mean that all sugar must be *quedan*ed, but I am no Philippine legal expert.
17. Although Villanueva is a venerable name in Negros, it is a pseudonym in this case. Since the planter is not a public figure, I opt not to use his real name, even though his dispute with Mr. Go was widely reported in Negros newspapers.

Chapter 5 The Great Importation War

1. The Makati Business Club is an organization to which most of the nation's largest corporations belong.
2. The word *"trapo"* is a double entendre. On one level it stands for the

English *tra*ditional *po*litician. But it is also a Tagalog word (from the Spanish) that means "dirty rag."

3. This was part of a general move to simplify the tariff structure. Under the now-suspended Executive Order No. 413, the highest tariff rate in a four-tier system would have become 30 percent. Sugar industry leaders, on the other hand, advocated a 100 percent tariff, but this was deemed to violate the Cairns Group agreement to liberalize agricultural trade, to which the Philippines is a signatory.

4. *Nata de coco* is a fermented, transluscent, coconut-based dessert product popular in Japan.

5. *Rationalization of Tariffs on Sugar, Molasses and Sugar Substitutes*, CONFED Position Paper, 1992. Although many continue to blame the government for high costs of production, in recent years the tariffs on fertilizers have been sharply reduced and in many instances eliminated. The tax incentives for mill improvement and refinery construction also had already been instituted, but the planters' confederation did not yet realize it.

6. In the midst of the import liberalization conflict, industry leaders, including Congressman Guanzon, asked Lacson to become head of the SRA. Lacson politely declined (*Today*, 11 July 1992). Lacson told me that he turned down offers for cabinet-level posts and declined to take over as SRA Administrator because he refused to divest himself of his diverse business holdings, as a new law required such office-holders to do.

7. Although the GATT Uruguay Round language on this question is hardly plain, my own reading of the relevant Article XI is that the Philippine sugar industry does *not* meet the criteria for permitting "quotas, import or export licenses or other measures" that prohibit or restrict importation. But the Article does permit "duties, taxes or other charges" and is silent on the question of how high these duties might be.

8. Despite ardent pleas from the Philippine left, both Mrs. Aquino and Mr. Ramos were committed to continuing to service the Marcos-era debt in order to prevent the dire financial consequences that would come with debt repudiation. This necessitated IMF involvement and further lending, thus giving the IMF the power to insist on "restructuring" some aspects of the Philippine economy.

9. Between the ratification of the new post-Marcos Constitution in February 1987 and March 1991, 33,905 bills were filed in the House of Representatives. The house acted upon 5,778, 343 were enacted into law, and 7 were vetoed by the president (National Statistics Office 1992: 68).

10. The head of a large planters' organization told me that Gamboa could never be an acceptable "leader of the industry," because he was per-

ceived as being too pro-consumer and "under the thumb of the Department of Agriculture." Interestingly, two articles appeared in the press during this period hinting at an acrimonious rift between Gamboa and Agriculture Secretary Roberto Sebastian. I think that no SRA administrator could ever be sufficiently pro-producer to satisfy most planters. Consumers, on the other hand, always perceived the SRA and its administrator as the government branch of the sugar industry, entirely co-opted by the producers.

11. A food exporter had to pay the VAT, but was legally entitled to receive a rebate from the government for the full amount. The majority of exporters with whom I spoke said that they had *never* received a VAT check from the government despite having filled out all the necessary forms. When the government and the sugar industry claimed that exporters were exempt from the VAT, so D-sugar cost the same as imported world-market sugar, they were correct only in the sense that the *quedan*s for raw sugar were bought from the planter or miller at world-market prices. After the refining and freighting fees and the trader mark-up, domestic refined world-market sugar generally cost more than imported sugar, even ignoring the VAT component.

12. Since the interview was conducted, Del Monte Philippines has become a subsidiary of Del Monte Pacific, Ltd., a publicly listed company on the Singapore Stock Exchange. Part of the company is owned by Macondray Holdings of Davao, which is a Philippine company (source: anonymous reviewer of this book's manuscript).

13. All imports are in multiples of twenty-one, since one container load of sugar equals twenty-one metric tons.

14. Not surprisingly, there was much acrimony and behind-the-scenes wrangling over this choice. Some industry leaders made it clear that they had no intention of being led by Coscolluela. Many planters scoffed at the very notion of having a single industry leader and interpreted the move as a power play by one particular planters' "group." One planter commented to me that, "It isn't the 1950s anymore."

15. A fascinating study of the 1992 election in the Negros haciendas is Rutten (1994).

16. Obviously, I read virtually all of these articles and studies while conducting my research; but I feel it best not to cite them by name in order to spare their authors embarrassment. One article revealed its PHILFOODEX provenance by citing the example of *nata de coco.* That columnist wrote, "An export industry is losing ground because of government policy pampering our lazy sugar barons." And, "Sugar barons claim that to allow cheap imported sugar to enter the country will affect badly the poor sugar tillers. The problem is that regardless of the state of the industry, whether it is in a boom or a recession, the plight

of our sugar workers has remained the same" (*Manila Chronicle*, 22 July 1994).
17. The Constitution allows for a certain number of representatives from under-represented "sectors" to be appointed by the president, for example women, labor, farmers, youth, the urban poor, mountain tribes, and the Muslim community.
18. The Department cited a study conducted by the Agricultural Policy Research and Advocacy Assistance Program at the University of the Philippines, Los Baños, and funded by USAID.

Chapter 6 Rationalization, Groupism, and the Chinese

1. Currently, Charlie Cojuangco is a congressman from Negros Occidental. His brother, Mark, is a congressman from Pangasinan in Luzon. Mark's given name is Marcos.
2. He also told me that he had heard about several instances in which a significant portion of the benefits meant for the workers had been appropriated by unscrupulous "labor leaders." Ironically, after this trader purchased the mill he "retrenched" (i.e., laid off) many of its workers, arguing that he needed to "rationalize" the mill's operations.
3. One Congressman associated with the sugar industry was quoted in a newspaper article as telling sugar producers not to worry about the impending hike in the minimum wage for farm workers since "the government will always support the industry by ensuring good sugar prices once salaries are adjusted" (*Today*, 24 Nov. 1993).
4. In a conversation about the retrenchment of six hundred workers at the BISCOM mill, one sugar consultant told me, "The Chinese manage for rationality."
5. Ironically, the Tagalog version ("Bayan Magiliw") is a translation of the English lyrics that were sung through the American colonial period, "Land of the Morning." The English was, in turn, a rendering of the original Spanish anthem written by Julian Felipe in 1898—the history of Philippine colonialism in a song!
6. The article's most remarkable line was as follows: "A former mayor who fought him for many years developed sentimental on how Armin C. Gustilo picked him up from the road, injured, assaulted and weeping from the *political* battles they fought. Then nursed him back to health, and he became his disciple." They must have been hard fought political battles to have left the mayor on that road "injured, assaulted and weeping."
7. Similar arguments are made in many of the articles in Hann and Dunn (1996).
8. Michael Pinches has documented how middle-class Filipinos frequently cite the Chinese as the group whose values and practices Fili-

pinos should emulate. He also describes the many methods that Filipino-Chinese businesspeople employ to portray themselves as first and foremost Filipinos. In Pinches's interviews with urban middle-class people, entrepreneurs, and business managers, not one person cited ownership of agricultural land as an important criterion of status or rank (1999: 292).
9. Of five "successful family businesses" profiled in Lee-Chua's (1997) study of Philippine elites, three are ethnic Chinese.
10. Aguilar (1998) argues that the propensity to gamble is *the* most defining cultural characteristic of sugar planters and that this propensity largely explains the way they transact their sugar and live their lives. I am doubtful that such a heterogeneous group can be so easily reduced to one essential trait, and indeed I myself know many sugar planters with no interest in gambling. Moreover, many planters I know are highly risk-adverse in their business dealings.

References

Abu-Lughod, Lila. 1991. "Writing Against Culture." In *Recapturing Anthropology: Working in the Present*. Richard G. Fox, ed. Santa Fe, N.Mex.: School of American Research.

Aguilar, Filomeno V. 1984. *The Making of Cane Sugar: Poverty, Crisis and Change in Negros Occidental*. Bacolod: Social Research Center, University of St. LaSalle.

———. 1994. "Beyond Inevitability: The Opening of Philippine Provincial Ports in 1855." *Journal of Southeast Asian Studies* 25: 70–90.

———. 1998. *Clash of Spirits: The History of Power and Sugar Planter Hegemony on a Visayan Island*. Honolulu: University of Hawai'i Press.

———. 2000. "The Republic of Negros." *Philippine Studies* 48: 26–52.

Akerlof, George. 1976. "The Economics of Caste and of the Rat Race and Other Woeful Tales." *Quarterly Journal of Economics* 90: 599–617.

Anderson, Benedict. 1987. "Cacique Democracy in the Philippines: Origins and Dreams." *New Left Review* 167: 3–31.

Angeles-Forster, Nora. 1995. *The Survival of Privilege: Strategies of Political Resilience of Oligarchies in the Philippines, 1946–1992*. Ph.D. Dissertation, Department of Political Science, Queens University, Kingston, Ontario.

Asad, Talal. 1983. "Anthropological Conceptions of Religion: Reflections on Geertz." *Man* 18: 237–259.

Attwood, Donald W. 1989. "Does Competition Help Co-operation?" *Journal of Development Studies* 26: 5–27.

———. 1992. *Raising Cane: The Political Economy of Sugar in Western India*. Boulder, Colo.: Westview Press.

Banfield, Edward C. 1958. *The Moral Basis of a Backward Society*. New York: Free Press.

Barth, Fredrik. 1987. *Cosmologies in the Making: A Generative Approach to Cultural Variation in Inner New Guinea*. New York: Cambridge University Press.

———. 1989. "The Analysis of Culture in Complex Societies." *Ethnos* 54: 120–142.

Baru, Sanjaya. 1990. *The Political Economy of Indian Sugar*. Delhi: Oxford University Press.

Bates, Robert H. 1981. *Markets and States in Tropical Africa: The Political Basis of Agricultural Policies*. Berkeley: University of California Press.

———. 1988. "Government and Agricultural Markets in Africa." In *Toward a Political Economy of Development: A Rational Choice Perspective*. Robert H. Bates, ed. Berkeley: University of California Press.

———. 1989. *Beyond the Miracle of the Market: The Political Economy of Agrarian Development in Kenya*. Cambridge: Cambridge University Press.

Baviskar, B. S. 1980. *The Politics of Development: Sugar Co-operatives in Maharastra*. Delhi: Oxford University Press.

Berger, Peter L. 1963. *Invitation to Sociology: A Humanistic Perspective*. Garden City, N.Y.: Anchor Press.

———. 1986. *The Capitalist Revolution: Fifty Propositions about Prosperity, Equality, and Liberty*. New York: Basic Books.

———, ed. 1990. *The Capitalist Spirit: Toward a Religious Ethic of Wealth Creation*. San Francisco: ICS Press.

Berger, Peter L., and Hsin-Huang Michael Hsiao, eds. 1988. *In Search of an East Asian Development Model*. New Brunswick, N.J.: Transaction Books.

Berlow, Alan. 1996. *Dead Season: A Story of Murder and Revenge on the Philippine Island of Negros*. New York: Pantheon Books.

Bhagwati, Jagdish. 1988. *Protectionism*. Cambridge, Mass.: MIT Press.

Biggart, Nicole Woolsey. 1991. "Explaining Asian Economic Organization: Toward a Weberian Institutional Perspective." *Theory and Society* 20: 199–232.

Billig, Michael S. 1991. "Stuck in Molasses: The Lack of Economic Diversification in Negros Occidental." *Pilipinas* 16: 19–43.

———. 1992a. "Sweet Reason: The Rationality of Growing Sugar on Negros." *Philippine Studies* 40: 153–182.

———. 1992b. Review of *The Negrense: A Social History of an Elite Class*, by Violeta B. Lopez-Gonzaga. *Pilipinas* 18: 87–90.

———. 1993. "Syrup in the Wheels of Progress: The Inefficient Organization of the Philippine Sugar Industry." *Journal of Southeast Asian Studies* 24: 122–147.

———. 1994. "The Death and Rebirth of Entrepreneurism on Negros Island, Philippines: A Critique of Cultural Theories of Enterprise." *Journal of Economic Issues* 28: 659–678.

———. 1997. "The Philippine 'Sugar Barons': Do Our Political Commitments Prevent Us from Taking Elite Culture Seriously?" Paper delivered at the annual meeting of the American Anthropological Association. Washington, D.C., November 1997.

———. 1999. "Keeping Our Politics Out of Others' Business." *Anthropology Newsletter* 40 (2, Feb. 1999): 62–64.

———. 2000. "Institutions and Culture: Neo-Weberian Economic Anthropology." *Journal of Economic Issues* 34: 771–788.

Brown, James G. 1987. *The International Sugar Industry: Developments and Prospects.* Washington, D.C.: The World Bank.

Cannell, Fenella. 1999. *Power and Intimacy in the Christian Philippines.* Cambridge: Cambridge University Press.

Cariño, Theresa C. 1998. *Chinese Big Business in the Philippines: Political Leadership and Change.* Singapore: Times Academic Press.

Central Bank. 1992. *Philippine Financial System—1991 Fact Book.* Manila: Central Bank.

Chandler, Alfred D. 1977. *The Visible Hand: The Managerial Revolution in American Business.* Cambridge, Mass.: Belknap Press.

———. 1984. "The Emergence of Managerial Capitalism." *Business History Review* 58: 473–503.

———. 1990. *Scale and Scope: The Dynamics of Industrial Capitalism.* Cambridge, Mass.: Belknap Press.

Chapman, William. 1987. *Inside the Philippine Revolution: The New People's Army and its Struggle for Power.* New York: W. W. Norton & Company.

Cheong, Caroline Mar Wai Jong. 1983. *The Chinese-Cantonese Family in Manila: A Study in Culture and Education.* Manila: Centro Escolar University.

Clifford, James. 1988. *The Predicament of Culture: Twentieth-Century Ethnography, Literature, and Art.* Cambridge, Mass.: Harvard University Press.

Clifford, James, and George E. Marcus, eds. 1986. *Writing Culture: The Poetics and Politics of Ethnography.* Berkeley: University of California Press.

Cohen, Abner. 1981. *The Politics of Elite Culture: Explorations in the Dramaturgy of Power in a Modern African Society.* Berkeley: University of California Press.

Collins, Joseph. 1989. *The Philippines: Fire on the Rim.* San Francisco: Institute for Food and Development Policy.

Collins, Randall. 1975. *Conflict Sociology.* New York: Academic Press.

———. 1986. *Weberian Sociological Theory.* Cambridge: Cambridge University Press.

———. 1994. *Four Sociological Traditions.* Oxford: Oxford University Press.

Covar, Rogelio R. 1990. "Factors Affecting Cane and Juice Quality." *Philippine Sugar Quarterly* 1 (2): 26–52.

Crapanzano, Vincent. 1986. "Hermes' Dilemma: The Masking of Subversion in Ethnographic Description." In *Writing Culture.* J. Clifford and G. E. Marcus, eds. Berkeley: University of California Press.

Cuesta, Angel M. 1980. *History of Negros.* Manila: The Historical Conservation Society.

Cullamar, Evelyn Tan. 1986. *Babaylanism in Negros: 1896–1907.* Quezon City: New Day Press.

Dacanay, Alexander Elemancil. 1982. *Growth and Development of the Sugar Manufacturing Sector, 1956–80.* Masters Thesis, Institute for Industrial Economics, Center for Research and Communication, Pasig City, Metro Manila.

Dahrendorf, Ralf. 1958. *Class and Class Conflict in Industrial Society.* Stanford: Stanford University Press.

David, Cristina C. 1989. "Philippines: Price Policy in Transition." In *Food Price Policy in Asia.* T. Sicular, ed. Ithaca, N.Y.: Cornell University Press.

De Los Reyes, Romana, and Sylvia Ma. G. Jopillo. 1991. *Pursuing Agrarian Reform in Negros Occidental.* Manila: Institute of Philippine Culture, Ateneo de Manila University.

De Soto, Hernando. 1989. *The Other Path: The Invisible Revolution in the Third World.* New York: Harper and Row.

———. 2000. *The Mystery of Capital.* New York: Basic Books.

Eisenstadt, S. N. 1954. "Reference Group Behavior and Social Integration: An Explorative Study." *American Sociological Review* 19: 175–185.

———. 1986. *A Sociological Approach to Comparative Civilizations: The Development and Directions of a Research Program.* Jerusalem: The Harry S. Truman Research Institute for the Advancement of Peace, Hebrew University.

Eisenstadt, S. N., and L. Roniger 1984. *Patrons, Clients, and Friends: Interpersonal Relations and the Structure of Trust in Society.* Cambridge: Cambridge University Press.

FAO. *FAOSTAT Database of Agricultural Production.* Rome: Food and Agriculture Organization. (Accessed at: http://apps.fao.org/).

Fallows, James M. 1987. "A Damaged Culture." *Atlantic Monthly* (Nov. 1987).

———. 1994. *Looking at the Sun: The Rise of the New East Asian Economic and Political System.* New York: Pantheon Books.

Feeny, David. 1993. "The Demand for and Supply of Institutional Arrangements." In *Rethinking Institutional Analysis and Development.* V. Ostrom, D. Feeny, and H. Picht, eds. San Francisco: Institute for Contemporary Studies.

Finch, Peter. 1991. *Sugarland.* New York: St. Martin's Press.

Finn, Janet L. 1998. *Tracing the Veins: Of Copper, Culture, and Community From Butte to Chuquicamata.* Berkeley: University of California Press.

Frank, Andre Gunder. 1967. *Capitalism and Underdevelopment in Latin America.* New York: Monthly Review Press.

Frydenlund, John E. 1995. "Reform the Sugar, Peanut, and Dairy Programs." *The Heritage Foundation Bulletin* 216. Washington, D.C.: The Heritage Foundation.

Fukuyama, Francis. 1995. *Trust: The Social Virtues and the Creation of Prosperity.* New York: The Free Press.

Geertz, Clifford. 1963. *Peddlers and Princes.* Chicago: University of Chicago Press.
———. 1973. *The Interpretation of Cultures.* New York: Basic Books.
———. 1980. *Negara: The Theatre State in Nineteenth-Century Bali.* Princeton: Princeton University Press.
———. 2000. *Available Light: Anthropological Reflections on Philosophical Topics.* Princeton: Princeton University Press.
Genova, José. 1988. *The Philippine Archipelago: Brief Notes on the Formation of Agricultural Colonies in the Island of Negros.* (English reprint of 1896 volume). Bacolod: Social Research Center, University of St. LaSalle.
Genovese, Eugene D. 1969. *The World the Slaveholders Made: Two Essays in Interpretation.* 1st ed. New York: Pantheon Books.
———. 1974. *Roll, Jordan, Roll: The World the Slaves Made.* 1st ed. New York: Pantheon Books.
———. 1992. *The Slaveholders' Dilemma: Freedom and Progress in Southern Conservative Thought, 1820–1860.* Columbia, S.C.: University of South Carolina Press.
———. 1994. *The Southern Tradition: The Achievement and Limitations of an American Conservatism.* Cambridge, Mass.: Harvard University Press.
Gerth, Hans H., and C. Wright Mills, eds. 1946. *From Max Weber: Essays in Sociology.* New York: Oxford University Press.
Gilder, George. 1981. *Wealth and Poverty.* New York: Basic Books.
———. 1984. *The Spirit of Enterprise.* New York: Simon and Schuster.
Ginsburg, Faye D. 1998. *Contested Lives: The Abortion Debate in an American Community* (updated ed.). Berkeley: University of California Press.
Gluckman, Max. 1955. *Custom and Conflict in Africa.* Oxford: Blackwell Press.
Goodell, Grace. 1995. "Another Way to Skin a Cat: The Spirit of Capitalism and the Confucian Ethic." *The National Interest* 42 (Winter 1995/96): 66–71.
Goodno, James B. 1991. *The Philippines: Land of Broken Promises.* London: Zed.
Goody, Jack. 1996. *The East in the West.* Cambridge: Cambridge University Press.
Gregory, C. A., and J. C. Altman. 1989. *Observing the Economy.* London: Routledge Press.
Hann, C. M.. 1998. "Introduction: The Embeddedness of Property." In *Property Relations: Renewing the Anthropological Tradition.* C. M. Hann, ed. Cambridge: Cambridge University Press.
Hann, Chris and Elizabeth Dunn, eds. 1996. *Civil Society: Challenging Western Models.* London: Routledge Press.
Harrison, Lawrence E. 1985. *Underdevelopment Is a State of Mind: The Latin American Case.* Center for International Affairs, Harvard University. Lanham, Md.: University Press of America.

———. 1992. *Who Prospers?: How Cultural Values Shape Economic and Political Success.* New York: Basic Books.
Harrison, Lawrence E., and Samuel P. Huntington, eds. 2000. *Culture Matters: How Values Shape Human Progress.* New York: Basic Books.
Hawes, Gary. 1987. *The Philippine State and the Marcos Regime: The Politics of Export.* Ithaca, N.Y.: Cornell University Press.
Hefner, Robert W. 1990. *The Political Economy of Mountain Java: An Interpretive History.* Berkeley: University of California Press.
Herzfeld, Michael. 1992. *The Social Production of Indifference: Exploring the Symbolic Roots of Western Bureaucracy.* Chicago: University of Chicago Press.
Himmelfarb, Gertrude. 1999. *One Nation, Two Cultures.* New York: Alfred A. Knopf.
Hofileña, Josefina Dalupan. 1996. "Life in the Occupied Zone: One Planter's Experience of War." *Journal of Southeast Asian Studies* 27: 82–94.
Hofstede, Geert. 1980. *Culture's Consequences: International Differences in Work-related Values.* Beverly Hills, Calif.: Sage Publications.
Hollnsteiner, Mary R. 1963. *The Dynamics of Power in a Philippine Municipality.* Quezon City: Community Development Research Center, University of the Philippines.
Huntington, Samuel P. 1996. *The Clash of Civilizations and the Remaking of World Order.* New York: Simon and Schuster.
Hutchcroft, Paul D. 1998. *Booty Capitalism: The Politics of Banking in the Philippines.* Ithaca, N.Y.: Cornell University Press.
———. "Colonial Masters, National Politicos, and Provincial Lords: Central Authority and Local Autonomy in the American Philippines, 1900–1913." *The Journal of Asian Studies* 59: 277–306.
Jagan, Larry, and John Cunnington. 1987. *Social Volcano: Sugar Workers in the Philippines.* London: W.O.W. Campaigns, Ltd.
Janelli, Roger L. (with Dawnhee Yim). 1993. *Making Capitalism: The Social and Cultural Construction of a South Korean Conglomerate.* Stanford: Stanford University Press.
Jones, Gregg R. 1989. *Red Revolution: Inside the Philippine Guerilla Movement.* Boulder, Colo.: Westview Press.
Joven, José R. 1990. *Primer on Land Reform and Taxation.* 2d ed. Quezon City: Rex Printing.
Junker, Laura Lee. 1994. "The Development of Centralized Craft Production Systems in A.D. 500–1600 Philippine Chiefdoms." *Journal of Southeast Asian Studies* 25: 1–30.
———. 1996. "Hunter-Gatherer Landscapes and Lowland Trade in Prehispanic Philippines." *World Archaeology* 27: 389–410.
———. 1999. *Raiding, Trading, and Feasting: The Political Economy of Philippine Chiefdoms.* Honolulu: University of Hawai'i Press.

Kaplan, Robert D. 1996. *The Ends of the Earth: A Journey to the Dawn of the 21st Century.* New York: Random House.
Kerkvliet, Benedict J. T. 1990. *Everyday Politics in the Philippines.* Berkeley: University of California Press.
———. 1995. "Toward a More Comprehensive Analysis of Philippine Politics: Beyond the Patron-Client, Factional Framework." *Journal of Southeast Asian Studies* 26: 401–419.
Kessler, Richard J. 1989. *Rebellion and Repression in the Philippines.* New Haven: Yale University Press.
Klitgaard, Robert. 1990. *Tropical Gangsters: One Man's Experience with Development and Decadence in Deepest Africa.* New York: Basic Books.
———. *Adjusting to Reality: Beyond 'State Versus Market' in Economic Development.* San Francisco: International Center for Economic Growth.
Kunio, Yoshihara. 1988. *The Rise of Ersatz Capitalism in South-East Asia.* Quezon City: Ateneo de Manila University Press.
Lacson, Daniel L. 1988. *Poverty and Adjustment in Negros Occidental, Philippines.* Washington, D.C.: Symposium on Poverty and Adjustment, The World Bank.
Landé, Carl. 1965. *Leaders, Factions, and Parties: The Structure of Philippine Politics.* New Haven: Southeast Asia Studies, Yale University.
Larkin, John A. 1993. *Sugar and the Origins of Modern Philippine Society.* Berkeley: University of California Press.
Ledesma, Antonio J., and Ma. Lourdes T. Montinola, eds. 1988. *The Implementation of Land Reform in Negros.* Bacolod: Social Research Center, University of St. LaSalle.
Lee-Chua, Queena N. 1997. *Successful Family Businesses: Dynamics of Five Filipino Business Families.* Quezon City: Ateneo de Manila University Press.
Lizares, Nicanor Padilla. 1993. *The Negros Sugar Industry: Coping with the Challenges of the 1990s.* Master's Thesis, Department of International Relations, Center for Research and Communication, Pasig City, Metro Manila.
LMC International. 1997. *A World Survey of Sugar and HFCS Field, Factory, and Freight Costs: 1997 Report.* Oxford, United Kingdom.
Lopez-Gonzaga, Violeta B. 1983. *Mechanization and Labor Employment: A Study of the Sugarcane Workers' Responses to Technological Change in Sugar Farming in Negros.* Bacolod: Social Research Center, University of St. LaSalle.
———. 1984. *The Sacadas in Negros: A Poverty Profile.* Bacolod: Social Research Center, University of St. LaSalle.
———. 1985. *Crisis and Poverty in Sugarlandia: The Case of Bacolod.* Bacolod: Social Research Center, University of St. LaSalle.
———. 1986. *Crisis in Sugarlandia: The Planters' Differential Perceptions and*

Responses and Their Impact on Sugarcane Workers' Households. Bacolod: Social Research Center, University of St. LaSalle.

———. 1987a. *Voluntary Land Sharing and Transfer Scheme in Negros.* Bacolod: Social Research Center, University of St. LaSalle.

———. 1987b. *Capital Expansion, Frontier Development, and the Rise of the Monocrop Economy in Negros (1850–1898).* Bacolod: Social Research Center, University of St. LaSalle.

———. 1989. *The Socio-Politics of Sugar: Wealth, Power Formation and Change in Negros (1899–1985).* Bacolod: Social Research Center, University of St. LaSalle.

———. 1991. *The Negrense: A Social History of an Elite Class.* Bacolod: Institute for Social Research and Development, University of St. LaSalle.

Lopez-Gonzaga, Violeta B., Virgilio Aguilar, and Ferris Fe Demegilio. 1988. *The Resource Base for Agrarian Reform and Development in Negros Occidental.* Bacolod: Social Research Center, University of St. LaSalle.

Lopez-Gonzaga, Violeta B., and Michelle Decena. 1990. "Negros in Transition: 1899–1905." *Philippine Studies* 38: 103–114.

Lord, Ron and Nydia Suarez. 1997. "Sugar and Sweeteners" (10 July 1997). Washington, D.C.: Economic Research Service, U.S. Department of Agriculture.

Lynch, Frank. 1964. *Four Readings in Philippine Values.* Quezon City: Ateneo de Manila University Press.

———. 1984. *Philippine Society and the Individual: Selected Essays of Frank Lynch, 1949–1976.* A. A. Yengoyan and P. Q. Makil, eds. Ann Arbor: Center for South and Southeast Asian Studies, University of Michigan.

Mackie, Jamie. 1992. "Changing Patterns of Chinese Big Business in Southeast Asia." In *Southeast Asian Capitalists.* Ruth McVey, ed. Ithaca, N.Y.: Southeast Asia Program, Cornell University.

———. 1998. "Business Success Among Southeast Asian Chinese: The Role of Culture, Values, and Social Structures." In *Market Cultures: Society and Morality in the New Asian Capitalisms.* Robert W. Hefner, ed. Boulder, Colo.: Westview Press.

Marcus, George E. (with Peter Dobkin Hall). 1992. *Lives in Trust: The Fortunes of Dynastic Families in Late Twentieth-Century America.* Boulder, Colo.: Westview Press.

Matthews, R.C.O. 1986. "The Economics of Institutions and the Sources of Growth." *The Economic Journal* 96: 903–918.

Mazumdar, Sucheta. 1998. *Sugar and Society In China: Peasants, Technology, and the World Market.* Cambridge, Mass.: Harvard University Asia Center, Monograph Series, no. 45.

McBeath, Gerald A. 1973. *Political Integration of the Philippine Chinese.* Berkeley: Center for South and Southeast Asian Studies, University of California, Monograph 8.

McCay, Bonnie J. 1998. *Oyster Wars and the Public Trust: Property, Law, and Ecology in New Jersey History.* Tucson, Ariz.: University of Arizona Press.

McCloskey, Dierdre N. 1996. *The Vices of Economists—The Virtues of the Bourgeoisie.* Amsterdam: Amsterdam University Press.

McCoy, Alfred W. 1982. "A Queen Dies Slowly: The Rise and Decline of Iloilo City." In *Philippine Social History.* A. W. McCoy and Ed. C. de Jesus, eds. Honolulu: University of Hawai'i Press.

———. 1983. "In Extreme Unction: The Philippine Sugar Industry under Martial Law." In *Political Economy of Philippine Commodities.* R. S. David, ed. Quezon City: Third World Studies Program, University of the Philippines.

———. 1984. *Priests on Trial.* Ringwood, Australia: Penguin Australia.

———. 1991. "The Restoration of Planter Power in La Carlota City." In *Local Perspectives on the Transition from Marcos to Aquino.* B.J.T. Kerkvliet and R. Mojares, eds. Manila: Ateneo de Manila University.

———, ed. 1993. *An Anarchy of Families: State and Family in the Philippines.* Madison: Center for Southeast Asian Studies, University of Wisconsin.

McVey, Ruth, ed. 1992. *Southeast Asian Capitalists.* Ithaca, N.Y.: Southeast Asia Program, Cornell University.

Meenahan, John M. 1985. "When Sweetness Goes." *Veritas,* October 27.

Merton, Robert K. 1957. *Social Theory and Social Structure.* Chicago: The Free Press of Glencoe.

Mills, C. Wright. 1956. *The Power Elite.* New York: Oxford University Press.

Mintz, Sidney. 1985. *Sweetness and Power: The Place of Sugar in Modern History.* New York: Penguin Books.

———. 2000. "Sows' Ears and Silver Linings: A Backward Look at Ethnography." *Current Anthropology* 41: 169–189.

Nader, Laura. 1972. "Up the Anthropologist—Perspectives Gained from Studying Up." In *Reinventing Anthropology.* Dell Hymes, ed. New York: Random House.

National Statistics Office. 1991. *The Philippines in Figures.* Manila: National Statistics Office.

———. 1992. *1992 Philippine Yearbook.* Manila: National Statistics Office.

Newman, Katherine S. 1999. *Falling From Grace: Downward Mobility in the Age of Affluence* (updated ed.). Berkeley: University of California Press.

North, Douglass C. 1990. *Institutions, Institutional Change and Economic Performance.* Cambridge: Cambridge University Press.

North, Douglass C., and Robert Paul Thomas. 1973. *The Rise of the Western World: A New Economic History.* Cambridge: Cambridge University Press.

O'Brien, Niall. 1987. *Revolution From the Heart.* New York: Oxford University Press.

———. 1993. *Island of Hope, Island of Tears.* Maryknoll, N.Y.: Orbis Books.

Ofreneo, R. E. 1987 (updated ed.). *Capitalism in Philippine Agriculture.* Quezon City: Foundation for Nationalist Studies.

Omohundro, John T. 1981. *Chinese Merchant Families in Iloilo: Commerce and Kin in a Central Philippine City.* Quezon City: Ateneo de Manila University Press.

Pandan, Raymundo T., ed. 1991. *The Agrarian Reform Process in Negros Occidental.* Bacolod: Institute for Social Research and Development, University of St. LaSalle.

Paxton, John, ed. 1982. *The Statesman's Year-Book, 1982–83.* London: Macmillan.

Pérez-López, Jorge F. 1991. *The Economics of Cuban Sugar.* Pittsburgh: University of Pittsburgh Press.

Pinches, Michael. 1996. "The Philippines' New Rich: Capitalist Transformation Amidst Economic Gloom." In *The New Rich in Asia: Mobile Phones, McDonalds, and Middle Class Revolution.* Richard Robison and David S. G. Goodman, eds. London: Routledge Press.

———. 1997. "Elite Democracy, Development, and People Power: Contending Ideologies and Changing Practices in Philippine Politics." *Asian Studies Review* 21: 104–120.

———. 1999. "Entrepreneurship, Consumption, Ethnicity, and National Identity in the Making of the Philippines' New Rich." In *Culture and Privilege in Capitalist Asia.* Michael Pinches, ed. London: Routledge Press.

Plant, Roger. 1987. *Sugar and Modern Slavery: A Tale of Two Countries.* London: Zed.

PSMA. 1993. *Facts and Figures on Philippine Sugar, 1970–1990.* Makati: Philippine Sugar Millers Association, Inc.

Putnam, Robert D. 1993. *Making Democracy Work: Civic Traditions in Modern Italy.* Princeton: Princeton University Press.

———. 2000. *Bowling Alone: The Collapse and Revival of American Community.* New York: Simon and Schuster.

Pye, Lucian W. 1985. *Asian Power and Politics: The Cultural Dimensions of Authority.* Cambridge, Mass.: Belknap Press.

Quirino, Carlos. 1974. *History of the Philippine Sugar Industry.* Manila: Kalayaan Press.

Riedinger, Jeffrey M. 1995. *Agrarian Reform in the Philippines: Democratic Transitions and Redistributive Reform.* Stanford, Calif.: Stanford University Press.

Roney, John C. 1991. "E.C. and U.S. Sugar Regimes: A Comparative Analysis of Supports and Costs." *Sugar y Azucar,* Nov. 1991: 26–32.

Rosenberg, Nathan and L. E. Birdzell, Jr. 1986. *How the West Grew Rich: The Economic Transformation of the Industrial World.* New York: Basic Books.

Rutten, Rosanne. 1982. *Women Workers of Hacienda Milagros: Wage Labor and Household Subsistence on a Philippine Sugar Plantation.* Amsterdam: Universiteit van Amsterdam.

———. 1994. "Courting the Workers' Vote: Rhetoric and Response in a Philippine Hacienda Region." *Pilipinas* 22: 1–34.

———. 1996. "Popular Support for the Revolutionary Movement CPP-NPA: Experiences in a Hacienda in Negros Occidental, 1978–1995." In *The Revolution Falters: The Left in Philippine Politics After 1986.* P. N. Abinales, ed. Ithaca, N.Y.: Southeast Asia Program Publications, Cornell University.

Sahlins, Marshall. 1999. "Two or Three Things that I Know about Culture." *Journal of the Royal Anthropological Institute* 5: 399–421.

Sandique, Rhea P. 1998. "RP Sugar Quota in U.S. increased by 27,411 MT." Bayanihan News Service, United Kingdom.

Sa-onoy, Modesto P. 1984. *The Philippine Sugar Trading Monopoly.* Bacolod: Negros Occidental Historical Commission.

———. 1992. *A History of Negros Occidental.* Bacolod: Today Publishers.

Schor, Juliet. 1998. *The Overspent American: Upscaling, Downshifting, and the New Consumer.* New York: Basic Books.

Schultz, Theodore W., ed. 1978. *Distortions of Agricultural Incentives.* Bloomington: University of Indiana Press.

Scott, James C. 1985. *Weapons of the Weak: Everyday Forms of Peasant Resistance.* New Haven: Yale University Press.

———. 1990. *Domination and the Arts of Resistance: Hidden Transcripts.* New Haven: Yale University Press.

Scott, William Henry. 1992. *Looking for the Prehispanic Filipino and Other Essays in Philippine History.* Quezon City: New Day Publishers.

Sidel, John T. 1989. "Beyond Patron-Client Relations: Warlordism and Local Politics in the Philippines." *Kasarinlan* 4: 19–30.

———. 1997. "Philippine Politics in Town, District, and Province: Bossism in Cavite and Cebu." *Journal of Asian Studies* 56: 947–966.

Skully, David W. 1998. "Auctioning Tariff Quotas for U.S. Sugar Imports." *Sugar and Sweetener* (Economic Research Service, USDA), May: 17–21.

Sowell, Thomas. 1994. *Race and Culture: A World View.* New York: Basic Books.

———. 1996. *Migrations and Culture: A World View.* New York: Basic Books.

Suarez, Nydia. 1997. "Origin of the U.S. Sugar Import Tariff-Rate Quota Shares." *Sugar and Sweetener* (Economic Research Service, USDA), Sept.: 14–15.

Szanton, David L. 1998. "Contingent Moralities: Social and Economic Investment in a Philippine Fishing Town." In *Market Cultures: Society and Morality in the New Asian Capitalisms.* Robert W. Hefner, ed. Boulder, Colo.: Westview Press.

Tan, Antonio S. 1984. *The Chinese Mestizos and the Formation of the Filipino Nationality*. Quezon City: University of the Philippines Press.
Thompson, E. P. 1966. *The Making of the English Working Class*. New York: Vintage Press.
Timberman, David G. 1991. *A Changeless Land: Continuity and Change in Philippine Politics*. Singapore: Institute for Southeast Asian Studies.
Timmer, C. Peter. 1986. *Getting Prices Right: The Scope and Limits of Agricultural Price Policy*. Ithaca, N.Y.: Cornell University Press.
Vandergeest, Peter, and Frederick H. Buttel. 1988. "Marx, Weber, and Development Sociology." *World Development* 16: 683–695.
Vayda, Andrew P. 1994. "Actions, Variations, and Change: The Emerging Anti-Essentialist View in Anthropology." In *Assessing Cultural Anthropology*. Robert Borofsky, ed. New York: McGraw-Hill.
Wallerstein, Immanuel. 1974. *The Modern World System*. New York: Academic Press.
Weber, Max. 1958 [1904–1905]. *The Protestant Ethic and the Spirit of Capitalism*. Translated by Talcott Parsons. New York: Charles Scribner's Sons.
———. 1968a. "'Objectivity' in Social Science." In *Readings in the Philosophy of the Social Sciences*. M. Brodbeck, ed. New York: Macmillan.
———. 1968b [1921–1922]. *Economy and Society: An Outline of Interpretive Sociology*. G. Roth and C. Wittich, ed. New York: Bedminster Press.
———. 1981. *General Economic History*. New Brunswick, N.J.: Transaction Publishers.
Wells, Miriam J. 1996. *Strawberry Fields: Politics, Class, and Work in California Agriculture*. Ithaca, N.Y.: Cornell University Press.
Wertheim, Wim F. 1995. "The Contribution of Weberian Sociology to Studies of Southeast Asia." *Journal of Southeast Asian Studies* 26: 17–29.
Wickberg, Edgar. 1965. *The Chinese in Philippine Life, 1850–1898*. New Haven: Yale University Press.
Wilkinson, Alec. 1989. *Big Sugar: Seasons in the Cane Fields of Florida*. New York: Knopf.
Williamson, Oliver E. 1985. *The Economic Institutions of Capitalism*. New York: Free Press.
Wolf, Eric R. 1999. *Envisioning Power: Ideologies of Dominance and Crisis*. Berkeley: University of California Press.
Wolfe, Alan. 1989. *Whose Keeper?: Social Science and Moral Obligation*. Berkeley: University of California Press.
World Bank. 1986. *Philippines Sugarlands Diversification Study*. Report #6042-PH. Washington, D.C.: World Bank.
World Bank, Asia Region. 1987. *Philippines Agricultural Sector Strategy Review*, vol. 2. Washington, D.C.: World Bank.
Yengoyan, Aram A. 1984. "Values and Institutions in the Philippines: The Social Anthropology of Frank Lynch." In *Philippine Society and the*

Individual: Selected Essays of Frank Lynch, 1949–1976. A. A. Yengoyan and P. Q. Makil, eds. Ann Arbor: Center for South and Southeast Asian Studies, University of Michigan.

Newspapers, Magazines, and Data Sources Cited.
Agribusiness Monitor. Pasig City, Metro Manila: Center for Research and Communication.
Annual Synopsis of Philippine Sugar Factories Performance Data. Manila and Bacolod: Sugar Regulatory Administration.
Asiaweek. Hong Kong: Time, Inc.
Asian Development Bank. Manila.
Associated Press.
Balita-L listserve. http://www.balita.org/news_archives.shtml.
The Bottler. Coca-Cola, Philippines. Manila.
Business World. Manila.
Central Bank of the Philippines Annual Reports. Manila.
CONFED (Confederation of Sugarcane Planters), Manila.
Economic Research Service. Washington, D.C.: USDA.
Facts and Figures on Philippine Sugar, 1970–1990. Manila: Philippine Sugar Millers Association.
Far Eastern Economic Review. Hong Kong: Dow Jones & Co.
The Financial Express. Manila.
Food and Agribusiness Monitor. Pasig City, Metro Manila: Center for Research and Communication.
Food and Agriculture Organization On-Line Datatbase. http://apps.fao.org.
General Agreement on Tariff and Trade (GATT).
Indian Express Newspapers. Bombay.
Inventory of Statistics Available in Government. Manila: National Statistical Coordination Board.
Manila Bulletin.
Manila Chronicle.
Manila Journal.
Manila Standard.
Manila Star
MSNBC On-Line. http://www.msnbc-com/news/.
National Federation of Sugarcane Workers. Bacolod.
National Statistics Office. Manila
Office of the United States Trade Representative. Washington, D.C.
Philippine Chamber of Food Manufacturers. Manila.
Philippine Daily Inquirer. Manila.
The Philippine Financial System Fact Book. Manila: The Central Bank of the Philippines.
Philippine Food Exporters Association (PHILFOODEX). Manila.

Philippine Headline News. Manila.
Philippine Magazine. Manila.
The Philippine Star. Manila.
Philippine Sugar Millers, Association. Makati. Web address: http://www/psma/com.ph.
Philippine Sugar Technologists Association (PHILSUTECH). Manila.
Philippine Times Journal. Manila.
Philsutech Sugar Journal. Manila.
SRA Newsletter. Manila and Bacolod: Sugar Regulatory Administration.
Sugar and Sweeteners Summary. Washington, D.C.: USDA.
Sugar and Sweeteners Yearbook. Washington, D.C.: USDA.
Sugar Industry Foundation, Inc. (SIFI). Bacolod.
Sugar Regulatory Administration. Manila.
Sugar Technologist. Manila.
Time Magazine. New York: Time, Inc.
Today. Bacolod.
United States Department of Agriculture On-Line Database. http://www.usda.gov/nass/.
Visayan Daily Star. Bacolod.
World Bank. Washington, D.C.
World Population Data Sheet. Washington, D.C.: Population Reference Bureau.
World Trade Organization Web-Site. http://www.wto.org/

Index

Abu-Lughod, Lila, 17, 291
advance contracts, 120, 174, 175, 181
advocacy: critique of, 11–13, 147, 271–273
agricultural knowledge and practices: of planters, 38, 49, 63–64, 83, 112, 127, 131, 153, 205, 213, 239, 244, 245, 248, 267, 268, 286n. 15
agsa, 38, 278n. 10. *See also* tenancy
Aguilar, Filomeno V., 33, 36–42, 45, 47, 48, 49, 52, 53, 57, 68, 277nn. 1, 4, 6, 7, 278nn. 9, 10, 11, 12, 286n. 15, 290n. 10, 291
Akerlof, George, 275n. 5, 291
Alonso, Nicolas, 142, 284n. 6
Altman, J. C., 4, 295
"American" planter, 202, 243–250
amo, 24, 204, 208, 210
Anderson, Benedict, 26, 291
Angeles-Forster, Nora, 26, 291
anthropology, 4–5, 6, 16, 31, 189, 230, 252, 253, 272, 273. *See also* advocacy; ethnographic methods; reflexivity
anti-national accusation, 149, 154, 170, 174, 176, 184, 188, 197, 215, 216, 217, 228, 256
apriorism, 145, 203, 225, 226, 240, 269, 271
Aquino, Corazon C. "Cory," 2, 78, 82, 114, 148, 151, 152, 204, 214, 280n. 25, 282n. 10, 285n. 8, 287n. 8
Araneta family, 52, 251, 253, 280n. 21; Amading, 253; Juan, 40
Arroyo, Gloria Macapagal, 157, 168, 190
Asad, Talal, 17, 291
ASEAN (Association of Southeast Asian Countries), 99, 163, 173, 175
Asian culture: and capitalism, 18, 275n. 3
aspartame, 29, 262

A-sugar, 103, 105, 107, 109, 110, 112–113
Attwood, Donald W., 285n. 11, 291
Australia: milk production, 173; sugar policies, 29, 91; sugar production and trade, 44, 60–61, 64, 94, 99, 124, 166, 177, 180, 181, 199, 281nn. 1, 2, 3, 4, 5, 281n. 7, 283n. 16
babaylanismo, 41, 278n. 12
Bacolod (city), 2, 76, 109, 152, 159, 185, 190, 191, 192, 244, 262; early history, 34; Estrada visit to, 257–258; papal visit to, 58
bagasse, 119, 124, 125, 133, 134, 135, 266, 285n. 12
Banfield, Edward C., 23–24, 291
bank centrals, 48, 49, 279n. 17
banking and finance, 78–82, 86–87, 130, 145, 221, 242, 258, 260, 261, 262; culture of, 252. *See also* credit and moneylending; crop loans
Barth, Fredrik, 17, 291
Baru, Sanjaya, 285n. 11, 291
Basic Christian Communities, 58
Batangas (province), 71, 72
Bates, Robert H., 218, 275n. 5, 283n. 1, 291–292
Baviskar, B. S., 285n. 11, 292
beer, 174, 284n. 7
beet sugar, 97, 283nn. 15, 17; lobbying of, 97; power of, 46, 50, 55–56; rise of, 40, 44, 99
Benedicto, Roberto S. "RSB," 56, 57, 58, 68, 83, 155, 218, 227, 246, 247, 280nn. 24, 25. *See also* Marcos, Ferdinand; restitution
Berger, Peter L., 6, 275n. 3, 276n. 9
Berlow, Alan, 58, 237, 275n. 1, 280n. 26, 292

305

beverage companies, 26, 70, 116, 120, 123, 156, 158, 167, 169, 172, 174–177, 199, 267, 284n. 7
Bhagwati, Jagdish, 194, 292
Bicol (region), 54, 72
bi-culturalism, 30–31, 177, 201, 202, 243–250
"Big Five" traders, 108–109, 132, 227, 239, 284n. 5, 286n. 13
Biggart, Nicole W., 275n. 3, 292
Billig, Michael S., 6, 12, 17, 27, 52, 83, 101, 191, 243, 277n. 1, 292; author's involvement, 140–142, 147, 155, 165, 189–194, 244, 247, 249, 271–272, 273
Binalbagan-Isabela Planters' Association (BIPA), 237, 238
Birdzell, L. E., 9, 300
BISCOM (Binalbagan-Isabela Sugar Company), 105, 136, 141, 237, 289n. 4
Board of Investment (BOI), 70–71, 87, 133, 170, 171, 183, 214
bodegas, 55, 56, 105, 107, 108, 111, 112, 114–115, 117, 118, 122, 123, 125, 128, 129, 134, 137, 138, 139, 220, 223
boilers (mills), 119, 127, 129, 133, 266
bonded warehouses, 151–152, 159, 164, 165, 166, 168, 169, 171, 177, 179, 182, 183, 198
boycott threats, 135, 136, 138, 150, 152, 155, 158, 173, 176, 179
Brazil, 92, 94, 99, 119, 199, 263, 264, 281nn. 1, 5, 283n. 16
Brown, James G., 154, 261, 263, 281n. 1, 293
B-sugar, 103–104, 105, 107, 109, 110, 112, 113, 167, 177, 180, 182; B1–sugar, 104, 110
bunker oil, 134, 285n. 12
Bureau of Internal Revenue (BIR), 80, 123, 130, 183. *See also* taxation
BUSCO (Bukidnon Sugar Company), 108, 132, 178, 179, 183, 239

cabo, 38, 205
CAFGUS (Citizens' Armed Forces Geographical Units), 115, 204
Cagayan (province), 54, 71, 72
Cagayan de Oro (province), 177

Camarines Sur (province), 71, 72
Canada, 91, 93, 96, 281n. 5
cane purchase experiment, 132–142, 144, 147, 267
cane purchase system, 46, 106–107, 120, 123, 124, 125–132, 144, 145, 146, 147, 223, 231, 281n. 7, 286n. 16
Canlaon (town and volcano), 136, 244
Canlubang sugar mill, 72–73, 279n. 16
Cannell, Fenella, 276n. 7, 293
capitalism, 144, 256, 259, 278n. 12; as ideal type, 21; transformation of, 4, 8, 251–262
carabao (water buffalo), 43, 44, 45, 85, 87, 278n. 14
Cariño, Theresa C., 242, 293
cattle, 74, 160, 173, 264
Cavite (province), 73, 262
Cebu (province and city), 33, 37, 71, 72, 133, 182, 258, 276n. 8, 277n. 2, 279n. 16
Central Bank of the Philippines, 79, 80, 81, 148, 149, 150, 155, 198, 293; CB-bills, 81–82
Central Luzon (region): bank lending in, 79; predominant role in early sugar production, 33, 38, 43; sugar production, 1, 72. *See also* Pampanga; Tarlac
centrals. *See* mills and millers
Chandler, Alfred D., 275n. 5, 293
Chapman, William, 26, 293
Cheong, Caroline Mar Wai Jong, 242, 293
Chikiamco, Calixto, 256
China, 8, 32, 33, 40, 45, 262, 278n. 11, 282n. 8, 285n. 11
Chinese: analysis of, 241–243; animosity toward, 28, 52, 121, 129, 139, 198, 202, 219, 220, 227, 239, 243; arrival in Pampanga, 42–43; definition of, 276n. 11; emulation of, 28, 202, 241, 242, 243, 253, 255, 259, 289n. 8 (*see also* reference groups); image of, 28, 30, 52, 55, 81, 121, 130, 137, 138, 139, 183, 198, 201, 202, 241, 242, 243, 262; purported advantage in obtaining credit, 81, 242; trading and, 55, 85, 108, 121, 129, 130, 132, 137, 140, 164,

176, 182, 183, 198, 219, 239, 241, 243, 254, 259, 290n. 9
Chinese mestizos, 241; 276n. 11; Iloilo elites, 34–36, 277n. 7; Pampanga elites, 42–43, 286n. 15
church: role of Philippine, 34, 58, 211, 240, 273
civil society, 5, 23–24, 227, 239, 240, 241, 269
Clifford, James, 17, 293
Coca-Cola, 70, 133, 156, 158, 163, 167, 169, 172; interview with executive of, 175–177
cockfighting, 38, 50, 76, 206, 244–245, 249. *See also* gambling
coconut, 32, 66, 75, 167
cogeneration, 119, 124, 129, 266
Cohen, Abner, 275n. 2, 293
Cojuangco, Eduardo "Danding," 83, 134, 136, 138, 145, 148, 176–177, 187, 218, 233, 248, 280n. 25; rationalization of farm, 205–208
Cojuangco family, 78, 122, 207, 222–223; Charlie, 206, 289n. 1; Mark, 289n. 1
collective action, 4, 10, 22–23, 26, 30, 47, 101, 114, 132, 146, 161, 170, 184, 185–186, 187, 193, 194, 195, 196, 197, 202, 227, 231, 235, 237, 240–241, 250, 261, 280nn. 20, 21. *See also* "groups" and "groupism"; "personalism"
Collins, Joseph, 26, 293
Collins, Randell, 10, 252, 293
Commodity Credit Corporation (CCC), 90, 96, 97, 221, 282n. 12
"communist" accusation, 21, 58, 88, 210, 213, 218
comparative advantage, 30, 68, 75, 100, 154, 158, 167, 215, 216, 217, 260, 263
competition: fear of, 126, 128, 129, 132, 153, 158, 164, 168, 179, 181, 183, 184, 212, 215, 216, 217, 219, 222, 224, 227, 261
Comprehensive Agrarian Reform Program (CARP), 59, 82–88, 101, 138, 144, 156, 160, 186, 187, 200, 205, 206, 213, 216, 246, 261, 262, 264, 268, 282nn. 10, 11; as example of property rights, 15, 101

CONFED, 89, 113–114, 115, 126, 150, 152, 159, 160, 161, 186, 190, 192, 208, 209, 224, 231, 232, 233, 234, 236, 255, 285nn. 8, 9, 286n. 16, 287n. 5
conflict: among elites, 103, 144, 145, 146, 252, 253, 254, 256, 257, 269, 271, 273, 276nn. 9, 10; as focus of study, 9–11, 13, 30, 143, 145, 193, 202, 252, 253, 257, 271, 273; food processors vs. government, 117, 118, 157, 167, 171, 179, 288n. 10; millers vs. food processors, 171–172, 184; planters vs. food processors, 102, 109–110, 112, 117, 150, 151, 154, 155, 156, 158, 159, 164, 166, 167, 168, 169, 175, 179, 181, 183, 184, 188–189, 195–196, 198, 216, 258; planters vs. government, 108, 111, 113–114, 115, 123, 149, 152, 155, 162, 163, 208, 221, 222, 231, 287n. 5, 288n. 10; planters vs. millers, 14, 47, 48, 52–53, 54, 116, 117, 118, 119, 122, 123, 124, 128, 129, 136, 138, 139, 140, 142, 160, 219, 231, 237, 253, 265, 280n. 21, 286n. 14; planters vs. planters, 114, 115, 197, 231; planters vs. traders, 35, 107, 108, 110, 111, 112, 120–121, 122, 124, 130, 135, 219, 220, 223, 239, 243. *See also* collective action
conflict of interest, 172, 176
Congress, Philippine, 68, 109, 159–160, 161, 181, 183, 184, 189–190, 191, 198, 231, 234, 261, 282n. 10, 287n. 9, 289n. 17. *See also* import "rationalization" bill; sugar bloc
consensus tradition, 251–252, 253
consolidation of sugar industry, 120, 121, 122, 235
consumer interests, 10, 15, 101, 102, 103, 107, 109, 114, 116–117, 129, 145, 146, 154, 158, 163, 164, 166, 167, 168, 169, 173, 174–175, 178, 180, 188, 196, 198, 199, 217, 226, 233, 234, 256, 257, 258, 261, 262, 263, 267, 268, 284n. 7, 287n. 10. *See also* food processing industries
cooperatives, 48, 58, 80, 85, 87, 88, 106, 117, 121, 124, 187, 210, 213, 235, 236
core sampling, 106, 128, 129, 283n. 3, 286n. 14

corn, 33, 72, 75–76, 101, 160, 264, 284n. 7
corruption, 21, 49, 115, 149, 162, 172, 177, 179, 188, 192, 230, 231, 237, 249, 256
Coscolluella, Rafael "Lito," 84, 140, 159–160, 184, 185, 186, 211, 233, 234, 235, 236, 282n. 11, 288n. 14
Covar, Rogelio, 61, 62, 280n. 3, 293
crab mentality (or "crabs-in-a-barrel"), 23, 126, 229, 230, 235, 237
Crapanzano, Vincent, 17, 293
credit and moneylending, 15, 33, 35, 36, 43, 45, 47, 49, 64, 78–79, 80, 81, 108, 116, 121, 130, 200, 203, 209, 242, 245, 278nn. 9, 13. *See also* banking and finance; crop loans
crisis of 1970s and 1980s, 1–2, 5, 55–59, 69, 153–154, 197, 217, 243, 262, 264, 272
crop loans, 35, 45, 49, 56, 76, 78–79, 80, 81, 82, 86–87, 130, 145, 163, 221, 264. *See also* banking and finance; credit and moneylending
C-sugar, 104, 105, 107, 108, 109, 110, 163
Cuba, 29, 44, 45, 47, 51, 54, 65, 90, 96, 119, 264, 281nn. 1, 5, 285n. 11
Cuesta, Angel M., 277n. 1, 293
Cullamar, Evelyn Tan, 41, 293
cultural change, 2, 145, 147, 177, 210, 211, 241–242, 243, 250, 254, 255, 256, 257, 258, 259, 260, 261, 265, 268, 289n. 8
cultural values: bourgeois, 3, 26, 28, 249, 254, 255, 256, 258, 272; changing, 129, 153, 177, 210, 211, 224, 227, 241, 242, 249, 255, 256, 268, 273, 289n. 8; and the Chinese, 239, 242, 243, 254, 255; discussion of, 240; and economic activity, 8, 17–18, 241, 242, 243, 255, 256–257, 275n. 3; about high fertility, 225–226; personalizing, 3, 177, 192–193. *See also* "groups" and "groupism"; paternalism
culture: American, 244–250, 254; boundaries of, 19–20, 251, 252, 253; conceptions of, 6, 16–22, 192–193, 201, 228, 242, 244, 249, 250, 252, 254, 269; heterogeneity of, 11, 19, 145–146, 251, 252, 254, 256, 259, 273; as ideal type, 16–23, 201, 228, 251, 252, 253, 268; and institutions, 143–147, 253, 255, 257, 259, 267, 268, 269; use of in Philippines, 129, 210, 211, 212, 242, 244, 249. *See also* essentialism; Philippine culture; planter culture
culturological school, 8–9, 25, 228, 229, 242
Cunningham, John, 277n. 1, 296
Customs, Bureau of, 149, 150, 151, 155, 179

Dacanay, Alexander Elemancil, 56, 65, 294
Dahrendorf, Ralf, 10, 294
Danao sugar mill, 135, 137
David, Cristina C., 101–102, 294
dead season, 39, 203
debt bondage, 37, 38, 43, 278n. 9
debt servicing, 80–81, 287n. 8
Decena, Michelle, 277n. 1, 298
Del Monte, 72, 150, 151, 156, 169, 288n. 12; interview with executive of, 177–179
De Los Reyes, Romana, 282n. 10, 294
Demegilio, Ferris Fe, 277n. 1, 298
Democratic and Independent Workers' Association (DIWA), 214, 248
Department of Agrarian Reform (DAR), 83, 84, 85, 86, 210. *See also* Comprehensive Agrarian Reform Program
Department of Agriculture, 101, 149, 162, 198, 200, 264, 288n. 10
Department of Environment and Natural Resources (DENR), 73
Department of Finance (DOF), 148, 159, 168, 185, 198, 214
Department of Labor and Employment (DOLE), 77, 114, 115
Department of Trade and Industry (DTI), 70, 163, 165
dependency: of workers, 25, 37, 39, 53, 204, 208, 209, 210, 211, 212, 224, 248, 250
De Soto, Hernando, 9, 15, 218, 294
de Venecia, Jose, 160
diversification, 15, 52, 73, 74–75, 80–81, 82, 83, 84, 119, 124, 153, 157, 160, 167,

186, 206, 210, 216, 223, 224, 233, 254, 262, 263, 264, 266, 268, 284n. 7
Dole (company), 72, 151, 156, 169, 177; interview with executive of, 179–182
Dominican Republic, 92, 283n. 16
Don Pedro sugar mill, 72, 183
D-sugar, 104, 105, 109, 110, 112, 118, 120, 151, 154, 155, 161, 163, 164, 165, 166, 167, 168, 170, 171, 174, 177, 178, 180, 181, 288n. 11
dumaans, 38, 40, 54, 204
"dumping" accusation, 2, 29, 98, 100, 152, 162, 163
Dunn, Elizabeth, 289n. 7, 295

economic anthropology, 269, 270; and ethnographic methods, 4–5, 270; and neo-Weberian approach, 6, 269, 270. *See also* anthropology; ethnographic methods; neo-Weberian approach
economics: as field of study and ideology, 4, 95, 127, 143, 144, 157, 158, 167, 181, 194, 206, 215, 217, 224–225, 226, 253, 269, 270, 271, 275n. 5
economic value of children, 225, 226
EDSA revolution, 2, 93, 101, 148, 232
Eisenstadt, S. N., 276nn. 7, 9, 10, 294
elites, 7, 26–27, 202, 209, 251, 255, 256, 257, 258, 259, 272, 290n. 9; conflict among, 27, 145, 146, 252, 253, 254, 256, 257, 272, 276nn. 9, 10; images of, 26–28, 198; loyalties of, 40, 44; and "studying up," 5, 144, 275n. 2, 276nn. 8, 9, 10. *See also* rural elites; urban elites
El Niño, 60, 62, 69, 104, 199
encargados, 38, 203, 205, 245
entrepreneurism, 1, 14, 17, 18, 27, 52, 68, 74–75, 107, 138, 195, 202, 205, 224, 241, 243, 245, 259, 276n. 8, 289n. 8
essentialism, 16, 17–20, 211, 228, 239, 240, 254, 268. *See also* culture, as ideal type; reification
Estrada, Joseph E. "Erap," 199, 257, 258, 267, 282n. 10
E-sugar, 104, 105, 111, 112, 118, 120, 154, 155, 165, 166, 174

ethnographic methods, 31, 189, 192–193, 270, 271
European Union: sugar policies, 29, 98–99, 154, 157, 160, 162, 166, 221; sugar production, 99, 184, 264, 283n. 17. *See also* beet sugar; quotas; sugar consumption, in Europe
exports, non-sugar, 148, 151, 158, 182, 260; coconut oil, 66; electronics, 66, 151, 260; garments, 65, 151, 153, 260. *See also* food processing industries, as exports

Fallows, James M., 8, 18, 228, 229, 230, 239, 294
"familism": as ideal type, 22–23
Far Eastern Economic Review, 148, 303
Farm Bills (U. S.), 92, 97, 98, 113, 282n. 13
"farmer": pejorative conception of, 130–131, 139, 145, 266, 267, 268
Federico, Ed, 213–214, 248
Feeny, David, 13, 294
"feudal" description, 1, 21, 117, 154, 161, 215, 254, 258, 262
Finch, Peter, 280n. 26, 296
Finn, Janet L., 10, 294
First Farmers sugar mill, 121, 236
Florida, 95, 96, 283n. 15
Food and Agriculture Organization (FAO), 57, 60, 61, 65, 89, 92, 99, 281n. 1
food processing industries, 10, 26, 99–100, 116, 117–118, 119–120, 159, 169, 184, 257, 258, 261, 263, 267; advocacy of import liberalization, 148, 151, 156, 163, 167, 168, 169, 178, 179, 188, 194; conflicts within, 156, 169, 170, 195, 196, 238; conflicts with sugar industry, 30, 100, 112, 114, 151, 156, 164–165, 169, 170, 171, 179, 184, 194, 195, 284n. 7; as exports, 26, 29, 104, 109, 111, 148, 151, 154, 159, 164, 166, 167, 169, 170, 174, 177, 178, 179, 181, 196, 288n. 11; image of, 154, 169–170, 179, 180, 188; importing sugar by, 30, 109, 111, 149, 151, 152, 158–159, 165, 166, 170, 173, 174, 175, 176, 177–179; opinions of cane pur-

chase, 140, 145–146; use of journalists by, 188–189. *See also* bonded warehouse; consumer interests
Fortich, Bishop Antonio, 58
France, 65, 99
Frank, Andre Gunder, 9, 294
"free market," 98, 99, 100, 102, 109, 135, 138, 144, 146, 148, 155, 156, 157, 163, 184, 188, 192, 194, 195, 197, 203, 205, 222, 227, 250, 257, 260, 271; advocacy of, 153, 154, 158, 168, 190, 195, 196, 206, 208, 214, 216, 223, 224, 257; as ideal type, 21–22, 30. *See also* rationalization
free-riding, 195, 240
free trade vs. protectionism, 148, 149, 153, 155, 162, 163, 166, 167, 169, 184, 190, 192, 194, 202–203, 208, 215, 216, 217, 223, 224, 257, 271. *See also* "free market"; protectionism; rationalization
Frydenlund, John E., 98, 294
Fukuyama, Francis, 8, 18, 23, 294

gambling, 50, 286n. 15, 290n. 10. *See also* cockfighting
Gamboa, Rodolfo "Dodol," 98, 99, 109, 114, 162, 185, 233, 234, 283n. 13, 284n. 6, 287n. 10; interview with, 162–164
Gaston, Yves Leopold, 34, 36, 277n. 5
GATT, 91, 97, 153, 157, 158, 161, 162, 163, 184, 185, 217, 258, 283n. 14, 287n. 7
Geertz, Clifford, 4, 20, 211, 252, 253, 275nn. 3, 4, 295
gender: and entrepreneurship, 28, 244, 245; and work, 204. *See also* masculinity
Generalized System of Preferences (GSP), 91, 282n. 13
Genovese, Eugene D., 12–13, 295
Gerth, Hans H., 12, 272, 295
Gilder, George, 8, 295
Ginsburg, Faye D., 10, 295
globalization, 4, 28–29, 153, 158, 192, 214, 215, 217, 223, 224, 250, 255, 256, 257, 258, 265, 268, 271
Go family, 132–142, 144, 145, 206, 219, 223, 237, 286n. 17; Alejandro "Andoy," 132, 133, 134, 135, 136, 137, 138, 139, 140, 141, 144, 145, 237, 267, 286n. 17; Alex, 138, 140, 141; Mary, 133
Goodell, Grace, 7, 295
Goodno, James B., 26, 295
Goody, Jack, 7, 295
Gregory, C. A., 4, 295
"groups" and "groupism," 22, 23, 30, 101, 191, 193, 195, 246, 252, 253, 255, 288n. 14; analysis of, 226–241; and civil society, 239–241; criticism of from within, 235, 246; as ideal types, 22, 23, 30, 201–202, 230. *See also* collective action; "personalism"
Guanzon, Romeo "Roming," 109, 110, 113–114, 115, 122, 150, 159, 200, 231, 233, 285n. 8, 287n. 6
Gustilo, Armando "Armin," 227, 232, 236, 280n. 25, 285nn. 8, 9, 289n. 6; Gustilo "group," 232, 234, 236, 237

"*hacenderos*," 1, 11, 35, 37, 38–40, 45, 47, 50, 106, 130, 198, 203, 205, 213, 278n. 9, 286n. 15. *See also* planters; "sugar barons"
Hacienda Luisita. *See* Luisita
Hann, Chris, 14, 289n. 7, 295
Hare-Hawes-Cutting bill, 50–51
Harrison, Lawrence E., 8, 9, 17–18, 295–296
hauling. *See* trucking and transloading
Hawai'i, 44, 45, 47, 96, 159, 177, 281n. 3, 283n. 15
Hawaiian-Philippines sugar mill, 132, 136, 141
Hawes, Gary, 33, 53, 56, 57, 58, 276n. 1, 280n. 24, 296
hectarage, 46–47, 48, 52, 57, 60–61, 63–64, 76, 78, 85, 117, 134, 236. *See also* Comprehensive Agrarian Reform Program
Hefner, Robert W., 275n. 3, 296
Herzfeld, Michael, 7, 296
high fructose corn syrup, 29, 92, 95, 96, 263
high value crops, 75, 84, 153, 160, 223, 224, 268. *See also* diversification

Himmelfarb, Gertrude, 8–9, 296
Hofileña, Josefina Dalupan, 280n. 19, 296
Hofstede, Geert, 18, 296
Hollnsteiner, Mary R., 276n. 7, 296
Hong Kong, 81, 118, 168, 170, 180, 181, 246
Hsiao, Hsin-Huang Michael, 275n. 3, 292
Huntington, Samuel P., 8, 9, 296
Hutchcroft, Paul D., 26, 296

ice cream, 116, 169, 172, 173, 182
ideal types, 7, 19–25, 201, 230, 260, 269, 270; culture as, 16–23, 31, 201, 228, 251, 252, 253, 268, 269; listing of, 21. *See also* neo-Weberian approach; Weber, Max
Iloilo (city), 34–35, 36; sugar port, 35, 45; textile production, 34–36, 277n. 7.
import liberalization, 114, 148, 149, 150, 152, 153, 154, 156, 157, 159, 163, 164, 165, 166, 167, 168, 169, 171, 175, 178, 179, 183, 184, 186, 194, 196, 199, 200, 216–217, 250, 258, 262, 287n. 6
import "rationalization" bill, 159, 160, 161, 162, 163, 164, 167, 168, 169, 170, 171, 173, 174, 175, 178, 179, 181, 183, 185, 186, 188, 189, 190, 194, 198, 214, 217, 224, 234
incorporation: of farms, 78, 130
India, 8, 44, 119, 124, 262, 281n. 1, 285n. 11
individual agency, 210–211, 235, 246, 250, 265, 268; and culture, 19–20, 225–226, 268
Indonesia, 29, 44, 111, 168, 252, 253, 260
infrastructural improvements, 2, 50, 155, 221, 260, 264
institutions: of capitalism, 256; creation of new, 14, 103, 143, 144, 145, 209, 241, 253, 256, 257, 267, 269; and culture, 14, 20, 31, 131, 143–147, 171, 202, 253, 257, 265, 267, 268, 269, 270; and efficiency, 30, 116, 125, 143, 144, 146, 147, 152, 171, 265, 267, 270; as ideal types, 20, 31, 269; and individual interests, 14, 103, 241, 256, 264;

of Philippine sugar, 101, 103, 112, 116–126, 129, 143, 144, 146–147, 171, 202, 264, 265–269; supply of and demand for, 13–14, 143–147
interest rates, 35, 76, 80–82, 85, 108, 155, 160, 163, 264
interests: competing, 11, 15, 103, 114, 161, 194, 202, 215, 226, 227, 239, 240, 250, 253, 256, 276n. 10; cultural construction of, 10, 13, 14, 19, 103, 144, 145, 146, 193, 203, 215, 224–225, 230, 253, 254, 269
International Monetary Fund (IMF), 57, 86, 148, 157, 161, 163, 185, 188, 214, 217, 287n. 8

Janelli, Roger L., 275n. 2, 296
Japan, 280n. 24; culture in, 228; land reform in, 82; lending to traders, 81; sugar consumption, 40, 120, 165, 262, 278n. 11, 284n. 4; sugar policies, 29, 93, 104, 158, 285n. 10
Jardine-Davies company, 132, 138, 139, 141
Jones, Gregg R., 26, 296
journalists: role in political debates, 161, 166, 179, 184–185, 186, 188, 191, 192, 193, 195, 231, 232, 233, 262, 288n. 16
Junker, Laura Lee, 277n. 4, 296

Kaplan, Robert D., 8, 297
kasamac, 42, 43, 54, 278n. 10
Kerkvliet, Benedict J. T., 276n. 7, 297
Kessler, Richard J., 26, 297
kinship, 22, 86, 227, 228, 230, 237, 238, 242, 246, 247; fictive, 229
Klitgaard, Robert, 218, 297
Kunio, Yoshihara, 26, 297

labor supply, 37–40, 49, 50, 68, 208, 278n. 9
labor unions, 48, 57–58, 87–88, 114, 185, 188, 204, 233–234, 248, 273, 283n. 13, 289n. 2; conflict among, 25, 88, 212–214, 238; groupism among, 238; opinions of rationalization, 25, 203, 212–214; opinions of workers, 25, 211, 213; red vs. yellow, 87–88, 213

312   Index

Lacson, Daniel L. "Bitay," 57, 58, 75, 77, 84, 152, 153, 157–158, 159, 185, 223, 224, 233, 234, 235, 287n. 6, 297; diversification plan, 75, 84, 224, 233

La Granja Agricultural Research and Extension Center, 66–67, 124. *See also* sugar research

Laguna (province), 48, 71, 72, 262, 279n. 15

Land Bank, 83, 84, 85, 88, 282n. 11. *See also* Comprehensive Agrarian Reform Program; Department of Agrarian Reform

Landé, Carl, 276n. 7, 297

land holdings. *See* hectarage

land reform. *See* Comprehensive Agrarian Reform Program

Larkin, John A., 32, 33, 34, 36, 38, 39, 41, 42, 43, 44, 46, 47, 48, 49, 52, 53, 276n. 1, 278n. 13, 279nn. 15, 16

Laurel-Langley Trade Agreement, 54, 55, 90

leaders, 1, 22, 23, 232, 239, 240; centrality of, 159, 184, 185, 190, 195, 227, 230, 235, 236, 237, 238, 287n. 10, 288n. 14. *See also* "groups" and "groupism"; sugar industry, leader of

Ledesma, Antonio J., 277n. 1, 282n. 10, 297

Lee-Chua, Queena N., 290n. 9, 297

leftist perspectives, 87–88, 188, 209–210, 213, 262, 287n. 8

letter of credit, 149, 150

Leyte (island), 71, 132

liens, 51, 67, 77, 89, 96, 115, 208, 233, 285n. 9

livelihood projects, 25, 209, 210, 213, 232, 235, 285n. 9

Lizares, Nicanor Padilla, 64, 297

LMC International, 64, 94, 297

lobbying, 45, 47, 48, 51, 77, 89, 90, 96, 97, 102, 111, 115, 148, 169, 170, 172, 174, 178, 179, 180, 195, 196, 224, 231, 282n. 13

Lomé Convention, 98, 99, 163. *See also* European Union, sugar policies

Loney, Nicholas, 34–35, 277n. 7

Lopez family, 52, 56–57, 251; Fernando, 56–57

Lopez-Gonzaga, Violeta B., 34, 36, 37, 41, 45, 50, 57, 68, 275n. 1, 277n. 1, 278n. 9, 297–298

Lord, Ron, 66, 298

Louisiana, 95, 96, 283n. 15

Luisita (Hacienda), 67, 70, 78, 121–122, 222

Luzuriaga, Eusebio de, 34, 36, 277n. 5

Lynch, Frank, 3, 276n. 7, 298, 303

Mackie, Jamie, 242, 298

Macondray and Company, 173, 288n. 12

Magna Carta of Small Farmers, 162, 185, 198

Magnolia, 173–174

Makati (city): as power center, 3, 198, 227, 255

Makati Business Club, 148, 261, 286n. 1

Malaysia, 66, 111, 168, 173, 175, 260

malnutrition, hunger, and starvation, 1–2, 50, 57, 59, 77, 85, 197, 205, 216, 217, 272

Manila, 26, 28, 34, 52, 73, 76, 102, 122, 159, 167, 183, 188, 189, 192, 244, 246, 250, 253, 258, 263, 276n. 8; bank lending in, 79; British occupation of, 32; opening to foreign trade, 32–33; port of, 32, 44, 284n. 4, 285n. 10; Spanish defeat, 40

Marcos, Ferdinand: policies toward sugar industry, 1–2, 54–59, 79, 82, 140, 155, 164, 168, 206, 218, 227, 247, 280nn. 24, 25, 284n. 5. *See also* Benedicto, Roberto S.; crisis of 1970s and 1980s

Marcos, Imelda, 58, 148, 247

Marcus, George E., 17, 275n. 2, 293, 298

Marxist economic anthropology, 6, 7, 8, 10, 143

masculinity, 2, 57, 131, 139

Matthews, R. C. O., 275n. 5, 298

Mauritius, 281n. 3, 283n. 3

Mazumdar, Sucheta, 285n. 11, 298

McBeath, Gerald A., 242, 298

McCay, Bonnie J., 10, 299
McCloskey, Deirdre N., 272, 299
McCoy, Alfred W., 26, 34, 35, 37, 46, 50, 58, 275n. 1, 276nn. 7, 11, 1, 277n. 1, 278n. 9, 280nn. 18, 26
mechanization: on sugar farms, 45, 50, 63, 68, 71, 87, 281n. 7
Meenahan, John M., 57, 299
mestizos. *See* Chinese mestizos
Mexico, 32, 33, 91, 93, 95–96, 281n. 5
middle class: rise of, 26, 27–28, 197, 240, 258, 259, 262, 289n. 8
military bases, 51, 53, 72, 92, 93, 113
milling contracts, 47, 48, 49, 52–53, 54, 76, 105, 122, 131, 132, 134, 136, 138, 141, 142, 219, 265, 279n. 16, 280n. 21, 285n. 8, 286n. 16
milling districts, 10, 22, 47, 55, 105, 125, 126, 132, 134, 135, 175, 218, 219, 224, 261, 268, 279n. 16
milling season, 47, 72, 77, 79, 107, 114, 123, 133, 134. *See also* dead season
mills and millers: capacity of, 2, 48, 60, 61, 71, 73, 107, 131, 133, 134, 135, 138; competition among, 105, 119, 125, 128, 135, 139–140, 141, 145, 219; consolidation of, 52–53, 54, 71, 73, 118, 120, 121, 122, 125, 126, 128, 219, 222, 251, 262; culture of, 140, 219, 243, 249, 251, 252, 254; diversification attempts, 74, 119; efficiency of, 49, 61, 62, 64, 69, 73, 106, 114, 118–119, 122–123, 125, 126, 136, 138, 139, 141, 143, 153, 154, 176, 222, 281nn. 3, 7, 283n. 3; on the farm, 42, 46, 49, 106, 116; gentlemen's agreement among, 135, 137, 140, 219; groupism among, 238–239; investment and improvement of, 118–119, 126–127, 128, 141, 183–184, 219, 249, 258, 266; location of, 71–72; marketing of sugar by, 73, 107, 116, 120, 124, 127, 128, 167, 170, 171, 175; opinions of cane purchase, 128, 139–140, 145, 266, 267; technological sophistication of, 1, 47, 49, 61–62, 69, 118, 126, 155, 239, 249, 266; transition to centrifugal, 46–47, 48, 106, 116, 144, 265. *See also* conflict, miller vs. food processors; conflict, planter vs. miller; traders, purchasing of mills by
Mills, C. Wright, 10, 12, 272, 295, 299
Mindanao (island), 41, 54, 71, 72, 84, 108, 115, 132, 160, 172, 177, 178, 179, 180, 245, 281n. 3
minimum wage, 64, 69, 77, 186, 204, 208, 213, 289n. 3. *See also* sugarcane workers, wages of
Mintz, Sidney, 16, 35, 257, 283n. 17
Mitra, Ramon, 114, 187
modern and modernization, 1, 4, 106, 117, 146, 147, 154, 158, 161, 166, 167, 179, 183, 188, 193, 200, 202, 252, 259, 260, 269, 285n. 7
molasses, 62, 71, 81, 93, 104, 105, 106, 119, 125, 127, 134, 153, 160, 164, 237, 264, 285n. 10, 286n. 13
Monetary Board, 148, 149, 150, 152, 153, 157
moneylending. *See* credit and moneylending
monocrop economy, 21, 41, 62, 262
monopsony, 22, 47, 55, 56, 220, 275n. 6
monosodium glutamate (MSG), 62, 160, 285n. 10
Montilla, Don Agustin, 34, 36, 277n. 5
Montinola, Jose Marie "Joe Marie," 233
Montinola, Ma. Lourdes T., 277n. 1, 282n. 10, 297
moscovado sugar, 46, 49, 278n. 14
Mount Pinatubo, 67, 69, 72
multinational companies, 10, 29, 149, 150, 151, 156, 164, 165, 169, 172, 175–183, 188, 198, 217; concern for reputation, 149, 156, 172, 175, 176, 179, 180, 188

NACUSIP (National Congress of Unions in the Sugar Industry of the Philippines), 212–213, 233
Nader, Laura, 5, 299
NAFTA (North American Free Trade Agreement), 91, 93, 95, 96, 281n. 5
nata de coco, 151, 165, 287n. 4, 288n. 16

National Economic Development Authority (NEDA), 149, 157, 168, 198, 214
National Federation of Sugarcane Planters (NFSP), 89, 109, 112, 113–114, 115, 126, 152, 156, 159, 200, 208, 231, 232, 233, 234, 255, 280n. 25, 285nn. 8, 9
National Federation of Sugarcane Workers (NFSW), 77, 87–88, 209–210, 213, 214, 234
National Sugar Trading Corporation (NASUTRA), 56, 57, 59, 284n. 5
Negros (island), 3, 5, 11, 27, 133, 244, 264; decline of tenancy, 38; expansion of sugar production, 35–37, 106; history of sugar production, 33–41, 53, 276n. 11, 277nn. 4, 7, 278nn. 10, 13, 279n. 18, 280n. 20; intermarriage, 36; references on history, 277n. 1; sugar production on, 1, 71–72, 76, 79, 86, 107, 123, 264. *See also* crisis of 1970s and 1980s
Negros Occidental (province), 2, 45, 71–72, 76, 79, 83, 84, 85, 121, 123, 128, 132, 140, 159, 160, 184, 185, 187, 192, 193, 206–207, 209, 236, 243, 244, 258, 262, 279n. 16, 284nn. 4, 6, 286n. 17, 289n. 1
Negros Oriental (province), 71–72, 134, 137
neo-liberal policies, 30, 148, 150, 152, 153, 154, 157, 158, 161, 188, 192, 194, 195, 197, 199, 214, 217, 258, 271
neo-mercantilism, 217, 218, 221–222, 226, 256, 261, 272
neo-Weberian approach, 6–16, 20, 143, 269, 270; causal eclecticism, 8, 20; conflict, 9–10, 143 (*see also* conflict); cultural embeddedness, 6; culture as ideal type, 16–22; ethical neutrality, 7, 12–13, 147, 272, 275n. 4 (*see also* advocacy; objectivity); features listed, 7. *See also* Weber, Max
nepotism, 172, 176–177
Nestle, 151, 156, 165, 173, 180; interview with executive of, 175
new institutional economics, 13–14, 143.
See also collective action; transaction costs
Newman, Katherine S., 10, 299
New People's Army (NPA), 58, 204, 210, 213, 214, 248
new rich (*nouveau riche*), 27, 258–259, 276n. 8; disparaging of, 259
New York Coffee, Sugar, and Cocoa Exchange, 282n. 12
Nicaragua, 90, 211
Non-government organizations (NGOs), 10, 23, 58, 59, 88, 209, 211, 229, 240
North, Douglass C., 9, 275n. 5, 299
North Negros Marketing Corporation, 73, 182; interview with officers of, 170

objectivity, 11–13, 146, 147, 165, 189, 193–194, 272, 273, 275n. 4. *See also* advocacy; Billig, Michael S., author's involvement; neo-Weberian approach, ethical neutrality
O'Brien, Niall, 58, 275n. 1, 277n. 1, 280n. 26, 299–300
Office of the United States Trade Representative, 90, 97
Ofreneo, R. E., 57, 300
Omohundro, John T., 242, 300
Osmeña, John H. R., 190

pacto de retrovendendo, 36, 43, 277n. 13
pakyaw, 39–40, 65, 204
Pambansang Awit (the national anthem), 229, 289n. 5
Pampanga (province), 67, 69, 160, 164, 174; contrast with Negros, 42–44, 53, 278nn. 10, 13; decline as sugar center, 3, 35, 71–72; history of sugar production, 41–44, 48–49, 278n. 10, 279n. 15; loyalties of elites, 44
Panay (island): as source of Negros population, 33–34, 37, 276n. 11; mills on, 71, 72, 281n. 3; sugar production on, 71–72, 79, 107. *See also* Iloilo
Pandan, Raymundo T., 282n. 10, 300
Pangasinan (province), 71, 148, 289n. 1
Papa Isio revolt, 41
Paras, Jerome, 137

particularism: virtue of, 20, 270, 271
paternalism, 39, 203–204, 207–208, 209, 210, 212, 226, 240, 248, 249, 250, 255, 256
patrimonial capitalism and patrimonial state, 27, 256, 257
patron-client relations: as ideal type, 24–25, 230; literature about, 276n. 7
Paxton, John, 65, 300
Pepsi-Cola, 70, 156, 158, 167, 169, 172–173; interview with executive of, 172–173; 7-Up brand, 172
Pérez-López, Jorge F., 285n. 11, 300
"personalism," 3, 192–193, 195, 228, 229, 230, 231, 239, 240, 248; as ideal type, 22–23, 229. *See also* "groups" and "groupism"
Pfleider family, 84
Philippine Association of Sugar Refiners, Inc. (PASRI), 89
Philippine Chamber of Food Manufacturers (PCFM), 169, 180, 238
Philippine culture, 19, 101, 177, 178, 192–93, 202, 210, 228, 229, 230, 239, 240, 242, 243, 251, 256, 259
Philippine Exchange Company (PHILEX), 55, 280n. 24
Philippine Food Exporters' Association (PHILFOODEX), 98, 156, 161, 178, 179, 180, 183, 188, 189, 193, 195, 196, 197, 214, 238, 240; conflicts within, 196, 238; interviews with officials of, 164–169
Philippine history, 228; annexation by U.S., 40–41, 277n. 2; Commonwealth period, 51–54, 279n. 17; Japanese occupation, 53, 280n. 19; Marcos era, 54–59; pre-Spanish period, 32, 277n. 4; references on, 276n. 1; revolution, 40, 44, 277n. 2; Spanish colonial period, 32–44; U.S. colonial period, 44–54, 106, 277n. 2, 289n. 5
Philippine National Bank (PNB), 47, 48, 49, 55, 56, 75, 79, 84, 86, 279n. 17
Philippine Securities and Exchange Commission, 73
Philippine Sugar Association (PSA), 47, 51

Philippine Sugar Commission (PHILSUCOM), 56, 57, 59, 68, 102, 115, 280n. 24
Philippine Sugar Millers' Association (PSMA), 71, 89, 158, 161, 170, 171, 176, 198, 199, 232, 238, 255, 300; competition with other association, 238
Philippine Sugar Technologists (PHILSUTECH), 125
picul, 32, 34, 61, 64, 76, 89, 105, 111, 115, 236, 281nn. 2, 3; definition of, 277n. 3
Pinches, Michael, 258, 259, 276n. 8, 289n. 8, 300
pineapple products, 120, 177, 179, 180, 264
planter culture, 19, 31, 39, 129, 138, 139, 186, 201, 203–204, 207, 219, 224, 227, 231, 235, 241, 242, 243, 248, 249, 250, 251, 252, 253, 254, 255, 269, 270, 290n. 10; and moral obligation, 5, 24, 207–208, 245, 250; and property rights, 126–132, 143, 147, 265, 267, 269, 270
planters: activities of, 74–75, 127, 186, 205, 235, 245, 246, 290n. 10; changing values of, 27, 52, 153, 204, 206, 210, 254, 255, 268; collective action by, 149, 150, 152, 166, 170, 184–186, 193, 224, 233–234, 235; contradictory views of, 204–205, 208, 210, 224; decline of political power, 2–3, 54–55, 84, 114, 129, 139, 143–144, 146, 156, 160, 184, 185, 186–187, 194, 197, 198, 218, 226, 227, 239, 242, 254, 255, 261, 265, 267, 268, 269, 272, 280n. 20; diversity among, 11, 76, 78, 107, 114, 117, 122, 135, 145, 164, 251, 254; early history of, 35–37, 49–50, 268; focus on America, 249–250; incomes, 76; interests of, 103, 116, 126, 166, 186, 188, 226; loyalties to associations, 237, 238, 246, 285n. 8; opinions of cane purchase, 13–14, 129–132, 135, 138, 139, 140, 145, 266, 267; resistance to Spanish, 40; self-image of, 128, 129, 130–131, 132, 194, 197, 199, 208, 226, 243–250, 255, 261, 266, 267, 268; sense of hierarchy, 235, 236. *See*

also conflict; *hacenderos;* "sugar barons"
Planters' Association of Southern Negros (PASON), 237, 238
planters' associations, 47, 53, 104, 107, 113, 116–117, 118, 122–123, 129, 132, 138, 141, 152, 209, 213, 219, 235, 237, 239, 246, 285nn. 8, 9; cooptation by mills, 123, 129, 136, 237, 238; proliferation and fissioning of, 236, 237, 238; voting procedures of, 235–236, 246
pole vaulting, 79–80, 85, 130
political action. *See* collective action
population growth, 66, 225, 263
power: balance of, 2, 3, 14, 26, 116, 122, 129, 143–144, 145, 146, 147, 194, 219, 220, 226, 227, 239, 241, 254, 255, 257, 261, 269; differing perceptions of, 128, 194, 233, 269; ideal type, 20, 269; of planters, 129, 146, 226, 254, 255, 261, 268, 280n. 20, 285n. 9
prawns, 62, 73, 74, 75, 80. *See also* diversification
private voluntary organizations (PVOs), 23, 28, 59, 209, 240
productivity, 2, 117; agricultural, 49, 61, 62–64, 69, 87, 153, 154; decline of, 60–70, 167; milling, 61, 62, 153, 154, 156; overall, 60–61, 64, 147, 153. *See also* sugar production
property rights, 13–16, 30, 46, 101, 103, 106, 115, 131, 137, 145, 147, 267, 286n. 16; implications for structure of incentives, 15–16, 101, 103, 116–126, 127, 129, 137, 143, 144, 146–147, 265, 268; institutionalization of, 103, 116, 143, 144, 147, 266–269. See also *quedan;* share system
protectionism, 26, 50, 69, 93, 94, 144, 148, 152, 153, 154, 155, 157, 158, 162, 163, 164, 167, 169, 172, 181, 184, 188, 192, 194, 196, 200, 216, 217, 223, 257, 260, 264, 271, 287n. 7
Puerto Rico, 44, 45, 47, 283n. 15
Putnam, Robert D., 23, 300
Pye, Lucian W., 8, 300

quedans, 79, 80, 81, 104–105, 106, 107, 109, 110, 111, 112, 114–115, 116–126, 130, 131, 132, 134, 137, 139, 141, 142, 144, 145, 146, 147, 154, 156, 159, 163, 170, 171, 172, 173, 175, 178, 180, 245, 257, 258, 265, 266, 267, 268, 285n. 10, 286n. 16, 287n. 7, 288n. 11
Quirino, Carlos, 32, 33, 47, 51, 276n. 1, 300
quotas, 2, 144, 153, 154, 155, 218, 264, 271, 287n. 7; advocacy for, 175, 218, 219, 226, 227, 261, 285n. 7; colonial era, 22, 51–54, 55, 116, 144, 219–220, 265, 268; European Union, 98–100, 157, 265; as source of pride, 95; U. S., 64, 65, 69, 88–98, 103, 110, 112–113, 120, 157, 163, 199, 214, 258, 265, 281n. 5, 283nn. 14, 16; in world sugar trade, 29, 100, 102

ramie, 74, 264, 282n. 8. *See also* diversification
Ramos, Fidel V., 58, 82, 114, 146, 148, 151, 187, 188, 199, 204, 206, 233, 282n. 10, 287n. 8
rationalization: advocacy for, 14, 134, 145, 153, 157, 158, 176, 178, 216, 248, 258, 260; analysis of, 202–226; central control (neo-mercantilist) conception of, 21–22, 157, 203, 207, 217–218, 220, 221, 222, 224, 226, 258, 260, 271; and conflict, 9, 15, 24–25, 30, 68–69, 136, 210, 226, 269; conflicting conceptions of, 16, 21–22, 134, 136, 138, 145, 201, 208, 209, 210, 212, 124, 216, 221, 222, 223, 224, 250, 258, 260; cultural contextualization of, 224–225, 226; free-market conception of, 21–22, 24, 202–203, 205–206, 207, 211, 214, 215, 216, 221, 223, 224, 258, 271, 289n. 2; of imports, 159, 176, 178, 214, 258 (*see also* import "rationalization" bill); as key concept, 9, 21–22, 30, 270, 271; Marcos-era, 1–2, 22, 55, 218; radical conception of, 209–210, 213 (*see also* leftist perspectives)
ratooning, 63, 199, 281n. 4

reference groups, 27, 241, 242, 243, 253, 255, 259, 276n. 9, 289n. 8. *See also* Chinese, emulation of
refineries, 70, 71, 89, 105, 122, 123, 124, 129, 133, 134, 135, 139, 152, 170, 171, 172, 176, 180, 181, 183, 220, 223, 267, 284n. 4; quality of, 70, 71, 133, 172, 173, 174, 175, 178, 179, 183
refining fees. *See* "tolling" fees
reflexivity, 13, 140–142, 189–194, 204–205, 244, 247, 249, 250, 272–273
reification: of culture, 4, 7, 18–20, 211, 254, 268. *See also* culture, as ideal type; essentialism
rent-seeking, 22, 23, 158, 250, 255, 256
Republic Act No. 809, 131–132, 137, 139, 286n. 16
resistance. *See* sugarcane workers, acts of resistance by
restitution, 59, 88, 155, 186, 208, 280n. 25
"restoration of planter power" perspective, 26, 254, 258, 260, 268
"retrenchment" of workers, 217, 223, 289nn. 2, 4
rice, 33, 42, 43, 48, 63, 72, 75, 86, 101, 102, 157, 160, 284n. 7
Riedinger, Jeffrey M., 282n. 10, 300
Roney, John C., 99, 300
Roniger, L., 276n. 7, 294
Rosenberg, Nathan, 9, 300
Rotary Clubs, 243, 245
rum, 33, 62, 263, 285n. 10, 286n. 13
rural agrarian elites: decline of, 3, 26–28, 30, 84, 111, 148, 192, 197, 215, 220, 227, 242, 254, 256, 257, 258, 259, 260, 272. *See also* elites; urban elites
Rutten, Rosanne, 203, 283n. 15, 301

sacadas, 39–40, 213
Sahlins, Marshall D., 16, 18, 301
San Carlos Planters' Association, 135, 136, 137, 138, 139, 140, 141, 142, 223, 237
San Carlos sugar mill, 132–142, 145, 179, 183, 206, 279n. 16. *See also* cane purchase experiment; Go family
Sandique, Rhea P., 283n. 14, 301

San Miguel, 70, 112, 156, 158, 163, 169, 173, 176, 284n. 7, 286n. 13; interview with executive of, 174–175
Sa-onoy, Modesto P., 40, 55, 111, 150, 277n. 1, 278n. 8, 280n. 24, 301
Saravia, Emilio, 36, 278n. 8
Schor, Juliet, 276n. 9, 301
Schultz, Theodore, W. 9, 301
Scott, James C., 25, 301
Scott, William Henry, 277n. 4, 301
Sebastian, Roberto S., 185, 288n. 10
secretariat, 185, 190, 233–234. *See also* SIFI, group
share system, 47, 49, 103, 105, 106, 116–126, 143, 144, 163, 200, 265, 266, 267, 268; early use of, 46–47, 49, 143, 265, 286n. 15; in other countries, 283nn. 2, 3; vs. alternatives, 13–14, 46, 103, 106, 116, 120, 123, 124, 125–132, 134, 137, 144, 146–147, 200, 223, 231, 258, 266, 267. *See also* cane purchase; property rights; *quedans*
Shemberg Manufacturing Company, 150, 164, 165; interview with executive of, 182–183
shipping problems, 155, 180–181, 221
Sidel, John T., 276n. 7, 301
SIFI (Sugar Industry Foundation, Inc.), 115, 208, 209, 211, 229, 232, 233, 235, 236, 285n. 9 (*see also* liens); SIFI "group," 209, 232, 233, 234, 236, 285n. 9 (*see also* "groups" and "groupism"); voting procedures for board, 236, 237
Singapore, 111, 118, 288n. 12; sugar policies, 93, 158; sugar production and trade, 70, 154, 166, 177, 178, 180, 181, 182, 184, 284n. 4
Skully, David W., 90, 91, 283nn. 14, 16, 301
slavery, 12–13, 168, 257
smuggling accusation, 140, 150, 152, 155, 159, 161, 164, 165, 166, 167, 177–178, 179, 182, 183
"social amelioration," 77, 208, 211, 233; fund, 115 (*see also* liens)
social security, 77, 115

soft drink companies. *See* beverage companies
South Africa, 90, 93, 281n. 3
South Cotabato (province), 179, 181, 182
Sowell, Thomas, 8, 301
Spanish-American war, 40–41, 277n. 2
spot buying, 172, 173, 174, 175
squatters, 84, 208
storage and stevedoring fees, 105, 107, 108, 136, 139, 218–219
Suarez, Nydia, 66, 91, 298, 301
subsidies, 55, 90, 97, 98, 99, 100, 152, 163, 167, 170, 184, 215, 217, 221, 222, 237, 264, 283–284n. 3; vs. price supports, 99, 221–222
sugar: quality of, 46, 69–70, 93–94, 106, 123, 133, 135, 139–140, 167, 169, 172, 173, 174, 175, 178, 179, 180
"sugar barons," 1, 49–50, 76, 84, 117, 156, 258, 262, 288n. 16; conspicuous consumption of, 1, 49–50, 153, 197, 205, 224, 258; disparaging of, 26, 117, 130, 154, 162, 166, 187, 215, 262; political influence of, 1, 54–55, 156, 161, 166, 187, 199, 258; use of image in media, 162, 187, 262. See also *hacenderos;* planters
sugar bloc (in Congress), 109, 132, 159, 160, 161–162, 167, 168, 187, 189, 198, 289n. 3
sugarcane: economies of scale, 87; quality of, 62–63, 69, 104, 127, 128, 135–136, 137, 139, 266, 286n. 14; varietals of, 49, 61, 62–63, 66–67, 76, 104, 124, 199, 206, 221, 281nn. 4, 6, 283n. 3
sugarcane workers, 1, 37–40, 42–44, 50, 53, 55, 57–58, 63–64, 85, 153, 197, 198, 203, 204, 207, 224, 225, 248, 258, 264, 283n. 13, 288n. 16; acts of resistance by, 25, 37, 41, 53, 207; "childlike" image of, 25, 204, 210, 211, 212, 248; culture of, 211, 251; opinion of cane purchase, 127; and rationalization, 24–25, 68–69, 203–213, 216, 248; reasons for high birth rate, 225; sharing profits with, 64, 159, 210, 212; use as excuse for protectionism, 152, 155, 157, 160, 167–168, 179, 181–182, 196, 197, 200, 216, 217, 222, 288n. 16; wages of, 39, 40, 53, 57, 64, 68–69, 77, 186, 204, 206, 210, 211, 289n. 3 (*see also* minimum wage)
sugar consumption: in Europe, 263, 278n. 11; in Philippines, 2, 54, 60, 66, 69, 89, 110, 113, 199, 214, 216, 263; in U.S., 44, 46, 88, 92, 98, 262, 263, 264, 287n. 11; in world, 262, 263, 264, 281n. 1
sugar exports, 2, 32, 33, 46, 54, 65–66, 89, 91, 93, 99, 100, 112–113, 120, 128, 158, 199, 214, 278n. 11, 281n. 5, 283n. 16
sugar imports, 65, 69, 89, 109, 111, 118, 148–149, 150, 151–152, 153, 154, 155, 156, 157, 158, 161, 163, 165, 166, 168, 170, 171, 173, 174, 175, 176, 177–178, 180, 181, 182, 183, 184, 198, 199, 200, 214, 215, 283n. 14, 288n. 13; other countries,' 92, 93, 99, 100, 166
sugar industry: conflicts within, 3, 9–10, 118, 152, 234 (*see also* conflict); image of, 3, 194, 196, 197, 250, 251, 262; leader of, 159, 184, 185, 190, 195, 227, 230, 233, 234, 235, 287n. 10, 288n. 14 (*see also* leaders); profits of, 49, 52, 75–76, 108, 118–119, 153, 168, 226, 263
sugarless *quedan* scams, 114–115, 122–123, 142, 221, 266
Sugar Orders, 103–104, 107, 112, 113, 180; conversions by, 104, 107–108, 109, 110, 111, 113, 131
sugar prices, 51, 55–56, 64, 69, 76, 90, 94–95, 96–97, 99, 101–102, 105, 107, 109, 100–111, 112, 113, 117, 125, 126, 127, 152, 154, 155, 158, 162, 163, 171, 172, 173, 175–176, 178, 181, 182, 217, 257, 263, 282n. 12, 284n. 4, 288n. 11; complaints by food processors about, 151, 152, 154, 156, 159, 165, 166, 167, 168, 170, 174, 175, 178, 181, 182; manipulation of, 48, 102, 108, 110, 129, 132, 220, 221, 227, 239, 241, 261, 271, 283n. 1, 289n. 3
sugar production, 32–35, 46, 51, 53, 57, 61, 63, 76, 116, 154, 163, 176, 199, 206, 257, 260, 263; costs of, 2, 49, 64,

76, 77, 78, 94, 95, 153, 200, 257, 258, 264, 283n. 15, 287n. 5; temperate vs. tropical, 29, 99, 100, 283nn. 15, 17; world, 281n. 1. *See also* productivity

Sugar Regulatory Administration (SRA), 10, 61, 66–68, 77, 89, 93, 94, 98, 99, 102, 106, 112, 114, 115, 117, 122, 125, 126, 129, 142, 149, 152, 156, 158, 171, 174, 185, 187, 191, 198, 220, 222, 231, 235, 261, 263, 281n. 3, 283n. 13, 284n. 6, 286n. 14, 287n. 6; apportionment to different markets, 103–104, 107, 108, 109, 110, 111, 113, 120, 163, 166, 178, 181 (*see also* Sugar Orders); institutional bloat, 67–68; make-up of board, 113–114, 146, 167, 231, 233; monitoring of imports, 149, 150, 151, 170, 177, 178; opinions of cane purchase, 125, 126, 140; opposition to import liberalization, 148, 155, 156, 159, 162 (*see also* import "rationalization" bill).

sugar research, 49, 66–67, 102, 127, 156, 185, 200, 221, 281n. 6; in other countries, 124. *See also* La Granja; Sugar Regulatory Administration

sugar restitution law. *See* restitution

"sunset industry," 2, 215, 254

sustainability, 63, 84, 88; as ideal type, 21

Szanton, David L., 242, 301

Taiwan, 81, 82, 94, 165, 168, 260; land reform in, 82

Tan, Antonio S., 242, 302

tariff rate quota (TRQ), 91, 92, 93, 96, 97, 113, 214, 283n. 16

tariffs and duties, 50, 70, 91, 92, 99, 149, 150, 151, 152, 153, 155, 157, 161, 163, 166, 168, 174–175, 176, 183, 185, 198, 199, 200, 214, 257, 258, 260, 264, 267, 287nn. 3, 5, 7; on inputs to sugar production, 78, 152, 155, 163, 221, 287n. 5. *See also* import liberalization

Tarlac (province), 67, 69, 78, 122, 280n. 25; decline as sugar center, 3, 71–72, opening of sugar land, 43

taxation, 70–71, 78, 80, 123, 130, 133, 152, 160, 167, 221, 260, 264, 287n. 5; "tax-ation" to NPA, 204. *See also* Bureau of Internal Revenue; value added, tax

tenancy, 38, 53; decline in Negros, 38; and land reform, 82; in Pampanga, 42–44, 53, 82. See also *agsa; samacan*

Texas, 95, 283n. 15

textile industry, 34–35, 65, 151, 153, 277n. 7, 282n. 8, 286n. 15. *See also* Chinese mestizos; exports, non-sugar; Iloilo

Thailand, 29, 62, 64, 65, 99, 102, 111, 118, 133, 154, 158, 168, 175, 199, 260; sugar production, 60–61, 281nn. 1, 5

Thomas, Robert Paul, 9, 299

Thompson, E. P., 9, 302

Timberman, David G., 26, 302

Timmer, C. Peter, 9, 302

tolling fees, 118, 124, 154, 166, 168, 170, 171, 178, 181, 284n. 4, 288n. 11. *See also* refineries

traders, 2, 10, 15, 43, 48, 50, 55, 56, 79, 81, 85, 102, 107, 108, 111, 117, 121, 155, 175, 182, 222, 239, 251, 254, 266; accusation of collusion by, 108, 109, 111, 117, 130, 146, 164, 182, 237, 239, 242; accusation of smuggling by, 111, 167, 179–180, 182–183 (*see also* smuggling accusation); diversity among, 107, 108, 117, 126, 127–128, 145, 254, 266, 285n. 5; groupism among, 238, 239; growing dominance of, 26, 143–144, 219, 255, 268; interests of, 103; marketing sugar by, 107, 116, 117, 118, 120, 124, 126, 127, 140, 146, 154, 166, 167, 168, 171, 172, 173, 175, 178, 180, 181, 284n. 4; molasses, 81, 285n. 10; opinions of cane purchase, 127–128, 140, 145, 146, 266; profits of, 2, 35, 55, 109, 110, 112, 117, 124, 126, 181; political connections of, 140, 176–177, 183, 284n. 5; purchasing of mills by, 11, 61–62, 83, 108, 114–115, 120–121, 124, 128, 132, 134, 140, 145, 146, 176, 183, 210, 219, 222, 241, 243, 251, 267, 286n. 13, 289n. 2. *See also* conflict, planters vs. traders

"tradesmen's" values, 50, 52, 241, 242, 243

transaction costs, 13, 15, 101, 116, 117, 118, 127, 132, 166, 176, 178, 266
"trapo," 148, 233, 286n. 2
treasury bills (T-bills), 81–82, 155, 160
trucking and transloading, 10–11, 47, 55, 71, 77–78, 104, 105, 107, 118, 125, 133, 134, 136, 137, 139, 149, 152, 218, 219, 280n. 22, 282n. 9; fees, 136

United States: annexation of the Philippines, 40–41, 44, 277n. 2; colonial rule, 44–54, 106, 289n. 5; sugar policies, 29, 48, 64, 88–98, 105, 154, 157, 158, 160, 162, 166, 281n. 5, 283n. 14 (*see also* quotas, U.S.); sugar production, 92, 95–96, 97, 113, 124, 264, 281n. 1. *See also* sugar consumption, in U.S.
United States Department of Agriculture (USDA), 66, 90, 91, 92, 97, 112, 173, 283n. 14
urban elites, 30, 194, 198, 226, 227, 242, 251, 255, 257, 258, 259, 260, 267; rise of, 3–4, 26–28, 111, 148, 202, 220, 254, 255, 256, 272, 276n. 8. *See also* elites; rural elites

value added, 30, 70, 93, 100, 117, 124, 151, 154, 260; misunderstanding of VAT, 171; tax (VAT), 118, 155, 159, 160, 166, 170–172, 178, 181, 182, 183, 288n. 11
Vandergeest, Peter, 275n. 3, 302
Vayda, Andrew P., 17, 302
veto, 161, 198, 287n. 9
Victorias Milling Company, 61, 63, 67, 70, 73–74, 80, 105, 107, 133, 135, 170, 175, 178, 179, 180, 182, 183, 236, 237, 284n. 4, 286n. 14
Visayas (islands), 41, 245, 277n. 7; bank lending in, 78; role in sugar production, 33, 35, 78, 279n. 14

Voluntary Offer for Sale (VOS), 83, 84, 85, 86, 206, 210. *See also* Comprehensive Agrarian Reform Program; Department of Agrarian Reform
votes: as political currency, 2, 146, 168, 186–187, 194, 197, 198, 207, 208, 227, 239, 248, 255–256, 261

wage labor system: rise of, 38–39, 53
Wallerstein, Immanuel, 9, 302
Weber, Max, 295, 302; continuing relevance of, 7, 143, 147, 201, 211; elective affinities, 8; ideal types (*See* ideal types); "is" vs. "ought," 147 (*see also* advocacy; neo-Weberian approach, ethical neutrality; objectivity); Protestant ethic thesis, 8; relevance to Asia, 7, 275n. 3; *Science as a Vocation*, 12, 272; strong thesis, 8; theory of capitalism, 6–7, 8; weak thesis, 8
Wells, Miriam J., 10, 302
Wertheim, Wim F., 275n. 3, 302
Wickberg, Edgar, 242, 302
Wilkinson, Alec, 95, 302
Williamson, Oliver E., 275n. 5, 302
Wolf, Eric R., 9, 302
Wolfe, Alan, 23, 302
World Bank, 59, 65, 78, 125, 302
world sugar market, 28–30, 55, 56, 64, 69, 88, 89, 97, 98, 99, 100, 104, 110, 112, 151, 154, 155, 162, 165, 166, 168, 175, 181. *See also* dumping; quotas
World Trade Organization (WTO), 97, 153, 157, 199, 200, 258, 265

Yengoyan, Aram A., 3, 302–303
Yulo, Arsenio "Buc-An," 61, 69, 93, 110, 114, 126, 158, 163, 233, 235, 261, 281n. 3, 284n. 6

Zaragoza, B., 281n. 6

About the Author

Michael S. Billig has degrees from Columbia (B.A., M.A.) and Harvard Universities (PhD) and is professor of anthropology at Franklin and Marshall College in Lancaster, Pennsylvania, where he has taught since 1986. He has conducted field research on the Philippine sugar industry since 1990, for which he received a Fulbright Senior Research Award in 1993–1994. His published articles have appeared in *Journal of Asian Studies, Philippine Studies, Pilipinas, Journal of Southeast Asian Studies,* and *Journal of Economic Issues,* among others. Billig's major research and teaching interests include economic anthropology, economic culture, property rights, class and culture, and anthropological theory. His writings have consistently affirmed the salience of culture as opposed to demographic, economic, and microfoundational reductionisms.

Production Notes for Billig / *Barons, Brokers, and Buyers: The Institutions and Cultures of Philippine Sugar*

Cover and interior designed by Santos Barbasa Jr. in Palatino with display type in Frutiger.

Composition by Josie Herr in QuarkXPress.

Printing and binding by The Maple-Vail Book Manufacturing Group.

Printed on 50 lb. New Age TCF, 440 ppi.